The Expositor's Bible
The General Epistles Of St. James And St. Jude

By

Alfred Plummer

The Expositor's Bible
The General Epistles Of St. James And St. Jude
by Alfred Plummer

ISBN: 978-93-61157-68-4

Published by

DOUBLE 9 BOOKS

2/13-B, Ansari Road
Daryaganj, New Delhi – 110002
info@double9books.com
www.double9books.com
Tel. 011-40042856

ABOUT THE AUTHOR

Alfred Plummer became an outstanding English theologian and biblical pupil regarded for his large contributions to biblical statement and exegesis. Plummer served as a prominent instructional, retaining the placement of Master of University College, Durham, and later because the Master of Balliol College, Oxford. His knowledge in biblical studies and his commitment to sound scholarship made him a reputable determine in theological circles. One of Alfred Plummer's incredible works is "The Expositor's Bible: The Pastoral Epistles," where he centered on offering insightful remark at the New Testament books of one Timothy, 2 Timothy, and Titus. The Pastoral Epistles are letters traditionally attributed to the Apostle Paul and addressed to early Christian leaders, offering steering on matters of doctrine and church employer. In "The Expositor's Bible: The Pastoral Epistles," Plummer brings his erudition to endure, imparting readers a thorough and scholarly exam of these critical biblical texts. His statement delves into ancient context, linguistic nuances, and theological implications, presenting pastors, scholars, and widespread readers with a precious useful resource for know-how and interpreting those epistles.

CONTENTS

INTRODUCTORY

CHAPTER I
THE CATHOLIC EPISTLES

THIS volume is to treat of the General Epistle of St. James and the General Epistle of St. Jude. According to the most common, but not invariable arrangement, they form the first and the last letters in the collection which for fifteen centuries has been known as the Catholic Epistles. The epithet "General," which appears in the titles of these Epistles in the English versions, is simply the equivalent of the epithet "Catholic," the one word being of Latin (*generalis*), the other of Greek (καθολικός) origin. In Latin, however, *e.g.* in the Vulgate, these letters are not called *Generales*, but *Catholicæ*.

The meaning of the term Catholic Epistles (καθολικαὶ ἐπιστολαι) has been disputed, and more than one explanation may be found in commentaries; but the true signification is not really doubtful. It certainly does not mean *orthodox* or *canonical*; although from the sixth century, and possibly earlier, we find these Epistles sometimes called the Canonical Epistles (*Epistolæ Canonicæ*), an expression in which "canonical" is evidently meant to be an equivalent for "catholic." This use is said to occur first in the *Prologus in Canonicas Epistolas* of the Pseudo-Jerome given by Cassiodorus (*De Justit. Divin. Litt.*, viii.); and the expression is used by Cassiodorus himself, whose writings may be placed between A.D. 540 and 570, the period spent in his monastery at Viviers, after he had retired from the conduct of public affairs. The term "catholic" is used in the sense of "orthodox" before this date, but not in connexion with these letters. There seems to be no earlier evidence of the opinion, certainly erroneous, that this collection of seven Epistles was called "Catholic" in order to mark them as Apostolic and authoritative, in distinction from other letters which were heterodox, or at any rate of inferior authority. Five out of the seven letters, viz. all but the First Epistle of St. Peter and the First Epistle of St. John, belong to that class of New Testament books which from the time of Eusebius (*H. E.* III. xxv. 4) have been spoken of as "disputed" (ἀντιλεγόμενα), *i.e.* as being up to the beginning of the fourth century not *universally* admitted to be canonical.[1] And it would have been almost a contradiction in terms if Eusebius had first called these Epistles "catholic" (*H. E.* II. xxiii. 25; VI. xiv. 1) in the sense of being universally accepted as authoritative, and had then classed them among the "disputed" books.

Nor is it accurate to say that these letters are called "catholic" because they are addressed to both Jewish and Gentile Christians alike, a statement which is not true of all of them, and least of all of the Epistle which generally stands first in the series; for the Epistle of St. James takes no account of Gentile Christians. Moreover, there are Epistles of St. Paul which are addressed to both Jews and Gentiles in the Churches to which he writes. So that this explanation of the term makes it thoroughly unsuitable for the purpose for which it is used, viz. to mark off these seven Epistles from the Epistles of St. Paul. Nevertheless, this interpretation is nearer to the truth than the former one.

The Epistles are called "Catholic" because they are not addressed to any particular Church, whether of Thessalonica, or Corinth, or Rome, or Galatia, but to the Church universal, or at any rate to a wide circle of readers. This is the earliest Christian use of the term "catholic," which was applied to the Church itself before it was applied to these or any other writings. "Wheresoever the bishop shall appear, there let the people be," says Ignatius to the Church of Smyrna (viii.), "just as where Jesus Christ is, *there is the Catholic Church*"—the earliest passage in Christian literature in which the phrase "Catholic Church" occurs. And there can be no doubt as to the meaning of the epithet in this expression. In later times, when Christians were oppressed by a consciousness of the slow progress of the Gospel, and by the knowledge that as yet only a fraction of the human race had accepted it, it became customary to explain "catholic" as meaning that which embraces and teaches the whole truth, rather than as that which spreads everywhere and covers the whole earth. But in the first two or three centuries the feeling was rather one of jubilation and triumph at the rapidity with which the "good news" was spreading, and of confidence that "there is not one single race of men, whether barbarians or Greeks, or whatever they may be called, nomads or vagrants, or herdsmen living in tents, among whom prayers and giving of thanks are not offered, through the name of the crucified Jesus, to the Father and Creator of all things" (Justin Martyr, *Trypho*, cxviii.); and that as "the soul is diffused through all the members of the body, Christians are scattered through all the cities of the world" (*Epistle to Diognetus*, vi.).[2] Under the influence of such exultation as this, which was felt to be in harmony with Christ's promise and command (Luke xxiv. 47; Matt. xxviii. 10), it was natural to use "catholic" of the universal extension of Christendom, rather than of the comprehensiveness of the truths of Christianity. And this meaning still prevails in the time of Augustine, who says that "the Church is called 'Catholic' in Greek, because it is diffused throughout the whole world" (*Epp.* lii. 1); although the later use, as meaning orthodox, in distinction to schismatical or heretical, has already begun; *e.g.* in the Muratorian Fragment, in which the writer speaks of heretical writing "which cannot be received into the Catholic Church; for wormwood is not suitable for mixing with honey" (Tregelles, pp. 20, 47; Westcott *On the Canon*, Appendix C, p. 500);[3] and the chapter in Clement of Alexandria on the priority of the Catholic Church to all heretical assemblies (*Strom.* VII. xvii).

The four Gospels and the Epistles of St. Paul were the Christian writings best known during the first century after the Ascension, and universally acknowledged as of binding authority[4]; and it was common to speak of them as "the Gospel" and "the Apostle," much in the same way as the Jews spoke of "the Law" and "the Prophets." But when a third collection of Christian documents became widely known another collective term was required by which to distinguish it from the collections already familiar, and the feature in these seven Epistles which seems to have struck the recipients of them most is the absence of an address to any local Church. Hence they received the name of Catholic, or General, or Universal Epistles. The name was all the more natural because of the number seven, which emphasized the contrast between these and the Pauline Epistles. St. Paul had written to seven particular Churches — Thessalonica, Corinth, Rome, Galatia, Philippi, Colossæ, and Ephesus; and here were seven Epistles without any address to a particular Church; therefore they might fitly be called "*General* Epistles." Clement of Alexandria uses this term of the letter addressed to the Gentile Christians "in Antioch and Syria and Cilicia" (Acts xv. 23) by the Apostles, in the so-called Council of Jerusalem (*Strom.* IV. xv.); and Origen uses it of the Epistle of Barnabas (*Con. Celsum* I. lxiii.), which is addressed simply to "sons and daughters," *i.e.* to Christians generally.

That this meaning was well understood, even after the misleading title "Canonical Epistles" had become usual in the West, is shown by the interesting Prologue to these Epistles written by the Venerable Bede, *c.* A.D. 712.[5] This prologue is headed, "Here begins the Prologue to the seven *Canonical* Epistles," and it opens thus: "James, Peter, John, and Jude published seven Epistles, to which ecclesiastical custom gives the name of *Catholic, i.e. universal.*"

The name is not strictly accurate, excepting in the cases of 1 John, 2 Peter, and Jude. It is admissible in a qualified sense of 1 Peter and James; but it is altogether inappropriate to 2 and 3 John, which are addressed, not to the Church at large, nor to a group of local Churches, but to individuals. But inasmuch as the common title of these letters was not the Epistles "to the Elect Lady" and "to Gaius," as in the case of the letters to Philemon, Titus, and Timothy, but simply the Second and Third of John, they were regarded as without address, and classed with the Catholic Epistles. And of course it was natural to put them into the same group with the First Epistle of St. John, although the name of the group did not suit them. At what date this arrangement was made is not certain; but there is reason for believing that these seven Epistles were already regarded as one collection in the third century, when Pamphilus, the friend of Eusebius, was making his famous library at Cæsarea. Euthalius (c. A.D. 450) published an edition of them, in making which he had collated "the accurate copies" in this library; and it is probable that he found the grouping already existing in those copies, and did not make it for himself. Moreover, it is probable that the copies at Cæsarea were made by Pamphilus himself; for the summary of the contents of the Acts published under the name of Euthalius is a mere copy of the summary given by Pamphilus, and it became the usual practice to place the Catholic Epistles immediately after the Acts. If, then, Euthalius got the summary of the Acts from Pamphilus, he probably got the arrangement from him also, viz. the putting of these seven Epistles into one group, and placing them next to the Acts.[6]

The order which makes the Catholic Epistles follow immediately after the Acts is very ancient, and it is a matter for regret that the influence of Jerome, acting through the Vulgate, has universally disturbed it in all Western Churches. "The connexion between these two portions (the Acts and the Catholic Epistles), commended by its intrinsic appropriateness, is preserved in a large proportion of Greek MSS. of all ages, and corresponds to marked affinities of textual history."[7] It is the order followed by Cyril of Jerusalem, Athanasius, John of Damascus, the Council of Laodicea, and also by Cassian. It has been restored by Tischendorf, Tregelles, and Westcott and Hort; but it is not to be expected that even their powerful authority will avail to re-establish the ancient arrangement.

The order of the books in the group of the Catholic Epistles is not quite constant; but almost always James stands first. In a very few authorities Peter stands first, an arrangement naturally preferred in the West, but not adopted even there, because the authority of the original order was too strong. A scholiast on the Epistle of James states that this Epistle has been placed before 1 Peter, "because it is *more catholic* than that of Peter," by which he seems to mean that whereas 1 Peter is addressed "to the elect who are sojourners of the Dispersion" in certain specified districts, the Epistle of James is addressed "to the twelve tribes which are of the Dispersion," without any limitation. The Venerable Bede, in the Prologue to the Catholic Epistles quoted above (p. 6), states that James is placed first, because he undertook to rule the Church of Jerusalem, which was the fount and source of that evangelic preaching which has spread throughout the world; or else because he sent his Epistle to the twelve tribes of Israel, who were the first to believe. And Bede calls attention to the fact that St. Paul himself adopts this order when he speaks of "James, and Cephas, and John, they who were reputed to be pillars" (Gal. ii. 9). It is possible, however, that the order James, Peter, John was meant to represent a belief as to the chronological precedence of James to Peter, and Peter to John; Jude being placed last because of its comparative insignificance, and because it was not at first universally admitted. The Syriac Version, which admits only James, 1 Peter, and 1 John, has the three in this order; and if the arrangement had its origin in reverence for the first Bishop of Jerusalem, it is strange that most of the Syriac copies should have a heading to the effect that these three Epistles of James, Peter, and John are by the three who witnessed the Transfiguration. Those who made and those who accepted this comment certainly had no idea of reverencing the first Bishop of Jerusalem, for it implies that the Epistle of James is by the son of Zebedee and brother of John, who was put to death by Herod. But it is probable that this heading is a mere blundering conjecture. If persons who believed the Epistle to be written by James the brother of John had fixed the order, they would have fixed it thus—Peter, James, John, as in Matt. xvii. 1; Mark v. 37; ix. 2; xiii. 3; xiv. 33; comp. Matt. xxvi. 37; or Peter, John, James, as in Luke viii. 51; ix. 28; Acts i. 13. But the former arrangement would be more reasonable than the latter, seeing that John wrote so long after the other two. The traditional order harmonizes with two facts which were worth marking—(1) that two of the three were Apostles, and must therefore be placed together; (2) that John wrote last, and must therefore be placed last; but whether or no the wish to mark these facts determined the order, we have not sufficient knowledge to enable us to decide.

How enormous would have been the loss had the Catholic Epistles been excluded from the canon of the New Testament it is not difficult to see. Whole phases of Christian thought would have been missing. The Acts and the Epistles of St. Paul would have told us of their existence, but would not have shown to us what they were. We should have known that there were serious differences of opinion even among the Apostles themselves, but we should have had a very imperfect knowledge as to their nature and reconciliation. We might have guessed that those who had been with Jesus of Nazareth throughout His ministry would not preach Christ in the same way as St. Paul, who had never seen Him until after the Ascension, but we should not have been sure of this; still less could we have seen in what the difference would have consisted; and we should have known very little indeed of the distinctive marks of the three great teachers who "were reputed to be pillars" of the Church. Above all, we should have known sadly little of the Mother Church of Jerusalem, and of the teaching of those many early Christians who, while heartily embracing the Gospel of Jesus Christ, believed that they were bound to hold fast not only to the morality, but to the discipline of Moses. Thus in many particulars we should have been left to conjecture as to how the continuity in the Divine Revelation was maintained; how the Gospel not merely superseded, but fulfilled, and glorified, and grew out of the Law.

All this has to a large extent been made plain to us by the providence of God in giving to us and preserving for us in the Church the seven Catholic Epistles. We see St. James and St. Jude presenting to us that Judaic form of Christianity which was really the complement, although when exaggerated it became the opposite, of the teaching of St. Paul. We see St. Peter mediating between the two, and preparing the way for a better comprehension of both. And then St. John lifts us up into a higher and clearer atmosphere, in which the controversy between Jew and Gentile has faded away into the dim distance, and the only opposition which remains worthy of a Christian's consideration is that between light and darkness, truth and falsehood, love and hate, God and the world, Christ and Antichrist, life and death.

[1] "Canonical" (κανονκός), from canon (κανών, connected with κάννα, "a reed or *cane*," "measuring-rod or ruler"), is used in both a passive and an active sense. A canonical book is primarily one which has been measured and tested, and secondarily that which is itself a measure or standard. Just as a cane, cut to the length of a yard-measure, thenceforth becomes a yard-measure itself, so the Scriptures were first of all tested as to their authority, and then became a standard for testing all other teaching; *i.e.* they became *canonical*.

[2] Comp. Ignatius, *Magn.* X.; Irenæus, *Hær.* I. x. 1, 2; III. iv. 2; V. xx. 1; Clement of Alexandria, *Strom.* VI., *sub-finem*; Tertullian, *Apol.* i., xxxvii.; *Adv. Judæos*, vii., xii., etc., etc.

[3] It has been remarked that this play upon words (*fel* and *mel*), which cannot be reproduced in English, is an argument against the theory of a Greek original.

[4] In the *Codex Sinaiticus* and some other authorities the Pauline Epistles are placed immediately after the Gospels, an arrangement which probably had its origin in the fact that for many early Christians these two groups constituted their New Testament. Among versions the Memphitic and the Thebaic have this order.

[5] It is omitted by Giles and other editors, but is given by Cave, in his *Historia Literaria* (I., p. 475), who says that it comes from an ancient MS. in the Library of Gonville and Caius College, Cambridge.

[6] Westcott *On the Canon*, pp. 362, 417, 3rd Ed.

[7] Westcott and Hort, II., p. 321; Scrivener, *Introduction to the Criticism of the N.T.* pp. 70, 74, 3rd Ed.

THE EPISTLE OF ST. JAMES

CHAPTER II
THE AUTHENTICITY OF THE
EPISTLE OF ST. JAMES

"James, a servant of God and of the Lord Jesus Christ." —Jas. i. 1.

THE question of the authenticity of this Epistle resolves itself into two parts—Is the Epistle the genuine product of a writer of the Apostolic age? if so, which of the persons of the Apostolic age who bore the name of James is the author of it? In answering the former of these two questions it is important to put it in the proper way. We have done a good deal towards the solution of a problem when we have learned to state it correctly; and the way in which we ought to approach the problem of the genuineness of this and other books of the New Testament is not, Why should we believe that these writings are what they profess to be? but, Why should we *refuse* to believe this? Have we any sufficient reason for reversing the decision of the fourth and fifth centuries, which possessed far more evidence on the question than has come down to us?

It must be remembered that that decision was not given mechanically or without consideration of doubts and difficulties; nor was it imposed by authority, until independent Churches and scholars had arrived at pretty much the same conclusion. And the decision, as soon as it was pronounced, was unanimously accepted in both East and West—a fact which was ample guarantee that the decision was universally recognized as correct; for there was no central authority of sufficient influence to force a suspected decision upon mistrustful Churches. Eusebius, it is true, classes most of the Catholic Epistles among the "disputed" (ἀντιλεγόμενα) books of the New Testament, without, however, affirming that he shared the doubts which existed in some quarters respecting them. This fact, which is sometimes rather hastily taken as telling altogether against the writings which he marks as "disputed," really tells *both* ways. On the one hand, it shows that doubts had existed respecting some of the canonical books; and these doubts must have had some reason (whether valid or not) for existing. On the other hand, the fact that the authority of these books was sometimes disputed in the third century shows that the verdict formally given and ratified at the Council of Laodicea (c. 364)[8] was given after due examination of the adverse evidence, and with a conviction that the doubts which had been raised were not justified; and the universal welcome which was accorded to the verdict throughout Christendom shows that the doubts which had been raised had ceased to exist. If, then, on the one hand we remember that misgivings once existed, and argue that these misgivings must have had some basis, on the other we must remember that these misgivings were entirely abandoned, and that there must have been reason for abandoning them. What reason, then, have we for disturbing the verdict of the fourth century, and reviving misgivings long ago put to rest?

Of course those who gave that verdict and those who ratified it were fallible persons, and no member of the English Church, at any rate, would argue that the question is closed and may not be reopened. But the point to be insisted upon is that the *onus probandi* rests with those who assail or suspect these books, rather than with those who accept them. It is not the books that ought, on demand, again and again to be placed on their trial, but the pleas of those who would once more bring them into court that ought to be sifted. These objectors deserve a hearing; but while they receive it, we have full right to stand by the decision of the fourth century, and refuse to part with, or even seriously to suspect, any of the precious inheritance which has been handed down to us. It may be confidently asserted that thus far no strong case has been made out against any of the five "disputed" Epistles, excepting 2 Peter; and with regard to that it is still true to affirm that the Petrine authorship remains, on the whole, a reasonable "working hypothesis."

Do not let us forget what the epithet "disputed," applied to these and one or two[9] other books of the New Testament, really means. It does *not* mean that at the beginning of the fourth century Eusebius found that these writings were *universally regarded with suspicion; that is a gross exaggeration of the import of the term*. Rather it means that these books were *not universally accepted*; that although they were, as a rule, regarded as canonical, and as part of the contents of the New Testament (ἐνδιάθηκοι γραφαί), yet in some quarters their authority was doubted or denied. And the reasons for these doubts were naturally not in all cases the same. With regard to 2 Peter, the doubt must have been as to its genuineness and authenticity. It claimed to be written by "Simon Peter, an Apostle of Jesus Christ" and a witness of the Transfiguration (2 Peter i. 1, 18); but the obscurity of its origin and other circumstances were against it. With regard to James, Jude, and 2 and 3 John the doubt was rather as to their Apostolicity. They did not claim to be written by Apostles. There was no reason for doubting the antiquity or the genuineness of these four books; but granting that they were written by the persons whose name they bore, were these persons Apostles? And if they were not, what was the authority of their writings? The doubts with regard to the Revelation and to the Epistle to the Hebrews were in part of the same character. Were they in the full sense of the term Apostolic, as having been written by Apostles, or at least under the guidance of Apostles? Eusebius says expressly that all these "disputed" books were "nevertheless *well known to most* people."[10]

And it is manifest that the doubts which Eusebius records were ceasing to exist. Only in some cases does he indicate, and that without open statement, that he himself was at all inclined to sympathize with them. And Athanasius, writing a very short time afterwards (A.D. 326), makes no distinction between acknowledged and disputed books, but places all seven of the Catholic Epistles, as of equal authority, immediately after the Acts of the Apostles.[11] Cyril of Jerusalem, in his Catechetical Lectures, written before his episcopate, c. A.D. 349, does the same (*Lect.* IV. x. 36). Some fifteen years later we have the Council of Laodicea, and near the end of the century the Council of Hippo, and the third Council of Carthage, giving formal ratification to these generally received views; after which all questioning for many centuries ceased. So that while the classification into "acknowledged" and "disputed" writings proves that each book was carefully scrutinized, and in various quarters independently, before it was admitted to the canon, the cessation of this distinction proves that the result of all this scrutiny was that the sporadic doubts and hesitations respecting certain of the books of the New Testament were finally put to rest.

And it must not be supposed that the process was one of general amnesty. While some books that had here and there been excluded were finally accepted, some that had here and there been included in the canon, such as the Epistles of Clement and of Barnabas and the Shepherd of Hermas, were finally rejected. The charge of uncritical or indiscriminate admission cannot be substantiated. The facts are quite the other way.

When we confine our attention to the Epistle of James in particular, we find that if the doubts which were here and there felt respecting it in the third century are intelligible, the universal acceptance which it met with in the fourth and following centuries is well founded. The doubts were provoked by two facts—(1) the Epistle had remained for some time unknown to a good many Churches; (2) when it became generally known it remained uncertain what the authority of the writer was, especially whether he was an Apostle or not. It is possible also that these misgivings were in some cases emphasized by the further fact that there is a marked absence of doctrinal teaching. In this Epistle the articles of the Christian faith are scarcely touched upon at all. Whether the apparent inconsistency with the teaching of St. Paul respecting the relation between faith and works, of which so much has been made since Luther's time, was discovered or not by those who were inclined to dispute the authority of this Epistle, may be doubted. But of course, if any inconsistency *was* believed to exist, that also would tell against the general reception of the letter as canonical.

That the Epistle should at first remain very little known, especially in the West and among the Gentile congregations, is exactly what we should expect from the character of the letter and the circumstances of its publication. It is addressed by a Jew to Jews, by one who never moved from the Church over which he presided at Jerusalem to those humble and obscure Christians outside Palestine who, by their conscientious retention of the Law side by side with the Gospel, cut themselves off more and more from free intercourse with other Christians, whether Gentile converts or more liberally-minded Jews. A letter which in the first instance was to be read in Christian *synagogues* (James ii. 2) might easily remain a long time without becoming known to Churches which from the outset had adopted the principles laid down in St. Paul's Epistle to the Galatians. The constant journeys of the Apostle of the Gentiles caused his letters to become well known throughout the Churches at a very early date. But the first Bishop of the Mother Church of Jerusalem had no such advantages. Great as was his influence in his own sphere, with a rank equal to that of an Apostle, yet he was not well known outside that sphere, and he himself seems never to have travelled beyond it, or even to have left the centre of it. With outsiders, who simply knew that he was not one of the Twelve, his influence would not be great; and a letter emanating from him, even if known to exist, would not be eagerly inquired after or carefully circulated. Gentile prejudice against Jewish Christians would still further contribute to keep in the background a letter which was specially addressed to Jewish Christians, and was also itself distinctly Jewish in tone. Nor would the exclusive class of believers to whom the letter was sent care to make it known to those Christians from whom they habitually kept aloof. Thus the prejudices of both sides contributed to prevent the Epistle from circulating outside the somewhat narrow circle to which it was in the first instance addressed; and there is therefore nothing surprising in its being unknown to Irenæus, Hippolytus, Tertullian, Cyprian, and the author of the Muratorian Canon. There is no sign that these writers *rejected* it; they had never heard of it.[12]

And yet the Epistle did become known at a very early date, at any rate to some outsiders, even in the West. It was almost certainly known to Clement of Rome, whose Epistle to the Church of Corinth (written *c.* A.D.

97) contains several passages, which seem to be reminiscences of St. James. And although not one of them can be relied upon as proving that Clement knew our Epistle, yet when they are all put together they make a cumulative argument of very great strength.[13] So cautious and critical a writer as Bishop Lightfoot does not hesitate to assert, in a note on Clement, chap. xii., "The instance of Rahab was doubtless suggested by Heb. xi. 31; James ii. 25; for *both these Epistles were known to St. Clement, and are quoted elsewhere.*" And the Epistle of St. James was certainly known to Hermas, a younger contemporary of Clement, and author of the *Shepherd*, which was written in the first half, and possibly in the first quarter, of the second century.[14] Origen, in the works of which we have the Greek original, quotes it once as "the Epistle current as that of James" (τῇ φερομένῃ Ἰακώβου ἐπιστολῇ — *In Johan.* xix. 6), and once (*In Psal.* xxx.) without any expression of doubt; and in the inaccurate Latin translations of others of his works there are several distinct quotations from the Epistle. So that it would seem to have reached Alexandria just as Clement, Origen's instructor and predecessor, left the city during the persecution under Septimius Severus (*c.* A.D. 202).[15]

But the conclusive fact in the external evidence respecting the Epistle is that it is contained in the Peshitto. This ancient Syriac Version was made in the second century, in the country in which the letter of James would be best known; and although the framers of this translation omitted 2 Peter, 2 and 3 John, and Jude, they admitted James without scruple. Thus the earliest evidence for this Epistle, as for that to the Hebrews, is chiefly Eastern; while that for Jude, as for 2 and 3 John, is chiefly Western.

And the evidence of the Peshitto is not weakened by the fact, if it be a fact, that there was a still earlier Syrian canon which contained none of the Catholic Epistles. There is no certain allusion to them or quotation from them in the Homilies of Aphrahat or Aphraates (*c.* A.D. 335); and in the "Doctrine of Addai" (A.D. 250-300) the clergy of Edessa are directed to read the Law and the Prophets, the Gospel, St. Paul's Epistles, and the Acts, no other canonical book being mentioned. In all Churches the number of Christian writings read publicly in the liturgy was at first small, and in no case were the Catholic Epistles the first to be used for this purpose.

The internal evidence, as we shall see when we come to examine it more closely, is even more strong than the external. The character of the letter exactly harmonizes with the character of James the first Bishop of Jerusalem, and with the known circumstances of those to whom the letter is addressed, and this in a way that no literary forger of that age could have reached. And there is no sufficient motive for a forgery, for the letter is singularly wanting in doctrinal statements. The supposed opposition to St. Paul will not hold;

a writer who wished to oppose St. Paul would have made his opposition much more clear. And a forger who wished to get the authority of St. James wherewith to counteract St. Paul's teaching would have made us aware that it was either an Apostle, the son of Zebedee or the son of Alphæus, or else the brother of the Lord, who was addressing us, and would not have left it open for us to suppose that the Epistle was from the pen of some unknown James, who had no authority at all equal to that of St. Paul. And let any one compare this Epistle with those of Clement of Rome, and of Barnabas, and of Ignatius, and mark its enormous superiority. If it were the work of a forger, what a perplexing fact this superiority would be! If it be the work either of an Apostle or of one who had Apostolic rank, everything is explained.

Luther's famous criticism on the Epistle, that it is "a veritable Epistle of straw," is amazing, and is to be explained by the fact that it contradicts his caricature of St. Paul's doctrine of justification by faith. There is no opposition between St. James and St. Paul, and there is sometimes no real opposition between St. James and Luther. And when Luther gives as his opinion that our Epistle was "not the writing of any Apostle" we can agree with him, though not in the sense in which he means it; for he starts from the erroneous supposition that the letter bears the name of the son of Zebedee. We must also bear in mind his own explanation of what is Apostolic and what is not. It has a purely subjective meaning. It does not mean what was written or not written by an Apostle or the equal of an Apostle. "Apostolic" means that which, in Luther's opinion, an Apostle *ought* to teach, and all that fails to satisfy this condition is not Apostolic. "Therein all true holy books agree, that they preach and urge Christ. That too is the right touchstone whereby to test all books—whether they urge Christ or not; for all Scripture testifies of Christ (Rom. iii. 21).... That which does not teach Christ is still short of Apostolic, even if it were the teaching of St. Peter or St. Paul. Again, that which preaches Christ, that were Apostolic, even if Judas, Annas, Pilate, and Herod preached it." The Lutheran Church has not followed him in this principle, which places the authority of any book of Scripture at the mercy of the likes and dislikes of the individual reader; and it has restored the Epistles to the Hebrews and of James and Jude to their proper places in the New Testament, instead of leaving them in the kind of appendix to which Luther had banished them and the Revelation. Moreover, the passage containing the statement about the "veritable Epistle of straw"[16] is now omitted from the preface to his translation. And with regard to this very point, his former friend and later opponent Andrew Rudolph Bodenstein, of Karlstadt, pertinently asked, "If you allow the Jews to stamp books with authority by receiving them, why do you refuse to grant as much power to the Churches of Christ, since the Church is not less than the Synagogue?" We have at least as much reason to trust the Councils of Laodicea, Hippo, and Carthage, which formally defined the limits of the New Testament, as we have to trust the unknown Jewish influences which fixed those of the Old. And when we examine for ourselves the evidence which is still extant, and which has greatly diminished in the course of fifteen hundred years, we feel that both on external and internal grounds the decision of the fourth century respecting the genuineness of the Epistle of St. James, as a veritable product of the Apostolic age and as worthy of a place in the canon of the New Testament, is fully justified.

[8] The date so frequently given, A.D. 363, cannot be substantiated, and on the whole is not probable. See Hefele, *History of the Church Councils*, II. vi. 93.

[9] The Epistle to the Hebrews and the Apocalypse.

[10] γνωρίμων δ' οὖν ὅμως τοῖς πολλοῖς (*H. E.* III. xxv. 3), where γνώριμος, as usual, indicates *familiar* knowledge. Eusebius is a desultory writer, and one has to gather his views from statements scattered over chaps. iii., xxiv., and xxv., some of which are not very precise. The following table seems to represent his opinion:—

CANONICAL Books (ἐνδιάθηκοι γραφαί)	*Universally acknowledged* (τὰ ὁμολογούμενα)	Four Gospels, Acts, fourteen Epistles of Paul (Hebrews ?), 1 John, 1 Peter, Apocalypse (?).
	Disputed (τὰ ἀντιλεγόμενα)	*As to authenticity*—2 Peter. *As to Apostolicity*—James, Jude, 2 and 3 John.
UNCANONICAL	*Orthodox*, but of no authority, because *defective*	*As to authenticity*—Acts of Paul, Shepherd, Apocalypse of Peter. *As to Apostolicity*—Epistle of Barnabas, Doctrines of the Apostles, Gospel according to Hebrews, Apocalypse (?).
	Heretical	Gospels of Peter, Thomas, Matthias, Acts of Andrew, John, etc., etc.

[11]   Epist. Fest. xxxix. The passage is given in full by Westcott On the Canon, Appendix D., xiv. The Ecclesiastical History of Eusebius cannot have been completed later than A.D. 325, but the earlier books were probably written about A.D. 313, soon after the Edict of Milan. See Bishop Lightfoot, Dict. of Chris. Biog., I., p. 322.

[12]   Harnack, *Das Neue Testament um das Jahr* 200 (Freiburg I. B., 1889), p. 79.

[13]

Compare Clement	with James.
x. 1	ii. 23.
xi. 2	i. 8; iv. 8.
xii. 1	ii. 25.
xvii. 6	iv. 14.
xxx. 2	iv. 6.
xxxi. 2	ii. 21.
xlvi. 5	iv. 1.
xlix. 5	x. 20.

[14] Salmon, *Introduction to the N.T.*, pp. 52, 582-91, 4th Ed. (Murray, 1889); Zahn, *Geschichte des Neutestamentlichen Kanons* (Erlangen, 1889), p. 962.

[15] If Zahn is right in thinking that Clement knew, and perhaps commented on, the Epistle of James, it may have become known in Alexandria somewhat earlier. A few passages in Clement have possible reminiscences of James; *e.g.* in *Strom.* II. v. he says of Abraham that he is found to have been expressly called the "friend" of God (James ii. 23); and in *Strom.* VI. xviii., in connexion with loving one's neighbour (the βασιλικὸς νόμος of James ii. 8), he speaks of being βασιλικοί (Zahn, *Geschichte des Neutestamentlichen Kanons*, I., pp. 322, 323—Erlangen, 1888). The *Hypotyposeis*, in which Clement perhaps treated of the Catholic Epistles, were written after he left Alexandria (*Ibid.*, p. 29).

[16] Or, more literally, "a right strawy Epistle"—"eine rechte strohern Epistel.... Denn sie doch keine evangelische Art an sich hat" (*Luther's Werke*, ed. Gustav Pfizer, Frankfurt, 1840, p. 1412; see also pp. 1423, 1424, and Westcott *On the Canon*, 3rd ed., pp. 448-54).

CHAPTER III
THE AUTHOR OF THE EPISTLE: JAMES THE BROTHER OF THE LORD

"James, a servant of God and of the Lord Jesus Christ." —Jas. i. 1

WE have still to consider the second half of the question as to the authenticity of this letter. Granting that it is a genuine Epistle of James, and a writing of the Apostolic age, to which of the persons in that age who are known to us as bearing the name of James is it to be attributed? The consensus of opinion on this point, though not so great as that respecting the genuineness of the letter, is now very considerable, and seems to be increasing.

The name James is the English form of the Hebrew name Yacoob (Jacob), which in Greek became Ἰάκωβος, in Latin Jacōbus, and in English James, a form which grievously blurs the history of the name. From having been the name of the patriarch Jacob, the progenitor of the Jewish race, it became one of the commonest of proper names among the Jews; and in the New Testament we find several persons bearing this name among the followers of Jesus Christ. It would be possible to make as many as six; but these must certainly be reduced to four, and probably to three.

These six are—

1. James the Apostle, the son of Zebedee and brother of John the Apostle (Matt. iv. 21; x. 2; xvii. 5; Mark x. 35; xiii. 3; Luke ix. 54; Acts xii. 2).

2. James the Apostle, the son of Alphæus (Matt. x. 3; Mark iii. 18; Luke vi. 15; Acts i. 13).

3. James the Little, the son of Mary the wife of Clōpas (John xix. 25), who had one other son, named Joses (Matt. xxvii. 56; Mark xv. 40).

4. James the brother of the Lord (Gal. i. 19), a relationship which he shares with Joses, Simon, and Judas (Matt. xiii. 55; Mark vi. 3) and some unnamed sisters.

5. James the overseer of the Church of Jerusalem (Acts xii. 17; xv. 13; xxi. 18; 1 Cor. xv. 7; Gal. ii. 9, 12).

6. James the brother of the Jude who wrote the Epistle (Jude i. 1).

Besides which, we have an unknown James, who was father of the Apostle Judas, not Iscariot (Luke v. 16); but we do not know that this James ever became a disciple.

Of these six we may safely identify the last three as being one and the same person; and we may probably identify James the Apostle, the son of Alphæus, with James the Little, the son of Mary and Clopas; in which case we may conjecture that the epithet of "the Little" (ὁ μικρός) was given him to distinguish him from the other Apostle James, the son of Zebedee. Clopas (not Cleophas, as in the A.V.) may be one Greek form of the Aramaic name Chalpai, of which Alphæus may be another Greek form; so that the father of this James may have been known both as Clopas and as Alphæus. But this is by no means certain. In the ancient Syriac Version we do not find both Alphæus and Clopas represented by Chalpai; but we find Alphæus rendered Chalpai, while Clopas reappears as Kleopha. And the same usage is found in the Jerusalem Syriac.

We have thus reduced the six to four or three; and it is sometimes proposed to reduce the three to two, by identifying James the Lord's brother with James the son of Alphæus. But this identification is attended by difficulties so serious as to seem to be quite fatal; and it would probably never have been made but for the wish to show that "brother of the Lord" does not mean brother in the literal sense, but may mean *cousin*. For the identification depends upon making Mary the wife of Clopas (and mother of James the son of Alphæus) identical with the sister of Mary the mother of the Lord, in the much-discussed passage John xix. 25; so that Jesus and James would be first cousins, being sons respectively of two sisters, each of whom was called Mary.[17]

The difficulties under which this theory labours are mainly these:—

1. It depends on an identification of Clopas with Alphæus, which is uncertain, though not improbable.

2. It depends on a further identification of Christ's "mother's sister" with "Mary the wife of Clopas" in John xix. 25, which is both uncertain and highly improbable. In that verse we almost certainly have four women, and not three, contrasted with the four soldiers just mentioned (vv. 23, 24), and arranged in two pairs: "His mother, and His mother's sister; Mary the wife of Clopas, and Mary Magdalene."

3. It assumes that two sisters were both called Mary.

4. No instance in Greek literature has been found in which "brother" (ἀδελφός) means "cousin." The Greek language has a word to express "cousin" (ἀνεψιός), which occurs Col. iv. 10; and it is to be noted that the

ancient tradition preserved by Hegesippus (c. A.D. 170) distinguishes James the first overseer of the Church of Jerusalem as the *"brother* of the Lord" (Eus. *H. E.* II. xxiii. 1), and his successor Symeon as the *"cousin* of the Lord" (IV. xxii. 4). Could Hegesippus have written thus if James were really a cousin? If a vague term such as "kinsman" (συγγενής) was wanted, that also might have been used, as in Luke i. 36, 58; ii. 44.

5. In none of the four lists of the Apostles is there any hint that any of them are the brethren of the Lord; and in Acts i. 13, 14, and 1 Cor. ix. 5, "the brethren of the Lord" are expressly distinguished from the Apostles. Moreover, the traditions of the age subsequent to the New Testament sometimes make James the Lord's brother one of the Seventy, but never one of the Twelve, a fact which can be explained only on the hypothesis that it was notorious that he was not one of the Twelve. The reverence for this James and for the title of Apostle was such that tradition would eagerly have given him the title had there been any opening for doing so.

6. The "brethren of the Lord" appear in the Gospels almost always with the mother of the Lord (Matt. xii. 46; Mark iii. 32; Luke viii. 19; John ii. 12); never with Mary the wife of Clopas; and popular knowledge of them connects them with Christ's mother, and not with any other Mary (Mark vi. 3; Matt. xiii. 55). "My brethren," in Matt. xxviii. 10, and John xx. 17, does not mean Christ's earthly relations, but the children of "My Father and your Father."

7. But the strongest objection of all is St. John's express statement (vii. 5) that "even His brethren did not believe on Him;" a statement which he could not have made if one of the brethren (James), and possibly two others (Simon and Judas), were already Apostles.

The identification of James the son of Alphæus with James the Lord's brother must therefore be abandoned, and we remain with three disciples bearing the name of James from which to select the writer of this Epistle—the son of Zebedee, the son of Alphæus, and the brother of the Lord. The father of Judas, not Iscariot, need not be considered, for we do not even know that he ever became a believer.

In our ignorance of the life, and thought, and language of the son of Zebedee and the son of Alphæus, we cannot say that there is anything in the Epistle itself which forbids us to attribute it to either of them; but there is nothing in it which leads us to do so. And there are two considerations which, when combined, are strongly against Apostolic authorship. The writer does not claim to be an Apostle; and the hesitation as to the reception of the Epistle in certain parts of the Christian Church would be extraordinary if the letter were reputed to be of Apostolic authorship. When we take either of these Apostles separately we become involved in further difficulties. It is not probable that any Apostolic literature existed in the lifetime of James the son of Zebedee, who was martyred, under Herod Agrippa I., *i.e.* not later than the spring of A.D. 44, when Herod Agrippa died. That any Apostle wrote an encyclical letter as early as A.D. 42 or 43 is so improbable that we ought to have strong evidence before adopting it, and the only evidence worth considering is that furnished by the Peshitto. The earliest MSS. of this ancient Syriac Version, which date from the fifth to the eighth century, call it an Epistle of James the Apostle; but evidence which cannot be traced higher than the fifth century respecting an improbable occurrence alleged to have taken place in the first century is not worth very much. Moreover, the scribes who put this heading and subscription to the Epistle may have meant no more than that it was by a person of Apostolic rank, or they may have shared the common Western error of identifying the brother of the Lord with the son of Alphæus. Editors of the Syriac Version in a much later age certainly do attribute the Epistle to the son of Zebedee, for they state that the three Catholic Epistles admitted to that version—James, 1 Peter, and 1 John—are by the three Apostles who witnessed the Transfiguration. The statement seems to be a blundering misinterpretation of the earlier title, which assigned it to James the Apostle. And if we attribute the letter to the son of Alphæus we get rid of one difficulty, only to fall into another; we are no longer compelled to give the Epistle so improbably early a date as A.D. 43, but we are left absolutely without any evidence to connect it with the son of Alphæus, *unless* we identify this Apostle with the brother of the Lord, an identification which has already been shown to be untenable.[18]

Therefore, without further hesitation, we may assign the Epistle to one of the most striking and impressive figures in the Apostolic age, James the Just, the brother of the Lord, and the first overseer of the Mother Church of Jerusalem.

Whether James was the brother of the Lord as being the son of Joseph by a former marriage, or as being the son of Joseph and Mary born after the birth of Jesus, need not be argued in detail. All that specially concerns us, for a right understanding of the Epistle, is to remember that it was written by one who, although for some time not a believer in the Messiahship of Jesus, was, through his near relationship, constantly in His society, witnessing His acts and hearing His words. This much, however, should be noted, that there is nothing in Scripture to warn us from understanding that Joseph and Mary had other children, and that "*first*born" in Luke ii. 7, and "till" in Matt. i. 25, appear to imply that they had; a supposition confirmed by contemporary belief (Mark vi. 3; Matt. xiii. 55), and by the constant attendance of these "brethren" on the mother of the Lord (Matt. xii. 46; Mark iii. 32; Luke viii. 19;

John ii. 12); that, on the other hand, the theory which gives Joseph children older than Jesus deprives Him of His rights as the heir of Joseph and of the house of David; seems to be of apocryphal origin (Gospel according to Peter, or Book of James); and like Jerome's theory of cousinship, appears to have been invented in the interests of ascetic views and of *à priori* convictions as to the perpetual virginity of the Blessed Virgin. The immense consensus of belief in the perpetual virginity does not begin until long after all historical evidence was lost. Tertullian appears to assume as a matter of course that the Lord's brethren are the children of Joseph and Mary, as if in his day no one had any other view (*Adv. Marc.*, IV. xix.; *De Carne Christi*, vii.).[19]

According to either view, James was the son of Joseph, and almost certainly was brought up with his Divine Brother in the humble home at Nazareth. His father, as St. Matthew tells us (i. 19) was a *just* or *righteous* man, like the parents of the Baptist (Luke i. 6), and this was the title by which James was known during his lifetime, and by which he is still constantly known. He is James "the Just" (ὁ δίκαιος). The epithet as used in Scripture of his father and others (Matt. i. 19; xxiii. 35; Luke i. 6; ii. 25; xxiii. 50; Acts x. 20; 2 Peter ii. 7), and in history of him, must not be understood as implying precisely what the Athenians meant when they styled Aristeides "the Just," or what we mean by being "just" now. To a Jew the word implied not merely being impartial and upright, but also having a studied and even scrupulous reverence for everything prescribed by the Law. The Sabbath, the synagogue worship, the feasts and fasts, purification, tithes, all the moral and ceremonial ordinances of the Law of the Lord—these were the things on which the just man bestowed a loving care, and in which he preferred to do more than was required, rather than the bare minimum insisted on by the Rabbis. It was in a home of which righteousness of this kind was the characteristic that St. James was reared, and in which he became imbued with that reverent love for the Law which makes him, even more than St. Paul, to be the ideal "Hebrew of Hebrews." For him Christ came "not to destroy, but to fulfil." Christianity turns the Law of Moses into a "royal law" (ii. 8), but it does not abrogate it. The Judaism which had been his moral and spiritual atmosphere during his youth and early manhood remained with him after he had learned to see that there was no antagonism between the Law and the Gospel.

It would be part of his strict Jewish training that he should pay the prescribed visits to Jerusalem at the feasts (John vii. 10); and he would there become familiar with the magnificent liturgy of the Temple, and would lay the foundation for that love of public and private prayer within its precincts which was one of his best-known characteristics in after-life. A love of prayer, and a profound belief in its efficacy, appear again and again in the pages of his Epistle (i. 5; iv. 2, 3, 8; v. 13-18). It was out of a strong personal experience that the man who knelt in prayer until "his knees became hard like a camel's" declared that "the supplication of a righteous man availeth much in its working."

Strict Judaism has ever a tendency to narrowness, and we find this tendency in the brethren of the Lord, in their attitude both towards their Brother, and also towards Gentile converts after they had accepted Him (Gal. ii. 12). Of the long period of silence during which Jesus was preparing Himself for His ministry we know nothing. But immediately after His first miracle, which they probably witnessed, they went down with Him, and His mother, and His disciples to Capernaum (John ii. 12), and very possibly accompanied Him to Jerusalem for the Passover. They would be almost certain to go thither to keep the feast. It was there that "many believed on His Name, beholding His signs which He did. But Jesus did not trust Himself unto them, for that He knew all men." He knew that when the immediate effect of His miracles had passed off the faith of these sudden converts would not endure. And this seems to have been the case with His brethren. They were at first attracted by His originality, and power, and holiness, then perplexed by methods which they could not understand (John vii. 3, 4), then inclined to regard Him as a dreamer and a fanatic (Mark iii. 21), and finally decided against Him (John vii. 5). Like many others among His followers, they were quite unable to reconcile His position with the traditional views respecting the Messiah; and instead of revising these views, as being possibly faulty, they held fast to them, and rejected Him. It was not merely in reference to the people of Nazareth, who had tried to kill Him (Luke iv. 29), but to those who were still closer to Him by ties of blood and home, that He uttered the sad complaint, "A prophet is not without honour, save in his own country, and among *his own kin*, and in *his own house*" (Mark vi. 4).

The fact that our Lord committed His mother to the keeping of St. John harmonizes with the supposition that at the time of the Crucifixion His brethren were still unbelievers. The Resurrection would be likely to open their eyes and dispel their doubts (Acts i. 14); and a special revelation of the risen Lord seems to have been granted to St. James (1 Cor. xv. 7), as to St. Paul; in both cases because behind the external opposition to Christ there was earnest faith and devotion, which at once found its object, as soon as the obstructing darkness was removed. After his conversion, St. James speedily took the first place among the believers who constituted the original Church of Jerusalem. He takes the lead, even when the chief of the Apostles are present. It is to him that St. Peter reports himself, when he is miraculously freed from prison (Acts xii. 17). It is he who presides at the so-called Council of Jerusalem (xv. 13; see esp. ver. 19). And it is to him that St. Paul specially turns on his last visit to Jerusalem, to report his success among the Gentiles (xxi. 17). St. Paul places him before St. Peter and St. John in mentioning those "who were reputed to be pillars" of the Church (Gal. ii. 9), and states that on his first visit to Jerusalem after his own conversion he stayed fifteen days with Peter, but saw no other of the Apostles, excepting James, the Lord's brother (Gal. i. 18, 19); a passage of disputed meaning, but which, if it does not imply that James was in some sense an Apostle, at least suggests that he was a person of equal importance. (Comp. Acts ix. 26-30.) Moreover, we find that at Antioch St. Peter himself allowed his attitude towards the Gentiles to be changed in deference to the representations of "certain that came from James," who had possibly misunderstood or misused their commission; but the narrowness already alluded to may have made St. James himself unable to move as rapidly as St. Peter and St. Paul in adopting a generous course with Gentile converts.

Unless there is a reference to St. James in Heb. xiii. 7, as among those who had once "had the lead over you," but are now no longer alive to speak the word, we must go outside the New Testament for further notices of him. They are to be found chiefly in Clement of Alexandria, Hegesippus, and Josephus. Clement (*Hypotyp*. VI. ap. Eus. *H. E.* II. i. 3) records a tradition that Peter, James, and John, after the Ascension of the Saviour, although they had been preferred by the Lord, did not contend for distinction, but that James the Just became Bishop of Jerusalem. And again (*Hypotyp*. VII.), "To James the Just, John, and Peter, the Lord, after the Resurrection, imparted the gift of knowledge (τὴν γνῶσιν); these imparted it to the rest of the Apostles, and the rest of the Apostles to the Seventy, of whom Barnabas was one. Now, there have been two Jameses—one the Just, who was thrown from the gable [of the Temple], and beaten to death by a fuller with a club, and another who was beheaded."[20] The narrative of Hegesippus is also preserved for us by Eusebius (*H. E.* II. xxiii. 4-18). It is manifestly legendary, and possibly comes from the Essene Ebionites, who appear to have been fond of religious romances. It is sometimes accepted as historical, as by Clement in the passage just quoted; but its internal improbabilities and its divergencies from Josephus condemn it. It may, however, contain some historical touches, especially in the general sketch of St. James; just as the legends about our own King Alfred, although untrustworthy as to facts, nevertheless convey a true idea of the saintly and scholarly king. It runs thus: "There succeeds to the charge of the Church, James, the brother of the Lord, in conjunction with the Apostles, the one who has been named Just by all, from the time of our Lord to our own time, for there were many called James.[21] Now, he was holy from his mother's womb. He drank neither wine nor strong drink; nor did he eat animal food. No razor ever came upon his head; he anointed not himself with oil; and he did not indulge in bathing. To him alone was it lawful to go into the Holy Place[22]; for he wore no wool, but linen. And he would go into the Temple alone, and would be found there kneeling on his knees and asking forgiveness for the people, so that his knees became dry and hard as a camel's, because he was always on his knees worshipping God and asking forgiveness for the people. On account, therefore, of his exceeding justness, he was called Just and Oblias, which is in Greek 'bulwark of the people' and 'justness,' as the prophets show concerning him. Some, then, of the seven sects among the people, which have been mentioned before by me in the *Memoirs*, asked him, What is the Door of Jesus? And he said that He was the Saviour. From which some believed Jesus is the Christ. But the sects aforesaid did not believe, either in the Resurrection or in One coming to recompense to each man according to his works. But as many as believed did so through James. When many, therefore, even of the rulers were believing, there was a tumult of the Jews and scribes and Pharisees, who said, It looks as if all the people would be expecting Jesus as the Christ. They came together, therefore, and said to James, We pray thee, restrain the people, for it has been led astray after Jesus, as though He were the Christ. We pray thee to persuade all that come to the day of the Passover concerning Jesus; for to thee we all give heed. For we bear witness to thee, and so do all the people, that thou art just, and acceptest not the person of any. Do thou, therefore, persuade the multitude not to be led astray concerning Jesus; for all the people and all of us give heed to thee. Stand, therefore, upon the gable of the Temple, that thou mayest be visible to those below, and that thy words may be readily heard by all the people. For on account of the Passover there have come together all the tribes, with the Gentiles also. Therefore the aforesaid scribes and Pharisees placed James upon the gable of the Temple, and cried to him and said, O just one, to whom we ought all to give heed, seeing that the people is being led astray after Jesus, who was crucified, tell us what is the Door of Jesus. And he answered with a loud voice, Why ask ye me concerning Jesus the Son of man? Even He sitteth in heaven, at the right of the Mighty Power, and He is to come on the clouds of heaven. And when many were convinced, and gave glory on the witness of James, and said, Hosannah to the Son of David, then again the same scribes and Pharisees said unto one another, We have done ill in furnishing such witness to Jesus. But let us go up, and cast him down, that they may be terrified, and not believe him. And they cried out, saying, Oh! oh! even the Just has been led astray. And they fulfilled the Scripture, which is written in Isaiah, Let us take away the Just One, for he is troublesome to us; therefore shall they eat the fruit of their deeds. So they went up, and cast down the Just, and said to one another, Let us stone James the Just. And they began to stone him, seeing that he was not dead from the fall, but turning round, knelt, and said, I pray Thee, Lord God and Father, forgive them, for they know not what they do. But whilst they were thus stoning him, one of the priests of the sons of Rechab, son of Rechabim,[23] to whom Jeremiah the prophet bears testimony, cried, saying, Stop! what are ye doing? The Just One is praying for you. And one of them, one of the fullers, took the club with which clothes are pressed, and brought it down on the head of the Just One. And in this way he bore witness. And they buried him on the spot by the Temple, and his monument still remains by the Temple. This man has become a true witness, to both Jews and Gentiles, that Jesus is the Christ. And straightway Vespasian lays siege to them." That is, Hegesippus regards the attack of the Romans as a speedy judgment on the Jews for the murder of James the Just, and consequently places it A.D. 69. This is probably several years too late. Josephus places it A.D. 62 or 63. His account is as follows:—

"Now, the younger Ananus, whom we stated to have succeeded to the high-priesthood, was precipitate in temper and exceedingly audacious, and he followed the sect of the Sadducees, who are very harsh in judging offenders, beyond all other Jews, as we have already shown. Ananus, therefore, as being a person of this character, and thinking that he had a suitable opportunity, through Festus being dead, and Albinus still on his journey (to Judæa), assembles a Sanhedrin of judges; and he brought before it the brother of Jesus who was called Christ (his name was James) and some others, and delivered them to be stoned, on a charge of being transgressors of the law. But as many as seemed to be most equitable among those in the city, and scrupulous as to all that concerned the laws, were grievously affected by this; and they send to the king [Herod Agrippa II.], secretly praying him to order Ananus to act in such a way no more; for that not even his first action was lawfully done. And some of them go to meet Albinus on his journey from Alexandria, and inform him that Ananus had no authority to assemble a Sanhedrin without his leave. And Albinus, being convinced by what they said, wrote in anger to Ananus, threatening to punish him for this. And for this reason King Agrippa took away the high-priesthood from him after he had been in office three months, and conferred it upon Jesus the son of Damnæus" (*Ant.* XX. ix. 1).

This account by Josephus contains no improbabilities, and should be preferred to that of Hegesippus. It has been suspected of Christian interpolation, because of the reference to Jesus Christ, whom Josephus persistently ignores in his writings. But a Christian who took the trouble to garble the narrative at all would probably have done so to more purpose, both as regards Jesus and James. In any case Hegesippus and Josephus agree in confirming the impression produced by the New Testament, that James the Just was a person held in the greatest respect by all in Jerusalem, whether Jews or Christians, and one who exercised great influence in the East over the whole Jewish race. We shall find that this fact harmonizes well with the phenomena of the Epistle, and it leads directly to the next question which calls upon us for discussion.

[17] The supposed relationship may be exhibited thus:—

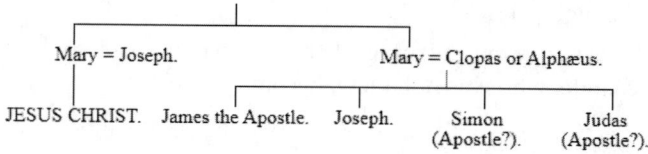

[18] It seems to be right to take this opportunity of preventing a name of great authority from being any longer quoted as favouring the identification. Dr. Döllinger, in his *Christenthum und Kirche in der Zeit der Grundlegung* (1860), translated by H. N. Oxenham as *The First Age of Christianity and the Church*, advocated the identification (chap. iii.). The venerable author told the present writer, in June, 1877, that he was convinced that his earlier opinion on this subject was entirely erroneous, and that the Apostle James of Alphæus was a different person from James Bishop of Jerusalem and brother of the Lord. He added that the Eastern Church had always distinguished the two, and that their identification in the West was due to the influence of Jerome.

The evidence of Martyrologies and Calendars is worth noting as indicating the tradition on the subject. The Hieronymian Martyrology and other early Roman Martyrologies commemorate James of Alphæus June 22nd, and James the Lord's brother December 27th; the Ambrosian Liturgy, James of Alphæus December 30th, and the Lord's brother May 1st; the Byzantine Calendar, James of Alphæus October 9th, and the Lord's brother October 23rd; the Egyptian and Ethiopic Calendars, James of Alphæus October 2nd, and the Lord's brother October 23rd.

[19] Alford, Farrar, Meyer, Schaff, Stier, Weiss, Wieseler, Winer, and others support this view. See also McClellan's

note on Matt. xiii. 55, and Plumptre's Introduction to St. James. Bishop Lightfoot contends for the Epiphanian theory.

[20] Comp. *Strom*. VI. viii., where Clement speaks of James, Peter, John, Paul (note the order) as possessing the true *gnosis*, and knowing all things.

[21] Hegesippus evidently distinguishes James the brother of the Lord from any of the Twelve.

[22] It is incredible that he should be allowed the privileges of the high priest.

[23] What is the meaning of this tautology? And could a Rechabite, who was not a Jew, become a priest?

CHAPTER IV
THE PERSONS ADDRESSED IN THE EPISTLE; THE JEWS OF THE DISPERSION

"James, a servant of God and of the Lord Jesus Christ, to the twelve tribes which are of the Dispersion, greeting."—James i. 1.

THESE words appear to be both simple and plain. At first sight there would seem to be not much room for any serious difference of opinion as to their meaning. The writer of the letter writes as "a servant of God and of the Lord Jesus Christ," *i.e.* as a Christian, "to the twelve tribes which are of the Dispersion," *i.e.* to the Jews who are living away from Palestine. Almost the only point which seems to be open to doubt is whether he addresses himself to all Jews, believing and unbelieving, or, as one might presume from his proclaiming himself at the outset to be a Christian, only to those of his fellow-countrymen who, like himself, have become "servants of the Lord Jesus Christ." And this is a question which cannot be determined without a careful examination of the contents of the Epistle.

And yet there has been very great difference of opinion as to the persons whom St. James had in his mind when he wrote these words. There is not only the triplet of opinions which easily grow out of the question just indicated, viz. that the letter is addressed to *believing Jews* only, to *unbelieving Jews* only, and to *both*: there are also the views of those who hold that it is addressed to Jewish and Gentile Christians regarded *separately*, or to the same regarded *as one body*, or to *Jewish Christians primarily*, with references to Gentile Christians and unconverted Jews, or finally to *Gentile Christians primarily*, seeing that they, since the rejection of Jesus by the Jews, are the true sons of Abraham and the rightful inheritors of the privileges of the twelve tribes.

In such a Babel of interpretations it will clear the ground somewhat if we adopt once more[24] as a guiding principle the common-sense canon of interpretation laid down by Hooker (*Eccles. Pol.* V. lix. 2), that "where a literal construction will stand, the farthest from the letter is commonly the worst." A literal construction of the expression "the twelve tribes of the Dispersion" will not only stand, but make excellent sense. Had St. James meant to address all Christians, regarded in their position as exiles from their heavenly home, he would have found some much plainer way of expressing himself. There is nothing improbable, but something quite the reverse, in the supposition that the first overseer of the Church of Jerusalem, who, as we have seen, was "a Hebrew of Hebrews," wrote a letter to those of his fellow-countrymen who were far removed from personal intercourse with him. So devoted a Jew, so devout a Christian, as we know him to have been, could not but take the most intense interest in all who were of Jewish blood, wherever they might dwell, especially such as had learned to believe in Christ, above all when he knew that they were suffering from habitual oppression and ill-treatment. We may without hesitation decide that when St. James says "the twelve tribes which are of the Dispersion" he means Jews away from their home in Palestine, and not Christians away from their home in heaven. For what possible point would the Dispersion (ἡ διασπορά) have in such a metaphor? Separation from the heavenly home might be spoken of as banishment, or exile, or homelessness, but not as "dispersion." Even if we confined ourselves to the opening words, we might safely adopt this conclusion, but we shall find that there are numerous features in the letter itself which abundantly confirm it.

It is quite out of place to quote such passages as the sealing of "the hundred and forty and four thousand ... out of every tribe of the children of Israel" (Rev. vii. 4-8), or the city with "twelve gates, ... and names written thereon, which are the names of the twelve tribes of the children of Israel" (Rev. xxi. 12). These occur in a book which is symbolical from the first chapter to the last, and therefore we know that the literal construction cannot stand. The question throughout is not whether a given passage is to be taken literally or symbolically, but what the passage in question symbolizes. Nor, again, can St. Peter's declaration that "ye are an elect race, a royal priesthood, a holy nation, a people for God's own possession" (1 Pet. ii. 9), be considered as at all parallel. There the combination of expressions plainly shows that the language is figurative; and there is no real analogy between an impassioned exhortation, modelled on the addresses of the Hebrew prophets, and the matter-of-fact opening words of a letter. The words have the clear ring of nationality, and there is nothing whatever added to them to turn the simple note into the complex sound of a doubtful metaphor. As Davidson justly remarks, "The use of the phrase *twelve tribes* is inexplicable if the writer intended all believers without distinction. The author makes no allusion to Gentile converts, nor to the relation between Jew and Gentile incorporated into one spiritual body."

Let us look at some of the features which characterize the Epistle itself, and see whether they bear out the view which is here advocated, that the persons addressed are Israelites in the national sense, and not as having been admitted into the spiritual "Israel of God" (Gal. vi. 16).

(1) The writer speaks of Abraham as "our father," without a hint that this is to be understood in any but the literal sense. "Was not Abraham our father justified by works, in that he offered up Isaac his son upon the altar?" (ii. 21). St. Paul, when he speaks of Abraham as "the father of all them that believe," clearly indicates this (Rom. iv. 11). (2) The writer speaks of his readers as worshipping in a "synagogue" (ii. 2), which may possibly mean that, just as St. James and the Apostles continued to attend the Temple services after the Ascension, so their readers are supposed to attend the synagogue services after their conversion. But at least it shows that the writer, in speaking of the public worship of those whom he addresses, naturally uses a word (συναγωγή) which had then, and continues to have, specially Jewish associations, rather than one (ἐκκλησία) which from the first beginnings of Christianity was promoted from its old political sphere to indicate the congregations, and even the very being, of the Christian Church. (3) He assumes that his readers are familiar not only with the life of Abraham (ii. 21, 23), but of Rahab (25), the prophets (v. 10), Job (11), and Elijah (17). These frequent appeals to the details of the Old Testament would be quite out of place in a letter addressed to Gentile converts. (4) God is spoken of under the specially Hebrew title of "the Lord of Sabaoth" (v. 4); and the frequent recurrence of "the Lord" throughout the Epistle (i. 7; iii. 9; iv. 10, 15; v. 10, 11, 15) looks like the language of one who wished to recall the name Jehovah to his readers. (5) In discountenancing swearing (v. 12) Jewish forms of oaths are taken as illustrations. (6) The vices which are condemned are such as were as common among the Jews as among the Gentiles—reckless language, rash swearing, oppression of the poor, covetousness. There is little or nothing said about the gross immorality which was rare among the Jews, but was almost a matter of course among the Gentiles. St. James denounces faults into which Jewish converts would be likely enough to lapse; he says nothing about the vices respecting which heathen converts, such as those at Corinth, are constantly warned by St. Paul. (7) But what is perhaps the most decisive feature of all is that he assumes throughout that for those whom he addresses the Mosaic Law is a binding and final authority. "If ye have respect of persons, ye commit sin, being convicted by the law as transgressors. ... If thou dost not commit adultery, but killest, thou art become a transgressor of the law" (ii. 9-11). "He that speaketh against a brother, or judgeth his brother, speaketh against the law, and judgeth the law" (iv. 11).

Scarcely any of these seven points, taken singly, would be at all decisive; but when we sum them up together, remembering in how short a letter they occur, and when we add them to the very plain and simple language of the address, we have an argument which will carry conviction to most persons who have no preconceived theory of their own to defend. And to this positive evidence derived from the presence of so much material that indicates Jewish circles as the destined recipients of the letter, we must add the strongly confirmatory negative evidence derived from the absence of anything which specially points either to Gentile converts or unconverted heathen. We may therefore read the letter as having been written by one who had been born and educated in a thoroughly Jewish atmosphere, who had accepted the Gospel, not as cancelling the Law, but as raising it to a higher power; and we may read it also as addressed to men who, like the writer, are by birth and education Jews, and, like him, have acknowledged Jesus as their Lord and the Christ. The difference between writer and readers lies in this, that he is in Palestine, and they not; that he appears to be in a position of authority, whereas they seem for the most part to be a humble and suffering folk. All which fits in admirably with the hypothesis that we have before us an Epistle written by the austere and Judaic-minded James the Just, written from Jerusalem, to comfort and warn those Jewish Christians who lay remote from his personal influence.

That it is Jewish *Christians*, and not unbelieving Jews, or Jews whether believing or not, who are addressed, is not open to serious doubt. There is not only the fact that St. James at the outset proclaims himself to be a Christian (i. 1), but also the statement that the wealthy oppressors of his poor readers "blaspheme the honourable Name by which ye are called," or more literally "which was called upon you," viz. the Name of Christ. Again, the famous paragraph about faith and works assumes that the faith of the readers and the faith of the writer is identical (ii. 7, 14-20). Once more, he expressly claims them as believers when he writes, "My brethren, hold not *the faith of our Lord Jesus Christ, the Lord of glory, with respect of persons*" (ii. 1). And if more be required, we have it in the concluding exhortations: "Be patient, therefore, brethren, *until the coming of the Lord*.... Stablish your hearts: for *the coming of the Lord* is at hand" (v. 7, 8).

Whether or no there are passages which glance aside at unbelieving Jews, and perhaps even some which are directly addressed to them, cannot be decided with so much certainty; but the balance of probability appears to be on the affirmative side in both cases. There probably are places in which St. James is thinking of unbelieving Israelites, and one or more passages in which he turns aside and sternly rebukes them, much in the same way as the Old Testament prophets sometimes turn aside to upbraid Tyre and Sidon and the heathen generally. "Do not the rich oppress you, and themselves drag you before the judgment-seats?" (ii. 6), seems to refer to rich unconverted Jews prosecuting their poor Christian brethren before the synagogue courts, just as St. Paul did when he was Saul the persecutor (Acts ix. 2). And "Do not they blaspheme the honourable Name by which *ye* are called?" can scarcely be said of Christians. If the blasphemers were Christians they would be said rather to blaspheme the honourable Name by which *they themselves* were called. *There* would lie the enormity—that the name of Jesus Christ had been "called upon them," and yet they blasphemed it. And when we come to look at the matter in detail we shall find reason for believing that the stern words at the beginning of chapter v. are addressed to unbelieving Jews. There is not one word of Christian, or even moral, exhortation in it; it consists entirely of accusation and threatening, and in this respect is in marked contrast to the equally stern words at the beginning of chapter iv., which are addressed to worldly and godless Christians.

To suppose that the rich oppressors so often alluded to in the Epistle are *heathen*, as Hilgenfeld does, confuses the whole picture, and brings no compensating advantage. The heathen among whom the Jews of the Dispersion dwelt in Syria, Egypt, Rome, and elsewhere, were of course, some of them rich, and some of them poor. But wealthy Pagans were not more apt to persecute Jews, whether Christians or not, than the needy Pagan populace. If there was any difference between heathen rich and poor in this matter, it was the fanatical and plunder-seeking mob, rather than the contemptuous and easy-going rich, who were likely to begin a persecution of the Jews, just as in Russia or Germany at the present time. And St. James would not be likely to talk of "the Lord of Sabaoth" (v. 4) in addressing wealthy Pagans. But the social antagonism so often alluded to in the Epistle, when interpreted to mean an antagonism between Jew and Jew, corresponds to a state of society which is known to have existed in Palestine and the neighbouring countries during the half-century which preceded the Jewish war of A.D. 66-70. (Comp. Matt. xi. 5; xix. 23, 24; Luke i. 53; vi. 20, 24; xvi. 19, 20.) During that period the wealthy Jews allied themselves with the Romans, in order more securely to oppress their poorer fellow-countrymen. And seeing that the Gospel in the first instance spread chiefly among the poor, this social antagonism between rich and poor Jews frequently became an antagonism between unbelieving and believing Jews. St. James, well aware of this state of things, from personal experience in Judæa, and hearing similar things of the Jews of the Dispersion in Syria, reasonably supposes that this unnatural tyranny of Jew over Jew prevails elsewhere also, and addresses all "the twelve tribes which are of the Diaspora" on the subject. [25] In any case his opportunities of knowing a very great deal respecting Jews in various parts of the world were large. Jews from all regions were constantly visiting Jerusalem. But the knowledge which he must have had respecting the condition of things in Palestine and Syria would be quite sufficient to explain what is said in this Epistle respecting the tyranny of the rich over the poor.

The *Diaspora*,[26] or *Dispersion of the Jews* throughout the inhabited world, had been brought about in various ways, and had continued through many centuries. The two chief causes were *forcible deportation* and *voluntary emigration*. It was a common policy of Oriental conquerors to transport whole populations, in order more completely to subjugate them; and hence the Assyrian and Babylonian conquerors of Israel carried away great multitudes of Jews to the East, sending Eastern populations to take their place. Pompey on a much smaller scale transported Jewish captives to the West, carrying hundreds of Jews to Rome. But disturbances in Palestine, and opportunities of trade elsewhere, induced large multitudes of Jews to emigrate of their own accord, especially to the neighbouring countries of Egypt and Syria; and the great commercial centres in Asia Minor, Alexandria, Antioch, Ephesus, Miletus, Pergamus, Cyprus, and Rhodes contained large numbers of Jews. While Palestine was the battle-field of foreign armies, and while newly founded towns were trying to attract population by offering privileges to settlers, thousands of Jews preferred the advantages of a secure home in exile to the risks which attended residence in their native country.

At the time when this Epistle was written three chief divisions of the Dispersion were recognized—the Babylonian, which ranked as the first, the Syrian, and the Egyptian. But the Diaspora was by no means confined to these three centres. About two hundred years before this time the composer of one of the so-called Sibylline Oracles could address the Jewish nation, and say, "But every land is full of thee,—aye and every ocean."[27] And there is abundance of evidence, both in the Bible and outside it, especially in Josephus and Philo, that such language does not go beyond the limits of justifiable hyperbole. The list of peoples represented at Jerusalem on the Day of Pentecost, "from every nation under heaven," tells one a great deal (Acts ii. 5-11. Comp. xv. 21, and 1 Macc. xv. 15-24). Many passages from Josephus might be quoted (*Ant.* XI. v. 2; XIV. vii. 2; *Bell. Jud.* II. xvi. 4; VII. iii. 3), as stating in general terms the same fact. But perhaps no original authority gives us more information than Philo, in his famous treatise *On the Embassy to the Emperor Caius*, which went to Rome (c. A.D. 40) to obtain the revocation of a decree requiring the Jews to pay divine homage to the Emperor's statue. In that treatise we read that "Jerusalem is the metropolis, not of the single country of Judæa, but of most countries, because of the colonies which she has sent out, as opportunity offered, into the neighbouring lands of Egypt, Phœnicia, Syria, and Cœlesyria, and the more distant lands of Pamphylia and Cilicia, most of Asia, as far as Bithynia and the utmost corners of Pontus; likewise unto Europe, Thessaly, Bœotia, Macedonia, Ætolia, Attica, Argos, Corinth, with the most parts and best parts of Greece. And not only are the continents full of Jewish colonies, but also the most notable of the islands—Eubœa, Cyprus, Crete—to say nothing of the lands beyond the Euphrates. For all, excepting a small part of Babylon and those satrapies which contain the excellent land around it, contain Jewish inhabitants. So that if my country were to obtain a share in thy clemency it would not be one city that would be benefited, but ten thousand others, situated in every part of the inhabited world—Europe, Asia, Libya, continental and insular, maritime and inland" (*De Legat. ad Caium* xxxvi., Gelen., pp. 1031-32). It was therefore an enormous circle of readers that St. James addressed when he wrote "to the twelve tribes which are of the Dispersion," although it seems to have been a long time before his letter became known to the most important of the divisions of the Diaspora, viz. the Jewish settlement in Egypt, which had its chief centre in Alexandria. We may reasonably suppose that it was the Syrian division which he had chiefly in view in writing, and it was to them, no doubt, that the letter in the first instance was sent. It is of this division that Josephus writes that, widely dispersed as the Jewish race is over the whole of the inhabited world, it is most largely mingled with Syria on account of its proximity, and especially in Antioch, where the kings since Antiochus had afforded them undisturbed tranquillity and equal privileges with the heathen; so that they multiplied exceedingly, and made many proselytes (*Bell. Jud.* VII. iii. 3).

The enormous significance of the Dispersion as a preparation for Christianity must not be overlooked. It showed to both Jew and Gentile alike that the barriers which had hedged in and isolated the hermit nation had broken down, and that what had ceased to be thus isolated had changed its character. A *kingdom* had become a *religion*. What henceforth distinguished the Jews in the eyes of all the world was not their country or their government, but their creed, and through this they exercised upon those among whom they were scattered an influence which had been impossible under the old conditions of exclusiveness. They themselves also were forced to understand their own religion better. When the keeping of the letter of the Law became an impossibility, they were compelled to penetrate into its spirit; and what they exhibited to the heathen was not a mere code of burdensome rites and ceremonies, but a moral life and a worship in spirit and truth. The universality of the services of the synagogue taught the Jew that God's worship was not confined to Jerusalem, and their simplicity attracted proselytes who might have turned away from the complex and bloody liturgies of the Temple. Even in matters of detail the services in the synagogue prepared the way for the services of the Christian

Church. The regular lessons—read from two divisions of Scripture, the antiphonal singing, the turning towards the east, the general Amen of the whole congregation, the observance of the third, sixth, and ninth hours as hours of prayer, and of one day in seven as specially holy—all these things, together with some others which have since become obsolete, meet us in the synagogue worship, as St. James knew it, and in the liturgies of the Christian Church, which he and the Apostles and their successors helped to frame. Thus justice once more became mercy, and a punishment was turned into a blessing. The captivity of the Jew became the freedom of both Jew and Gentile, and the scattering of Israel was the gathering in of all nations unto God. "He hath scattered abroad; He hath given to the poor: His righteousness abideth for ever" (Ps. cxii. 9; 2 Cor. ix. 9).

[24] See *The Pastoral Epistles* in this series, pp. 285-6.

[25] See Salmon, *Introduction to the N.T.*, p. 502, 4th ed. (Murray, 1889); Renan, *L'Antechrist*, p. xii.; Ewald, *History of Israel*, vol. vii., p. 451, Eng. Tr. (Longmans, 1885); Weiss, *Introduction to the N.T.*, vol. ii., pp. 102-3 (Hodder and Stoughton, 1888).

[26] See the immense amount of information collected in Schürer, *The Jewish People in the Time of Christ*, div. ii., vol. ii., pp. 219-327; also Westcott's article "Dispersion," in Smith's *Dict. of Bible*; Herzog and Plitt, *Real-Encykl.*, vol. vii., pp. 203-8; and esp. Philo, *Legat. ad Caium*.

[27] Πᾶσα δὲ γαῖα σέθεν πλήρης καὶ πᾶσα θάλασσα.

CHAPTER V
THE RELATION OF THIS EPISTLE TO THE WRITINGS OF ST. PAUL AND OF ST. PETER. THE DATE OF THE EPISTLE. THE DOCTRINE OF JOY IN TEMPTATION

"Count it all joy, my brethren, when ye fall into manifold temptations, knowing that the proof of your faith worketh patience. And let patience have its perfect work, that ye may be perfect and entire, lacking in nothing."— James i. 2-4.

THIS passage at once raises the question of the relation of this Epistle to other writings in the New Testament. Did the writer of it know any of the writings of St. Paul or of St. Peter? It is contended in some quarters that the similarity of thought and expression in several passages is so great as to prove such knowledge, and it is argued that such knowledge tells against the genuineness of the Epistle. In any case the question of the *date* of the Epistle is involved in its relation to these other documents; it was written after them, if it can be established that the author of it was acquainted with them.

With Dr. Salmon[28] we may dismiss the coincidences which have been pointed out by Davidson and others between expressions in this Epistle and the Epistles to the Thessalonians, Corinthians, and Philippians. Some critics seem to forget that a large number of words and phrases were part of the common language, not merely of Jews and early Christians, but of those who were in the habit of mixing much with such persons. We can no more argue from such phrases as "be not deceived" (1 Cor. vi. 9; xv. 33; Gal. vi. 7, and James i. 16), "but some one will say" (1 Cor. xv. 35, and James ii. 18), "a transgressor of the law" (Rom. ii. 25, 27, and James ii. 11), "fruit of righteousness" (Phil. i. 11, and James iii. 18), or from such words as "entire" (1 Thess. v. 23, and James i. 4), "transgressor" used absolutely (Gal. ii. 18, and James ii. 9), and the like, that when they occur in two writings the author of one must have read the other, than we can argue from such phrases as "natural selection," "survival of the fittest," and the like that the writer who uses them has read the works of Darwin. A certain amount of stereotyped phraseology is part of the intellectual atmosphere of each generation, and the writers in each generation make common use of it. In such cases even striking identity of expressions may prove nothing as to the dependence of one author upon another. The obligation is not of one writer to another, but of both to a common and indefinite source. In other words, both writers quite naturally make use of language which is current in the circles in which they live.[29]

Some of the coincidences between the Epistle of James and the Epistle to the *Romans* are of a character to raise the question whether they can satisfactorily be explained by considerations of this kind, and one of these more remarkable coincidences occurs in the passage before us. St. James writes, "Knowing that the proof of your faith worketh patience." St. Paul writes, "Knowing that tribulation worketh patience; and patience, probation" (Rom. v. 3). In this same chapter we have another instance. St. James says, "Be ye doers of the word, and not hearers only" (i. 22). St. Paul says, "Not the hearers of a law are just before God, but the doers of a law shall be justified" (Rom. 13). There is yet a third such parallel. St. James asks, "Whence come fightings? Come they not hence, even of your pleasures which war in your members?" (iv. 1). St. Paul laments, "I see a different law in my members, warring against the law of my mind" (Rom. vii. 23).[30]

The effect of this evidence will be different upon different minds. But it may reasonably be doubted whether these passages, even when summed up together, are stronger than many other strange coincidences in literature, which are known to be accidental. The second instance, taken by itself, is of little weight; for the contrast between hearers and doers is one of the most hackneyed commonplaces of rhetoric. But assuming that a *primâ facie* case has been established, and that one of the two writers has seen the Epistle of the other, no difficulty is created, whichever we assume to have written first. The Epistle to the Romans was written in A.D. 58, and might easily have become known to St. James before A.D. 62. On the other hand, the Epistle of St. James may be placed anywhere between A.D. 45 and 62, and in that case might easily have become known to St. Paul before A.D. 58. And of the two alternatives, this latter is perhaps the more probable. We shall find other reasons for placing the Epistle of St. James earlier than A.D. 58; and we may reasonably suppose that had he read the Epistle to the Romans, he would have expressed his meaning respecting justification somewhat differently. Had he wished (as some erroneously suppose) to oppose and correct the teaching of St. Paul, he would have done so much more unmistakably. And as he is really quite in harmony with St. Paul on the question, he would, if he had read him, have avoided words which look like a contradiction of St. Paul's words.

It remains to examine the relations between our Epistle and the First Epistle of St. Peter. Here, again, one of the coincidences occurs in the passage before us. St. James writes, "Count it all joy, when ye enter into manifold temptations; knowing that the proof of your faith worketh patience;" and St. Peter writes, "Ye greatly rejoice, though now for a little while, if need be, ye have been put to grief in manifold temptations, that the proof of your faith ... might be found" (1 Peter i. 6, 7). Here there is the thought of rejoicing in trials common to both passages, and the expressions for "manifold temptations" and "proof of your patience" are identical in the two places. This is remarkable, especially when taken with other coincidences. On the other hand, the fact that some of the language is common to all three Epistles (James, Peter, and Romans) suggests the possibility that we have here one of the "faithful sayings" of primitive Christianity, rather than one or two writers remembering the writings of a predecessor.

In three places St. James and St. Peter both quote the same passages from the Old Testament. In i. 10, 11 St. James has, "*As the flower of the grass* he shall pass away. For the sun ariseth with the scorching wind, and *withereth the grass; and the flower* thereof *falleth*," where the words in italics are from Isaiah xl. 6-8. St. Peter (i. 24) quotes the words of Isaiah much more completely and consecutively, and in their original sense; he does not merely make a free use of portions of them. Again, in iv. 6 St. James quotes from Prov. iii. 34, "God resisteth the proud, but giveth grace to the humble." In v. 5 St. Peter quotes exactly the same words. Lastly, in v. 20 St. James quotes from Prov. x. 12 the expression "covereth sins." In iv. 8 St. Peter quotes a word more of the original, "love covereth sins." And it will be observed that both St. James and St. Peter change "covereth *all* sins" into "covereth *a multitude* of sins."

Once more we must be content to give a verdict of "Not proven." There is a certain amount of probability, but nothing that amounts to proof, that one of these writers had seen the other's Epistle. Let us, however, assume that echoes of one Epistle are found in the other; then, whichever letter we put first, we have no chronological difficulty. The probable dates of death are, for St. James A.D. 62, for St. Peter A.D. 64-68. Either Epistle may be placed in the six or seven years immediately preceding A.D. 62, and one of the most recent critics[31] places 1 Peter in the middle of the year A.D. 50, and the Epistle of James any time after that date. But there are good reasons for believing that 1 Peter contains references to the persecution under Nero, that "fiery trial" (iv. 12) in which the mere being a Christian would lead to penal consequences (iv. 16), and in which, for conscience' sake, men would have to "endure griefs, suffering wrongfully" (ii. 19), thereby being "partakers of Christ's sufferings" (iv. 13). In which case 1 Peter cannot be placed earlier than A.D. 64, and the Epistle of James must be the earlier of the two. And it seems to be chiefly those who would make our Epistle a forgery of the second century (Brückner, Holtzmann) who consider that it is James that echoes 1 Peter, rather than 1 Peter that reproduces James. There is a powerful consensus of opinion[32] that if there is any influence of one writer upon the other, it is St. James who influences St. Peter, and not the other way.

We must not place the Epistle of St. James in or close after A.D. 50. The crisis respecting the treatment of Gentile converts was then at its height (Acts xv.); and it would be extraordinary if a letter written in the midst of the crisis, and by the person who took the leading part in dealing with it, should contain no allusion to it. The Epistle must be placed either before (A.D. 45-49) or some time after (A.D. 53-62) the so-called Council of Jerusalem. There is reason for believing that the controversy about compelling Gentiles to observe the Mosaic Law, although sharp and critical, was not very lasting. The *modus vivendi* decreed by the Apostles was on the whole loyally accepted, and therefore a letter written a few years after it was promulgated would not of necessity take any notice of it. Indeed, to have revived the question again might have been impolitic, as implying either that there was still some doubt on the point, or that the Apostolic decision had proved futile.

In deciding between the two periods (A.D. 45-49 and 53-62) for the date of the Epistle of St. James, we have not much to guide us if we adopt the view that it is independent of the writings of St. Peter and of St. Paul. There is plenty in the letter to lead us to suppose that it was written before the war (A.D. 66-70) which put an end to the tyranny of the wealthy Sadducees over their poorer brethren, before controversies between Jewish and Gentile Christians such as we find at Corinth had arisen or become chronic, and before doctrinal controversies had sprung up in the Church; also that it was written at a time when the coming of Christ to judgment was still regarded as near at hand (v. 8), and by some one who could recollect the words of Christ independently of the Gospels, and who therefore must have stood in close relationship to Him. All this points to its having been written within the lifetime of James the Lord's brother, and by such a person as he was; but it does not seem to be decisive as to the difference between *c.* A.D. 49 and *c.* A.D. 59. We must be content to leave this undecided. But it is worth while pointing out that if we place it earlier than A.D. 52 we make it the earliest book in the New Testament. The First Epistle to the Thessalonians was written late in A.D. 52 or early in 53; and excepting our Epistle, and *perhaps* 1 Peter, there is no other writing in the New Testament that can reasonably be placed at so early a date as 52.

"Count it all joy, my brethren, when ye fall into manifold temptations." "My brethren," with or without the epithet "beloved," is the regular form of address throughout the Epistle (16, 19; ii. 1, 5, 14; iii. 1, 10, 12; v. 12), in one or two places the "my" being omitted (iv. 11; v. 7, 9, 19). The frequency of this brotherly address seems to indicate how strongly the writer feels, and wishes his readers to feel, the ties of race and of faith which bind them together.

In "Count it all joy," *i.e.* "Consider it as nothing but matter for rejoicing,"[33] we miss a linguistic touch which is evident in the Greek, but cannot well be preserved in English. In saying "joy" (χάραν) St. James is apparently carrying on the idea just started in the address, "greeting" (χαίρειν), *i.e.* "wishing joy." "I wish you *joy*; and you must account as pure *joy* all the troubles into which you may fall." This carrying on a word or thought from one sentence into the next is characteristic of St. James, and reminds us somewhat of the style of St. John. Thus "The proof of your faith worketh *patience*. And let *patience* have its perfect work" (i. 3, 4). "*Lacking* in nothing. But if any of you *lacketh* wisdom" (4, 5). "Nothing *doubting*: for he that *doubteth* is like the surge of the sea" (6). "The lust, when it hath conceived, beareth *sin*; and the *sin*, when it is full grown, bringeth forth death" (15). "Slow to *wrath*: for the *wrath* of man worketh not the righteousness of God" (19, 20). "This man's *religion* is vain. Pure *religion* and undefiled before our God and Father is this" (26, 27). "In many things we all *stumble*. If any man *stumbleth* not in word" (iii. 2). "Behold, how much wood is kindled by how small a *fire*! And the tongue is a *fire*" (iii. 5, 6). "Ye have not, because ye *ask* not. Ye *ask*, and receive not" (iv. 2, 3). "Your gold and your silver are *rusted*; and their *rust* shall be for a testimony against you" (v. 3). "We call them blessed which *endured*: ye have heard of the *endurance* of Job" (v. 11).

It is just possible that "*all* joy" (πᾶσαν χάραν) is meant exactly to balance "*manifold* temptations" (πειρασμοῖς ποικίλοις). Great *diversity* of troubles is to be considered as in reality *every kind* of joy. Nevertheless, the troubles are not to be of our own making or seeking. It is not when we inflict suffering on ourselves, but when we "fall into" it, and therefore may regard it as placed in our way by God, that we are to look upon it as a source of joy rather than of sorrow. The word for "fall into" (περιπίπτειν) implies not only that what one falls into is unwelcome, but also that it is unsought and unexpected. Moreover, it implies that this unforeseen misfortune is large enough to encircle or overwhelm one. It indicates a *serious* calamity. The word for "temptations" in this passage is the same as is used in the sixth petition of the Lord's Prayer; but the word is not used in the same sense in both places. In the Lord's Prayer all kinds of temptation are included, and especially the internal solicitations of the devil, as is shown by the next petition: "Lead us not into temptation, but deliver us from the tempter." In the passage before us internal temptations, if not actually excluded, are certainly quite in the background. What St. James has principally in his mind are *external* trials, such as poverty of intellect (ver. 5), or of substance (ver. 9), or persecution (ii. 6, 7), and the like; those worldly troubles which test our faith, loyalty, and obedience, and tempt us to abandon our trust in God, and to cease to strive to please Him. The trials by which Satan was allowed to tempt Job are the kind of temptations to be understood here.[34] They are material for spiritual joy, because (1) they are opportunities for practising virtue, which cannot be learned without practice, nor practised without opportunities; (2) they teach us that we have here no abiding city, for a world in which such things are possible cannot be a lasting home; (3) they make us more Christlike; (4) we have the assurance of Divine support, and that no more will ever be laid upon us than we, relying upon that support, can bear; (5) we have the assurance of abundant compensation here and hereafter.

St. James here is only echoing the teaching of his Brother: "Blessed are ye when men shall reproach you, and persecute you, and say all manner of evil against you falsely, for My sake. Rejoice, and be exceeding glad; for great is your reward in heaven" (Matt. v. 11, 12). In the first days after Pentecost he had seen the Apostles acting in the very spirit which he here enjoins, and he had himself very probably taken part in doing so, "rejoicing that they were counted worthy to suffer dishonour for the Name" (Acts v. 41. Comp. iv. 23-30). And as we have already seen in comparing the parallel passages, St. Peter (1 Peter 1, 6) and St. Paul (Rom. v. 3) teach the same doctrine of rejoicing in tribulation.

As St. Augustine long ago pointed out, in his letter to Anastasius (*Ep.* cxlv. 7, 8), and Hooker also (*Eccl. Pol.* V. xlviii. 13), there is no inconsistency in teaching such doctrine, and yet praying, "Lead us not into temptation." Not only is there no sin in shrinking from both external trials and internal temptations, or in desiring to be freed from such things; but such is the weakness of the human will, that it is only reasonable humility to pray to God not to allow us to be subjected to severe trials. Nevertheless, when God, in His wisdom, has permitted such things to come upon us, the right course is, not to be cast down and sorrowful, as though something quite intolerable had overtaken us, but to rejoice that God has thought us capable of enduring something for His sake, and has given us the opportunity of strengthening our patience and our trust in Him.

This doctrine of joy in suffering, which at first sight seems to be almost superhuman, is shown by experience to be less hard than the apparently more human doctrine of resignation and fortitude. The effort to be resigned, and to suffer without complaining, is not a very inspiriting effort. Its tendency is towards depression. It does not lift us out of ourselves or above our tribulations. On the contrary, it leads rather to self-contemplation and a brooding over miseries. Between mere resignation and thankful joy there is all the difference that there is between mere obedience and affectionate trust. The one is submission; the other is love. It is in the long run easier to rejoice in tribulation, and be thankful for it, than to be merely resigned and submit patiently. And therefore this "hard saying" is really a merciful one, for it teaches us to endure trials in the spirit that will make us feel them least. It is not only "a good thing to sing praises unto our God;" it is also "a joyful and pleasant thing to be thankful" (Ps. cxlvii. 1).

And here it may be noticed that St. James is no Cynic or Stoic. He does not tell us that we are to anticipate misfortune, and cut ourselves off from all those things the loss of which might involve suffering; or that we are to trample on our feelings, and act as if we had none, treating sufferings as if they were non-existent, or as if they in no way affected us. He does not teach us that as Christians we live in an atmosphere in which excruciating pain, whether of body or mind, is a matter of pure indifference, and that such emotions as fear or grief under the influence of adversity, and hope or joy under the influence of prosperity, are utterly unworthy and contemptible. There is not a hint of anything of the kind. He points out to us that temptations, and especially external trials, are really blessings, if we use them aright; and he teaches us to meet them in that conviction. And it is manifest that the spirit in which to welcome a blessing is the spirit of joy and thankfulness.

St. James does not bid us accept this doctrine of joy in tribulation upon his personal authority. It is no philosopher's *ipse dixit*. He appeals to his readers' own experience: "Knowing that the proof of your faith worketh patience." "Knowing" (γινώσκοντες), *i.e.* "in that ye are continually finding out and getting to know." The verb and the tense indicate progressive and continuous knowledge, as by the experience of daily life; and this teaches us that proving and testing not only brings to light, but brings into existence, patience. This patience (ὑπομονή), this abiding firm under attack or pressure, must be allowed full scope to regulate all our conduct; and then we shall see why trials are a matter for joy rather than sorrow, when we find ourselves moving onwards towards, not the barrenness of Stoical "self-sufficiency" (αὐτάρκεια), but the fulness of Divine perfection. "That ye may be perfect and entire,[35] lacking in nothing," is perhaps one of the many reminiscences of Christ's words which we shall find in this letter of the Lord's brother. "Ye therefore shall be perfect, as your heavenly Father is perfect" (Matt. v. 48).

[28] *Introduction to the N.T.*, pp. 509-10, 4th Ed.

[29] It is quite possible that both St. Paul and St. James derive the phrase "a transgressor of the law" from the remarkable addition to the canonical Gospels which is found in Codex D (Beza) after Luke vi. 4: "The same day He beheld a certain man working on the Sabbath, and said to him, Man, if thou knowest what thou art doing, blessed art thou; but if thou knowest not thou art accursed and *a transgressor of the law*." Note that in Rom. ii., where the phrase occurs twice (vv. 25, 27), the address "O man" also occurs twice. Comp. Gal. ii. 18, and see A. Resch, *Agrapha; Aussercanonische Evangelienfragmente* (Leipzig, 1889), pp. 36, 189-92.

[30] In order to do justice to these coincidences one must look at them in the original Greek; but to those who cannot read Greek the accuracy of the Revised Version gives a very fair idea of the amount of similarity.

1. γινώσκοντες ὅτι τὸ δοκίμιον ὑμῶν τῆς πίστεως κατεργάζεται ὑπομονήν (James i. 3): εἰδότεσ ὅτι ἡ θλίπσις ὑπομονὴν κατεργάζεται, ἡ δὲ ὑπομον δοκιμήν (Rom. v. 3).

2. γίνεσθε δὲ ποιηταὶ λόγου καὶ μὴ ἀκροαταὶ μόνον (James i. 22): οὐ γὰρ οἱ ἀκροαταὶ νόμου δίκαιοι παρὰ τῷ θεῷ, ἀλλ' οἱ ποιηταὶ νόμοι δικαιωθήσονται (Rom. ii. 13).

3. ἐκ τῶν ἡδονῶν ὑμῶν τῶν στρατευομένων ἐν τοῖς μέλεσιν ὑμῶν (James iv. 1): ἕτερον νόμον ἐν τοῖς μελεσίν μου ἀντιστρατευόμενον τῳ νόμῳ τοῦ νοός μου (Rom vii. 23).

[31] B. Weiss, *Introduction to the N.T.*, vol. ii., pp. 106, 150 (Hodder and Stoughton, 1888).

[32] Beyschlag's revision of Meyer's *Brie des Jacobus* (Göttingen, 1888), p. 22.

[33] This rendering has been questioned; but it is justified by such expressions as πᾶσαν ἀληθείην μυθήσομαι, "I will tell nothing but what is true" (Hom. Od. xi. 507). See *Pastoral Epistles* in this series, p. 392.

[34] See F. D. Maurice, *Unity of the N.T.* (Parker, 1854), p. 318.

[35] On the strength of the word for "entire" (ὁλόκληρος), which occurs nowhere else in the New Testament, excepting 1 Thess. v. 23, it has been asserted that the writer of this Epistle must have seen that passage. The adjective is used in the Septuagint of whole, unhewn stones, *saxis informibus et impolitis* (Deut. xxvii. 6), and in Josephus of entire animals used for sacrifice (*Ant.* III. ix. 2). It is fairly common in Plato and Aristotle. The substantive ὁλοκληρία occurs in Acts iii. 16, of the "perfect soundness" given to the impotent man, and in the Septuagint (Isa. i. 6), of the "soundness" which was wholly wanting in Israel. If St. James did not get his knowledge of the word simply from his knowledge of the Greek language, which is manifestly very complete, he probably derived it from the Septuagint. It is absurd to base an argument as to acquaintance with 1 Thessalonians on so common a word.

CHAPTER VI
THE RELATION OF THIS EPISTLE TO THE BOOKS OF ECCLESIASTICUS AND OF THE WISDOM OF SOLOMON. THE VALUE OF THE APOCRYPHA, AND THE MISCHIEF OF NEGLECTING IT

"But if any of you lacketh wisdom, let him ask of God, who giveth to all liberally, and upbraideth not; and it shall be given him. But let him ask in faith, nothing doubting: for he that doubteth is like the surge of the sea driven by the wind and tossed. For let not that man think that he shall receive anything of the Lord; a double-minded man, unstable in all his ways." —St. James i. 5-8.

THE previous section led us to the question as to the relation of this Epistle to certain Christian writings, and in particular to the Epistle of St. Paul to the Romans, and to the First Epistle of St. Peter. The present section, combined with the preceding one, raises a similar question—the relation of our Epistle to certain Jewish writings, and especially the Books of Ecclesiasticus and the Wisdom of Solomon.

The two sets of questions are not parallel. In the former case, even if we could determine that the writer of one Epistle had certainly seen the Epistle of the other, we should still be uncertain as to which had written first. Here, if the similarity is found to be too great to be accounted for by common influences acting upon both writers, and we are compelled to suppose that one has made use of the writing of the other, there cannot be any doubt as to the side on which the obligation lies. The Book of Ecclesiasticus certainly, and the Book of Wisdom possibly, had come into circulation long before St. James was born. And if, with some of the latest writers[36] on the subject, we place the Book of Wisdom as late as A.D. 40, it nevertheless was written in plenty of time for St. James to have become acquainted with it before he wrote his Epistle. Although some doubts have been expressed on the subject, the number of similarities, both of thought and expression, between the Epistle of St. James and Ecclesiasticus is too great to be reasonably accounted for without the supposition that St. James was not only acquainted with the book, but fond of its contents. And it is to be remembered, in forming an opinion on the subject, that there is nothing intrinsically improbable in the supposition that St. James had read Ecclesiasticus. Indeed, the improbability would rather be the other way. Even if there were no coincidences of ideas and language between our Epistle and Ecclesiasticus, we know enough about St. James and about the circulation of Ecclesiasticus to say that he was likely to become acquainted with it. As Dr. Salmon remarks on the use of the Apocrypha generally, "The books we know as Apocrypha are nearly all earlier than the New Testament writers, *who could not well have been ignorant of them*; and therefore coincidences between the former and the latter are not likely to have been the result of mere accident."[37]

But it will be worth while to quote a decided expression of opinion, on each side of the question immediately before us, from the writings of scholars who are certainly well qualified to give a decided opinion. On the one hand, Bernhard Weiss says, "It has been incorrectly held by most that the author adheres very closely to Jesus Sirach.... But it must be distinctly denied that there is anywhere an echo of the Book of Wisdom."[38] On the other hand, Dr. Edersheim, after pointing out the parallel between Ecclus. xii. 10, 11, and James v. 3, concludes, "In view of all this it *cannot be doubted* that both the simile and the expression of it in the Epistle of St. James were derived from Ecclesiasticus." And then he gives some more coincidences between the two writings, and sums up thus: "But if the result is to *prove beyond doubt* the familiarity of St. James with a book which at the time was evidently in wide circulation, it exhibits with even greater clearness the immense spiritual difference between the standpoint occupied in Ecclesiasticus and that in the Epistle of St. James."[39] And Archdeacon Farrar quotes with approval an estimate that St. James "alludes more or less directly to the Book of the Wisdom of Solomon at least five times, but to the Book of Ecclesiasticus more than fifteen times.... The fact is the more striking because in other respects St. James shows no sympathy with Alexandrian speculations. There is not in him the faintest tinge of Philonian philosophy; on the contrary, he belongs in a marked degree to the school of Jerusalem. He is a thorough Hebraiser, a typical Judaist. All his thoughts and phrases move normally in the Palestinian sphere. This is a curious and almost unnoticed phenomenon. The "sapiential literature" of the Old Testament was the *least* specifically Israelite. It was the direct precursor of Alexandrian morals. It deals with mankind, and not with the Jew. Yet St. James, who shows so much partiality for this literature, is of all the writers of the New Testament the least Alexandrian, and the most Judaic."[40]

Let us endeavour to form an opinion for ourselves; and the only way in which to do this with thoroughness is to place side by side, in the original Greek, the passages in which there seems to be coincidence between the two writers. Want of space prevents this from being done here. But some of the most striking coincidences shall be placed in parallel columns, and where the coincidence is inadequately represented by the English Version the Greek shall be given also. Other coincidences, which are not drawn out in full, will be added, to enable students who care to examine the evidence more in detail to do so without much trouble. Two Bibles, or, still better, a Septuagint and a Greek Testament, will serve the purpose of parallel columns.

It will be found that by far the greater number of coincidences occur in the first chapter, a fact which suggests the conjecture that St. James had been reading Ecclesiasticus shortly before he began to write. In the middle of the Epistle there is very little that strongly recalls the son of Sirach. In the last chapter there are one or two striking parallels; but by far the larger proportion is in the first chapter.

ECCLESIASTICUS.	ST. JAMES.
1. A patient man will bear for a time, and afterward joy shall spring up unto him (i. 23). My son, if thou come to serve the Lord, prepare thy soul for temptation (πειρασμόν). Set thy heart aright, and constantly endure.... Whatsoever is brought upon thee take cheerfully, and be patient when thou art changed to a low estate. For gold is tried (δοκιμάζεται) in the fire, and acceptable men in the furnace of adversity (ii. 1-5).	Count it all joy, my brethren, when ye fall into manifold temptations (πειρασμοῖς), knowing that the proof (τὸ δοκίμιον) of your faith worketh patience. And let patience have her perfect work, that ye may be perfect and entire, lacking in nothing (i. 2-4). Blessed is the man that endureth temptation (πειρασμόν); for when he hath been approved (δόκιμος γενόμενος), he shall receive the crown of life (i. 12).
2. If thou desire wisdom (σοφίαν), keep the commandments, and the Lord shall give her unto thee (i. 26). I desired wisdom (σοφίαν) openly in my prayer.... The Lord hath given me a tongue for my reward (li. 13, 22). Thy desire for wisdom (σοφίας) shall be given thee (vi. 37. Comp. xliii. 33). [A fool] will give little, and will upbraid (ὀνειδίσει) much (xx. 15). After thou hast given, upbraid (ὀνείδιζε) not (xli. 22. Comp. xviii. 18).	But if any of you lacketh wisdom (σοφίαν), let him ask of God, who giveth to all men liberally, and upbraideth not (μὴ ὀνειδίζοντος); and it shall be given him (i. 5).

3. Distrust not the fear of the Lord; and come not unto Him with a double heart (i. 28).

But let him ask in faith, nothing doubting: for he that doubteth is like the surge of the sea driven by the wind and tossed. For let not that man think that he shall receive anything of the Lord; a double-minded man, unstable in all his ways (i. 6-8. Comp. iv. 8).

Woe be to fearful hearts, and faint hands, and the sinner that goeth two ways (ii. 12). Be not faint-hearted when thou makest thy prayer (vii. 10. Comp. xxxiii. 2; xxxv. 16, 17).

4. Exalt not thyself, lest thou fall, and bring dishonour upon thy soul (i. 30). The greater thou art, the more humble thyself, and thou shalt find favour before the Lord (iii. 18. Comp. xxxi. 1-9).

But let the brother of low degree glory in his high estate; and the rich in that he is made low (i. 9, 10).

5. Say not thou, It is through the Lord that I fell away: for thou oughtest not to do the things that He hateth. Say not thou, He hath caused me to err: for He hath no need of the sinful man (xv. 11, 12).

Let no man say, when he is tempted, I am tempted of God: for God cannot be tempted with evil, and He Himself tempteth no man (i. 13).

6. Be swift in thy listening (ταχὺς ἐν ἀκροάσει σου); and with patience give answer (v. 11).

Let every man be swift to hear (ταχὺς εἰς τὸ ἀκοῦσαι), slow to speak, slow to wrath (i. 19).

7. Thou shalt be to him as one that hath wiped a mirror (ἔσοπτρον), and shalt know that it is not rusted (κατίωται) for ever (xii. 11).
  Like as bronze rusteth (ἰοῦται), so is his wickedness (xii. 10).
  Lose money through a brother and a friend, and let it not rust (ἰωθήτω) under the stone unto loss (xxix. 10).

He is like unto a man beholding his natural face in a mirror (ἐν ἐσόπτρῳ).... Your gold and your silver are rusted (κατίωται); and their rust (ἰός) shall be a testimony against you (i. 23; v. 3).

8. He that looketh in (ὁ παρακύπτων) through her windows, i.e. the windows of wisdom (xiv. 23).
  A fool peepeth in (παρακύπτει) at the door (xxi. 23).

He that looketh into (ὁ παρακύψας) the perfect law (i. 25).

9. A prey of lions are wild asses in the wilderness; so the fodder of the rich are the poor (οὕτω νομαὶ πλουσίων πτωχοί: xiii. 19. Comp. xiii. 3, 17, 18). But ye have dishonoured the poor man (τὸν πτωχόν). Do not the rich (οἱ πλούσιοι) oppress you, and themselves drag you before the judgment-seats? (ii. 6).

It will be observed that of these nine examples all come out of the first two chapters of St. James, and six are from the first two chapters of Ecclesiasticus. This fact is worth considering in estimating the probabilities of St. James being under the influence of this earlier and popular book. Owing to recent reading, or some other cause, he seems to have been specially familiar with the opening chapters of Ecclesiasticus. Probably most persons who study these coincidences will be of the opinion that Bernhard Weiss is needlessly cautious and sceptical when he refuses to assent to the common opinion that in some portions of the Epistle St. James closely follows the Wisdom of Jesus, the son of Sirach. The strongest coincidence is the seventh in the table. The word for "to rust" (κατιόω) occurs nowhere else either in the Septuagint or in the New Testament, and the passages in Ecclesiasticus and St. James "are the only Biblical passages in which the figure of rust as affecting unused silver and gold occurs" (Edersheim). The fifth instance is also very striking.

Let us now look at some of the coincidences between the Book of the Wisdom of Solomon and the Epistle of St. James.

WISDOM.

ST. JAMES.

1. The hope of the ungodly is like thistle-down carried away by the wind; like a thin froth that is driven away by the blast, and like smoke is dispersed by the wind (v. 14. Comp. μαρανθῆναι in ii. 8). He that doubteth is like the surge of the sea driven by the wind and tossed.... As the flower of the grass he shall pass away.... So also shall the rich man fade away (μαρανθήσεται) in his ways (i. 6, 10, 11).

2. In eternity it weareth a crown and triumpheth (iv. 2). When he hath been approved he shall receive the crown of life, which the Lord promised to them that love Him (i. 12).

3. The alterations of the solstices and the change of seasons (τροπῶν ἀλλαγὰς καὶ μεταβολὰς καιρῶν: vii. 18). With whom can be no variation, neither shadow of turning (παρ᾽ ᾧ οὐκ ἔνι παραλλαγὴ ἢ τροπῆς ἀποσκίασμα: i. 17).

4. Let us oppress (καταδυναστεύσωμεν) the poor righteous man.... Let us examine him with despitefulness and torture (ii. 10, 19).	Ye have dishonoured the poor man. Do not the rich oppress (καταδυναστεύουσιν) you, and themselves drag you before the judgment-seats? (ii. 6).
5. For the lowest is pardonable by mercy; but mighty men shall be mightily chastised (vi. 6).	For judgment is without mercy to him that hath showed no mercy: mercy glorieth against judgment (ii. 13).
6. What hath pride profited us? or what good hath riches with our vaunting (ἀλαζονείας) brought us? All those things are passed away like a shadow, and as a post that hasted by, etc. etc.; even so we, as soon as we were born, came to an end" (v. 8-14).	Go to now, ye that say, To-day or to-morrow we will go into this city, and spend a year there, and trade and get gain: whereas ye know not what shall be on the morrow. What is your life? For ye are a vapour, that appeareth for a little time, and then vanisheth away.... But now ye glory in your vauntings (ἀλαζονίαις): all such glorying is evil (iv. 13-16).
7. Let us lie in wait for the righteous (τὸν δίκαιον).... Let us condemn him (καταδικάσωμεν) with a shameful death (ii. 12, 20).	Ye have condemned (κατεδικάσατε), ye have killed the righteous one (τὸν δίκαιον); he doth not resist you (v. 6).

It will at once be perceived that these parallels are neither so numerous nor so convincing as those which have been pointed out between Ecclesiasticus and the Epistle of St. James; but they are sufficient to make a *primâ facie* case of considerable probability, whatever date we assign to the Book of Wisdom. This probability is strengthened by the fact that this book, with the rest of the Apocrypha or deutero-canonical writings, constituted to a large extent the *religious literature of the Jews of the Dispersion*; and therefore in writing to such Jews St. James would be likely to make conscious allusions to writings with which his hearers would be sure to be familiar; a consideration which strengthens the case as regards the coincidences with Ecclesiasticus, as well as regards those with the Wisdom of Solomon. Even if the probability as to the Alexandrian origin of Wisdom were a certainty, and if the conjectural date A.D. 40 were established, there would be nothing surprising in its becoming well known in Jerusalem within twenty years of its production. It is, therefore, far too strong an assertion when Weiss declares that "it must be distinctly denied that there is anywhere [in the Epistle of St. James] an echo of the Book of Wisdom." All that one can safely say is that the evidence for his acquaintance with the book does not approach to proof.

But the use of these two books of the Apocrypha by writers in the New Testament does not depend upon the question whether St. James makes use of them or not. If this were the place to do it, it might be shown that other coincidences, both of language and thought, far too numerous and too strong to be all of them accidental, occur in the writings of St. Peter, St. Paul, and St. John.[41] Such things also occur outside the New Testament in the Epistles of Clement and of Barnabas; while Clement of Alexandria frequently quotes Ecclesiasticus with the introductory formula, "The Scripture saith."

These facts go a long way towards proving that the neglect of the Apocrypha which is so prevalent among ourselves is a thing which cannot be defended, either by an appeal to Scripture or by the practice of the primitive Church; for both the one and the other show a great respect for these deutero-canonical writings. That the New Lectionary omits a good deal of what used to be read publicly in church is not a thing to be lamented. We gladly sacrifice portions of the Apocrypha in order to obtain more of Ezekiel and Revelation. It is the neglect of them in private reading that is so much to be deplored. Passages which are too grotesque and too unspiritual to be edifying when read to a mixed congregation are nevertheless full of instruction, and throw most valuable light both on the Old and on the New Testament. The Apocryphal writings, instead of being a worthless interpolation between the Old Testament and the New, like a block of paltry buildings disfiguring two noble edifices, are among our best means of understanding how the Old Testament led up to the New, and prepared the way for it. They show us the Jewish mind under the combined influences of Jewish Scriptures, Gentile culture, and new phases of political life, and being gradually brought into the condition in which it either fiercely opposed or ardently accepted the teaching of Christ and His Apostles. A huge chasm yawns between Judaism as we leave it at the close of the Old Testament canon, and as we find it at the beginning of the Gospel history; and we have no better material with which to bridge the chasm than the writings of the Apocrypha. This is well brought out, not only in the commentary on the Apocrypha already quoted more than once, but also in a valuable review of the commentary from which some of what follows is taken.[42]

The neglect of the Apocrypha has not been by any means entirely accidental. It is partly the result of a deliberate protest against the action of the Council of Trent in placing these books on a level with the books of the Old and New Testament. In the seventeenth century we find the learned John Lightfoot writing, "Thus sweetly and nearly should the two

Testaments join together, and thus Divinely should they kiss each other, but that the wretched Apocrypha doth thrust in between." And the fact that many people are now unable to recognize or appreciate an allusion to the Apocrypha is by no means the most serious result of this common neglect of its contents. Appreciation of the Bible in general, and especially of those books in which the Old and New Testaments come most in contact, is materially diminished in consequence. The Apocrypha is not a barrier, but a bridge; it does not separate, but unite the two Covenants. What thoughtful reader can pass from the Old to the New Testament without feeling that he has entered another world? He is still in Palestine, still among the Jews; but how different from the Palestine and the Judaism of Ezra, and Nehemiah, and Malachi! He "finds mention of persons, and sects, and schools of which he can find no trace in the Old Testament. He comes upon beliefs and opinions for which the earlier canon does not even furnish a clue. He discovers institutions long settled, and dominating the religious life of the people, of which the Old Testament supplies not even the name. He finds popular ideas, religious terms and phrases in current use wholly unlike those of ancient psalmists and prophets." And there is no literature that can explain all these changes to him either so surely or so fully as the Apocrypha. It supplies instances of the early use of New Testament words, of old words in new senses. It throws light upon the growth of the popular conception of the Messiah. It illuminates still more the development of the doctrine of the Logos. Above all, it helps us to see something of the evolution of that strange religious system which became the raw material out of which the special doctrines of Pharisees, Sadducees, and Essenes were formed, and which had a powerful influence upon Christianity itself.

The neglect of the Apocrypha has been greatly increased by the widespread practice of publishing Bibles without it, and even of striking out from the margins of these mutilated Bibles all references to it. And this mischief has lately been augmented by the fact that the Revised Version omits it. Yet no portion of the Bible was in greater need of revision. The original texts used by the translators of 1611 were very bad; and perhaps in no part of the Authorized Version are utterly faulty translations more abundant. A comparison of the quotations given above with the text of the Authorized Version of Wisdom and Ecclesiasticus will show that considerable changes have been made in order to bring the quotations into harmony with the true readings of the Greek text, and thus give a fair comparison with the words of St. James.

Books which the writers of the New Testament found worthy of study, and from which they derived some of their thoughts and language, ought not to be lightly disregarded by ourselves. We cannot disregard them without loss; and it is the duty of every reader of the Bible to see that his apprehension of the Old and New Testaments is not hindered through his ignorance of those writings which interpret the process of transition from the one to the other. Neglect of the helps to understanding His Word which God has placed easily within our reach may endanger our possession of that wisdom which St. James here assures us will be given to every one who asks for it in faith.

A discussion of that heavenly wisdom, and of the efficacy of prayer offered in faith, will be found in the expositions of later passages in the Epistle.[43]

[36] Grätz, Noack, Plumptre, F. W. Farrer.

[37] *The Speaker's Commentary, Apocrypha*, vol. i., p. xli. (Murray, 1888).

[38] *Introduction to the N.T.*, vol. ii., pp. 114, 115 (Hodder and Stoughton, 1888).

[39] *The Speaker's Commentary, Apocrypha*, vol. ii., pp. 22, 23 (Murray 1888).

[40] *The Early Days of Christianity*, vol. i., pp. 517-18. Dr. Salmon leaves the question undecided (*Introduction to N.T.*, p. 511).

[41] See Dr. Salmon's *General Introduction* to the Apocrypha in the *Speaker's Commentary*, vol. i., pp. xli., xlii.

[42] *Edinburgh Review*, No. 345, January, 1889, pp. 58-95.

[43] See on iii. 13-18, and on v. 13-18. In connexion with this subject the Inaugural Lecture of Professor Margoliouth, on *The Place of Ecclesiasticus in Semitic Literature* (Clarendon Press, 1890), and his defence of the position there maintained in the pages of the *Expositor*, should be studied. It is *possible* that from the language of Ecclesiasticus we may be able to demonstrate that the late date assigned by recent critics to certain books in the Old Testament is quite untenable for the language of them is centuries older than that of Ecclesiasticus.

CHAPTER VII
THE EXALTATION OF THE LOWLY, AND THE FADING AWAY OF THE RICH. THE METAPHORS OF ST. JAMES AND THE PARABLES OF CHRIST

"But let the brother of low degree glory in his high estate: and the rich in that he is made low: because as the flower of the grass he shall pass away. For the sun ariseth, with the scorching wind, and withereth the grass; and the flower thereof falleth, and the grace of the fashion of it perisheth: so also shall the rich man fade away in his goings." —St. James i. 9-11.

IN this section St. James returns to what is the main thought of the first chapter, and one of the main thoughts of the whole Epistle, viz. the blessedness of enduring temptations, and especially such temptations as are caused by external trials and adversity. He adds another thought which may help to console and strengthen the oppressed Christian.

The Revisers have quite rightly restored the "But" (δέ) at the beginning of this section. There seems to be absolutely no authority for its omission; and we may conjecture that the earlier English translators ignored it, because it seemed to them to be superfluous, or even disturbing. The Rhemish Version, made from the Vulgate (*Glorietur autem*), is the only English Version which preserves it; and Luther (*Ein Bruder aber*) preserves it also. The force of the conjunction is to connect the advice given in this section with the items of advice already given. They form a connected series. "Count it all joy, when ye fall into manifold temptations.... But (δέ) let patience have its perfect work. ... But (δέ) if any lacketh wisdom, let him ask of God.... But (δέ) let him ask in faith.... But (δέ) let the brother of low degree glory in his high estate: and the rich in that he is made low."

The meaning of this last item in the series is by no means clear. Various interpretations have been suggested, and it is difficult or even impossible to arrive at a conclusive decision as to which of them is the right one. But we may clear the ground by setting aside all explanations which would make "the brother of low degree" (ὁ ταπεινός) to mean the Christian who is lowly in heart (Matt. xi. 29), and "the rich" (ὁ πλούσιος) the Christian who is rich in faith (ii. 5) and in good works (1 Tim. vi. 18). Both words are to be understood literally. The lowly man is the man of humble position, oppressed by poverty, and perhaps by unscrupulous neighbours (ii. 3), and the rich man, here, as elsewhere in this Epistle, is the man of wealth who very often oppresses the poorer brethren (i. 11; ii. 6; v. 1).

What, then, is the meaning of the "high estate" (ὕψος) in which the brother of low degree is to glory, and of the "being made low" (ταπείνωσις), in which the rich man is to do the same? At first sight one is disposed to say that the one is the heavenly birthright, and the other the Divine humiliation, in which every one shares who becomes a member of Christ; in fact, that they are the same thing looked at from different points of view; for what to the Christian is promotion, to the world seems degradation. If this were correct, then we should have an antithesis analogous to that which is drawn out by St. Paul, when he says, "He that was called in the Lord, being a bond-servant, is the Lord's freeman: likewise he that was called, being free, is Christ's bond-servant" (1 Cor. vii. 22). But on further consideration this attractive explanation is found not to suit the context. What analogy is there between the humiliation in which every Christian glories in Christ and the withering of herbage under a scorching wind? Even if we could allow that this metaphor refers to the fugitive character of earthly possessions, what has that to do with Christian humiliation, which does not depend upon either the presence or the absence of wealth? Moreover, St. James says nothing about the fugitiveness of riches: it is the rich man *himself*, and not his wealth, that is said to "pass away," and to "fade away in his goings." Twice over St. James declares this to be the destiny of the rich man; and the wording is such as to show that when the writer says that "the rich man shall fade away in his goings" he means the man, and not his riches. "His goings," or "journeys," very likely refers to his "going into this city to spend a year there, and trade, and get gain" (iv. 13); *i.e.* he wastes himself away in the pursuit of wealth. But what could be the meaning of *wealth* "fading away *in its journeys*"? Evidently, we must not transfer what is said of the rich man himself to his possessions.

It is a baseless assumption to suppose that the rich man here spoken of is a Christian at all. "The brother of low degree" is contrasted, not with the *brother* who is rich, but with the rich man, whose miserable destiny shows that he is not "a brother," *i.e.* not a believer. The latter is the wealthy Jew who rejects Christ. Throughout this Epistle (ii. 6, 7; v. 1-6) "rich" is a term of reproach. This is what is meant by the Ebionite tone of the Epistle; for poverty is the condition which Ebionism delights to honour. In this St. James seems to be reproducing the thoughts both of Jesus Christ and of Jesus the son of Sirach. "Woe unto you that are rich! for ye have received your consolation. Woe unto you, ye that are full now! for ye shall hunger" (Luke

vi. 25, 26. Comp. Matt. xix. 23-25). "The rich man hath done wrong, and is very wroth besides: the poor man is wronged, and he must intreat also.... An abomination to the proud is lowliness; so the poor are abomination to the rich" (Ecclus. xiii. 3, 20).

But when we have arrived at the conclusion that the "being made low" does not refer to the humiliation of the Christian, and that the rich man here threatened with a miserable end is not a believer, a new difficulty arises. What is the meaning of the wealthy unbeliever being told to *glory* in the degradation which is to prove so calamitous to him? In order to avoid this difficulty various expedients have been suggested. Some propose a rather violent change of *mood*—from the imperative to the indicative. No verb is expressed, and it is said that instead of repeating "let him glory" from the previous clause, we may supply "he glories," as a statement of fact rather than an exhortation. The sentence will then run, "But let the brother of low degree glory in his high estate; but (δέ) the rich *glorieth* in his being made low;" *i.e.* he glories in what degrades him and ought to inspire him with shame and grief. Others propose a still more violent change, viz. of *verb*; they would keep the imperative, but supply a word of opposite meaning: "so let the rich man *be ashamed* of his being made low." Neither of these expedients seems to be necessary, or indeed to be a fair treatment of the text.[44] It is quite possible to make good sense of the exhortation, without any violent change either of mood or of verb. In the exhortation to the rich man St. James speaks in severe irony: "Let the brother of low degree glory in his high estate; and the rich man—what is he to glory in?—let him glory in the only thing upon which he can count with certainty, viz. his being brought low; because as the flower of the grass he shall pass away." Such irony is not uncommon in Scripture. Our blessed Lord Himself makes use of it sometimes, as when He says of the hypocrites that they have their reward, and have it in full (ἀπέχουσι: Matt. vi. 2, 5, 16).

Whether or no this interpretation be accepted—and no interpretation of this passage has as yet been suggested which is free from difficulty—it must be clearly borne in mind that no explanation can be correct which does not preserve the connexion between the humiliation of the rich man and his passing away as the flower of the grass. This fading away *is* his humiliation, *is* the thing in which he is to glory, if he glories in anything at all. The inexorable "because" must not be ignored or explained away by making the wealth of the rich man shrivel up, when St. James twice over says that it is the rich man himself who fades away.

The metaphor here used of the rich man is common enough in the Old Testament. Man "cometh forth like a flower, and is cut down" (ὥσπερ ἄνθος ἀνθῆσαν ἐξέπεσεν LXX.), says Job, in his complaint (xiv. 2); and, "As for man, his days are as grass; as a flower of the field, so he flourisheth. For the wind passeth over it, and it is gone; and the place thereof shall know it no more," says the Psalmist (ciii. 15, 16). But elsewhere, with a closer similarity to the present passage, we have this transitory character specially attributed to the ungodly, who "shall soon be cut down like the grass, and wither as the green herb" (Ps. xxxvii. 2). None of these passages, however, are so clearly in St. James's mind as the words of Isaiah: "All flesh is grass, and all the goodliness thereof is as the flower of the field: the grass withereth, the flower fadeth; because the breath of the Lord bloweth upon it: surely the people is grass. The grass withereth, the flower fadeth; but the word of our God shall stand for ever" (Isa. xl. 6, 7). Here the words of St. James are almost identical with those of the Septuagint (ὡς ἄνθος χόρτου· ἐξηράνθη ὁ χόρτος καὶ τὸ ἄνθος ἐξέπεσεν ... ἐξηράνθη χόρτος, ἐξέπεσεν τὸ ἄνθος); and, as has been already pointed out (p. 59), this is one of the quotations which our Epistle has in common with that of St. Peter (1 Peter i. 24).

"Grass" throughout is a comprehensive term for herbage, and the "flower of grass" does not mean the bloom or blossom of grass in the narrower sense, but the wild flowers, specially abundant and brilliant in the Holy Land, which grow among the grass. Thus, in the Sermon on the Mount, what are first called "the lilies (τὰ κρίνα) of the field" are immediately afterwards called "the grass (τὸν χόρτον) of the field" (Matt. vi. 28, 30).

"The scorching wind" (ὁ καύσων) is one of the features in the Epistle which harmonize well with the fact that the writer was an inhabitant of Palestine. It is the furnace-like blast from the arid wilderness to the east of the Jordan. "Yea, behold, being planted, shall it prosper? shall it not utterly wither when the east wind toucheth it? It shall wither in the beds where it grew" (Ezek. xvii. 10). "God prepared a sultry east wind; and the sun beat upon the head of Jonah, that he fainted" (Jonah iv. 8). The fig-tree, olives, and vine (iii. 12) are the chief fruit-trees of Palestine; and "the early and latter rain" (v. 7) points still more clearly to the same district.

It has been remarked with justice that whereas St. Paul for the most part draws his metaphors from the scenes of human activity—building, husbandry, athletic contests, and warfare—St. James prefers to take his metaphors from the *scenes of nature*. In this chapter we have "the surge of the sea" (ver. 6) and "the flower of the grass" (ver. 10). In the third chapter we have the "rough winds" driving the ships, the "wood kindled by a small fire," "the wheel of nature," "every kind of beasts and birds, of creeping things, and things in the sea," "the fountain sending forth sweet water," "the fig-tree and vine" (vv. 4, 5, 6, 7, 11, 12). In the fourth chapter human life is "a vapour, that appeareth for a little time, and then vanisheth away" (ver. 14). And in the last chapter, besides the moth and the rust, we have "the fruit of the earth," and "the early and latter rain" (vv. 2, 3, 7, 18).

These instances are certainly very numerous, when the brevity of the Epistle is considered. The love of nature which breathes through them was no doubt learned and cherished in the village home at Nazareth, and it forms another link between St. James and his Divine Brother. Nearly every one of the natural phenomena to which St. James directs attention in this letter are used by Christ also in His teaching. The surging of the sea (Luke xxi. 25), the flowers of the field (Matt. vi. 28), the burning of wood (John xv. 6), the birds of the air (Matt. vi. 26; viii. 20; xiii. 4, 32), the fountain of sweet water (John iv. 10-14; vii. 38), the fig-tree (Matt. vii. 16; xxi. 19; xxiv. 32), the vine (John xv. 1-5), the moth (Matt. vi. 19), the rust (Matt. vi. 19), and the rain (Matt. v. 45; vii. 25). In some cases the use made by St. James of these natural objects is very similar to that made by our Lord, and it may well be that what he writes is a reminiscence of what he had heard years before from Christ's lips; but in other cases the use is quite different, and must be assigned to the love of nature, and the recognition of its fitness for teaching spiritual truths, which is common to the Lord and His brother. Thus, when St. James asks, "Can a fig-tree, my brethren, yield olives, or a vine figs?" we seem to have an echo of the question in the Sermon on the Mount, "Do men gather grapes of thorns, or figs of thistles?" And when St. James tells the rich oppressors that their "garments are moth-eaten; their gold and their silver are rusted," is he not remembering Christ's charge, "Lay not up for yourselves treasures upon the earth, where moth and rust do consume, and where thieves break through and steal"? But in most of the other cases there is little or no resemblance between the similes of Christ and the figurative use of the same natural phenomena made by St. James. Thus, while Jesus uses the flowers of the field to illustrate God's care for every object in the universe, and the superiority of the glory which He bestows over that with which man adorns himself, St. James teaches thereby the transitory character of the glory which comes of riches; and while Christ points to the rain as illustrating God's bounty to good and bad alike, St. James takes it as an illustration of His goodness in answer to patient and trusting prayer.

It is manifest that in this matter St. James is partly following a great example, but partly also following the bent of his own mind. The first, without the second, would hardly have given us so many examples of this kind of teaching in so small a space. St. John had equal opportunities with St. James of learning this method of teaching from Christ, and yet there are scarcely any examples of it in his Epistles. Possibly his opportunities were even greater than those of St. James; for although he was at most the cousin of the Lord, whereas St. James was His brother, yet he was present during the whole of Christ's ministry, whereas St. James was not converted until after the Resurrection. But there is this great difference between Christ's teaching from nature and that of St. James: St. James recognizes in the order and beauty of the universe a revelation of Divine truth, and makes use of the facts of the external world to teach spiritual lessons; the incarnate Word, in drawing spiritual lessons from the external world, could expound the meaning of a universe which He Himself had made. In the one case it is a disciple of nature who imparts to us the lore which he himself has learned; in the other it is the Master of nature, who points out to us the meaning of His own world, and interprets to us the voices of the winds and the waves, which obey Him.

> [44] 1 Tim. iv. 3, where commanding is understood from forbidding, is not strictly parallel: "forbidding to marry, *and commanding* to abstain from meats." The context is such as to prevent any misunderstanding of the loosely worded sentence. See Moulton's Winer, p. 777; also Bede, who rightly remarks, "Subauditur a superiore versa, *glorietur*. Quod per irrisionem quæ Græce ironia vocatur, dictum esse constat ... ut humiliatus in æternum pereat cum purpurato illo divite qui Lazarum despexit egentem."

CHAPTER VIII
THE SOURCE OF TEMPTATIONS AND THE REALITY OF SIN. THE DIFFICULTIES OF THE DETERMINIST

"Blessed is the man that endureth temptation: for when he hath been approved, he shall receive the crown of life, which the Lord promised to them that love Him. Let no man say when he is tempted, I am tempted of God: for God cannot be tempted with evil, and He Himself tempteth no man: but each man is tempted when he is drawn away by his own lust and enticed. Then the lust, when it hath conceived, beareth sin: and the sin, when it is full-grown, bringeth forth death. Be not deceived, my beloved brethren. Every good gift and every perfect boon is from above, coming down from the Father of lights, with whom can be no variation, neither shadow that is cast by turning. Of His own will He brought us forth by the word of truth, that we should be a kind of first-fruits of His creatures." — St. James i. 12-18.

After the slight digression respecting the short-lived glory of the rich man, St. James returns once more to the subject with which the letter opens — the blessing of trials and temptations as opportunities of patience, and the blessedness of the man who endures them, and thus earns "the crown of life, which the Lord has promised to them that love Him." These last words are very interesting as being a record of *some utterance of Christ's not preserved in the Gospels,* of which we have perhaps other traces elsewhere in the New Testament (1 Pet. v. 4; Rev. ii. 10; 2 Tim. iv. 8).[45] They imply a principle which qualifies what goes before, and leads on to what follows. The mere endurance of temptations and afflictions will not win the promised crown, unless temptations are withstood, and afflictions endured in the right spirit. The proud self-reliance and self-repression of the Stoic has nothing meritorious about it. These trials must be met in a spirit of loving trust in the God who sends or allows them. It is only those who love and trust God who have the right to expect anything from His bounty. This St. James continually insists on. Let not the double-minded man, with his affections and loyalty divided between God and Mammon, "think that he shall receive anything of the Lord" (i. 7). God has chosen the poor who are "rich in *faith*" to be "heirs of the kingdom which He promised *to them that love Him"* (ii. 5). And this love of God is quite incompatible with love of the world. "Whosoever therefore would be a friend of the world maketh himself an enemy of God" (iv. 4).

It is the loving withstanding of temptation, then, that wins the crown of life: the mere being tempted tends rather to death. "Lust, when it hath conceived, beareth sin: and the sin, when it is full-grown, bringeth forth death." With these facts before him, the loving Christian will never say, when temptations come, that they come from God. It cannot be God's will to seduce him from the path of life to the path of death. The existence of temptations is no just ground of complaint against God. Such complaints are an attempt to shift the blame from himself to his Creator. The temptations proceed, not from God, but from the man's own evil nature; a nature which God created stainless, but which man of his own free will has debased. To tempt is to try to lead astray; and one has only to understand the word in its true sense to see how impossible it is that God should become a tempter. By a simple but telling opposition of words St. James indicates where the blame lies. God *"Himself* tempteth no man (πειράζει δὲ αὐτὸς οὐδένα); but each man is tempted when by his *own* lust he is drawn away and enticed" (ὑπὸ τῆς ἰδίας ἐπιθυμίας ἐξελκόμενος καὶ δελεαζόμενος). It is his own evil desire which plays the part of the temptress, drawing him out from his place of safety by the enticement of sinful pleasure.[46] So that the fault is in a sense doubly his. The desire which tempts proceeds from his own evil nature, and the will which consents to the temptress is his own. Throughout the passage St. James represents the evil desire as playing the part of Potiphar's wife. The man who withstands such temptation is winning the promised crown of life; the man who yields has for the offspring of his error death. The one result is in accordance with God's will, as is proved by His promising and bestowing the crown; the other is not, but is the natural and known consequence of the man's own act.

At the present time there is a vehement effort being made in some quarters to shift the blame of man's wrong-doing, if not on to God (and He is commonly left out of the account, as unknown or non-existing), at any rate on to those natural laws which determine phenomena. We are asked to believe that such ideas as moral freedom and responsibility are mere chimæras, and that the first thing which a reasonable person has to do, in raising himself to a higher level, is to get rid of them. He is to convince himself that character and conduct are the necessarily evolved result of inherited endowments, developed in certain circumstances, over neither of which the man has any control. He did not select the qualities of body and mind which he received from his parents, and he did not make the circumstances in which he has had to live since his birth. He could no more help acting as he did on any given occasion than he could help the size of his heart or the colour of his brain. He is no more responsible for the acts which he produces than a tree is responsible for its leaves. And of all senseless delusions and senseless wastes of power, those which are involved in the feeling of remorse are the worst. In remorse we wring our hands over deeds which we could not possibly have avoided doing, and reproach ourselves for emitting what we could not by any possibility have done. Ethiopians might as reasonably blame themselves for their black skins, or be conscience-stricken for not having golden hair, as any human being feel remorse for what he has done or left undone in the past. Whatever folly a man may have committed, he eclipses it all by the folly of self-reproach.

Positivism will indeed have worked marvels when it has driven remorse out of the world; and until it has succeeded in doing so, it will remain confronted by an unanswerable proof—as universal as the humanity which it professes to worship—that its moral system is based upon a falsehood. Whether or no we admit the belief in a God, the fact of self-reproach in every human heart remains to be accounted for. And it is a fact of the most enormous proportions. Think of the years of mental agony and moral torture which countless numbers of the human race have endured since man became a living soul, because men have invariably reproached themselves with the folly and wickedness which they have committed. Think of the exquisite suffering which remorse has inflicted on every human being who has reached years of reflexion. Think of the untold misery which the misdeeds of men have inflicted upon those who love and would fain respect them. It may be doubted whether all other forms of human suffering, whether mental or bodily, are more than as a drop in the ocean, compared with the agonies which have been endured through the gnawing pangs of remorse for personal misconduct, and of shame and grief for the misconduct of friends and relations. And if the Determinist is right, all this mental torture, with its myriad stabs and stings through centuries of centuries, is based on a monstrous delusion. These bitter reproachers of themselves and of those dearest to them might have been spared it all, if only they had known that not one of the acts thus blamed and lamented in tears of blood could have been avoided.

Certainly the Positivist, who shuts God out from his consideration, has a difficult problem to solve, when he is asked how he accounts for a delusion so vast, so universal, and so horrible in its consequences; and we do not wonder that he should exhaust all the powers of rhetoric and invective in the attempt to exorcize it. But his difficulty is as nothing compared with the difficulties of a thinker who endeavours to combine Determinism with Theism, and even with Christianity. What sort of a God can He be who has allowed, who has even ordained, that every human heart should be wrung with this needless, senseless agony? Has any savage, any inquisitor, ever devised torture so diabolical? And what kind of a Saviour and Redeemer can He be who has come from heaven, and returned thither again, without saying one word to free men from their blind, self-inflicted agonies; who, on the contrary, has said many things to confirm them in their delusions? Whence came moral evil and the pangs of remorse, if there is no such thing as free will? They must have been fore-ordained and created by God. The Theist has no escape from that. If God made man free, and man by misusing his freedom brought sin into the world, and remorse as a punishment for sin, then we have *some* explanation of the mystery of evil. God neither willed it nor created it; it was the offspring of a free and rebellious will. But if man was never free, and there is no such thing as sin, then the madman gnawing his own limbs in his frenzy is a reasonable being and a joyous sight, compared with the man who gnaws his own heart in remorse for the deeds which the inexorable laws of his own nature compelled him, and still compel him, to commit.

Is there, or is there not, such a thing as sin? That is the question which lies at the bottom of the error against which St. James warns his readers, and of the doctrines which are advocated at the present time by Positivists and all who deny the reality of human freedom and responsibility. To say that when we are tempted we are tempted by God, or that the Power which brought us into existence has given us no freedom to refuse the evil and to choose the good, is to say that sin is a figment of the human mind, and that a conscious revolt of the human mind against the power of holiness is impossible. On such a question the appeal to human language, of which Aristotle is so fond, seems to be eminently suitable; and the verdict which it gives is overwhelming. There is probably no language, there is certainly no civilized language, which has no word to express the idea of sin. If sin is an illusion, how came the whole human race to believe in it, and to frame a word to express it?[47] Can we point to any other word in universal, or even very general use, which nevertheless represents a mere chimæra, believed in as real, but actually non-existent? And let us remember that this is no case in which self-interest, which so fatally warps our judgment, can have led the whole human race astray. Self-interest would lead us entirely in the opposite direction. There is no human being who would not enthusiastically welcome the belief that what seem to him to be grievous sins are no more a matter of reproach to him than the beatings of his heart or the winkings of his eyes. Sometimes the conscience-stricken offender, in his efforts to excuse his acts before the judgment-seat of his higher self, tries to believe this. Sometimes the Determinist philosopher endeavours to prove to him that he ought to believe it. But the stern facts of his own nature and the bitter outcome of all human experience are too strong for such attempts. In spite of all specious excuses, and all plausible statements of philosophic difficulties, his conscience and his consciousness compel him to confess, "It was my own lust that enticed me, and my own will that consented."

How serious St. James considers the error of attempting to make God responsible for our temptations is shown both by the earnest and affectionate insertion of "Be not deceived,[48] my beloved brethren," and also by the pains which he takes to disprove the error. After having shown the true source of temptation, and explained the way in which sin and death are generated, he points out how incredible it is on other grounds that God should become a tempter. How can the Source of every good gift and every perfect boon[49] be also a source of temptations to sin? How can the Father of lights be one who would lead away His creatures into darkness? If what we know of human nature ought to tell us whence temptations to sin are likely to come, what we know of God's nature and of His dealings with mankind ought to tell us whence such things are *not* likely to come.

And He is far above those heavenly luminaries of which He is the Author. *They* are not always bright, and are therefore very imperfect symbols of His holiness. In their revolutions they are sometimes overshadowed. The moon is not always at the full, the sun is sometimes eclipsed, and the stars suffer changes in like manner. In Him there is no change, no loss of light, no encroachment of shadow. There is never a time at which one could say that through momentary diminution in holiness it had become possible for Him to become a tempter.

Nor are the brightness and beneficence which pervade the material universe the chief proofs of God's goodness and of the impossibility of temptations to sin proceeding from Him. It was "of His own will" that He rescued mankind from the state of death into which their rebellious wills had brought them, and by a new revelation of Himself in "the Word of truth," *i.e.* the Gospel, brought them forth again, born anew as Christians, to be, like the first-born under the Law, "a kind of first-fruits of His creatures."[50]

When, therefore, we sum up all the known facts of the case, there is only one conclusion at which we can justly arrive. There is the nature of God, so far as it is known to us, utterly opposed to evil. There is the nature of man, as it has been debased by himself, constantly bringing forth evil. There is

God's goodness, as manifested in the creation of the universe and in the regeneration of man. It is a hopeless case to try to banish remorse by making God responsible for man's temptations and sin.

There is only one way of getting rid of remorse, and that is to confess sin—to confess its reality, to confess it to God, and if need be to man. No man ever yet succeeded in justifying himself by laying the blame of his sins on God. But he may do so by laying the sins themselves upon "the Lamb of God, who taketh away the sins of the world," and by washing his stained robes, "and making them white in the blood of the Lamb." That done, remorse will have no power over him; and instead of fruitlessly accusing God, and seeking vain substitutes for the service of God, he will humbly "give Him glory," and "serve Him day and night in His temple" (Joshua vii. 19; Rev. vii. 15).

Note.—The difficult expression (τροπῆς ἀποσκίασμα) rendered in the Authorized Version "shadow of turning," and in the Revised "shadow that is cast by turning," has received a great variety of translations and explanations. The Old Latin, *modicum obumbrationis*, like the Greek commentators, makes ἀποσκίασμα = σκιά = "shade, trace, small amount." It is doubtful whether the rare compound ἀποσκίασμα ever acquired this meaning; but the opinion of Greeks on this point is of great weight, and certainly this meaning makes good sense. The Vulgate, *vicissitudinis obumbratio*, is as difficult as the Greek; and Augustine's *momenti obumbratio* comes from the false reading ῥοπῆς. "Shadow cast by turning" does not seem to be very helpful, whether we interpret "turning" to mean the revolutions of the sun or of the earth, or the changes of nature generally. Perhaps the genitive is the genitive of quality, "shadow of change" for "changing shadow;" so Stier and Theil, *wechselnde Beschattung*, and Stolz *abwechselnde Verdunkelung*. Comp. ἀκροατὴς ἐπιλησμονῆς (i. 25), and, see the *Expositor*, Sept. 1889, pp. 228-30.

[45] In the *Acta Philippi, Apocal. Apocr.*, ed. Tischendorf, p. 147, we have, "Blessed is he who hath his raiment white; for he it is who receiveth the crown of joy." See A. Resch, *Agrapha; Aussercanonische Evangelienfragmente* (Leipzig, 1889), p. 254.

[46] The punctuation and order of words in both A.V. and R.V. seem to be faulty: "enticed," quite as much as "drawn away," belongs to "by his own lust." Moreover, the metaphor is not seduction from the right road, but alluring out of security into danger.

[47]   See R. H. Hutton on *The Service of Man*, in the *Contemporary Review*, April, 1887, p. 492.

[48]   Or, "led astray" (πλανᾶσθε). The word implies fundamental departure from the truth (v. 19; John vii. 47; 1 John i. 8; ii. 26; iii. 7; Rev. xviii. 23).

[49] The words form an hexameter in the original, which may be either accidental or a quotation: πᾶσα δόσις ἀγαθὴ καὶ πᾶν δώρημα τελειον ("Every gift that is good, and every boon that is perfect").

[50] See F. D. Maurice, *Unity of the N.T.* (Parker, 1854), pp. 320-23.

CHAPTER IX
THE DELUSION OF HEARING WITHOUT
DOING. THE MIRROR OF GOD'S WORD

"But be ye doers of the word, and not hearers only, deluding your own selves. For if any one is a hearer of the word, and not a doer, he is like unto a man beholding his natural face in a mirror: for he beholdeth himself, and goeth away, and straightway forgetteth what manner of man he was. But he that looketh into the perfect law, the law of liberty, and so continueth, being not a hearer that forgetteth, but a doer that worketh, this man shall be blessed in his doing."—St. James i. 22-25.

HERE we reach what on the whole seems to be the main thought of the Epistle—*the all-importance of Christian activity and service.* The essential thing, without which other things, however good in themselves, become insignificant or worthless, or even mischievous, is *conduct.* Everything else, if not accompanied by practice, by avoiding evil and doing good, is vain. In Bishop Butler's words, religion "does not consist in the knowledge and belief even of fundamental truth," but rather in our being brought "to a certain temper and behaviour;" or as St. John puts it still more simply, only "he who *doeth* righteousness is righteous." Suffering injuries, poverty, and temptations, hearing the Word, teaching the Word, faith, wisdom (i. 2, 9, 12, 19; ii. 14-26; iii. 7-13), are all of them excellent; but if they are not accompanied by a holy life, a life of prayer and gentle words and good deeds, they are valueless.

There are two or three other leading thoughts, but they are all of them subordinated to this main thought of the necessity for Christian conduct as well as Christian belief and wisdom. One of these secondary thoughts has already been noticed more than once—the blessedness of enduring temptations and other trials; it is specially prominent in the first and last chapters (i. 2-4, 12; v. 7-11). Another of the secondary topics which have a prominent place in the letter is the peril of much speaking. It introduces and closes the section which lies immediately before us (i. 19, 26), and it is dwelt upon at length in the third chapter. Yet a third topic which cannot fail to attract the attention of the reader is the preference given to the poor over the rich as regards their spiritual opportunities, and the stern warnings addressed to all those whose wealth leads them to become tyrannical. This subject is specially prominent in the first, second, and last chapters (i. 10, 11; ii. 1-7; v. 1-6). But all these matters are looked at from the point of view of Christian conduct and service. They are not in any one case the idea which binds together the whole Epistle, but they lead up to it and emphasize it. If we were to single out one verse as in a special way summing up the teaching of the whole letter, we could hardly find one more suitable for the purpose than the first of the four which stand at the head of the present chapter: "Be ye doers of the word, and not hearers only, deluding your own selves." It will be worth while to examine this simple and most practical exhortation somewhat in detail.

It is one of the many sayings in the Epistle which irresistibly remind us of the teaching of Jesus Christ; not as being a quotation from any of His recorded discourses, but as being an independent reproduction of the substance of His conversation by one who was quite familiar with it, but was not familiar with the written Gospels. Had the writer of this letter been well acquainted with any of the four Gospels, he could hardly have escaped being influenced by them, and the echoes of Christ's teaching which we find in its pages would have been more closely in accordance with the reports of His words which they contain. This feature of the Epistle harmonizes well with its being written by the Lord's brother, who must have been very familiar with the Lord's teaching, and who wrote before A.D. 62, *i.e.* at a time when perhaps not one of our Gospels was written, and when certainly none of them can have had a very wide circulation. More will be said upon this point hereafter : for the present it suffices to point out the resemblance between this warning against the delusion of thinking that hearing without doing is of any avail, and the warning which closes the Sermon on the Mount: "Every one which heareth these words of Mine, and doeth them, shall be likened unto a wise man, which built his house upon the rock.... And every one that heareth these words of Mine, and doeth them not, shall be likened unto a foolish man, which built his house upon the sand: and the rain descended, and the floods came, and the winds blew, and smote upon that house; and it fell: and great was the fall thereof" (Matt. vii. 24-27).

"Be ye doers of the Word." Both verb and tense are remarkable (γίνεσθε): "*Become* doers of the Word." True Christian practice is a thing of growth; it is a process, and a process which has already begun, and is continually going on. We may compare, "*Become* ye therefore wise as serpents, and harmless as doves" (Matt. x. 16); "Therefore *become* ye also ready" (xxiv. 44); and "*Become* not faithless, but believing" (John xx. 27; where see Westcott's note). "Become doers of the Word" is more expressive than "Be doers of the Word," and a good deal more expressive than "Do the Word." A "doer of the Word" (ποιητὴς λόγου) is such by profession and practice; the phrase expresses a habit. But one who merely incidentally performs what is prescribed may be said to "do the Word." By the "Word" is meant what just before has been called the "implanted Word" and the "Word of truth" (w. 21, 18), and what in this passage is also called "the perfect law, the law of liberty" (ver. 25), *i.e.* the Gospel. The parable of the Sower illustrates in detail the meaning of becoming an habitual doer of the implanted Word.

"And not hearers only." The order of the words in the Greek is a little doubtful, the authorities being very much divided; but the balance is in favour of taking "only" closely with "hearers" (μὴ ἀκροαταὶ μόνον rather than μὴ μόνον ἀκροαταί); "Be not such as are mere hearers and nothing more." The word for "hearer" occurs nowhere else in the New Testament, excepting in the singularly similar passage in the Epistle to the Romans, which is one of the passages that give support to the theory that either St. Paul had seen this Epistle, or St. James had seen St. Paul's: "Not the hearers (ἀκροαταί) of a law are just before God, but the doers of a law shall be justified," (Rom. ii. 13; see above, p. 57). The verb (ἀκροάομαι) does not occur in the New Testament; but another cognate substantive (ἀκροατήριον), meaning "a place of hearing," is found in the Acts (xxv. 23). In classical Greek this group of words indicates *attentive* listening, especially in the case of those who attend the lectures of philosophers and the addresses of public speakers. It is thus used frequently in Plato, Aristotle, Thucydides, and Plutarch. It is somewhat too hastily concluded that there is nothing of this kind included either in this passage or in Rom. ii. 13. Possibly that is the very thing to which both St. James and St. Paul allude. St. James, in the address which he made to the so-called Council of Jerusalem, says, "Moses from generations of old hath in every city them that preach him, being read in the synagogues every Sabbath" (Acts xv. 21). The Jews came with great punctiliousness to these weekly gatherings, and listened with much attention to the public reading and exposition of the Law; and too many of them thought that with that the chief part of their duty was performed. This habitual public testimony of respect for the Mosaic Law and the traditional interpretations of it, and this zeal to acquire a knowledge of its contents and an insight into its meaning, was the main portion of what was required of them. This, St. James tells them, is miserably insufficient, whether what they hear be the Law or the Gospel, the Law with or without the illumination of the life of Christ. "Being swift to hear" (ver. 19) and to understand is well, but "apart from works it is barren." It is the habitual practice in striving to *do* what is heard and understood that is of value. "Not a hearer that forgetteth, but a doer that worketh" is blessed, and "blessed in his doing." To suppose that mere hearing brings a blessing is "deluding your own selves." Bede rightly quotes Rev. i. 3 in illustration: "Blessed are they that hear the words of the prophecy, and *keep* the things which are written therein."

The word here used for deluding (παραλογιζόμενοι) is found nowhere else in the New Testament, excepting in one passage in the Epistle to the Colossians (ii. 4), in which St. Paul warns them against allowing any one to "delude them with persuasiveness of speech." But the word is fairly common both in ordinary Greek and in the Septuagint. Its meaning is to mislead with fallacious reasoning, and the substantive (παραλογισμός) is the Aristotelian term for a fallacy. The word does not necessarily imply that the fallacious reasoning is known to be fallacious by those who employ it. To express that we should rather have the word which is used in 2 Peter i. 16 to characterize "cunningly devised fables" (σεσοφισμένοι μῦθοι). Here we are to understand that the victims of the delusion do not, although they might, see the worthlessness of the reasons upon which their self-contentment is based. It is precisely in this that the danger of their position lies. Self-deceit is the most subtle and fatal deceit. The mere knowledge of the law derived from their attentive listening to it does but increase their evil case, if they do not practise it. "To him that knoweth to do good, and doeth it not, to him it is sin" (iv. 17).

The Jews have a saying that the man who hears without practising is like a husbandman who ploughs and sows, but never reaps. Such an illustration, being taken from natural phenomena, would be quite in harmony with the manner of St. James; but he enforces his meaning by employing a far more striking illustration. He who is a hearer and not a doer "is like unto a man beholding his natural face in a mirror." Almost all the words in this sentence are worthy of separate attention.

"Is like unto a *man*" (ἔοικεν ἀνδρί). St. James uses the more definite word, which usually excludes women, and sometimes boys also. He does not say, "is like unto a *person*" (ἀνθρώπῳ), which would have included both sexes and all ages. A somewhat quaint explanation has been suggested by Paes, and adopted as probable elsewhere; viz. that men, as a rule, give only a passing look to themselves in the glass; whereas it is a feminine weakness to be fond of attentive observations. But it is fatal to this suggestion that the word here used for beholding (κατανοεῖν) means to fix one's mind upon, and consider attentively. It is the word used in "Consider the ravens," and "Consider the lilies" (Luke xii. 24, 27). Moreover, the Greeks sometimes do what we very frequently do in speaking of the human race; they employ the male sex as representative of both. This usage is found in the New Testament; *e.g.* "The queen of the South shall rise up in the judgment with *the men* (τῶν ἀνδρῶν) of this generation, and shall condemn them.... *The men* (ἄνδρες) of Nineveh shall stand up in the judgment with this generation, and shall condemn it" (Luke xi. 31, 32). Here it is impossible that the women are not included. And this use of "man" (ἀνήρ) in the sense of human being is specially common in St. James. We have it four times in this chapter (vv. 8, 12, 20, 23), and again in the second (ver. 2) and third (ver. 2).

This man, then, attentively studies his natural face in a mirror. The words for "his natural face" literally mean "the face of his birth" (τὸ πρόσωπον τῆς γενέσεως αὐτοῦ), *i.e.* the features with which he was born; and the mirror would be a piece of polished metal, which, however excellent, would not reflect the features with the clearness and fidelity of a modern looking-glass. Hence the necessity for attentive observation, the result of which is that the man recognizes his own face beyond all question. But what follows? "He beheld himself, and he has gone away, and he straightway forgot what manner of man he was." The perfect tense between two aorists gives a lively simplicity to the narration (κατενόησεν ... ἀπελήλυθεν ... ἐπελάθετο). This is represented as a common case, though not an invariable one. Most of us know our own features sufficiently well to recognize them in a good representation of them, but do not carry in our minds a very accurate image of them. But what has all this to do with being hearers, and not doers, of the Word?

The spoken or written Word of God is the mirror. When we hear it preached, or study it for ourselves, we can find the reflexion of ourselves in it, our temptations and weaknesses, our failings and sins, the influences of God's Spirit upon us, and the impress of His grace. It is here that we notice one marked difference between the inspiration of the sacred writers and the inspiration of the poet and the dramatist. The latter show us *other people* to the life; Scripture shows us *ourselves.*

> "Our mirror is a blessed book,
> Where out from each illumined page
> We see one glorious image look,
> All eyes to dazzle and engage,
>
> The Son of God; and that indeed
> We see Him as He is we know,
> Since in the same bright glass we read
> The very life of things below.
>
> Eye of God's Word, where'er we turn
> Ever upon us! thy keen gaze

Can all the depths of sin discern,
Unravel every bosom's maze.

Who that has felt thy glance of dread
Thrill through his heart's remotest cells,
About his path, about his bed,
Can doubt what Spirit in thee dwells?"[51]

Keble's metaphor is somewhat more elaborate than St. James's. He represents the Bible as a mirror, out of which the reflected image of the Son of God looks upon us and reads our inmost selves. St. James supposes that in the mirror we see ourselves reflected. But the thought is the same, that through hearing or reading God's Word our knowledge of our characters is quickened. But does this quickened knowledge last? does it lead to action, or influence our conduct? Too often we leave the church or our study, and the impression produced by the recognition of the features of our own case is obliterated. "We straightway forget what manner of men we are," and the insight which has been granted to us into our own true selves is just one more wasted experience.

But this need not be so, and in some cases a very different result may be noticed. Instead of merely looking attentively for a short time, he may *stoop down and pore over it*. Instead of forthwith going away, he may *continue* in the study of it. And instead of straightway forgetting, he may prove a mindful *doer that worketh*. Thus the three parts of the two pictures are made exactly to balance. The word for "looking into" is an interesting one (παρακύπτειν). It indicates bending forward to examine earnestly. It is used of Peter looking into the sepulchre (Luke xxiv. 12, a verse of doubtful genuineness); and of Mary Magdalene doing the same (John xx. 11); and of the angels desiring to look into heavenly mysteries (1 Peter i. 12). He who does this recognizes God's Word as being "the perfect law, the law of liberty." The two things are the same. It is when the law is seen to be perfect that it is found to be the law of liberty. So long as the law is not seen in the beauty of its perfection, it is not loved, and men either disobey it or obey it by constraint and unwillingly. It is then a law of bondage. But when its perfection is recognized men long to conform to it; and they obey, not because they must, but because they choose. To do what one likes is freedom, and they like to obey. It is in this way that the moral law of the Gospel becomes "the law of liberty," not by imposing fewer obligations than the moral law of the Jew or of the Gentile, but by infusing into the hearts of those who welcome it a disposition and a desire to obey. Christian liberty is never licence. It is not the relaxation of needful restraints, but the spontaneous acceptance of them as excellent in themselves and beneficial to those who observe them. It is the difference between a code imposed by another, and a constitution voluntarily adopted. To be made to work for one whom one fears is slavery and misery; to choose to work for one whom one loves is freedom and happiness. The Gospel has not abolished the moral law; it has supplied a new and adequate motive for fulfilling it.

"Being not a hearer that forgetteth." Literally, "having become not a hearer of forgetfulness" (οὐκ ἀκροατὴς ἐπιλησμονῆς γενόμενος); *i.e.* having by practice come to be a hearer, who is characterized, not by forgetfulness of what he hears, but by attentive performance of it.[52] The unusual word "forgetfulness" occurs nowhere else in the New Testament, nor in classical Greek; but it is found in Ecclesiasticus (xi. 27), "The affliction of an hour causeth forgetfulness of pleasure;" and this adds a trifle to the evidence that St. James was acquainted with that book . "A hearer of forgetfulness" exactly balances, both in form and in thought, "a doer of work;" and this is well brought out by the Revisers, who turn *both* genitives by a relative clause: "a hearer that forgetteth," and "a doer that worketh." The Authorized Version is much less happy: "a forgetful hearer, but a doer of *the* work." There is no article in the Greek, and the translation of one genitive by an adjective, and of the other by a genitive, is unfortunate. "A doer of *work*" (ποιητὴς ἔργου), or "a doer that *worketh*," is an expression that emphasizes just what St. James wishes to emphasize, viz. the necessity of actively practising what is attentively heard. "A doer" would have sufficed, but "a doer that worketh" makes the idea of habitual action still more prominent.

"This man shall be blessed in his doing" (ἐν τῇ ποιήσει). Once more we have a word which is found nowhere else in the New Testament, but occurs in Ecclesiasticus (xix. 20), and with much the same meaning as here: "All wisdom is fear of the Lord; and in all wisdom there is doing of the law" (ποίησις νόμου). The correspondence between the meaning of St. James and the meaning of the son of Sirach is very close. Mere knowledge without performance is of little worth: it is in the doing that a blessing can be found.

The danger against which St. James warns the Jewish Christians of the Dispersion is as pressing now as it was when he wrote. Never was there a time when interest in the Scriptures was more keen or more widely spread, especially among the educated classes; and never was there a time when greater facilities for gratifying this interest abounded. Commentaries, expositions, criticisms, introductions, helps of all kinds, exegetical, homiletic, historical, and textual, suitable both for learned and unlearned students, multiply year by year. But it is much to be feared that with many of us the interest in the sacred writings which is thus roused and fostered remains to a very large extent a literary interest. We are much more eager to know all *about* God's Word than from it to learn His will respecting ourselves, that we may do it; to prove that a book is genuine than to practise what it enjoins. We study Lives of Christ, but we do not follow the life of Christ. We pay Him the empty homage of an intellectual interest in His words and works, but we do not the things which He says. We throng and press Him in our curiosity, but we obtain no blessing, because in all our hearing and learning there is no true wisdom, no fear of the Lord, and no doing of His Word.

[51] *The Christian Year*, St. Bartholomew's Day.

[52] This "characterizing genitive" is not exactly a Hebraism, like "children of wrath," "son of perdition," "son of light," and the like; but the use of the genitive in place of an adjective is more common in Oriental languages, and therefore in Greek which is under Oriental influences. See p. 122.

CHAPTER X
THE CHRISTOLOGY OF ST. JAMES. THE PRACTICAL UNBELIEF INVOLVED IN SHOWING A WORLDLY RESPECT OF PERSONS IN PUBLIC WORSHIP

"My brethren, hold not the faith of our Lord Jesus Christ, the Lord of glory, with respect of persons. For if there come into your synagogue a man with a gold ring, in fine clothing, and there come in also a poor man in vile clothing; and ye have regard to him that weareth the fine clothing, and say, Sit thou here in a good place; and ye say to the poor man, Stand thou there, or sit under my footstool; are ye not divided in your own mind, and become judges with evil thoughts?" —St. James ii. 1-4.

AS has been stated already, in a previous chapter , one of Luther's main objections to this Epistle is that it does not "preach and urge Christ." "It teaches Christian people, and yet does not once notice the Passion, the Resurrection, the Spirit of Christ. The writer names Christ a few times; but he teaches nothing of Him, but speaks of general faith in God."

This indictment has been more fully drawn out by a modern writer. "The author's stand-point is Jewish rather than Christian. The ideas are cast in a Jewish mould. The very name of Christ occurs but twice (i. 1; ii. 1), and His atonement is scarcely touched. We see little more than the threshold of the new system. It is the teaching of a Christian Jew, rather than of one who had reached a true apprehension of the essence of Christ's religion. The doctrinal development is imperfect. It is only necessary to read the entire Epistle to perceive the truth of these remarks. In warning his readers against transgression of the law by partiality to individuals, the author adduces Jewish rather than Christian motives (ii. 8-13). The greater part of the third chapter, respecting the government of the tongue, is of the same character, in which Christ's example is not once alluded to, the illustrations being taken from objects in nature. The warning against uncharitable judgment does not refer to Christ, or to God, who puts His Spirit in the hearts of believers, but to the law (iv. 10-12). He who judges his neighbour judges the law. The exhortation to feel and act under constant remembrance of the dependence of our life on God belongs to the same category (iv. 13-17). He that knows good without doing it is earnestly admonished to practise virtue and to avoid self-security, without reference to motives connected with redemption. Job and the Prophets are quoted as examples of patience, not Christ; and the efficacy of prayer is proved by the instance of Elias, without allusion to the Redeemer's promise (v. 17). The Epistle is wound up after the same Jewish fashion, though the opportunity of mentioning Christ, who gave Himself a Sacrifice for sin, presented itself naturally."[53]

All this may be admitted, without at all consenting to the conclusion which is drawn from it. Several other considerations must be taken into account before we can form a satisfactory opinion respecting the whole case. Few things are more misleading, in the interpretation of Scripture, than the insisting upon one set of facts and texts, and passing over all that is to be found on the other side. In this manner the most opposite views may be equally proved from Scripture. Universalism and the eschatology of Calvin, Pelagianism and Fatalism, Papalism and Presbyterianism.

First, both logically and chronologically the teaching of St. James precedes that of St. Paul and of St. John. To call it "retrograde" when compared with either of them is to call a child retrograde when compared with a man. St. Paul had to feed his converts with milk before he fed them with meat, and the whole of the congregations addressed by St. James in this letter must have been at a comparatively early stage of development. In some respects even the Mother Church of Jerusalem, from which his letter was written, did not get beyond these early stages. Before it had done so the centre of Christendom had moved from Jerusalem to Antioch; and to Jerusalem it never returned. It was useless to build a structure of doctrine before a foundation of morality had been laid. Advent must come before Christmas, and Lent before Easter. The manifold significance of the great truths of the Incarnation and the Resurrection would not be well appreciated by those who were neglecting some of the plainest principles of the moral law; and to appeal to the sanctions which every Jew from his childhood had been accustomed to regard as final was probably in the long-run more convincing than to remind these converts of the additional sanctions which they had admitted when they entered the Christian Church. Moreover, there are passages in the Epistle which seem to show that St. James at times looks aside to address Jews who are not Christians at all, and it may be that even when He addresses Christian converts he deliberately prefers arguments which would weigh with Jew and Christian alike to those which would appeal to the latter only. Like St. Paul himself, he was willing to become to the Jews a Jew, that he might win the Jews. Besides which, we must allow something for the bias of his own mind. To his death he remained in many respects, not only a saintly shepherd of the Christian Church, but also a Hebrew of Hebrews. He is the last Jewish prophet as well as the first Christian bishop, a Hebrew Rabbi inside the Church; and even if the condition of his readers had not made it desirable to lay much stress upon the Law and the Old Testament, the associations of a lifetime would have led him frequently to those old sources of truth and morality, all the more so as no authoritative Christian literature was as yet in existence. It was part of his mission to help in creating such a literature. He sets one of the first, it may be the very first, of the mystic stones, which, although apparently thrown together without order or connexion, form so harmonious and so complete a whole; and alike in the solidity of its material and in the simplicity of its form this Epistle is well fitted to be one of the first stones in such a building.

But it is easy to go away with an exaggerated view of the so-called deficiencies of this letter as regards distinctly Christian teaching. The passage before us is a strong piece of evidence, and even if it stood alone it would carry us a long way. Moreover, the strength of it is not much affected by the ambiguity of construction which confronts us in the original. It is impossible to say with absolute certainty how the genitive "of glory" (τῆς δόξης) ought to be taken; but the Revisers are possibly right: "Hold not the faith of our Lord Jesus Christ, (the Lord) of glory, with respect of persons."[54] Nor does it much matter whether we take the Greek negative (μὴ ... ἔχετε) as an imperative, "Do not go on holding;" or as an interrogative which expects a negative reply, "Do ye hold?" In any case we have the Divinity of Jesus Christ, and the fact of His being an object of faith to Christians, placed before us in clear language. No mere Jew, and no Ebionite who believed that Jesus was a mere man, could have written thus. And the words with which the Epistle opens are scarcely less marked: "James, of God and of the Lord Jesus Christ a bond-servant." In both passages the title "Lord," which in the Old Testament means Jehovah, is given to Jesus Christ, and in the opening words God and the Lord Jesus are placed side by side as equal. Moreover, St. James, who might have claimed honour as the brother of the Lord, prefers to style himself His bond-servant. He has "known Christ after the flesh," few more closely and intimately, and he knows from experience how little such knowledge avails: "henceforth knows he Him so no more." He who does the will of God is the true brother of the Lord, and it is this kind of relationship to Christ that he wishes to secure for his readers.

Nor do these two passages, in which Jesus Christ is mentioned by name, stand alone. There is the question, "Do not they blaspheme the honourable Name by which ye were called?" The honourable Name, which had been "called upon" them, is that of Christ, and if it can be blasphemed it is a Divine Name (ii. 7). The Second Advent of Christ, "the coming of the Lord," is a thing for which Christians are to wait patiently and longingly (v. 7-9), and the office which He will then discharge is that of the Divine Judge of all mankind. "The coming of the Lord is at hand. Murmur not, brethren, one against another, that ye be not judged: behold, the Judge standeth before the doors" (v. 8, 9).

Nor have we yet exhausted the passages which in this singularly practical and undoctrinal Epistle point clearly to the central doctrine of the Divinity of Christ and His eternal relation to His Church. "Is any among you sick? Let him call for the elders of the Church; and let them pray over him, anointing him with oil in the Name of the Lord: and the prayer of faith shall save him that is sick, and the Lord shall raise him up" (v. 14, 15). As in the case of the man healed at the Beautiful Gate of the Temple (Acts iii. 6, 16) it is "in the Name of Jesus Christ of Nazareth, ... whom God raised from the dead, even in this Name," that the sick man is to be restored. And some interpreters (Dorner and Von Soden) think that Christ is included, or even exclusively intended, in "One is the Lawgiver and the Judge" (iv. 12. Comp. v. 9). Thus Liddon: "Especially noteworthy is his assertion that the Lord Jesus Christ, the Judge of men, is not the delegated representative of an absent Majesty, but is Himself the Legislator enforcing His own laws. The Lawgiver, he says, is One Being with the Judge who can save and can destroy; the Son of man, coming in the clouds of heaven, has enacted the law which He thus administers."[55] But without taking into account expressions of which the interpretation is open to doubt, there is quite enough to show us that the Divinity of Jesus Christ, His redeeming death, His abiding power, and His return to judgment are the basis of the moral teaching of St. James, and are never long absent from his thoughts. Expressions, some of which no mere Jew or Ebionite could have used, and others which no such imperfect believer would have been likely to use, abound in this short Epistle, in spite of its simple and practical character.[56]

"My brethren, hold not the faith of our Lord Jesus Christ, the Lord of glory, with respect of persons." These words open a new section of the letter, as the renewed address indicates; and although the Epistle is not a set treatise, capable of analysis, but a letter, in which the subjects to be treated are loosely strung together in the order in which they occur to the writer, yet the connexion between the two very different subjects of this section and the preceding one can be traced. The previous section teaches that much hearing is better than much talking, and that much hearing is worthless without corresponding conduct. This section denounces undue respect of persons, and especially of wealthy persons during public worship. The connecting thoughts are religious worship and the treatment of the poor. The conduct which is true devotion is practical benevolence, moral purity, and unworldliness. This conclusion suggests a new subject, worldly respect of persons in public worship. That is the very reverse of pure devotion. To *profess* one's belief in Jesus Christ, the Lord of glory, and at the same time *show* one's belief in the majesty of mere money, is grievously incongruous. St. James is not making any attack on differences of rank, or asserting that no man is to be honoured above another. He is pointing out that reverence for the wealthy is no part of Christianity, and that such reverence is peculiarly out of place in the house of God, especially when it brings with it a corresponding disregard of the poor.

"If there come into your *synagogue*." This is one of several improvements which the Revisers have introduced into this passage. The Authorized Version has "assembly," which obscures the fact that the letter is written in those very early days of the Church in which the Jewish Christians still attended the worship of the Temple and the synagogue, or if they had a separate place of worship, spoke of it under the old familiar name. The latter is probably what is meant here. St. James, in writing to Christians, would hardly speak of a Jewish place of worship as "*your* synagogue," nor would he have rebuked Christians for the way in which different persons were treated in a synagogue of the Jews. The supposition that "the article (τὴν συναγωγὴ ὑμῶν) indicates that the *one* synagogue of the entire Jewish Christian Dispersion is meant, *i.e.* their religious community symbolically described by the name of the Jewish place of worship," is quite unfounded, and against the whole context. A typical incident—perhaps something which had actually been witnessed by St. James, or had been reported to him—is made the vehicle of a general principle (comp. i. 11). That the reference is to judicial courts often held in synagogues is also quite gratuitous, and destroys the contrast between "pure religion" and worldly respect of persons in public worship.

Another improvement introduced by the Revisers is a uniform translation of the word (ἐσθής) capriciously rendered "apparel," "raiment," and "clothing." Only one word is used in the Greek, and it is misleading to use three different words in English. By a quaint misuse of the very passage before us, the translators of 1611 defend their want of precision in such matters, and avow that in many cases precision was deliberately sacrificed to variety and to a wish to honour as many English words as possible by giving them a place in the Bible! In ordinary copies of the Authorized Version the Address to King James is commonly given, the far more instructive Address to the Reader never. Near the close of it the translators say as follows:—

"Another thing we think good to admonish thee of (gentle Reader) that we have not tied ourselves to an uniformity of phrasing, or to an identity of words, as some peradventure would wish we had done, because they observe, that some learned men some where, have been as exact as they could that way. Truly, that we might not vary from the sense of that which we had translated before, if the word signified the same thing in both places (for there be some words that be not of the same sense every where) we were especially careful, and made a conscience, according to our duty. But, that we should express the same notion in the same particular word; as for example, if we translate the *Hebrew* or *Greek* word once by *Purpose*, never to call it *Intent*; if one where *Journeying*, never *Travelling*; if one where *Think*, never *Suppose*; if one where *Pain*, never *Ache*; if one where *Joy*, never *Gladness*, etc. Thus to mince the matter, we thought to savour more of curiosity than wisdom, and that rather it would breed scorn in the Atheist, than bring profit to the godly Reader. For is the kingdom of God become words or syllables? why should we be in bondage to them if we may be free, use one precisely, when we may use another no less fit, as commodiously? A godly Father in the primitive time shewed himself greatly moved, that one of new-fangleness called κράββατοω σκίμπους though the difference be little or none (Niceph. Call. viii. 42); and another reporteth, that he was much abused for turning *Cucurbita* (to which reading the people had been used) into *Hedera* (Jerome *in iv. Jonæ*. See S. Augustine, *Epist.* 71). Now if this happen in better times, and upon so small occasions, we might justly fear hard censure, if generally we should make verbal and unnecessary changings. We might also be charged (by scoffers) with some unequal dealing towards a great number of good English words. For as it is written of a certain great Philosopher, that he should say, that those logs were happy that were made images to be worshipped; for their fellows, as good as they, lay for blocks behind the fire: so if we should say, as it were, unto certain words, Stand up higher, have a place in the Bible always, and to others of a like quality, Get ye hence, be banished for ever, we might be taxed peradventure with S. James his words, namely, *To be partial in our selves and judges of evil thoughts.*"[57]

In the passage before us the repetition of one and the same word for "clothing" is possibly not accidental. The repetition accentuates the fact that such a thing as clothing is allowed to be the measure of a man's merit. The rich man is neither the better nor the worse for his fine clothes, the poor man neither the better nor the worse for his shabby clothes. The error lies in supposing that such distinctions have anything to do with religion, or ought to be recognized in public worship; and still more in supposing that any one, whether rich or poor, may at such a time be treated with contumely.

"Are ye not divided in your own mind, and become judges with evil thoughts?" Here, as in the first verse, there is a doubt whether the sentence is an interrogation or not. In the former case the meaning is the same, whichever way we take it; for a question which implies a negative answer (μή interrogative) is equivalent to a prohibition. In the present case the meaning will be affected if we consider the sentence to be a statement of fact, and the number of translations which have been suggested is very large. In both cases we may safely follow the Vulgate and *all* English versions in making the first verse a prohibition, and the fourth a question. "Are ye not divided in your own mind?" Or more literally, "Did ye not doubt in yourselves?" *i.e.* on the typical occasion mentioned. At the outset St. James says, "Hold not the faith of our Lord Jesus Christ with respect of persons." But the conduct described respecting the treatment of the gold-ringed man and the squalidly clothed man shows that they do have respect of persons in their religion, and that shows that genuine faith in Christ is wanting. Such behaviour proves that they *doubt* in themselves. They are not single-hearted believers in the Lord Jesus, but double-minded doubters (i. 6, 7), trying to make the best of both worlds, and to serve God and Mammon.

The word rendered "doubt" (διακρίνεσθαι) *may* mean "distinguish:" "Do ye not make distinctions among yourselves?" It is so taken by Renan (*L'Antéchrist*, p. 49) and others. This makes sense, but it is rather obvious sense; for of course to give a rich man a good place, and a poor man a bad one, is making distinctions. It seems better to adhere to the meaning which the word certainly has in the preceding chapter (i. 6), as well as elsewhere in the New Testament (Matt. xxi. 21; Mark xi. 23; Acts x. 20; Rom. iv. 20; xiv. 23), and understand it as referring to the want of faith in Christ and in His teaching which was displayed in a worldly preference for the rich over the poor, even in those services in which His words were to be taught and His person adored.

"Judges *with* evil thoughts" is an improvement on the more literal but misleading "judges *of* evil thoughts" (κριταὶ διαλογισμῶν πονηρῶν). The meaning of the genitive case is that the evil thoughts *characterize* the judges, as in such common phrases as "men *of* evil habits," "judges *of* remarkable severity" (see above on "hearers of forgetfulness," p. 108). The word for "thoughts" is one which in itself suggests evil, even without any epithet. It is the word used of the reasonings of the Pharisees, when they taxed our Lord with blasphemy for forgiving sins (Luke v. 22. Comp. xxiv. 38). St. Paul uses it of those who are "vain in their reasonings" (Rom. i. 21; 1 Cor. iii. 20), and couples with it "murmurings" (Phil. ii. 14) as congenial company. Those men who, even while engaged in the public worship of God, set themselves up as judges to honour the rich and condemn the poor, were not holding the faith of Jesus Christ, but were full of evil doubts, questionings, and distrust.

[53] Davidson, *Introduction to the Study of the N.T.* vol. i. pp. 327, 328, 2nd ed. (Longmans, 1882).

[54] There is, however, a good deal to be said for Bengel's suggestion, that τῆς δόξης is in apposition with τοῦ κυρίου ἡμ. Ἰ. Χριστοῦ, *i.e.* "the faith of our Lord Jesus Christ, (who is) the Glory." Comp. Luke ii. 32; Eph. i. 7; 1 Peter iv. 14; 2 Peter i. 17; Col. i. 27; John i. 14. See J. B. Mayor's note in the *Expositor*, Sept., 1889, pp. 225-28.

[55] *Bampton Lectures*, Lect. VI, p. 433 (Rivingtons, 1867).

[56] Among these should be included the phrases which St. James uses to indicate the Gospel revelation: "the Word of truth" (i. 18); "the implanted Word" (i. 21); "the perfect law, the law of liberty" (i. 25); "the royal law" (ii. 8).

[57] From the *Exact Reprint Page for Page of the A.V. published in the Year MDCXI.* (Oxford, 1833). See also Trench *On the A.V. of the N.T.*, pp. 83-101, and Lightfoot *On a Fresh Revision of the N.T.*, pp. 33-59, for some excellent remarks on the harm done by making differences in the English where there is no difference in the Greek. In the present passage, besides the threefold translation of ἐσθής, there is a double translation of λαμπρός ("*goodly* apparel" and "gay clothing"), and also of εἰσέλθῃ ("come" and "come in"). In 1 John ii. 24 we have the same word (μένειν) translated in three different ways ("abide," "remain," "continue") in the same verse, entirely destroying the effect of St. John's impressive repetition.

CHAPTER XI
THE INIQUITY OF RESPECTING THE RICH AND DESPISING THE POOR. THE SOLIDARITY OF THE DIVINE LAW

"Hearken, my beloved brethren; did not God choose them that are poor as to the world to be rich in faith, and heirs of the kingdom which He promised to them that love Him? But ye have dishonoured the poor man. Do not the rich oppress you, and themselves drag you before the judgment-seats? Do not they blaspheme the honourable Name by the which ye are called? Howbeit if ye fulfil the royal law, according to the Scripture, Thou shalt love thy neighbour as thyself, ye do well: but if ye have respect of persons, ye commit sin, being convicted by the law as transgressors. For whosoever shall keep the whole law, and yet stumble in one point, he is become guilty of all." —St. James ii. 5-10.

ST. JAMES is varied in his style. Sometimes he writes short, maxim-like sentences, which remind us of the Book of Proverbs; sometimes, as in the passage before us, he is as argumentative as St. Paul. Having condemned worldly respect of persons as practical infidelity, he proceeds to prove the justice of this estimate; and he does so with regard to both items of the account: these respecters of persons are utterly wrong, both in their treatment of the poor and in their treatment of the rich. The former is the worse of the two; for it is in flat contradiction of the Divine decree, and is an attempt to reverse it. God has said one thing about the poor man's estate, and these time-servers, publicly in the house of God, say another.

"Hearken, my beloved brethren." He invites their attention to an affectionate and conclusive statement of the case. "Did not God choose them that are poor as to the world to be rich in faith, and heirs of the kingdom? But *ye* have dishonoured the poor man." By the humble life which, by Divine decree, God's Son led upon the earth, by the social position of the men whom He chose as His Apostles and first disciples, by blessings promised to the poor and to the friends of the poor, both under the Law and under the Gospel, God has declared His special approbation of the poor man's estate. "But *ye*" (ὑμεῖς δέ, with great emphasis on the pronoun) "have dishonoured the poor man." With Haman-like impiety ye would disgrace "the man whom the King delights to honour."

Let us not misunderstand St. James. He does not say or imply that the poor man is promised salvation on account of his poverty, or that his poverty is in any way meritorious. That is not the case, any more than that the wealth of the rich is a sin. But so far as God has declared any preference, it is for the poor, rather than for the rich. The poor man has fewer temptations, and he is more likely to live according to God's will, and to win the blessings that are in store for those who love Him. His dependence upon God for the means of life is perpetually brought home to him, and he is spared the peril of trusting in riches, which is so terrible a snare to the wealthy. He has greater opportunities of the virtues which make man Christlike, and fewer occasions of falling into those sins which separate him most fatally from Christ. But opportunities are not virtues, and poverty is not salvation. Nevertheless, to a Christian a poor man is an object of reverence, rather than of contempt.

But the error of the worldly Christians whom St. James is here rebuking does not end with dishonouring the poor whom God has honoured; they also pay special respect to the rich. Have the rich, as a class, shown that they deserve anything of the kind? Very much the reverse, as experience is constantly proving. "Do not the rich oppress you, and themselves drag you before the judgment-seats? Do not they blaspheme the honourable Name by the which ye are called?" Unless we consider the "synagogue" mentioned above to be a Jewish one, in which Christians still worship, as in the Temple at Jerusalem, the gold-ringed worshipper is to be understood as a Christian; and reasons have been given above for believing that the "synagogue" is a Christian place of worship. But in any case the rich oppressors here spoken of are not to be thought of as exclusively or principally Christian. They are the wealthy as a class, whether converts to Christianity or not; and apparently, as in chap. v. 1-6, it is the wealthy unbelieving Jews who are principally in the writer's mind. St. James is thinking of the rich Sadducees, who at this period (A.D. 35-65) were among the worst oppressors of the poorer Jews, and of course were specially bitter against those who had become adherents of "the Way," and who seemed to them to be renegades from the faith of their forefathers. It was precisely to this kind of oppression that St. Paul devoted himself with fanatical zeal previous to his conversion (Acts ix. 1, 2; 1 Tim. i. 13; 1 Cor. xv. 9; Phil. iii. 6).

"The judgment-seats" before which these wealthy Jews drag their poorer brethren may be either heathen or Jewish courts (comp. 1 Cor. vi. 2, 4), but are probably the Jewish courts frequently held in the synagogues. The Roman government allowed the Jews very considerable powers of jurisdiction over their own people, not only in purely ecclesiastical matters, but in civil matters as well. The Mosaic Law penetrated into almost all the relations of life, and where it was concerned it was intolerable to a Jew to be tried by heathen law. Consequently the Romans found that their control over the Jews was more secure, and less provocative of rebellion, when the Jews were permitted to retain a large measure of self-government. This applied not only to Palestine, but to all places in which there were large settlements of Jews. Even in the New Testament we find ample evidence of this. The high priest grants Saul "letters to *Damascus*, unto the synagogues," to arrest all who had become converts to "the Way" (Acts ix. 2). And St. Paul before Herod Agrippa II. declares that, in his fury against converts to Christianity, he "persecuted them even unto *foreign* cities" (Acts xxvi. 11). Most, if not all, of the five occasions on which he himself "received of the Jews forty stripes save one" (2 Cor. xi. 24) must have been during his travels outside Palestine. The proconsul Gallio told the Jews of Corinth, not only that they might, but that they must, take their charges against Paul, for breaking Jewish law, to a Jewish tribunal; and when they ostentatiously beat Sosthenes before his own tribunal, for some Jewish offence, he abstained from interfering. It is likely enough that provincial governors, partly from policy, partly from indifference, allowed Jewish officials to exercise more power than they legally possessed; but they possessed quite enough to enable them to handle severely those who contravened the letter or the traditional interpretation of the Mosaic Law. That the dragging before the judgment-seats refers to bringing Christians before Roman magistrates, in a time of persecution, is a gratuitous hypothesis which does not fit the context. It was the mob, rather than the rich, that in the earlier persecutions acted in this way. The rich were contemptuously indifferent. There is, therefore, no evidence here that the letter was written during the persecution under Domitian or under Trajan. Nevertheless, their Christianity, rather than their debt, was probably the reason why these poor Jewish Christians were prosecuted in the synagogue courts by the wealthy Jews.

So far from this passage being evidence that the Epistle was written at a time long after the death of St. James, it is, as Renan has carefully shown, almost a proof that it was written during his lifetime. As regards the relations between rich and poor, "the Epistle of James is a perfect picture of the Ebionim at Jerusalem in the years which preceded the revolt." The destruction of Jerusalem "introduced so complete a change into the situation of Judaism and of Christianity, that it is easy to distinguish a writing subsequent to the catastrophe of the year 70 from a writing contemporary with the third Temple. Pictures evidently referring to the internal contests between the different classes in Jerusalem society, such as that which is presented to us in the Epistle of James, are inconceivable after the revolt of the year 66, which put an end to the reign of the Sadducees."[58] These were the times when women bought the priesthood for their husbands from Herod Agrippa II., and went to see them officiate, over carpets spread from their own door to the Temple; when wealthy priests were too fastidious to kill the victims for sacrifice without first putting on silk gloves; when their kitchens were furnished with every appliance for luxurious living, and their tables with every delicacy; and when, supported by the Romans, to whom they truckled, they made war upon the poor priests, who were supported by the people. Like Hophni and Phinehas, they sent out their servants to collect what they claimed as offerings, and if payment was refused the servants took what they claimed by force. Facts like these help us to understand the strong language used here by St. James, and the still sterner words at the beginning of the fifth chapter. In such a state of society the mere possession of wealth certainly established no claims upon the reverence of a Christian congregation; and the fawning upon rich people, degrading and unchristian at all times, would seem to St. James to be specially perilous and distressing then.

"Do not they blaspheme the honourable Name by which ye are called?" The last clause literally means "which was called upon you" (τὸ ἐπικληθὲν ἐφ' ὑμᾶς); and we need not doubt that the reference is to the Name of Christ which was invoked upon them at their baptism; *quod invocatum est super vos*, as the Vulgate has it. The same expression is found in the Septuagint of those who are called by God's Name (2 Chron. vii. 14; Jer. xiv. 9; xv. 16; Amos ix. 12). Some have suggested that the name here indicated is that of "poor," or of "brethren," or of "Christian;" but none of these is at all probable. It may be doubted whether the last was already in common use; and "blaspheme" would be a very strong expression to use of any of them; whereas both it and "honourable" are quite in keeping if the name be that of Christ. The word rendered "honourable" (καλόν) cannot be adequately translated. It is the same as that which is rendered "good" when we read of "the *Good* Shepherd" (John x. 11). It suggests what is beautiful, noble, and good, as opposed to what is foul, mean, and wicked; and such is the Name of Christ, which is called in a special sense "*the* Name" (Acts v. 41; 3 John 7. Comp. Ignatius, *Eph.* iii., vii.; *Philad.* x.; Clem. Rom. ii., xiii.). That the blasphemers are not Christians is shown by the clause "which was called upon *you.*" Had Christians been intended, St. James would have written "Do not they blaspheme the honourable Name which was called upon *them?*" That they blasphemed the Name in which they were baptized would have been such an aggravation of their offence that he would not have failed to indicate it. These blasphemers were no doubt Jews; and St. James has in his mind the anathemas against Jesus Christ which were frequent utterances among the Jews, both in the synagogues and in conversation. St. Paul alludes to these when he says, "No man speaking in the Spirit of God saith, Jesus is anathema;" and Justin Martyr writes, "That which is said in the Law, Cursed is every one that hangeth on a tree, confirms our hope which is hung upon the crucified Christ, not as if God were cursing that crucified One, but because God foretold that which would be done by all of you (Jews) and those like you.... And you may see with your eyes this very thing coming to pass; for in your synagogues you curse all those who from Him have become Christians" (*Trypho*, xcvi.). The text, "Cursed is every one that hangeth on a tree," was a favourite one with the Jews in their controversies with Christians, as St. James would know well (see Gal. iii. 13); and all this tends to show that he refers to literal blasphemy by word of mouth, and not to the virtual blasphemy which is involved in conduct that dishonours Christ.

His argument, therefore, amounts to this, that the practice of honouring the rich for their riches is (quite independently of any dishonour done to the poor) doubly reprehensible. It involves the meanness of flattering their own oppressors, and the wickedness of reverencing those who blaspheme Christ. It is a servile surrender of their own rights, and base disloyalty to their Lord.

But perhaps (the argument continues) some will defend this respect paid to the rich as being no disloyalty to Christ, but, on the contrary, simple fulfilment of the royal law, "Thou shalt love thy neighbour as thyself." Be it so, that the rich as a class are unworthy of respect and honour, yet nevertheless they are our neighbours, and no misconduct on their side can cancel the obligation on our side to treat them as we should wish to be treated ourselves. We ourselves like to be respected and honoured, and therefore we pay respect and honour to them. To those who argue thus the reply is easy. Certainly, if that is your motive, ye do well. But why do you love your neighbour as yourselves if he chances to be rich, and treat him like a dog if he chances to be poor? However excellent your reasons for honouring the wealthy may be, you still do not free yourselves from the blame of showing an unchristian respect of persons, and therefore of committing sin, "being convicted by the law as transgressors."

The law of loving one's neighbour as oneself is a "royal law," not as having emanated from God or from Christ as King, still less as being a law which binds even kings, or which makes kings of those who observe it. It is a royal law, as being sovereign over other laws, inasmuch as it is one of those two on which "hang all the Law and the Prophets" (Matt. xxii. 40). Indeed, either of the two may be interpreted so as to cover the whole duty of man. Thus St. Paul says of this royal law, "The whole law is fulfilled in one word, even in this, Thou shalt love thy neighbour as thyself" (Gal. v. 14). And St. John teaches the same truth in a different way, when he declares that "he that loveth not his brother whom he hath seen cannot love God whom he hath not seen" (1 John iv. 20). The expression "royal law" occurs nowhere else, either in the New Testament or in the Septuagint, but it is found in a dialogue entitled Minos, which is sometimes wrongly attributed to Plato. It is one which might readily occur to any one as a name for a supreme moral principle.

"Whosoever shall keep the whole law, and yet stumble in one point, he is become guilty of all."[59] The law is the expression of one and the same principle—love; and of one and the same will—the will of God. Therefore he who deliberately offends against any one of its enactments, however diligently he may keep all the rest, is guilty of offending against the whole. His guiding principle is not love, but selfishness—not God's will, but his own. He keeps nine tenths of the law because he likes to do so, and he breaks one tenth because he likes to do so. The fact of his wilful disobedience proves that his obedience is not the fruit of love or loyalty, but of self-seeking. If we ask what his character is, the answer must be, "He is a lawbreaker." These respecters of persons claimed to be observers of the law, because they treated their rich neighbours as they would have liked to be treated themselves. St. James shows them that, on the contrary, they are transgressors of the law, because they pick and choose as to what neighbours shall be treated thus kindly. They keep the law when it is convenient to keep it, and break it when it is inconvenient to keep it. Such keeping of the law is in its essence, not obedience, but disobedience. He who follows honesty only because honesty is the best policy is not an honest man, and he who obeys the law only because obedience suits him is not an obedient man. There is no serving God with reservations. However small the reservation may be, it vitiates all the rest. In order to *"fulfil* the law" (a rare expression, found only here and in Rom. ii. 27), we must keep it all round, independently of our own likes and dislikes.

St. James is not here countenancing the severity of Draco, that small crimes deserve death, and that there is no worse punishment for great crimes; nor yet the paradox of the Stoics, that the theft of a penny is as bad as parricide, because in either case the path of virtue is left, and one is drowned as surely in seven feet of water as in seventy fathoms. He is not contending that all sins are equal, and that to break one of God's commands is as bad as to break them all. What he maintains is that no one can claim to be a fulfiller of the law in virtue of his extensive obedience so long as there is any portion of the law which he wilfully disobeys. Why does he disobey in this? Because it pleases him to do so. Then he would disobey in the rest if it pleased him to do so. The motive of his conduct is not submission, but self-will. He is in character "a transgressor of the law."

Both defects are common enough still, and are likely to remain so. Paying respect to *persons, dignities,* and *positions* is a frequent form of meanness, especially in the manner here condemned, of courting the rich and slighting the poor. It is a Christian duty to respect the rank or the office of those whom God has placed in a position superior to ourselves, and it is also a Christian duty to reverence those who by God's grace are leading lives of virtue and holiness; but it is unchristian partiality to honour a man merely for his wealth, or to dishonour him merely for his poverty. And secondly, we are all of us prone to plead, both before the world and our own consciences, the particulars in which we do *not* offend as a set-off against those in which we *do.* To detect ourselves thus balancing a transgression here, against many observances there, ought at once to startle us into the conviction that the whole principle of our lives must be faulty. Our aim is, not to love God, or to obey Him, but to get to heaven, or at least to escape hell, *on the cheapest terms.*

[58] *L'Antechrist,* pp. xi.-xiii., 49-54.

[59] This text caused St. Augustine much perplexity. He sent a long discussion of it to Jerome, asking for his opinion. Augustine's solution is that the whole law hangs on the love of God, and that every transgression is a breach of love (*Ep.* CLXVII. iv. 16).

CHAPTER XII
FAITH AND WORKS: THREE VIEWS OF THE RELATION OF THE TEACHING OF ST. JAMES TO THE TEACHING OF ST. PAUL. THE RELATION OF LUTHER TO BOTH

"What doth it profit, my brethren, if a man say he hath faith, but have not works? can that faith save him? If a brother or sister be naked, and in lack of daily food, and one of you say unto them, Go in peace, be ye warmed and filled; and yet ye give them not the things needful to the body; what doth it profit? Even so faith, if it have not works, is dead in itself. Yea, a man will say, Thou hast faith, and I have works: show me thy faith apart from thy works, and I by my works will show thee my faith. Thou believest that God is One; thou doest well: the devils also believe, and shudder. But wilt thou know, O vain man, that faith apart from works is barren? Was not Abraham our father justified by works, in that he offered up Isaac his son upon the altar? Thou seest that faith wrought with his works, and by works was faith made perfect; and the Scripture was fulfilled which saith, And Abraham believed God, and it was reckoned unto him for righteousness; and he was called the friend of God. Ye see that by works a man is justified, and not only by faith. And in like manner was not also Rahab the harlot justified by works, in that she received the messengers, and sent them out another way? For as the body apart from the spirit is dead, even so faith apart from works is dead."—St. James ii. 14-26.

THIS famous passage has been quoted in full, because one needs to have the whole of it before one in order to appreciate the value of the arguments used on this side and on that as to its relation to the teaching of St. Paul on the connexion between faith and works; for which purpose mere extracts will not do; and also because considerable changes, some of them important, have been made throughout the passage by the Revisers, and these will influence the impression derived from reading the passage as a whole.

It might be thought that here, at any rate, we have got, in this singularly practical and undogmatic Epistle, a paragraph which is, both in intention and in effect, distinctly doctrinal. It seems at first sight to be a careful exposition of St. James's views as to the nature and value of faith and its relation to conduct. But a little attention will prove to us that throughout the passage St. James is as practical in his aim as in any part of the letter, and that whatever doctrinal teaching there may be in the passage is there because the practical purpose of the writer could not be fulfilled without involving doctrine, and not at all because the writer's object is to expound or defend an article of the Christian faith. He has *agenda* rather than *credenda* in his mind. An orthodox creed is assumed throughout. What needs to be produced is not right belief, but right action.

In this affectionate pastoral St. James passes in review the defects which he knows to exist in his readers. They have their good points, but these are sadly marred by corresponding deficiencies. They are swift to hear, but also swift to speak and slow to act. They believe in Jesus Christ; but they dishonour Him by dishonouring His poor, while they profess to keep the law of charity by honouring the rich. They are orthodox in a Monotheistic creed; but they rest content with that, and their orthodoxy is as barren as a dead tree. It is with this last defect that St. James is dealing in the passage before us. And as so often (i. 12, 19; ii. 1; iii. 1, 13; iv. 1, 13; v. 1, 7, 13), he clearly states his main point first, and then proceeds to enforce and elucidate it.

"What doth it profit, my brethren, if a man say he hath faith, but have not works? Can that faith save him?" "*That* faith" is literally "*the* faith," or "*his* faith;" viz. such faith as he professes, a faith that produces nothing. There is no emphasis on "say." St. James is not insinuating that the man says he has faith, when he really has none. If that were the case, it would be needless to ask, "Can his faith save him?" The question then would be, "Can his *profession* of faith save him?" But St. James nowhere throws doubt on the truth of the unprofitable believer's professions, or on the possibility of believing much and doing nothing. Why, then, does he put in the "say"? Why not write, "If a man have faith"? Perhaps in order to indicate that in such cases the man's own statement is all the evidence there is that he has faith. In the case of other Christians their works prove them to be believers; but where there are no works you can only have the man's word for it that he believes. The case is parallel to that sketched by our blessed Lord, which St. James may have in his mind. "Not every one that saith unto Me, Lord, Lord, shall enter into the kingdom of heaven; but he that *doeth* the will of My Father which is in heaven. Many will say to Me in that day, Lord, Lord, did we not prophesy by Thy Name, and by Thy Name cast out devils, and by Thy Name do many mighty works? And then will I profess unto them, I never knew you; depart from Me, ye that work iniquity" (Matt. vii. 21-

23). In this case it is manifest that the profession of faith is not mere empty hypocrisy; it is not a saying of "Lord, Lord," to one who is not believed to be the Lord. It is a faith that can remove mountains, but divorced from the love which makes it acceptable. The two, which God hath joined together, have by man's self-will been put asunder.

The relation, therefore, of the teaching of St. James to that of His Divine Brother is clear: the two are in perfect harmony. What is its relation to the teaching of St. Paul? Omitting minor differences, there are in the main three answers to this question: (1) The writer of this Epistle is deliberately contradicting and correcting the teaching of St. Paul. (2) St. James is correcting prevalent misunderstandings, or is anticipating probable misunderstandings, of the teaching of St. Paul. (3) St. James writes without reference to, and possibly without knowledge of, the precise teaching of the Apostle of the Gentiles respecting the relation between faith and works.

(1) Those who hold the first of these three views naturally maintain that the Epistle is not genuine, but the production of some one of a later age than St. James, who wished to have the great authority of his name to cover an attack upon the teaching of St. Paul. Thus F. C. Baur maintains that "the doctrine of this Epistle must be considered as intended to correct that of Paul." This, which is taken from the second edition of his work on the *Life and Work of St. Paul*, published after his death in 1860, by his pupil Zeller, may be taken as his matured opinion. In his history of the *Christian Church of the First Three Centuries*, published in 1853, he expresses himself a little less positively: "It is impossible to deny that the Epistle of James presupposes the Pauline doctrine of justification. And if this be so, its tendency is distinctly anti-Pauline, though it may not be aimed directly against the Apostle himself. The Epistle contends against a one-sided conception of the Pauline doctrine, which was dangerous to practical Christianity." In both works alike Baur contends that the Epistle of James cannot be genuine, but is the product of some unknown writer in the second century. The opinions that our Epistle is directed against the teaching of St. Paul, and that it is not genuine, naturally go together. It is against all probability that St. James, who had supported St. Paul in the crisis at Jerusalem in A.D. 50 (Acts xv.), and who had given to him and Barnabas the right hand of fellowship (Gal. ii. 9), should attack St. Paul's own teaching. But to deny the authenticity of the Epistle, and place it in a later age, does not really avoid the difficulty of the supposed attack on St. Paul, and it brings with it other difficulties of a no less serious character. In any case the letter is addressed to *Jewish* Christians (i. 1); and what need was there to put *them* on their guard against the teaching of a man whom they regarded with profound distrust, and whose claim to be an Apostle they denied? It would be as reasonable to

warn Presbyterians against the doctrine of the Infallibility of the Pope. Besides all which, as Renan has shown, the letter sketches a state of things which would be inconceivable after the outbreak of the war which ended in the destruction of Jerusalem; *i.e.* it cannot be placed later than A.D. 66.

Dr. Salmon justly observes, "To a disciple of Baur there is no more disappointing document than this Epistle of James. Here, if anywhere in the New Testament, he might expect to find evidence of anti-Pauline rancour. There is what looks like flat contradiction between this Epistle and the teaching of St. Paul.... But that opposition to Paul which, on a superficial glance, we are disposed to ascribe to the Epistle of James, disappears on a closer examination. I postpone for the moment the question whether we can suppose that James intended to contradict Paul; but whether he intended it or not, he has not really done so; he has denied nothing that Paul has asserted, and asserted nothing that a disciple of Paul would care to deny. On comparing the language of James with that of Paul, all the distinctive expressions of the latter are found to be absent from the former. St. Paul's thesis is that a man is justified not by works of the law, but by the faith of Jesus Christ. James speaks only of works without any mention of the law, and of faith without any mention of Jesus Christ, the example of faith which he considers being merely the belief that there is one God. In other words, James is writing not in the interests of Judaism, but of morality. Paul taught that faith in Jesus Christ was able to justify a man uncircumcised and unobservant of the Mosaic ordinances.... For this Pauline teaching James not only has no word of contradiction, but he gives no sign of ever having heard of the controversy which, according to Baur, formed the most striking feature in the early history of the Church.... Whatever embarrassment the apparent disagreement between the Apostles has caused to orthodox theologians is as nothing in comparison with the embarrassment caused to a disciple of Baur by their fundamental agreement."[60]

We may, therefore, safely abandon a theory which involves three such difficulties. It assigns a date to the Epistle utterly incompatible with its contents. It makes the writer warn Jewish Christians against teaching which they, of all Christians, were least likely to find attractive. And after all, the warning is futile; for the writer's own teaching is fundamentally the same as that which it is supposed to oppose and correct. Besides all which, we may say with Reuss that this Tübingen criticism is mere baseless ingenuity. It "overlooks the unique originality of the Epistle;" and to ascribe to the writer of it "any ulterior motives at all is simply a useless display of acuteness."[61]

(2) This last remark will not predispose us to regard with favour the second hypothesis mentioned above—that in this passage St. James is correcting prevalent misunderstandings, or is anticipating probable

misunderstandings, of the teaching of St. Paul. There is no trace of any such intention, or of any anxiety on the subject. The purpose of the passage is not doctrinal at all, but, like the rest of the Epistle, eminently practical. The writer's object throughout is to inculcate the necessity of right conduct. Readiness in hearing the Word of God is all very well, and correctness of belief in God is all very well; but without readiness to do what pleases Him it is as useless as a dead vine. Whether St. James remembered the words, "We reckon that a man is justified by faith apart from the works of the law" (Rom. iii. 28), must remain doubtful; for, as has been pointed out in a previous exposition (p. 57), there is some reason for believing that he had seen the Epistle to the Romans. But there is no reason for believing that he was acquainted with the parallel statement in the Epistle to the Galatians, "We being Jews by nature, and not sinners of the Gentiles, yet knowing that a man is not justified by the works of the law, save through faith in Jesus Christ, even we believe on Jesus Christ, that we might be justified by faith in Christ, and not by the works of the law; because by the works of the law shall no flesh be justified" (ii. 15, 16). Of one thing, however, we may feel confident, that, had St. James been intending to give the true meaning of either or both of these statements by St. Paul, in order to correct or obviate misunderstanding, he would not have worded his exposition in such a way that it would be possible for a hasty reader to suppose that he was contradicting the Apostle of the Gentiles instead of merely explaining him. He takes no pains to show that while St. Paul speaks of works *of the law, i.e.* ceremonial observances, he himself is speaking of good works generally, which St. Paul no less than himself regarded as a necessary accompaniment and outcome of living faith.

Moreover, was there any likelihood that the Jewish Christians would thus misinterpret St. Paul? Among Gentile Christians there was danger of this, because they misunderstood the meaning of the Christian liberty which he so enthusiastically preached. But with Jewish converts the danger was that they would refuse to listen to St. Paul in anything, not that they would be in such a hurry to accept his teaching that they would go away with a wrong impression as to what he really meant. And precisely that doctrine of St. Paul which was so liable to be misunderstood St. James proclaims as clearly as St. Paul does in this very Epistle. He also declares, more than once, that the Gospel is the "law of *liberty*" (i. 25; ii. 12). Had St. James been writing to Gentiles, there might have been some reason for his putting his readers on their guard against misinterpreting St. Paul's manner of preaching the Gospel: in writing "to the twelve tribes which are of the Dispersion" there was little or no reason for so doing.

(3) We fall back, therefore, upon the far more probable view that in this passage St. James is merely following the course of his own argument, without thinking of St. Paul's teaching respecting the relation between faith and works. How much of St. Paul's teaching he knew depends upon the date assigned to this Epistle, whether before A.D. 50 or after A.D. 60. At the later date St. James must have known a good deal, both from St. Paul himself, and also from the many Jews of the Dispersion, who had heard the preaching of the Apostle in his missionary journeys, had seen some of his letters, and brought both good and evil reports of his work to the Church at Jerusalem. Each year, at the Passover and other festivals, James would receive multitudes of such visitors. But it does not follow that because he knew a good deal about St. Paul's favourite topics, and his manner of presenting the faith to his hearers, therefore he has his teaching in his mind in writing to Jewish converts. The passage before us is thoroughly intelligible, if it is treated on its own merits without any reference to Pauline doctrine; and not only so, but we may say that it becomes more intelligible when so treated.

At the opening of the Epistle St. James insists on the necessity of *faith*: "knowing that the proof of your faith worketh patience" (ver. 3); and "Let him ask in faith, nothing doubting" (ver. 6). Then he passes on to insist upon the necessity of *practice*: "Be ye doers of the Word, and not hearers only, deluding your own selves" (ver. 22); and "Being not a hearer that forgetteth, but a doer that worketh" (ver. 25). At the beginning of the second chapter he does exactly the same. He first assumes that as a matter of course his hearers have *faith* (ver. 1), and then goes on to show how this must be accompanied by the *practice* of charity and mercy towards all, and especially towards the poor (vv. 2-13). The passage before us is precisely on the same lines.

It is assumed that his readers profess to have *faith* (vv. 14, 19); and St. James does not dispute the truth of this profession. But he maintains that unless this faith is productive of a corresponding *practice*, its existence is not proved, and its utility is disproved. It is as barren as a withered tree, and as lifeless as a corpse. Three times over he asserts, with simple emphasis, that faith apart from practice is dead (vv. 17, 20, 26). All which tends to show that the present paragraph comes quite naturally in the course of the exhortation, without any ulterior motive being assumed to explain it. It is in close harmony with what precedes, and thoroughly in keeping with the practical aim of the whole letter. We see how easily it might have been written by any one who was in earnest about religion and morality, without having heard a word about St. Paul's teaching respecting faith in Christ and works of the law.

It has been already pointed out that a letter addressed by a Jewish Christian to Jewish Christians would not be very likely to take account of St. Paul's doctrine, whether rightly or wrongly understood. It has also been shown that St. James, as is natural in such a letter, makes frequent appeals to the Old Testament, and also has numerous coincidences with portions of that now much-neglected Jewish literature which forms a connecting-link between the Old and the New, especially with the Books of Wisdom and Ecclesiasticus. It was in the period in which that literature was produced that discussions as to the value of faith in God, as distinct from the fear of God, and in particular as to the faith of Abraham, the friend of God, began to be common among the Jews, especially in the Rabbinical schools. We find evidence of this in the Apocrypha itself. "Abraham was a great father of many people, ... and when he was proved he was found faithful" (Ecclus. xliv. 19, 20). "Was not Abraham found faithful in temptation, and it was imputed unto him for righteousness?" (1 Macc. ii. 52), where the interrogative form of sentence may have suggested the interrogation of St. James. It will be observed that in these passages we have the adjective "faithful" (πιστός); not yet the substantive "faith" (πίστις). But in the composite and later work which in our Bibles bears the name of the Second Book of Esdras we have faith frequently spoken of. "The way of truth shall be hidden, and the land shall be barren of faith" (v. 1). "As for faith, it shall flourish, corruption shall be overcome, and the truth, which hath been so long without fruit, shall be declared" (vi. 28). "Truth shall stand, and faith shall wax strong" (vii. 34). And in two remarkable passages faith is spoken of in connexion with works. "And every one that shall be saved, and shall be able to escape by his works, and by faith, whereby ye have believed, shall be preserved from the said perils, and shall see My salvation" (ix. 7, 8). "These are they that have works and faith towards the Most Mighty" (xiii. 23). With Philo faith and the faith of Abraham are common topics. He calls it "the queen of the virtues," and the possessor of it "will bring a faultless and most fair sacrifice to God." Abraham's faith is not easy to imitate, so hard is it to trust in the unseen God rather than in the visible creation; whereas he without wavering believed that the things which were not present were already present, because of His most sure faith in Him who promised.[62]

Other instances might be quoted from Jewish literature; but these suffice to show that the nature of faith, and the special merit of Abraham's faith, were subjects often discussed among Jews, and were likely to be familiar to those whom St. James addresses. This being so, it becomes probable that what he has in his mind is not Pauline doctrine, or any perversion of it, but some Pharisaic tenet respecting these things. The view that faith is formal orthodoxy—the belief in one God—and that correctness of belief suffices for the salvation of a son of Abraham, seems to be the kind of error against which St. James is contending. About faith in Christ or in His Resurrection there is not a word. It is the cold Monotheism which the self-satisfied Pharisee has brought with him into the Christian Church, and which he supposes will render charity and good works superfluous, that St. James is condemning. [63] So far from this being a contradiction to St. Paul, it is the very doctrine which he taught, and almost in the same form of words. "*What doth it profit* (τί ὄφελος), my brethren," asks St. James, "if a man say he hath faith, but have not works?" "If I have all faith, so as to remove mountains, but have not love, I am nothing," says St. Paul. "And if I bestow all my goods to feed the poor, and if I give my body to be burned, but have not love, *it profiteth me nothing*" (οὐδὲω ὠφελοῦμαι).

St. Paul and St. James are thus found to be agreed. It remains to be shown that in spite of his own statements to the contrary, Luther was as fully agreed with the latter as with the former. When he writes about St. James, Luther's prejudices lead him to disparage a form of teaching which he has not been at the pains to comprehend. But when he expounds St. Paul he does so in words which would serve excellently as an exposition of the teaching of St. James. In his preface to the Epistle to the Romans he writes thus: "But faith is a Divine work in us, that changes us and begets us anew of God (John i. 13); and kills the old man, makes of us quite other men in heart, courage, mind, and strength, and brings the Holy Spirit with it. Oh, it is a living, active, energetic, mighty thing, this faith, *so that it is impossible that it should not work what is good without intermission. It does not even ask whether good works are to be done, but before one asks it has done them, and is ever doing.* But he who does not do such works is a man without faith, is fumbling and looking about him for faith and good works, and knows neither the one nor the other, yet chatters and babbles many words about both.

"Faith is a living, deliberate confidence in the grace of God, so sure that it would die a thousand times for its trust. And such confidence and experience of Divine grace make a man merry, bold, and joyful towards God and all creatures; all which the Holy Spirit does in faith. Hence the man without compulsion becomes willing and joyful to do good to every one, to serve every one, to endure everything, for the love and praise of God, who has shown him such grace. Therefore *it is impossible to sever works from faith; yea, as impossible as to sever burning and shining from fire.*"[64]

[60] *Introduction to the N.T.*, 4th ed. (Murray, 1889), pp. 504, 506, a work which may be most heartily commended to every student of the New Testament.

[61] *History of the Sacred Scriptures of the N.T.*, translated by E. L. Houghton (Edinburgh: T. and T. Clark, 1884), p. 143.

[62] See the passages quoted by Hatch, *Essays in Biblical Greek*, pp. 85-87 (Oxford, 1889).

[63] This kind of error is alluded to by Justin Martyr, in his *Dialogue with the Jew Trypho*: "Blessed is the man to whom the Lord will not impute sin; that is, who receives remission of his sins from God as having repented of his sins; but not as ye deceive yourselves, and some other (Jews) who resemble you in this, who say that even if they are sinners, but attain to a knowledge of God, the Lord will not impute sin to them" (cxli., p. 370, D).

[64] *Werke*, ed. Gustav Pfizer, Frankfurt am Main, 1840, p. 1415.

CHAPTER XIII
THE FAITH OF THE DEMONS; THE FAITH OF ABRAHAM; AND THE FAITH OF RAHAB THE HARLOT

"Thou believest that God is One; thou doest well: the devils also believe, and shudder."

"Was not Abraham our father justified by works, in that he offered up Isaac his son upon the altar?"

"And in like manner was not also Rahab the harlot justified by works, in that she received the messengers, and sent them out another way?" —St. James ii. 19, 21, 25.

In the preceding chapter several points of great interest were passed over, in order not to obscure the main issue as to the relation of this passage to the teaching of St. Paul. Some of these may now be usefully considered.

Throughout this volume, as in the companion volume on the Pastoral Epistles and other volumes for which the present writer is in no way responsible, the Revised Version has been taken as the basis of the expositions. There may be reasonable difference of opinion as to its superiority to the Authorized Version for public reading in the services of the Church, but few unprejudiced persons would deny its superiority for purposes of private study and both private and public exposition. Its superiority lies not so much in happy treatment of difficult texts, as in the correction of a great many small errors of translation, and above all in the substitution of a great many true or probable readings for others that are false or improbable. And while there are not a few cases in which there is plenty of room for doubt whether the change, even if clearly a gain in accuracy, was worth making, there are also some in which the uninitiated student wonders why no change was made. The passage before us contains a remarkable instance. Why has the word "devils" been retained as the rendering of δαιμόνια, while "demons" is relegated to the margin?

There are two Greek words, very different from one another in origin and history, which are used both in the Septuagint and in the New Testament to express the unseen and spiritual powers of evil. These are διάβολος and δαιμόνιον, or in one place δαίμων (Matt. xlii. 31; *not* Mark v. 12, or Luke vii. 29, or Rev. xvi. 14 and xviii. 2). The Scriptural usage of these two words is quite distinct and very marked. Excepting where it is used as an adjective (John vi. 70; 1 Tim. iii. 11; 2 Tim. iii. 3; Titus ii. 3), διάβολος is one of the names of Satan, the great enemy of God and of men, and the prince of the spirits of evil. It is so used in the Books of Job and of Zechariah, as well as in Wisdom ii. 24, and also throughout the New Testament, viz. in the Gospels and Acts, the Catholic and Pauline Epistles, and the Apocalypse. It is, in fact, a proper name, and is applied to one person only. It commonly, but not invariably (1 Chron. xxi. 1; Ps. cviii. [cix.] 5) has the definite article. The word δαιμόνιον, on the other hand, is used of those evil spirits who are the messengers and ministers of Satan. It is thus used in Isaiah, the Psalms, Tobit, Baruch, and throughout the New Testament. It is used also of the false gods of the heathen, which were believed to be evil spirits, or at least the productions of evil spirits, who are the inspirers of idolatry; whereas Satan is never identified with any heathen divinity. Those who worship false gods are said to worship "demons," but never to worship "the devil." Neither in the Old Testament nor in the New are the two words ever interchanged. Satan is never spoken of as a δαίμων or δαιμόνιον, and his ministers are never called διάβολοι. Is it not a calamity that this very marked distinction should be obliterated in the English Version by translating both Greek words by the word "devil," especially when there is another word which, as the margin admits, might have been used for one of them? The Revisers have done immense service by distinguishing between *Hades*, the abode of departed spirits of men, and *Hell* or *Gehenna*, the place of punishment (iii. 6). Why did they reject a similar opportunity by refusing to distinguish *the devil* from *the demons* over whom he reigns? This is one of the suggestions of the American Committee which might have been followed with great advantage and (so far as one sees) no loss.

St. James has just been pointing out the advantage which the Christian who has works to show has over one who has only faith. The one can prove that he possesses both; the other cannot prove that he possesses either. The works of the one are evidence that the faith is there also, just as leaves and fruit are evidence that a tree is alive. But the other, who possesses only faith, cannot prove that he possesses even that. He says that he believes, and we may believe his statement; but if any one doubts or denies the truth of his profession of faith he is helpless. Just as a leafless and fruitless tree may be alive; but who is to be sure of this? We must note, however, that in this case the statement is *not* doubted. "Thou *hast* faith, and I have works;" the possibility of possessing faith without works is not disputed. And again, "Thou *believest* that God is One;" the orthodox character of the man's creed is not called in question. This shows that there is no emphasis on "say" in the opening verse, "If a man *say* he hath faith, but have not works;" as if such a profession were incredible And this remains equally true if, with some of the best editors, we turn the statement of the man's faith into a question, "Dost thou believe that God is One?" For "Thou doest well" shows that the man's orthodoxy is not questioned. The object of St. James is not to prove that the man is a hypocrite, and that his professions are false; but that, *on his own showing*, he is in a miserable condition. He may plume himself upon the correctness of his Theism; but as far as that goes, he is no better than the demons, to whom this article of faith is a source, not of joy and strength, but of horror.

It is most improbable that, if he had been alluding to the teaching of St. Paul, St. James would have selected the Unity of the Godhead as the article of faith held by the barren Christian. He would have taken faith in Christ as his example. But in writing to Jewish Christians, without any such allusion, the selection is very natural. The Monotheism of his creed, in contrast with the foolish "gods many, and lords many," of the heathen, was to the Jew a matter of religious and national pride. He gloried in his intellectual and spiritual superiority to those who could believe in a plurality of deities. And there was nothing in Christianity to make him think less highly of this supreme article of faith. Hence, when St. James desires to give an example of the faith on which a Jewish Christian, who had sunk into a dead formalism, would be most likely to rely, he selects this article, common to both the Jewish and the Christian creed, "I believe that God is One." "Thou doest well" is the calm reply; and then follows the sarcastic addition, "The demons also believe—and shudder."

Is St. James here alluding to the belief mentioned above, that the gods of the heathen are demons? They, of all evil spirits, might be supposed to know most about the Unity of God, and to have most to fear in reference to it. "They sacrificed unto demons, which were no God," we read in Deuteronomy (xxxii. 17). And again, in the Psalms, "They sacrificed their sons and their daughters unto demons" (cvi. 37. Comp. xcvi. 5). In these passages the Greek word δαιμόνια represents the Elilim or Shedim, the nonenities who were allowed to usurp the place of Jehovah.[65] And St. Paul affirms, "That the things which the Gentiles sacrifice, they sacrifice to demons, and not to God" (1 Cor. x. 20). It is quite possible, therefore, that St. James is thinking of demons as objects of idolatrous worship, or at any rate as seducing people into such worship, when he speaks of the demons' belief in the Unity of God.

But a suggestion which Bede makes, and which several modern commentators have followed, is well worth considering. St. James may be thinking of the demons which possessed human beings, rather than those which received or promoted idolatrous worship. Bede reminds us of the many demons who went out at Christ's command, crying out that He was the Son of God, and especially of the man with the legion among the Gadarenes, who expressed not only belief, but horror: "What have I to do with Thee, Jesus, Son of the most high God? I adjure Thee by God, that Thou torment me not." Without falling into the error of supposing that demons can mean demoniacs, we may imagine how readily one who had witnessed such scenes as those recorded in the Gospels might attribute to the demons the expressions of horror which he had heard in the words and seen on the faces of those whom demons possessed. Such expressions were the usual effect of being confronted by the Divine presence and power of Christ, and were evidence both of a belief in God and of a dread of Him. St. James, who was then living with the Mother of the Lord, and sometimes followed His Divine Brother in His wanderings, would be almost certain to have been a witness of some of these healings of demoniacs. And it is worth noting that the word which in the Authorized Version is rendered "tremble," and in the Revised "shudder" (φρίσσειν), expresses *physical horror*, especially as it affects the hair; and in itself it implies a body, and would be an inappropriate word to use of the fear felt by a purely spiritual being. It occurs nowhere else in the New Testament; but in the Septuagint we find it used in the Book of Job: "Then a spirit passed before my face; the hair of my flesh stood up" (iv. 15). It is a stronger word than either "fear" or "tremble," and strictly speaking can be used only of men and other animals.

This horror, then, expressed by the demons through the bodies of those whom they possess, is evidence enough of faith. Can faith such as that save any one? Is it not obvious that a faith which produces, not works of love, but the strongest expressions of fear, is not a faith on which any one can rely for his salvation? And yet the faith of those who refuse to do good works, because they hold that their faith is sufficient to save them, is no better than the faith of the demons. Indeed, in some respects it is worse. For the sincerity of the demons' faith cannot be doubted; their terror is proof of it: whereas the formal Christian has nothing but cold professions to offer. Moreover, the demons are under no self-delusion; they know their own terrible condition. For the formalist who accepts Christian truth and neglects Christian practice there is a dreadful awakening in store. There will come a time when "believe and shudder" will be true also of him. "But, before it is too late, willest thou to get to know, O vain man, that faith apart from works is barren?"

"Wilt thou know" does not do justice to the full meaning of the Greek (θέλεισ γνῶναι). The meaning is not, "I would have you know," but, "Do you wish to have acquired the knowledge?" You profess to know God and to believe in Him; do you desire to know what faith in Him really means? "O vain man" is literally, "O empty man," *i.e.* empty-headed, empty-handed, and empty-hearted. Empty-headed, in being so deluded as to suppose that a dead faith can save; empty-handed, in being devoid of true spiritual riches; empty-hearted, in having no real love either for God or man. The epithet seems to be the equivalent of *Raca*, the term of contempt quoted by our Lord as the expression of that angry spirit which is akin to murder (Matt. v. 22). The use of it by St. James may be taken as an indication that the primitive Church saw that the commands in the Sermon on the Mount are not rules to be obeyed literally, but illustrations of principles. The sin lies not so much in the precise term of reproach which is employed as in the spirit and temper which are felt and displayed in the employment of it. The change from "dead" (A.V.) to "barren" (R.V.) is not a change of translation, but of reading (νεκρά to ἀργή), the latter term meaning "*workless*, idle, unproductive" (Matt. xx. 3, 6; 1 Tim. v. 13; Titus i. 12; 2 Peter i. 8). Aristotle (*Nic. Eth.*, I. vii. 11) asks whether it is likely that every member of a man's body should have a function or work (ἔργον) to perform, and that man as a whole should be functionless (ἀργός). Would nature have produced such a vain contradiction? We should reproduce the spirit of St. James's pointed interrogation if we rendered "that faith without fruits is fruitless."

In contrast with this barren faith, which makes a man's spiritual condition no better than that of the demons, St. James places two conspicuous instances of living and fruitful faith—Abraham and Rahab. The case of "Abraham our father" would be the first that would occur to every Jew. As the passages in the Apocrypha (Wisdom x. 5; Ecclus. xliv. 20; 1 Macc. ii. 52) prove, Abraham's faith was a subject of frequent discussion among the Jews, and this fact is quite enough to account for its mention by St. James, St. Paul (Rom. iv. 3; Gal. iii. 6), and the writer of the Epistle to the Hebrews (xi. 17), without supposing that any one of them had seen the writings of the others. Certainly there is no proof that the writer of this Epistle is the borrower, if there is borrowing on either side. It is urged that between the authors of this Epistle and that to the Hebrews there must be dependence on one side or the other, because each selects not only Abraham, but Rahab, as an example of faith; and Rahab is so strange an example that it is unlikely that two writers would have selected it independently. There is force in the argument, but less than at first sight appears. The presence of Rahab's name in the genealogy of the Christ (Matt. i. 5), in which so few women are mentioned, must have given thoughtful persons food for reflexion. Why was such a woman singled out for such distinction? The answer to this question cannot be given with certainty. But whatever caused her to be mentioned in the genealogy may also have caused her to be mentioned by St. James and the writer of Hebrews; or the fact of her being in the genealogy may have suggested her to the authors of these two Epistles. This latter alternative does not necessarily imply that these two writers were acquainted with the written Gospel of St. Matthew, which was perhaps not in existence when they wrote. The genealogy, at any rate, was in existence, for St. Matthew no doubt copied it from official or family registers. Assuming, however, that it is not a mere coincidence that both writers use Abraham and Rahab as examples of fruitful faith, it is altogether arbitrary to decide that the writer of the Epistle to the Hebrews wrote first. The probabilities are the other way. Had St. James known that Epistle, he would have made more use of it.

The two examples are in many respects very different. Their resemblance consists in this, that in both cases faith found expression in action, and this action was the source of the believer's deliverance. The case of Abraham, which St. Paul uses to prove the worthlessness of "works of the law" in comparison with a living faith, is used by St. James to prove the worthlessness of a dead faith in comparison with works of love which are evidence that there is a living faith behind them. But it should be noticed that a different episode in Abraham's life is taken in each Epistle, and this is a further reason for believing that neither writer refers to the other. St. Paul appeals to Abraham's faith in believing that he should have a son when he was a hundred, and Sarah ninety years of age (Rom. iv. 19). St. James appeals to Abraham's faith in offering up Isaac, when there seemed to be no possibility of the Divine promise being fulfilled if Isaac was slain. The latter required more faith than the former, and was much more distinctly an *act* of faith; a work, or series of works, that would never have been accomplished if there had not been a very vigorous faith to inspire and support the doer. The *result* (ἐξ ἔργων) was that Abraham was "justified," *i.e.* he was accounted righteous, and the reward of his faith was with still greater solemnity and fulness than on the first occasion (Gen. xv. 4-6) promised to him: "By Myself have I sworn, saith the Lord, *because thou hast done this thing*, and hast not withheld thy son, thine only son; that in blessing I will bless thee, and in multiplying I will multiply thy seed as the stars of heaven, and as the sand which is upon the sea-shore; and thy seed shall possess the gate of his enemies; and in thy seed shall all the nations of the earth be blessed; *because thou hast obeyed My voice*" (Gen. xxii. 16-18).

With the expression "was justified *as a result of* works" (ἐξ ἔργων ἐδικαιώθη), which is used both of Abraham and of Rahab, should be compared our Lord's saying, "By thy words thou shalt be justified, and by thy words thou shalt be condemned" (Matt. xii. 37), which are of exactly the same form; literally, "*As a result* of thy words thou shalt be accounted righteous, and *as a result* of thy words thou shalt be condemned" (ἐκ τῶν λόγων σου δικαιωθήσῃ, καὶ ἐκ τῶν λόγων σου καταδικασθήσῃ); that is, it is from the consideration of the words in the one case, and of the works in the other, that the sentence of approval proceeds; they are the *source* of the justification. Of course from the point of view taken by St. James words are "works;" good words spoken for the love of God are quite as much fruits of faith and evidence of faith as good deeds. It is not impossible that his phrase is an echo of expressions which he had heard used by Christ.

That the words rendered "offered up Isaac his son upon the altar" really mean this, and not merely "brought Isaac his son as a victim up to the altar," is clear from other passages where the same phrase (ἀναφέρειν ἐπὶ τὸ θυσιαστήριον) occurs. Noah "offering burnt offerings on the altar" (Gen. viii. 20) and Christ "offering our sins on the tree" (1 Pet. ii. 24) might be interpreted either way, although the *bringing up* to the altar and to the tree does not seem so natural as the *offering on them*. But a passage in Leviticus about the offerings of the leper is quite decisive: "Afterward he shall kill the burnt offering: and the priest shall offer the burnt offering and the meal offering upon the altar" (xiv. 19, 20). It would be very unnatural to speak of bringing the victim up to the altar after it had been slain. (Comp. Baruch i. 10; 1 Macc. iv. 53.) The Vulgate, Luther, Beza, and all English versions agreed in this translation; and it is not a matter of small importance, not a mere nicety of rendering. In all completeness, both of will and deed, Abraham had actually surrendered and offered up to God his only son, when he laid him bound upon the altar, and took the knife to slay him—to slay that son of whom God had promised, "In Isaac shall thy seed be called." Then "was the Scripture fulfilled;" *i.e.* what had been spoken and partly fulfilled before (Gen. xv. 6) received a more complete and a higher fulfilment. Greater faith hath no man than this, that a man gives back His own promises unto God. The real but incomplete faith of believing that aged parents could become the progenitors of countless thousands had been accepted and rewarded. Much more, therefore, was the perfect faith of offering to God the one hope of posterity accepted and rewarded. This last was a *work* in which his faith co-operated, and which proved the complete development of his faith; by it "was faith made perfect."

"He was called the Friend of God." Abraham was so called in Jewish tradition; and to this day this is his name among his descendants the Arabs, who much more commonly speak of him as "the Friend" (*El Khalil*), or "the Friend of God" (*El Khalil Allah*), than by the name Abraham. Nowhere in the Old Testament does he receive this name, although our Versions, both

Authorized and Revised, would lead us to suppose that he is so called. The word is found neither in the Hebrew nor in existing copies of the Septuagint. In 2 Chron. xx. 7, "Abraham Thy friend" should be "Abraham Thy beloved;" and in Isaiah xli. 8, "Abraham My friend" should be "Abraham whom I loved." In both passages, however, the Vulgate has the rendering *amicus*, and some copies of the Septuagint had the reading "friend" in 2 Chron. xx. 7, while Symmachus had it in Isa. xli. 8 (See Field's *Hexapla*, I., p. 744; II., p. 513). Clement of Rome (x., xvii.) probably derived this name for Abraham from St. James. But even if Abraham is nowhere styled "the Friend of God," he is abundantly described as being such. God talks with him as a man talks with his friend, and asks, "Shall I hide from Abraham that which I do?" (Gen. xviii. 17); which is the very token of friendship pointed out by Christ. "No longer do I call you servants; for the servant knoweth not what his lord doeth: but I have called you friends; for all things that I heard from My Father I have made known unto you" (John xv. 15). It is worthy of note that St. James seems to intimate that the word is not in the sacred writings. The words, "And Abraham believed God, and it was reckoned unto him for righteousness," are introduced with the formula, "The Scripture was fulfilled which saith." Of the title "Friend of God" it is simply said "he was called," without stating by whom.[66]

"*In like manner* was not also Rahab the harlot justified by works?" It is because of the similarity of her case to Abraham's, both of them being a contrast to the formal Christian and the demons, that Rahab is introduced. In her case also faith led to action, and the action had its result in the salvation of the agent. If there had been faith without action, if she had merely believed the spies without doing anything in consequence of her belief, she would have perished. She was glorified in Jewish tradition, perhaps as being a typical forerunner of proselytes from the Gentile world; and it may be that this accounts for her being mentioned in the genealogy of the Messiah, and consequently by St. James and the writer of the Epistle to the Hebrews. The Talmud mentions a quite untrustworthy tradition that she married Joshua, and became the ancestress of eight persons who were both priests and prophets, and also of Huldah the prophetess. St. Matthew gives Salmon the son of Naasson as her husband; he may have been one of the spies.

But the contrast between Abraham and Rahab is almost as marked as the similarity. He is the friend of God, and she is of a vile heathen nation and a harlot. His great act of faith is manifested towards God, hers towards men. His is the crowning act of his spiritual development; hers is the first sign of a faith just beginning to exist. He is the aged saint, while she is barely a catechumen. But according to her light, which was that of a very faulty moral standard, "she did what she could," and it was accepted.

These contrasts have their place in the argument, as well as the similarities. The readers of the Epistle might think, "Heroic acts are all very suitable for Abraham; but we are not Abrahams, and must be content with sharing his faith in the true God; we cannot and need not imitate his acts." "But," St. James replies (and he writes ὁμοίως δέ, not καὶ ὁμοίως), "there is Rahab, Rahab the heathen, Rahab the harlot; at least you can imitate her." And for the Jewish Christians of that day her example was very much in point. She welcomed and believed the messengers, whom her countrymen persecuted, and would have slain. She separated herself from her unbelieving and hostile people, and went over to an unpopular and despised cause. She saved the preachers of an unwelcome message for the fulfilment of the Divine mission with which they had been entrusted. Substitute the Apostles for the spies, and all this is true of the believing Jews of that age. And as if to suggest this lesson, St. James speaks not of "young men," as Joshua vi. 23, nor of "spies," as Hebrews xi. 31, but of "messengers," a term which is as applicable to those who were sent by Jesus Christ as to those who were sent by Joshua.

Plutarch, who was a young man at the time when this Epistle was written, has the following story of Alexander the Great, in his "Apothegms of Kings and Generals": The young Alexander was not at all pleased with the successes of his father, Philip of Macedon. "My father will leave me nothing," he said. The young nobles who were brought up with him replied, "He is gaining all this for you." Almost in the words of St. James, though with a very different meaning, he answered, "*What does it profit* (τί ὄφελος;), if I possess much and *do* nothing?" The future conqueror scorned to have everything done for him. In quite another spirit the Christian must remember that if he is to conquer he must not suppose that his heavenly Father, who has done so much for him, has left him nothing to do. There is the fate of the barren fig-tree as a perpetual warning to those who are royal in their professions of faith, and paupers in good works.

[65] Döllinger, *The Gentile and the Jew*, II., pp. 384, 386, Eng. Tr., *Heidenthum und Judenthum*, pp. 825, 827.

[66] The following story is given by Mahometan commentators on the passage, "God took Abraham for His friend," which occurs in the fourth chapter of the Koran, entitled *Nessa*, or "Women:" Abraham was the father of the poor, and in a famine he emptied his granaries to feed them. Then he sent to one of his friends, who was a great lord in

Egypt, for corn. But the friend said, "We also are in danger of famine. The corn is not wanted for Abraham, but for his poor. I must keep it for our own poor." And the messengers returned with empty sacks. As they neared home they feared being mocked for their failure; so they filled their sacks with sand, and came in well laden. In private they told Abraham of his friend's refusal, and Abraham at once retired to pray. Meanwhile Sarah opened one of the sacks, and found excellent flour in it, and with this began to bake bread for the poor. When Abraham returned from prayer he asked Sarah whence she obtained the flour. "From that which your friend in Egypt has sent," she replied. "Say rather from that which the true Friend has sent, that is God; for it is He who never fails us in our need." At the moment when Abraham called God his Friend God took Abraham also to be His friend. (See the notes in Sale's *Koran*; D'Herbelot's *Bibliothèque Orientale*, Maestricht, 1776, p. 13; Bishop Thirlwall's *Letters to a Friend*, Bentley, 1882, pp. 63, 64).

Eusebius (*Præp. Evan.* IX. xix., p. 420) quotes Alexander Polyhistor (*c.* B.C. 80) as stating that Molon (Josephus, *Contra Apionem*, II. xiv.) interpreted the name Abraham as meaning the "Father's Friend" (πατρὸς φίλος), probably through a misspelling of the name. (See Lightfoot's note on Clem. Rom. x.)

CHAPTER XIV
THE HEAVY RESPONSIBILITIES OF TEACHERS. THE POWERS AND PROPENSITIES OF THE TONGUE. THE SELF-DEFILEMENT OF THE RECKLESS TALKER

"Be not many teachers, my brethren, knowing that we shall receive heavier judgment. For in many things we all stumble. If any stumble not in word, the same is a perfect man, able to bridle the whole body also. Now if we put the horses' bridles into their mouths, that they may obey us, we turn about their whole body also. Behold, the ships also, though they are so great, and are driven by rough winds, are yet turned about by a very small rudder, whither the impulse of the steersman willeth. So the tongue also is a little member, and boasteth great things. Behold, how much wood is kindled by how small a fire! And the tongue is a fire: the world of iniquity among our members is the tongue, which defileth the whole body, and setteth on fire the wheel of nature, and is set on fire by hell. For every kind of beasts and birds, of creeping things and things in the sea, is tamed, and hath been tamed by mankind: but the tongue can no man tame; it is a restless evil, it is full of deadly poison." — St. James iii. 1-8.

FROM the "idle faith" (πίστις ἀργή) St. James goes on to speak of the "idle word" (ῥῆμα ἀργόν). The change from the subject of faith and works to that of the temptations and sins of speech is not so abrupt and arbitrary as at first sight appears. The need of warning his readers against sins of the tongue has been in his mind from the first. Twice in the first chapter it comes to the surface. "Let every man be swift to hear, slow to speak, slow to wrath" (ver. 19), as if being slow to hear and swift to speak were much the same as being swift to wrath. And again, "If any man thinketh himself to be religious, while he bridleth not his tongue, but deceiveth his heart, this man's religion is vain" (ver. 26). And now the subject of barren faith causes him to return to the warning once more. For it is precisely those who neglect good works that are given to talk much about the excellence of their faith, and are always ready to instruct and lecture others. That *controversies* about faith and works suggested to him this section about offences of the tongue, is a gratuitous hypothesis. St. James shows no knowledge of any such controversies. As already pointed out, the purpose of the preceding section (ii. 14-26) is not controversial or doctrinal, but purely practical, like the rest of the Epistle. The paragraph before us is of the same character; it is against those who substitute words for works.

St. James is entirely of Carlyle's opinion that in the majority of cases, if "speech is silvern, silence is golden;" but he does not write twenty volumes to prove the truth of this doctrine. "In noble uprightness, he values only the strict practice of concrete duties, and hates talk" (Reuss); and while quite admitting that teachers are necessary, and that some are called to undertake this office, he tells all those who desire to undertake it that what they have to bear in mind is its perils and responsibilities. And it is obvious that true teachers must always be a minority. There is something seriously wrong when the majority in the community, or even a large number, are pressing forward to teach the rest.

"Be not many teachers, my brethren;" or, if we are to do full justice to the compact fulness of the original, "Do not many of you become teachers." St. James is not protesting against a usurpation of the ministerial office; to suppose this is to give far too specific a meaning to his simple language. The context points to no such sin as that of Korah and his company, but simply to the folly of incurring needless danger and temptation. In the Jewish synagogues any one who was disposed to do so might come forward to teach, and St. James writes at a time when the same freedom prevailed in the Christian congregations. "Each had a psalm, had a teaching, had a revelation, had a tongue, had an interpretation.... All could prophesy one by one, that all might learn and all be comforted" (1 Cor. xiv. 26, 31). But in both cases the freedom led to serious disorders. The desire to be called of men "Rabbi, Rabbi," told among Jews and Christians alike, and many were eager to expound who had still the very elements of true religion to learn. It is against this general desire to be prominent as instructors both in private and in public that St. James is here warning his readers. The Christian Church already has its ministers distinct from the laity, to whom the laity are to apply for spiritual help (v. 14); but it is not an invasion of their office by the laity to which St. James refers, when he says, "Do not many of you become teachers." These Jewish Christians of the Dispersion were like those at Rome to whom St. Paul writes; each of them was confident that his knowledge of God and the Law made him competent to become "a guide of the blind, a light of them that are in darkness, a corrector of the foolish, a teacher of babes, having in the Law the form of knowledge and of the truth" (Rom. ii. 17 *ff.*). But in teaching others they forgot to teach themselves; they failed to see that to preach the law without being a doer of the law was to cause God's name to be blasphemed among the Gentiles; and that to possess faith and do nothing but talk was but to increase their own condemnation; for it was to place themselves among those who are condemned by Christ because "they say and do not" (Matt. xxiii. 3). The phrase "to receive judgment" (κρῖμα λαμβάνειν) is in *form* a neutral one: the judgment may conceivably be a favourable one, but in *usage* it implies that the judgment is adverse (Mark xii. 40; Luke xx. 47; Rom. xiii. 2). Even without the verb "receive" this word "judgment" in the New Testament generally has the meaning of a *condemnatory* sentence (Rom. ii. 2, 3; iii. 8; v. 16; 1 Cor. xi. 29; Gal. v. 10; 1 Tim. iii. 6; v. 12; 1 Pet. iv. 17; 2 Pet. ii. 3; Jude 4; Rev. xvii. 1; xviii. 20). And there is no reason to doubt that such is the meaning here; the context requires it. The fact that St. James with affectionate humility and persuasiveness includes himself in the judgment—"*we* shall receive"—by no means proves that the word is here used in a neutral sense. In this he is like St. John, who breaks the logical flow of a sentence in a similar manner, rather than seem not to include himself: "If any man sin, *we* have an Advocate" (1 John ii. 1); *he* is as much in need of the Advocate as others. So also here, St. James, as being a teacher, shares in the heavier condemnation of teachers. It was the conviction that the word is not neutral, but condemnatory, which produced the rendering in the Vulgate, "knowing that ye receive greater condemnation" (*scientes quoniam majus judicium sumitis*), it being thought that St. James ought not to be included in such a judgment.

But this is to miss the point of the passage. St. James says that "in many things we stumble—*every one of us.*" He uses the strong form of the adjective (ἅπαντες for πάντες), and places it last with great emphasis. Every one of us sins, and therefore there is condemnation in store for every one of us. But those of us who are teachers will receive a heavier sentence than those of us who are not such; for our obligations to live up to the law which we know, and profess, and urge upon others, are far greater. Heaviest of all will be the condemnation of those who, without being called or qualified, through fanaticism, or an itch for notoriety, or a craze for controversy, or a love of fault-finding, push themselves forward to dispense instruction and censure. They are among the fools who "rush in where angels fear to tread," and thereby incur responsibilities which they need not, and ought not, to have incurred, because they do not possess the qualifications for meeting them and discharging them. The argument is simple and plain: "Some of us must teach. All of us frequently fall. Teachers who fall are more severely judged than others. Therefore do not many of you become teachers."

In what sphere is it that we most frequently fall? Precisely in that sphere in which the activity of teachers specially lies—in speech. "If any stumbleth not in word, the same is a perfect man." St. James is not thinking merely of the teacher who never makes a mistake, but of the man who never sins with the tongue. There is an obvious, but by no means exclusive, reference to teachers, and that is all. To every one of us, whatever our sphere in life, the saying comes home that one who offends not in word is indeed a *perfect* man. By "perfect" (τέλειος) he means one who has attained full spiritual and moral development, who is "perfect and entire, lacking in nothing" (i. 4). He is no longer a babe, but an adult; no longer a learner, but an adept. He is a full and complete man, with perfect command of all the faculties of soul and body. He has the full use of them, and complete control over them. The man who can bridle the most rebellious part of his nature, and keep it in faultless subjection, can bridle also the whole. This use of "perfect," as opposed to what is immature and incomplete, is the commonest use of the word in the New Testament. But sometimes it is a religious or philosophical term, borrowed from heathen mysteries or heathen philosophy. In such cases it signifies the *initiated*, as distinct from novices. Such a metaphor was very applicable to the Gospel, and St. Paul sometimes employs it (1 Cor. ii. 6; Col. i. 28); but it may be doubted whether any such thought is in St. James's mind here, although such a metaphor would have suited the subject. He who never stumbles in word can be no novice, but must be fully initiated in Christian discipline. But the simpler interpretation is better. He who can school the tongue can school the hands and the feet, the heart and the brain, in fact "the whole body," the whole of his nature, and is therefore a perfect man.

In his characteristic manner, St. James turns to natural objects for illustrations to enforce his point. "Now if we put the horses' bridles into their mouths, that they may obey us, we turn about their whole body." The changes made here by the Revisers are changes caused by a very necessary correction of the Greek text (εἰ δέ instead of ἴδε, which St. James nowhere else uses, or ἰδού, which here has very little evidence in its favour); for the text has been corrupted in order to simplify a rather difficult and doubtful construction. The uncorrupted text may be taken in two ways. *Either*, "But if we put the horses' bridles into their mouths, that they may obey us, and so turn about their whole body"—(much more ought we to do so to ourselves); this obvious conclusion being not stated, but left for us to supply at the end of an unfinished sentence. *Or*, as the Revisers take it, which is simpler, and leaves nothing to be understood. A man who can govern his tongue can govern his whole nature, just as a bridle controls, not merely the horse's mouth, but the whole animal. This first metaphor is suggested by the writer's own language. He has just spoken of the perfect man *bridling* his whole body, as before he spoke of the impossibility of true religion in one who does not *bridle* his tongue (i. 26); and this naturally suggests the illustration of the horses.

The argument is *à fortiori* from the horse to the man, and still more from the ship to the man, so that the whole forms a climax, the point throughout being the same, viz. the smallness of the part to be controlled in order to have control over the whole. And in order to bring out the fact that the ships are a stronger illustration than the horses, we should translate, "Behold, *even* the ships, though they are so great," etc., rather than "Behold, the ships *also*, though they are so great." First the statement of the case (ver. 2), then the illustration from the horses (ver. 3), then *"even* the ships" (ver. 4), and finally the application, "so the tongue *also*" (ver. 5). Thus all runs smoothly. If, as is certainly the case, we are able to govern irrational creatures with a small bit, how much more ourselves through the tongue; for just as he who has lost his hold of the reins has lost control over the horse, so he who has lost his hold on his tongue has lost control over himself. The case of the ship is still stronger. It is not only devoid of reason, but devoid of life. It cannot be taught obedience. It offers a dead resistance, which is all the greater because of its much greater size, and because it is driven by rough winds; yet its whole mass can be turned about by whoever has control of the little rudder, to lose command of which is to lose command of all. How much more, therefore, may we keep command over ourselves by having command over our tongues! There is nothing more in the metaphor than this. We may, if we please, go on with Bede, and turn the whole into a parable, and make the sea mean human life, and the winds mean temptations, and so on; but we must beware of supposing that anything of that kind was in the mind of St. James, or belongs to the explanation of the passage. Such symbolism is read into the text, not extracted from it. It is legitimate as a means of edifying, but it is not interpretation.

The expression "rough winds" (σκληρῶν ἀνέμων) is peculiar, "rough" meaning hard or harsh, especially to the touch, and hence of what is intractable or disagreeable in other ways (1 Sam. xxv. 3; Matt. xxv. 24; John vi. 60; Acts xxvi. 14; Jude 15). Perhaps in only one other passage in Greek literature, previous to this Epistle, is it used as an epithet of wind, viz. in Prov. xxvii. 16, a passage in which the Septuagint differs widely from the Hebrew and from our versions. St. James, who seems to have been specially fond of the sapiential books of Scripture, may have derived this expression from the Proverbs.

"So the tongue also is a little member, and boasteth great things." The tongue, like the bit and the rudder, is only a very small part of the whole, and yet, like them, it can do great things. St. James says, "boasteth great things," rather than "doeth great things," not in order to insinuate that the tongue boasts of what it cannot or does not do, which would spoil the argument, but in order to prepare the way for the change in the point of the argument. Hitherto the point has been *the immense influence which the small organ of speech has over our whole being,* and the consequent need of controlling it when we want to control ourselves. We must take care to begin the control in the right place. This point being established, the argument takes a somewhat different turn, and the necessity of curbing the tongue is shown, not from its great power, but from its *inherent malignity.* It can be made to discharge good offices, but its natural bent is towards evil. If left unchecked, it is certain to do incalculable mischief. The expression "boasteth great things" marks the transition from the one point to the other, and in a measure combines them both. There are great things done; that shows the tongue's power. And it boasts about them; that shows its bad character.[67]

This second point, like the first, is enforced by two illustrations taken from the world of nature. The first was illustrated by the power of bits and rudders; the second is illustrated by the capacity for mischief in fire and in venomous beasts. "Behold, what a fire kindles what a wood!" is the literal rendering of the Greek, where "what a fire" evidently means "how small a fire," while "what a wood" means "how large a wood." The traveller's camp-fire is enough to set a whole forest in flames, and the camp-fire was kindled by a few sparks. "Fire," it is sometimes truly said, "is a good servant, but a bad master," and precisely the same may with equal truth be said of the tongue. So long as it is kept under control it does excellent service; but directly it can run on unchecked, and lead instead of obeying, it begins to do untold mischief. We sometimes speak of men whose "*pens* run away with them;" but a far commoner case is that of persons whose *tongues* run away with them, whose untamed and unbridled tongues say things which are neither seriously thought nor (even at the moment) seriously meant. The habit of saying "great things" and using strong language is a condition of constant peril, which will inevitably lead the speaker into evil. It is a reckless handling of highly dangerous material. It is playing with fire.

Yes, "the tongue is a fire. The world of iniquity among our members is the tongue, which defileth the whole body." The right punctuation of this sentence cannot be determined with certainty, and other possible arrangements will be found in the margin of the Revised Version; but on the whole this seems to be the best. The one thing that is certain is that the "so" of the Authorized Version—"*so* is the tongue among our members"—is not genuine; if it were, it would settle the construction and the punctuation in favour of what is at least the second best arrangement: "The tongue is a fire, that world of iniquity: the tongue is among our members that which defileth the whole body." The meaning of "the world of iniquity" has been a good deal discussed, but is not really doubtful. The ordinary colloquial signification is the right one. The tongue is a boundless store of mischief, an inexhaustible source of evil, a universe of iniquity; *universitas iniquitatis*, as the Vulgate renders it. It contains within itself the elements of all unrighteousness; it is charged with endless possibilities of sin. This use of "world" (κόσμος) seems not to occur in classical Greek; but it is found in the Septuagint of the Proverbs, and again in a passage where the Greek differs widely from the Hebrew. What is still more remarkable, it occurs immediately after the mention of sins of speech: "An evil man listeneth to the tongue of the wicked; but a righteous man giveth no heed to false lips. The faithful man has the whole *world* of wealth; but the faithless not even a penny" (xvii. 4).

"*Is* the tongue." The word for "is" must be observed (not ἐστι, nor ὑπάρχει, but καθίσταται). Its literal meaning is "constitutes itself," and it occurs again in iv. 4, where the Revisers rightly translate it "maketh himself:" "Whosoever would be a friend of the world *maketh himself* an enemy of God." The tongue was not created by God to be a permanent source of all kinds of evil; like the rest of creation, it was made "very good," "the best member that we have." It is by its own undisciplined and lawless career that it *makes itself* "the world of iniquity," that it *constitutes itself* among our members as "that which defileth our whole body." This helps to explain what St. James means by "*unspotted*" (ἄσπθλον) or "undefiled" (i. 27). He who does not bridle his tongue is not really religious. Pure religion consists in keeping in check that "which *defileth* (ἡ σπιλοῦσα) our whole body." And the tongue defiles us in three ways;—by suggesting sin to ourselves and others; by committing sin, as in all cases of lying and blasphemy; and by excusing or defending sin. It is a palmary instance of the principle that the best when perverted becomes the worst—*corruptio optimi fit pessima*.

It "setteth on fire the wheel of nature, and is set on fire by hell." We must be content to leave the precise meaning of the words rendered "the wheel of nature" (τὸν τροχὸν τῆς γενέσεως) undetermined. The general meaning is evident enough, but we cannot be sure what image St. James had in his mind when he wrote the words. The one substantive is obviously a metaphor, and the other is vague in meaning (as the latter occurs i. 23, the two passages should be compared in expounding); but what the exact idea to be conveyed by the combination is, remains a matter for conjecture. And the conjectures are numerous, of which one must suffice. The tongue is a centre from which mischief radiates; that is the main thought. A wheel that has caught fire at the axle is at last wholly consumed, as the fire spreads through the spokes to the circumference. So also in society. Passions kindled by unscrupulous language spread through various channels and classes, till the whole cycle of human life is in flames. Reckless language first of all "defiles the whole" nature of the man who employs it, and then works destruction far and wide through the vast machinery of society. And to this there are no limits; so long as there is material, the fire will continue to burn.

How did the fire begin? How does the tongue, which was created for far other purposes, acquire this deadly propensity? St. James leaves us in no doubt upon that point. It is an inspiration of the evil one. The enemy, who steals away the good seed, and sows weeds among the wheat, turns the immense powers of the tongue to destruction. The old serpent imbues it with his own poison. He imparts to it his own diabolical agency. He is perpetually setting it on fire (present participle) from hell.

The second metaphor by which the malignant propensity of the tongue is illustrated is plain enough. It is an untamable, venomous beast. It combines the ferocity of the tiger and the mockery of the ape with the subtlety and venom of the serpent. It can be checked, can be disciplined, can be taught to do good and useful things; but it can never be tamed, and must never be trusted. If care and watchfulness are laid aside, its evil nature will burst out again, and the results will be calamitous.

There are many other passages in Scripture which contain warnings about sins of the tongue: see especially Proverbs xvi. 27, 28; Ecclus. v. 13, 14, and xxviii. 9-23, from which St. James may have drawn some of his thoughts. But what is peculiar to his statement of the matter is *this*, that *the reckless tongue defiles the whole nature of the man who owns it*. Other writers tell us of the mischief which the foul-mouthed man does to others, and of the punishment which will one day fall upon himself. St. James does not lose sight of that side of the matter, but the special point of his stern warning is the insisting upon the fact that unbridled speech is a *pollution* to the man that employs it. Every faculty of mind or body with which he has been endowed is contaminated by the subtle poison which is allowed to proceed from his lips. It is a special application of the principle laid down by Christ, which was at first a perplexity even to the Twelve, "The things which proceed out of the man are those that defile the man" (Mark vii. 15, 20, 23). The emphasis with which Christ taught this ought to be noticed. On purpose to insist upon it, "He called to Him the multitude *again*, and said unto them, Hear ye *all* of you, and *understand*: there is nothing from without the man, that going into him can defile him; but the things which proceed out of the man are those that defile the man." And He repeats this principle a second and a third time to His disciples privately. "Are ye so without understanding also?... That which proceedeth out of the man, that defileth the man.... All these things proceed from within, and defile the man." If even an unspoken thought can defile, when it has not yet proceeded farther than the heart, much greater will be the pollution if the evil thing is allowed to come to the birth by passing the barrier of the lips. This flow of evil from us means nothing less than this, that we have made ourselves a channel through which infernal agencies pass into the world. Is it possible for such a channel to escape defilement?

[67] There is a story that Amasis, King of Egypt, sent a sacrifice to Bias the sage, asking him to send back the best part and the worst; and Bias sent back the tongue.

CHAPTER XV
THE MORAL CONTRADICTIONS
IN THE RECKLESS TALKER

"Therewith bless we the Lord and Father; and therewith curse we men, which are made after the likeness of God: out of the same mouth cometh forth blessing and cursing. My brethren, these things ought not so to be. Doth the fountain send forth from the same opening sweet water and bitter? Can a fig-tree, my brethren, yield olives, or a vine figs? neither can salt water yield sweet." —St. James iii. 9-12.

IN these concluding sentences of the paragraph respecting sins of the tongue St. James does two things—he shows the moral chaos to which the Christian who fails to control his tongue is reduced, and he thereby shows such a man how vain it is for him to hope that the worship which he offers to Almighty God can be pure and acceptable. He has made himself the channel of hellish influences. He cannot at pleasure make himself the channel of heavenly influences, or become the offerer of holy sacrifices. The fires of Pentecost will not rest where the fires of Gehenna are working, nor can one who has become the minister of Satan at the same time be a minister to offer praise to God.

When those who would have excused themselves for their lack of good works pleaded the correctness of their faith, St. James told them that such faith was barren and dead, and incapable of saving them from condemnation. Similarly, the man who thinks himself to be religious, and does not bridle his tongue, was told that his religion is vain (i. 26). And in the passage before us St. James explains how that is. His religion or religious worship (θρησκεία) is a mockery and a contradiction. The offering is tainted; it comes from a polluted altar and a polluted priest. A man who curses his fellow men, and then blesses God, is like one who professes the profoundest respect for his sovereign, while he insults the royal family, throws mud at the royal portraits, and ostentatiously disregards the royal wishes. It is further proof of the evil character of the tongue that it is capable of lending itself to such chaotic activity. "Therewith bless we the Lord and Father," i.e. God in His might and in His love; "and therewith curse we men, which are made after the likeness of God." The heathen fable tells us the apparent contradiction of being able to blow both hot and cold with the same breath; and the son of Sirach points out that "if thou blow the spark, it shall burn; if thou spit upon it, it shall be quenched; and both these come out of thy mouth" (Ecclus. xxviii. 12). St. James, who may have had this passage in his mind, shows us that there is a real and a moral contradiction which goes far beyond either of these: "Out of the same mouth cometh forth blessing and cursing." Well may he add, with affectionate earnestness, "My brethren, these things ought not so to be."

Assuredly they ought not; and yet how common the contradiction has been, and still is, among those who seem to be, and who think themselves to be, religious people! There is perhaps no particular in which persons professing to have a desire to serve God are more ready to invade His prerogatives than in venturing to denounce those who differ from themselves, and are supposed to be therefore under the ban of Heaven. "They have a zeal for God, but not according to knowledge. For being ignorant of God's righteousness, and seeking to establish their own, they do not subject themselves to the righteousness of God" (Rom. x. 2, 3). Hence they rashly and intemperately "curse whom the Lord hath not cursed, and defy whom the Lord hath not defied" (Num. xxiii. 8). There are still many who believe that not only in the psalms and hymns in which they bless the Lord, but also in the sermons and pamphlets in which they fulminate against their fellow-Christians, they are "offering service to God" (John xvi. 2). There are many questions which have to be carefully considered and answered before a Christian mouth, which has been consecrated to the praise of our Lord and Father, ought to venture to utter denunciations against others who worship the same God and are also His offspring and His image. Is it quite certain that the supposed evil is something which God abhors; that those whom we would denounce are responsible for it; that denunciation of *them* will do any good; that this is the proper time for such denunciation; that *we* are the proper persons to utter it? About every one of these questions the most fatal mistakes are constantly being made. The singing of *Te Deums* after massacres and *dragonnades* is perhaps no longer possible; but alternations between religious services and religious prosecutions, between writing pious books and publishing exasperating articles, are by no means extinct. For one case in which harm has been done because no one has come forward to denounce a wrongdoer, there are ten cases in which harm has been done because some one has been indiscreetly, or inopportunely, or uncharitably, or unjustly denounced. "Praise is not seasonable (ὡραῖος) in the mouth of a sinner" (Ecclus. xv. 9); and whatever may have been the writer's meaning in the difficult passage in which it occurs, we may give it a meaning that will bring it into harmony with what St. James says here. The praise of God is not seasonable in the mouth of one who is ever sinning in reviling God's children.

The illustrations of the fountain and the fig-tree are among the touches which, if they do not indicate one who is familiar with Palestine, at any rate agree well with the fact that the writer of this Epistle was such. Springs tainted with salt or with sulphur are not rare, and it is stated that most of those on the eastern slope of the hill-country of Judæa are brackish. The fig-tree, the vine, and the olive were abundant throughout the whole country; and St. James, if he looked out of window as he was writing, would be likely enough to see all three. It is not improbable that in one or more of the illustrations he is following some ancient saying or proverb. Thus, Arrian, the pupil of Epictetus, writing less than a century later, asks, "How can a vine grow, not vinewise, but olivewise, or an olive, on the other hand, not olivewise, but vinewise? It is impossible, inconceivable." It is possible that our Lord Himself, when He used a similar illustration in connexion with the worst of all sins of the tongue, was adapting a proverb already in use. In speaking of "the blasphemy against the Spirit" He says, "Either make the tree good, and its fruit good; or make the tree corrupt, and its fruit corrupt: for the tree is known by its fruit. Ye offspring of vipers, how can ye, being evil, speak good things? for out of the abundance of the heart the mouth speaketh. The good man out of his good treasure bringeth forth good things; and the evil man out of his evil treasure bringeth forth evil things. And I say unto you, That every idle word that men shall speak, they shall give account thereof in the day of judgment" (Matt. xii. 33-36). And previously, in the Sermon on the Mount, where He is speaking of deeds rather than of words, "By their fruits ye shall know them. Do men gather grapes of thorns, or figs of thistles? Even so every good tree bringeth forth good fruit, but the corrupt tree bringeth forth evil fruit. A good tree cannot bring forth evil fruit, neither can a corrupt tree bring forth good fruit" (Matt. vii. 16-18).

Can it be the case that while physical contradictions are not permitted in the lower classes of unconscious objects, moral contradictions of a very monstrous kind are allowed in the highest of all earthly creatures? The "double-minded man," who prays and doubts, receives nothing from the Lord, because his petition is only in form a prayer; it lacks the essential characteristic of prayer, which is faith. But the double-tongued man, who blesses God and curses men, what does he receive? Just as the double-minded man is judged by his doubts, and not by his forms of prayer, so the double-tongued man is judged by his curses, and not by his forms of praise. In each case one or the other of the two contradictories is not real. If there is prayer, there are no doubts; and if there are doubts, there is no prayer—no prayer that will avail with God. So also in the other case: if God is sincerely and heartily blessed, there will be no cursing of His children; and if there is such cursing, God cannot acceptably be blessed; the very words of praise, coming from such lips, will be an offence to Him.

But it may be urged, our Lord Himself has set us an example of strong denunciation in the woes which He pronounced upon the scribes and Pharisees; and again, St. Paul cursed Hymenæus and Alexander (1 Tim. i. 20), the incestuous person at Corinth (1 Cor. v. 5), and Elymas the sorcerer (Acts xiii. 10). Most true. But firstly, these curses were uttered by those who could not err in such things. Christ "knew what was in man," and could read the hearts of all; and the fact that St. Paul's curses were supernaturally fulfilled proves that he was acting under Divine guidance in what he said. And secondly, these stern utterances had their source in love; not, as human curses commonly have, in hate. It was in order that those on whom they were pronounced might be warned, and schooled to better things, that they were uttered; and we know that in the case of the sinner at Corinth the severe remedy had this effect; the curse was really a blessing. When *we* have infallible guidance, and when *we* are able by supernatural results to prove that we possess it, it will be time enough to begin to deal in curses. And let us remember *the proportion* which such things bear to the rest of Christ's words and of St. Paul's words, so far as they have been preserved for us. Christ wrought numberless miracles of mercy: besides those which are recorded in detail, we are frequently told that "He healed many that were sick with divers diseases, and cast out many devils" (Mark i. 34); that "He had healed many" (iii. 10); that "wheresoever He entered, into villages, or into cities, or into the country, they laid the sick in the market-places, and besought Him that they might touch if it were but the border of His garment; and as many as touched Him were made whole" (vi. 56); and so forth (John xxi. 25). But He wrought only one miracle of judgment, and that was upon a tree, which could teach the necessary lesson without feeling the punishment (Mark xi. 12-23). All this applies with much force to those who believe themselves to be called upon to denounce and curse all such as seem to them to be enemies of God and His truth: but with how much more force to those who in moments of anger and irritation deal in execrations on their own account, and curse a fellow-Christian, not because he seems to them to have offended God, but because he has offended themselves! That such persons should suppose that their polluted mouths can offer acceptable praises to the Lord and Father, is indeed a moral contradiction of the most startling kind. And are such cases rare? Is it so uncommon a thing for a man to attend church regularly, and join with apparent devotion in the services, and yet think little of the grievous words which he allows himself to utter when his temper is severely tried? How amazed and offended he would be if he were invited to eat at a table which had been used for some disgusting purpose, and had never since been cleansed! And yet he does not hesitate to "defile his whole body" with his unbridled tongue, and then offer praise to God from this polluted source!

Nor is this the only contradiction in which such a one is involved. How strange that the being who is lord and master of all the animal creation should be unable to govern himself! How strange that man's chief mark of superiority over the brutes should be the power of speech, and that he should use this power in such a way as to make it the instrument of his own degradation, until he becomes lower than the brutes! They, whether tamed or untamed, unconsciously declare the glory of God; while he, with his noble powers of consciously and loyally praising Him, by his untamed tongue reviles those who are made after the image of God, and thus turns his own praises into blasphemies. Thus does man's rebellion reverse the order of nature and frustrate the will of God.

The writer of this Epistle has been accused of exaggeration. It has been urged that in this strongly worded paragraph he himself is guilty of that unchastened language which he is so eager to condemn; that the case is over-stated, and that the highly coloured picture is a caricature. Is there any thoughtful person of large experience that can honestly assent to this verdict? Who has not seen what mischief may be done by a single utterance of mockery, or enmity, or bravado; what confusion is wrought by exaggeration, innuendo, and falsehood; what suffering is inflicted by slanderous suggestions and statements; what careers of sin have been begun by impure stories and filthy jests? All these effects may follow, be it remembered, from a single utterance in each case, may spread to multitudes, may last for years. One reckless word may blight a whole life. "Many have fallen by the edge of the sword, but not so many as have fallen by the tongue" (Ecclus. xxviii. 18). And there are persons who habitually pour forth such things, who never pass a day without uttering what is unkind, or false, or impure. When we look around us, and see the moral ruin which in every class of society can be traced to reckless language—lives embittered, and blighted, and brutalized by words spoken and heard—can we wonder at the severe words of St. James, whose experience was not very different from our own? Violent and uncharitable language had become one of the besetting sins of the Jews, and no doubt Jewish Christians were by no means free from it. "Curse the whisperer and the double-tongued," says the son of Sirach, "for such have destroyed many that were at peace" (Ecclus. xxviii. 13). To which the Syriac Version adds a clause not given in the Greek, nor in our Bibles: "Also *the third tongue,* let it be cursed; for it has laid low many corpses." This expression, "third tongue," seems to have come into use among the Jews in the period between the Old and New Testament. It means a slanderous tongue, and it is called "third" because it is fatal to three sets of people—to the person who utters the slander, to those who listen to it, and to those about whom it is uttered. "A third tongue hath tossed many to and fro, and driven them from nation to nation; and strong cities hath it pulled down, and houses of great men hath it overthrown" (Ecclus. xxviii. 14); where not only the Syriac, but the Greek, has the interesting expression "third tongue," a fact obscured in our version.

The "third tongue" is as common and as destructive now as when the son of Sirach denounced it, or St. James wrote against it with still greater authority; and we all of us can do a great deal to check the mischief, not merely by taking care that we keep our own tongues from originating evil, but by refusing to repeat, or if possible even to listen to, what the third tongue says. Our unwillingness to hear may be a discouragement to the speaker, and our refusal to repeat will at least lessen the evil of his tale. We shall have saved ourselves from becoming links in the chain of destruction.

There is one kind of sinful language to which the severe sayings of St. James specially apply, although the context seems to show that it was not specially in his mind—impure language. The foul tongue is indeed a "world of iniquity, which defileth the whole body, and setteth on fire the wheel of nature, and is set on fire by hell." In no other case is the self-pollution of the speaker so manifest, or the injury to the listener so probable, so all but inevitable. Foul stories and impure jests and innuendoes, even more clearly than oaths and curses, befoul the souls of those who utter them, while they lead the hearers into sin. Such things rob all who are concerned in them, either as speakers or listeners, of two things which are the chief safeguards of virtue—the fear of God, and the fear of sin. They create an atmosphere in which men sin with a light heart, because the grossest sins are made to look not only attractive and easy, but amusing. What can be made to seem laughable is supposed to be not very serious. There is no more devilish act that a human being can perform than that of inducing others to believe that what is morally hideous and deadly is "pleasant to the eye and good for food." And this devil's work is sometimes done merely to raise a laugh, merely for something to say. Does any one seriously maintain that the language of St. James is at all too strong for such things as these? We hardly need his authority for the belief that a filthy tongue pollutes a man's whole being, and owes its inspiration to the evil one.

It is of angry, ill-tempered, unkind words that we do not believe this so readily. Words that are not false or calumnious, not running out into blasphemies and curses, and certainly not tainted with anything like impurity, do not always strike us as being as harmful as they really are, not only to others, whom they irritate or sadden, but to ourselves, who allow our characters to be darkened by them. The captious word, that makes everything a subject for blame; the discontented word, that would show that the speaker is always being ill-treated; the biting word, that is meant to inflict pain; the sullen word, that throws a gloom over all who hear it; the provoking word, that seeks to stir up strife—of all these we are most of us apt to think too lightly, and need the stern warnings of St. James to remind us of their true nature and of their certain consequences. As regards *others*, such things wound tender hearts, add needlessly and enormously to the unhappiness of mankind, turn sweet affections sour, stifle good impulses, create and foster bad feelings, embitter in its smallest details the whole round of daily life. As regards *ourselves*, indulgence in such language weakens and warps our characters, blunts our sympathies, deadens our love for man, and therefore our love for God. "In particular it makes prayer either impossible or half useless. Whether we know it or not, the prayer that comes from a heart indulging in evil temper is hardly a prayer at all. We cannot really be face to face with God; we cannot really approach God as a Father; we cannot really feel like children kneeling at His feet; we cannot really be simply affectionate and truthful in what we say to Him, if irritation, discontent, or gloom, or anger, is busy at our breasts. An undisciplined temper shuts out the face of God from us. We may see His holy Law, but we cannot see Himself. We may think of Him as our Creator, our Judge, our Ruler, but we cannot think of Him as our Father, nor approach Him with love."[68] "Salt water cannot yield sweet."

It was once pleaded on behalf of a man who had been criticized and condemned as unsatisfactory, that he was "a good man, all but his temper." "All but his temper!" was the not unreasonable reply; "as if temper were not nine tenths of religion." "If any man stumbleth not in word, the same is a *perfect* man."

[68] *Sermons preached in Rugby School Chapel*, by the Rev. Frederick Temple, D.D. (Macmillan, 1867), pp. 324, 325.

CHAPTER XVI
THE WISDOM THAT IS FROM BELOW

"Who is wise and understanding among you? let him show by his good life his works in meekness of wisdom. But if ye have bitter jealousy and faction in your heart, glory not, and lie not against the truth. This wisdom is not a wisdom that cometh down from above, but is earthly, sensual, devilish. For where jealousy and faction are, there is confusion and every vile deed." —St. James iii. 13-16.

THIS section, which again looks at first sight like an abrupt transition to another subject, is found, upon closer examination, to grow quite naturally out of the preceding one. St. James has just been warning his readers against the lust of teaching and talking. Not many of them are to become teachers, for the danger of transgressing with the tongue, which is great in all of us, is in them at a maximum, because teachers must talk. Moreover, those who teach have greater responsibilities than those who do not; for by professing to instruct others they deprive themselves of the plea of ignorance, and they are bound to instruct by example of good deeds, as well as by precept of good words. From this subject he quite naturally passes on to speak of the difference between the wisdom from above and the wisdom from below; and the connexion is twofold. It is those who possess only the latter wisdom, and are proud of their miserable possession, who are so eager to make themselves of importance by giving instruction; and it is the fatal love of talk, about which he has just been speaking so severely, that is one of the chief symptoms of the wisdom that is from below.

This paragraph is, in fact, simply a continuation of the uncompromising *attack upon sham religion* which is the main theme throughout a large portion of the Epistle. St. James first shows how useless it is to be an eager hearer of the word, without also being a doer of it. Next he exposes the inconsistency of loving one's neighbour as oneself if he chances to be rich, and neglecting or even insulting him if he is poor. From that he passes on to prove the barrenness of an orthodoxy which is not manifested in good deeds, and the peril of trying to make words a substitute for works. And thus the present section is reached. Throughout the different sections it is the empty religiousness which endeavours to avoid the *practice* of Christian virtue, on the plea of possessing zeal, or faith, or knowledge, that is mercilessly exposed and condemned. "Deed, deeds, deeds," is the cry of St. James; "these ought ye to have done, and not to have left the other undone." Without Christian practice, all the other good things which they possessed or professed were savourless salt.

"Who is wise and understanding among you?" (τίς σοφὸς καὶ ἐπιστήμων ἐν ὑμῖν). The same two words meet us in the questionings of Job (xxviii. 12): "Where shall wisdom (σοφία) be found? and where is the place of understanding (ἐπιστήμη)?"[69] Of all the words which signify some kind of intellectual endowment, e.g. "prudence" (φρόνησις), "knowledge" (γνῶσις or ἐπίγνωσις), and "understanding" (ἐπιστήμη or σύνεσισ), "wisdom" (σοφία) always ranks as highest. It indicates, as Clement of Alexandria defines it (*Strom.* I. v.), "the understanding of things human and Divine, and their causes." It is the word which expresses the typical wisdom of Solomon (Matt. xii. 42; Luke xi. 31), the inspiration of St. Stephen (Acts vi. 10), and the Divine wisdom of Jesus Christ (Matt. xiii. 54; Mark vi. 2; and comp. Luke xi. 49 with Matt. xxiii. 34). It is also employed in the heavenly doxologies which ascribe wisdom to the Lamb and to God (Rev. v. 12; vii. 12). St. James, therefore, quite naturally employs it to denote that excellent gift for which Christians are to pray with full confidence that it will be granted to them (i. 5, 6), and which manifests its heavenly character by a variety of good fruits (iii. 17).

Whether we are to understand any very marked difference between the two adjectives ("wise" and "understanding") used in the opening question, is a matter of little moment. The question taken as a whole amounts to this: Who among you professes to have superior knowledge, spiritual or practical? The main thing is not the precise scope of the question, but of the answer. Let every one who claims to have a superiority which entitles him to teach others *prove* his superiority by his good *life*. Once more it is a call for deeds, and not words—for conduct, and not professions. And St. James expresses this in a specially strong way. He might have said simply, "Let him by his conduct show his wisdom," just as he said above, "I by my works will show thee my faith." But he says, "Let him show by his good life his works in meekness of wisdom." Thus the necessity for *practice* and *conduct*, as distinct from mere knowledge, is enforced twice over; and besides that, the particular character of the conduct, the atmosphere in which it is to be exhibited, is also indicated. It is to be done "in *meekness* of wisdom." There are two characteristics here specified which we shall find are given as the infallible signs of the heavenly wisdom; and their opposites as signs of the other. The heavenly wisdom is fruitful of good deeds, and inspires those who possess it with gentleness. The other wisdom is productive of nothing really valuable, and inspires those who possess it with contentiousness. The spirit of strife, and the spirit of meekness; those are the two properties which chiefly distinguish the wisdom that comes from heaven from the wisdom that comes from hell.

This test is a very practical one, and we can apply it to ourselves as well as to others. How do we bear ourselves in argument and in controversy? Are we serene about the result, in full confidence that truth and right should prevail? Are we desirous that truth should prevail, even if that should involve *our* being proved to be in the wrong? Are we meek and gentle towards those who differ from us? or are we apt to lose our tempers, and become heated against our opponents? If the last is the case we have reason to doubt whether our wisdom is of the best sort. He who loses his temper in argument has begun to care more about himself, and less about the truth. He has become like the many would-be teachers rebuked by St. James; slow to hear, and swift to speak; unwilling to learn, and eager to dogmatize; much less ready to know the truth than to be able to say something, whether true or false.

The words "by his good life" (ἐκ τῆς καλῆς ἀναστροφῆς) are a change made by the Revisers for other reasons than the two which commonly weighed with them. As already stated, their most valuable corrections are those which have been produced by the correction of the corrupt Greek text used by previous translators. Many more are corrections of mistranslations of the correct Greek text. The present change of "good *conversation*" into "good *life*" comes under neither of these two heads. It has been necessitated by a change which has taken place in the English language during the last two or three centuries. Words are constantly changing their meaning. "Conversation" is one of many English words which have drifted from their old signification; and it is one of several which have undergone change since the Authorized Version was published, and in spite of the enormous influence exercised by that version. For there can be no doubt that our Bible has retained words in use which would otherwise have been dropped, and has kept words to their old meaning which would otherwise have undergone a change. This latter influence, however, fails to make itself felt where the changed meaning still makes sense; and that is the case with the passages in which "conversation" (as a rendering of ἀναστροφή) occurs in the New Testament. "Conversation" was formerly a word of much wider meaning, and its gradual restriction to intercourse by word of mouth is unfortunate. Formerly it covered the whole of a man's *walk* in life (*Lebenswandel*), his going out and coming in, his behaviour or conduct. Wherever he "turned himself about" and lived, there he had his "conversation" (*conversatio*, from *conversari*, the exact equivalent of ἀναστροφή, from ἀναστρέφεσθαι). It was exactly the word that was required by the translators of the Greek

Testament. In the Septuagint it does not occur until the Apocrypha (Tobit iv. 14). But it causes serious misunderstanding to restrict the meaning of all the passages in which the word occurs to "conversation" in the modern sense, as if speaking were the only thing included; and the Revisers have done very rightly in removing this source of misunderstanding; but they have been unable to find any one expression which would serve the purpose, and hence have been compelled to vary the translation. Sometimes they give "manner of life" (Gal. i. 13; Eph. iv. 22; 1 Tim. iv. 12; 1 Peter i. 18); iii. 16; once "manner of living" (1 Peter i. 15); three times "behaviour" (1 Peter ii. 12; iii. 1, 2); three times "life" (Heb. xiii. 7; 2 Peter ii. 7; and here); and once "living" (2 Peter iii. 11). These different translations are worth collecting together, inasmuch as they give a good idea of the scope of "conversation" in the old sense,[70] which really represents the word used by St. James. That "conversation," with the modern associations which inevitably cling to it now, should be used in the passage before us, is singularly unfortunate. It not only misrepresents, but it almost reverses the meaning of the writer. So far from telling a man to show his wisdom by what he *says* in his intercourse with others, St. James rather exhorts him to show it by saying as little as possible, and doing a great deal. Let him show out of a noble life the conduct of a wise man in the gentle spirit which befits such. In modern language, let him in the fullest sense be a Christian gentleman.

"In *meekness* of wisdom." On this St. James lays great stress. He has already told his readers to "receive with meekness the implanted word" (i. 21), and what implies the same thing, although the word is not used, to "be swift to hear, slow to speak, slow to wrath" (i. 19). And in the passage before us he insists with urgent repetition upon the peaceable and gentle disposition of those who possess the wisdom from above (vv. 17, 18). The Christian grace of meekness is a good deal more than the rather second-rate virtue which Aristotle makes to be the mean between passionateness and impassionateness, and to consist in a due regulation of one's angry feelings (*Eth. Nic.* IV. v.). It includes submissiveness towards God, as well as gentleness towards men; and it exhibits itself in a special way in giving and receiving instruction, and in administering and accepting rebuke. It was, therefore, just the grace which the many would-be teachers, with their loud professions of correct faith and superior knowledge, specially needed to acquire. The Jew, with his national contempt for all who were not of the stock of Israel, was always prone to self-assertion, and these Christian Jews of the Dispersion had still to learn the spirit of their own psalms. "The meek will He guide in judgment; and the meek will He teach His way" (xxv. 9). "The meek shall inherit the land, and shall delight themselves in the abundance of peace" (xxxvii. 11). "The Lord upholdeth the meek" (cxlvii. 6).

"He shall beautify the meek with salvation" (cxlix. 4). In all these passages the Septuagint has the adjective (πραεῖς) of the substantive used by St. James (πραΰτης). "But if," instead of this meekness, "ye have bitter jealousy and faction in your heart, glory not, and lie not against the truth." With a gentle severity St. James states as a mere supposition what he probably knew to be a fact. There was plenty of bitter zealousness and party spirit among them; and from this fact they could draw their own conclusions. It was an evil from which the Jews greatly suffered; and a few years later it hastened, if it did not cause, the overthrow of Jerusalem. This "jealousy" or zeal (ζῆλος) itself became a party name in the fanatical sect of the Zealots. It was an evil from which the primitive Church greatly suffered, as passages in the New Testament and in the sub-Apostolic writers prove; and can we say that it has ever become extinct? The same conclusion must be drawn now as then.

Jealousy or zeal may be a good or a bad thing according to the motive which inspires it. God Himself is called "a jealous God," and is said to be "clad with zeal as a cloak" (Isa. lix. 17), and to "take to Him jealousy for complete armour" (Wisdom v. 17). To Christ His disciples applied the words, "The zeal of Thine house shall eat me up" (John ii. 17). But more often the word has a bad signification. It indicates "zeal not according to knowledge" (Rom. x. 2), as when the high priest and Sadducees arrested the Apostles (Acts v. 17), or when Saul persecuted the Church (Phil. iii. 6). It is coupled with strife (Rom. xiii. 13), and is counted among the works of the flesh (Gal. v. 20). To make it quite plain that it is to be understood in a bad sense here, St. James adds the epithet "bitter" to it, and perhaps thereby recalls what he has just said about a mouth that utters both curses and blessings being as monstrous as a fountain spouting forth both bitter water and sweet. Moreover, he couples it with "faction" (ἐριθεία), a word which originally meant "working for hire," and especially "weaving for hire" (Isa. xxxviii. 12), and thence any ignoble pursuit, especially political canvassing, intrigue, or factiousness (Arist. *Pol.* V. ii. 6; iii. 9; Rom. ii. 8; Phil. i. 16; ii. 3). This also St. Paul classes among the works of the flesh (Gal. v. 20). What St. James seems to refer to in these two words is bitter religious animosity; a hatred of error (or what is supposed to be such), manifesting itself, not in loving attempts to win over those who are at fault, but in bitter thoughts, and words, and party combinations.

"Glory not, and lie not against the truth." To glory with their tongues of their superior wisdom, while they cherished jealousy and faction in their hearts, was a manifest lie, a contradiction of what they must know to be the truth. In their fanatical zeal for the truth they were really lying against the truth, and ruining the cause which they professed to serve. Of how many a controversialist would that be true; and not only of those who have entered the lists against heresy and infidelity, but of those who are preaching a crusade against vice! "The whole Christianity of many a devotee consists only, we may say, in a bitter contempt for the sins of sinners, in a proud and loveless contention with what it calls the wicked world" (Stier).

"This wisdom is not a wisdom that cometh down from above, but is earthly, sensual, devilish." The wisdom which is exhibited in such a thoroughly unchristian disposition is of no heavenly origin. It may be a proof of intellectual advantages of some kind, but it is not such as those who lack it need pray for (i. 5), nor such as God bestows liberally on all who ask in faith. And then, having stated what it is not, St. James tells in three words, which form a climax, what the wisdom on which they plume themselves, in its nature, and sphere, and origin, really is. *It belongs to this world,* and has no connexion with heavenly things. *Its activity is in the lower part of man's nature,* his passions and his human intelligence, but it never touches his spirit. And in its origin and manner of working *it is demoniacal.* Not the gentleness of God's Holy Spirit, but the fierce recklessness of Satan's emissaries, inspires it. Just as there is a faith which a man may share with demons (ii. 19), and a tongue which is set on fire by hell (iii. 6), so there is a wisdom which is demoniacal in its source and in its activity.

The second of the three terms of condemnation used by St. James (ψυχικός) cannot be adequately rendered in English, for "psychic" or "psychical" would convey either no meaning or a wrong one. It does not occur in the Septuagint, but is found six times in the New Testament—four times in the First Epistle to the Corinthians (ii. 14; xv. 44, 46), where most English versions have "natural;" once in Jude (19), where Tyndale, Cranmer, and the Genevan have "fleshly," the Rhemish, the Authorized, and the Revised "sensual;" and once here, where Genevan, Rhemish, Authorized, and Revised all give "sensual," the last placing "natural or animal" in the margin.[71] When man's nature is divided into body and soul, or flesh and spirit, every one understands that the body or flesh indicates the lower and material part, the soul or spirit the higher and immaterial part. But when a threefold division is made, into body, soul, and spirit, we are apt to allow the more simple and more familiar division to disturb our ideas. "Soul" is allowed to keep its old meaning, and to be understood as much more allied with "spirit" than with "body" or "flesh." This causes serious misunderstanding. When the soul is distinguished, not only from the flesh, but from the spirit, it represents a part of our nature which is much more closely connected with the former than with the latter. The "natural" or "sensual" man, though higher than the carnal man, who is the slave of his animal passions, is far below the spiritual man, who is ruled by the highest portion of his nature, which is under the guidance of the Holy Spirit. The natural man does not soar above the things of this world. His inspirations are not heavenly. "Of the earth he is, and of the earth he speaketh." The wisdom from above is heavenly, spiritual, Divine; the wisdom from below is earthly, sensual, devilish.

Does this seem to be an exaggeration? St. James is ready to justify his strong language. "For where jealousy and faction are, there is confusion and every vile deed." And who are the authors of confusion and vile deeds? Are they to be found in heaven, or in hell? Is confusion, or order, the mark of God's work? If one wished to sum up succinctly the manner in which the activity of demons specially exhibits itself, could one do so better than by saying "confusion and every vile deed"? "God is not a God of confusion, but of peace," says St. Paul, using the very word that we have here (1 Cor. xiv. 33); and every one heartily assents to the doctrine. The reason and conscience of every man tell him that disorder cannot in origin be Divine; it is part of that ruin which Satanic influences have been allowed to make in a universe which was created "very good." Jealousy and faction mean anarchy; and anarchy means a moral chaos in which every vile deed finds an opportunity. We know, therefore, what to think of the superior wisdom which is claimed by those in whose hearts jealousy and faction reign supreme. It may have a right to the name of wisdom, just as a correct belief about the nature of God may have a right to the name of faith, even when it remains barren, and therefore powerless to save. But an inspiration which prompts men to envy and intrigue, because, when many are rushing to occupy the post of teacher, others find a hearing more readily than themselves, is the inspiration of Cain and of Korah, rather than of Moses or of Daniel. The professed desire to offer service to God is really only a craving to obtain advancement for self. Self-seeking of this kind is always ruinous. It both betrays and aggravates the rottenness that lurks within. It was immediately after there had been a contention among the Apostles, "which of them was accounted to be greatest" (Luke xxii. 24), that they "all forsook Him and fled."

Note.—A portion of Dr. Newman's description of a gentleman will serve to illustrate what has been said above. It occurs in his *Discourses addressed to the Catholics of Dublin.* "It is almost a definition of a gentleman to say that he is one who *never inflicts pain.* He is mainly occupied in merely removing the obstacles which hinder the free and unembarrassed action of those about him, and he concurs with their movements rather than takes the initiative himself. He carefully avoids whatever may cause a jar or a jolt in the minds of those with whom he is cast—all clashing of opinion, or collision of feeling, all restraint, or suspicion, or gloom, or resentment; his great concern being to make every one at their ease and at home. He has his eyes on all his company; he is tender towards the bashful, gentle towards the distant, and merciful towards the absurd. He guards against unseasonable allusions, or topics which may irritate. He has no ears for slander or gossip, is scrupulous in imputing motives to those who interfere with him, and interprets everything for the best."

[69] Comp. also Deut. i. 13, and iv. 6, where we have the same combination.

[70] That "conversation" should also have been used as a rendering of πολίτευμα (Phil. iii. 20; comp. i. 27) and τρόπος (Heb. xiii. 5) is very unfortunate.

[71] Purvey has "beastly" in all six places, which is a translation of the *animalis* of the Vulgate: "earthly, beastly, fiendly" is his triplet. See p. 453.

CHAPTER XVII
THE WISDOM THAT IS FROM ABOVE

"But the wisdom that is from above is first pure, then peaceable, gentle, easy to be entreated, full of mercy and good fruits, without variance, without hypocrisy. And the fruit of righteousness is sown in peace for them that make peace." —St. James iii. 17, 18.

AT the beginning of his Epistle St. James exhorts those of his readers who feel their lack of wisdom to pray for it. It is one of those good and perfect gifts from above, which come down from the Father of lights, who "giveth to all liberally, and upbraideth not" (i. 5, 17). He now, after having sketched its opposite, states, in a few clear, pregnant words, what the characteristics of this heavenly gift of wisdom are. In both passages he probably had in his mind, and wished to suggest to the minds of his readers, well-known utterances on the same subject in the Books of Proverbs, Ecclesiasticus, and Wisdom.

"My son, if thou cry after discernment, and lift up thy voice for understanding; if thou seek her as silver, and search for her as for hid treasures; then shalt thou understand the fear of the Lord, and find the knowledge of God. For the Lord giveth wisdom; out of His mouth cometh knowledge and understanding" (Prov. ii. 3-6).

Again, the magnificent "Praise of Wisdom" in the twenty-fourth chapter of Ecclesiasticus, in which Wisdom is made to tell her own glories, opens thus: "I came forth from the mouth of the Most High, and covered the earth like a cloud;" and it continues, "Then the Creator of all things gave me a commandment, and He that created me caused my tabernacle to rest, and said, Let thy dwelling be in Jacob, and thine inheritance in Israel. Before time was, from the beginning, He created me, and until times cease I shall in nowise fail" (vv. 3, 8, 9).

And in the similar passage in the Book of Wisdom, in which the praise of Wisdom is put into the mouth of Solomon, he says, "Wisdom, which is the worker of all things, taught me.... She is the breath of the power of God, and a pure emanation from the glory of the Almighty: therefore doth no defiled thing fall into her. For she is the effulgence ($\dot{\alpha}\pi\alpha\dot{\nu}\gamma\alpha\sigma\mu\alpha$: Heb. i. 3) of the everlasting light, the unspotted mirror of the power of God, and the image of His goodness. And being one, she can do all things; and remaining in herself, she maketh all things new; and in all generations entering into holy souls, she maketh them friends of God, and prophets. For God loveth nothing but him that dwelleth with wisdom" (vii. 22, 25-28).

Three thoughts are conspicuous in these passages. Wisdom originates with God. It is consequently pure and glorious. God bestows it upon His people. These thoughts reappear in St. James, and to them he adds another, which scarcely appears in the earlier writers. Wisdom is "peaceable, gentle, easy to be entreated, full of mercy, and good fruits." In Proverbs we do indeed read that "all her paths are peace" (iii. 17); but the thought is not followed up. It does not seem to occur to the son of Sirach; and not one of the twenty-one epithets which the writer of Wisdom piles up in praise of this heavenly gift (vii. 22, 23) touches upon its peaceable and placable nature. It was left to the Gospel to teach, both by the example of Christ and by the words of His Apostles, how inevitably the Divine wisdom produces, in those who possess it, gentleness, self-repression, and peace.

"But the wisdom that is from above is first pure, then peaceable, gentle, easy to be entreated." The "first" and the "then" may be seriously misunderstood. St. James does *not* mean that the heavenly wisdom cannot be peaceable and gentle until all its surroundings have been made pure from everything that would oppose or contradict it; in other words, that the wise and understanding Christian will first free himself from the society of all whom he believes to be in error, and then, but not till then, will he be peaceable and gentle. That is, so long as folly and falsehood remain, they must be denounced, and made either to recant or to retire; for only when they have disappeared will wisdom show itself easy to be entreated. Purity, i.e. freedom from all that would dim the brightness of truth, must precede peace, and there can be no peace until it is obtained.

This interpretation contradicts the context, and makes St. James teach the opposite of what he says very plainly in the sentences which precede, and in those which follow, the words which we are considering. It tries to enlist him on the side of partisanship and persecution, at the very moment when he is pleading most earnestly against them. He is stating a logical, and not a chronological order, when he declares that true wisdom is "first pure, then peaceable." In its inmost being it is pure; among its very various external manifestations are the six or seven beneficent qualities which follow the "then." If there were no one to be gentle to, no one coming to entreat, no one needing mercy, the wisdom from above would still be pure; therefore this quality comes first.

When the author of the Book of Wisdom says that wisdom is "a pure emanation from the glory of God: therefore can no defiled thing fall into her" (vii. 25), he is thinking of a pure stream, into which no foul ditch is able to empty its polluting contents, or of a pure ray of light, which does not admit of mixture with anything that would colour or darken it. He does not use the word for pure which we have here (ἁγνός), but one which signifies "unmixed," and hence "unsullied" (εἰλικρινής), and which occurs Phil. i. 10 and 2 Pet. iii. 1. The word used here by St. James is akin to "holy" (ἅγιος), and primarily signifies what is associated with religious awe (ἄγος), and hence "hallowed," especially by sacrifice. From this it became narrowed in meaning to what is free from the pollution of unchastity or bloodshed. As a Biblical word it sometimes has this narrow meaning; but generally it implies freedom from all stain of sin, and therefore is not far removed in meaning from "holy." But it is worth noting that whereas Christ and good men are spoken of as both pure and holy, yet God is called holy, but never pure. Divine holiness cannot be assailed by any polluting influence. Human holiness, even that of Christ, can be so assailed, and in resisting the assault it remains "pure."

In the passage before us "pure" must certainly not be limited to mean simply "chaste." The word "sensual," applied to the wisdom from below, does not mean unchaste, but living wholly in the world of sense; and the purity of the heavenly wisdom does not consist merely in victory over temptations of the flesh, but in freedom from worldly and low motives. Its aim is that truth should become known and prevail, and it condescends to no ignoble arts in prosecuting this aim. Contradiction does not ruffle it, and hostility does not provoke it to retaliate, because its motives are thoroughly disinterested and pure. Thus, its peaceable and placable qualities flow out of its purity. It is *first* pure, *then* peaceable." It is because the man who is inspired with it has no ulterior selfish ends to serve that he is gentle, sympathetic, and considerate towards those who oppose him. He strives, not for victory over his opponents, but for truth both for himself and for them; and he knows what it costs to arrive at truth. We have a noble illustration of this temper in some of the opening passages of St. Augustine's treatise against the so-called *Fundamental Letter* of Manichæus. He begins thus:—

"My prayer to the one true God Almighty, of whom, and through whom, and in whom are all things, has been and is, that in refuting and disproving the heresy of you Manichæans, to which you adhere perchance more through thoughtlessness than evil intent, He would give me a mind composed and tranquil, and aiming rather at your amendment than your discomfiture.... It has been our business, therefore, to prefer and choose the better part, that we might have an opportunity for your amendment, not in contention, and strife, and persecutions, but in gentle consolation, affectionate exhortation, and quiet discussion; as it is written, The Lord's servant must not strive, but be gentle towards all, teachable, forbearing, in meekness correcting them that oppose themselves....

"Let those rage against you who know not with what toil truth is found, and how difficult it is to avoid errors.... Let those rage against you who know not with how great difficulty the eye of the inner man is made whole, so that it can behold its Sun.... Let those rage against you who know not with what sighs and groans it is made possible, in however small a degree, to comprehend God. Finally, let those rage against you who have never been deceived by such an error as that whereby they see you deceived....

"Let neither of us say that he has already found the truth. Let us seek it as if it were unknown to us both. For it can be sought for with zeal and unanimity only if there be no rash assumption that it has been found and is known."

And to the same effect, although in a different key, a critical writer of our own day has remarked that "by an intellect which is habitually filled with the wisdom which is from heaven, in all its length and breadth, 'objections' against religion are perceived at once to proceed from imperfect apprehension. Such an intellect cannot rage against those who give words to such objections. It sees that the objectors do but intimate the partial character of their own knowledge."[72]

It will be observed that while the writer just quoted speaks about the *intellect*, St. James speaks about the *heart*. The difference is not accidental, and it is significant of a difference in the point of view. The modern view of wisdom is that it is a matter which mainly consists in the strengthening and enrichment of the intellectual powers. Increase of capacity for acquiring and retaining knowledge; increase in the possession of knowledge: this is what is meant by growth in wisdom. And by knowledge is meant acquaintance with the nature and history of man, and with the nature and history of the universe. All this is the sphere of the intellect rather than of the heart. The purification and development of the moral powers, if not absolutely excluded from the scope of wisdom, is commonly left in the background and almost out of sight. What St. James says here is fully admitted: the highest wisdom keeps a man from the bitterness of party spirit. But why? Because his superior intelligence and information tell him that the opposition of those who dissent from him is the result of ignorance, which requires, not insult and abuse, but instruction. St. James does not dissent from this view, but he adds to it. There are further and higher reasons why the truly wise man does not rail at others, or try to browbeat and silence them. Because, while he abhors folly, he loves the fool, and would win him over from his foolish ways; because he desires not only to impart knowledge, but to increase virtue; and because he knows that strife means confusion, and that gentleness is the parent of peace. Christians are charged to be "wise as serpents, but *harmless as doves*."

The Scriptural view of wisdom does not contradict the modern one, but it is taken from the other side. In it the education of the moral and spiritual powers is the main thing, while intellectual advancement is in the background or out of sight. There is nothing in the teaching of Christ or his Apostles that is hostile to intellectual progress; but neither by His example, nor by the directions which His disciples received or delivered, do we find that culture was regarded as part of, or necessary to, or even a very desirable companion for, the Gospel. Neither Christ nor any one of His immediate followers came forward as a great promoter of intellectual pursuits. Why is this? It would perhaps be a sound and sufficient answer to say, that valuable as such work would have been, there was much more serious and important work to be done. To convert men from sin to righteousness was far more urgent than to improve their minds. But there is more to be said than this. That perverse generation had to "turn, and become as little children," before it could enter into the kingdom of heaven. To develop a man's intellectual powers is not always the best way to make him "humble himself as a little child." Increase of knowledge may make a Newton feel like a child picking up pebbles on the shore of truth, but it is apt to make "the natural man" less childlike. But for no one, whether catechumen, or convert, or mature Christian, can the cultivation of his intellect be as pressing a duty as the cultivation of his heart. "To speak with the tongues of men and of angels," and to "know all mysteries and all knowledge," is as nothing in comparison with love. And it is in some measure possible to see why this is so. Man's moral nature certainly suffered, and ruinously suffered, at the Fall. It is not so certain that his intellectual nature suffered also. If it did suffer, it suffered *through* the moral nature, because depravation of the heart depraved the brain. In neither case would there be any necessity for the Gospel to pay special attention to the regeneration of the intellect. If man's intellect was unscathed by his fall from innocence, it could continue its natural development, and go on from strength to strength towards perfection. If, however, the loss of innocence has entailed a loss of mental capacity, then the wound inflicted on the intellectual nature through the moral nature must be healed in the same way. First purify the heart and regenerate the will, and then the recovery of the intellect will follow in due course.[73] It is easy to reach the intellect through the heart, and this is what the wisdom that is from above aims at doing. If we begin with the intellect, we shall very likely end there; and in that case the man is not raised from his degradation, but equipped with additional powers of mischief. "Into a soul that deviseth evil, wisdom will not enter, nor yet dwell in a body that is sunk in sin" (Wisdom i. 4).

"Full of mercy and good fruits." The wisdom from above is not only peaceable, reasonable, and conciliatory, when under provocation or criticism, it is also eager to take the initiative in doing all the good in its power to those whom it can reach or influence. Thus it goes hand in hand with that pure and undefiled religion which visits "the fatherless and widows in their affliction" (i. 27). Just as St. James has no sympathy with a faith which does not clothe the naked and feed the hungry, and offer of its best to God (ii. 15, 16, 21), nor with a tongue which blesses God and curses men (ii. 9), so he has no belief in the heavenly character of a wisdom which holds itself aloof in calm superiority to all cavil and complaint, with a condescending air of passionless impartiality. The intellectual miser, who gloats over the treasures of his own accumulated knowledge, and smiles with lofty indifference upon the criticisms and squabbles of the imperfectly instructed, has no share in the wisdom that is from above. He is peaceful and moderate, not out of love and sympathy, but because his time is too precious to be wasted in barren controversy, and because he is too proud to place himself on a level with those who would dispute with him. No selfish arrogance of this kind has any place in the character of the truly wise. His wisdom not only enlightens his intellect, but warms his heart and strengthens his will. He believes that "the wise man alone is king," and that "the wise man alone is happy," yet not because he has the crown of knowledge and abundance of intellectual enjoyment, but because he "fulfils the royal law, Thou shalt love thy neighbour as thyself" (ii. 8), and because happiness is to be found in promoting the happiness of others.

"Without variance, without hypocrisy." These are the last two of the goodly qualities which St. James gives as marks of the heavenly wisdom. Similarity in sound, which cannot well be preserved in English, has evidently had something to do with their selection (ἀδιάκριτος, ἀνυπόκριτος). The first of the two has perplexed translators, and the English versions give us considerable choice: "without variance," "without wrangling," "without partiality," "without doubtfulness," "without judging." Purvey has for the two epithets "deeming without feigning," following the Sixtine edition of the Vulgate, which has *judicans sine simulatione*, instead of *non judicans, sine simulatione*. The word occurs nowhere else either in the Old or in the New Testament; but it is cognate with a word which St. James uses twice at the beginning of this Epistle (διακρινόμενος: i. 6), and which is there rendered "doubting" or "wavering." Of the various possible meanings of the word before us we may therefore prefer "without doubtfulness." The wisdom from above is unwavering, steadfast, single-minded. Thus Ignatius charges the Magnesians (xv.) to "possess an unventuring spirit" (ἀδιάκριτον πνεῦμα), and tells the Trallians (i.) that he has "learned that they have a mind unblameable and unwavering in patience" (ἀδιάκριτον ἐν ὑπομονῇ). And Clement of Alexandria (*Pæd*. II. iii., p. 190) speaks of "unwavering faith" (ἀδιακρίτῳ πίστει), and a few lines farther on he reminds his readers, in words that suit our present subject, that "wisdom is not bought with earthly coin, nor is sold in the market, but in heaven." If he had said that wisdom is not sold in the market, but *given* from heaven, he would have made the contrast both more pointed and more true.

"The fruit of righteousness is sown in peace for them that make peace." The Greek may mean either "*for* them that make peace," or "*by* them that make peace;" and we need not attempt to decide. In either case it is the peacemakers who sow the seed whose fruit is righteousness, and the peacemakers who reap this fruit. The whole process begins, progresses, and ends in peace.

It is evident that the heavenly wisdom is pre-eminently a *practical* wisdom. It is not purely or mainly intellectual; it is not speculative; it is not lost in contemplation. Its object is to increase holiness rather than knowledge, and happiness rather than information. Its atmosphere is not controversy and debate, but gentleness and peace. It is full, not of sublime theories or daring hypotheses, but of mercy and good fruits. It can be confident without wrangling, and reserved without hypocrisy. It is the twin sister of that heavenly love which "envieth not, vaunteth not itself, seeketh not its own, is not provoked, taketh no account of evil."

[72] Mark Pattison, Essays: Life of Bishop Warburton, vol. ii., pp. 163, 164 (Oxford: 1889).

[73] See Jellett's Thoughts on the Christian Life, p. 49 (Dublin: 1884).

CHAPTER XVIII
ST. JAMES AND PLATO ON LUSTS AS THE CAUSES OF STRIFE; THEIR EFFECT ON PRAYER

"Whence come wars, and whence come fightings among you? come they not hence, even of your pleasures which war in your members? Ye lust, and have not: ye kill and covet, and cannot obtain: ye fight and war; ye have not, because ye ask not. Ye ask, and receive not, because ye ask amiss, that ye may spend it in your pleasures." —St. James iv. 1-13.

THE change from the close of the third chapter to the beginning of the fourth is startling. St. James has just been sketching with much beauty the excellences of the heavenly wisdom, and especially its marked characteristic of always tending to produce an atmosphere of peace, in which the seed that produces the fruit of righteousness will grow and flourish. Gentleness, good-will, mercy, righteousness, peace—these form the main features of his sketch. And then he abruptly turns upon his readers with the question, "Whence come wars, and whence come sightings among you?"

The sudden transition from the subject of peace to the opposite is deliberate. Its object is to startle and awaken the consciences of those who are addressed. The wisdom from below produces bitter jealousy and faction; the wisdom from above produces gentleness and peace. Then how is to be explained the origin of the wars and fightings which prevail among the twelve tribes of the Dispersion? That ought to set them thinking. These things must be traced to causes which are earthly or demoniacal rather than heavenly; and if so, those who are guilty of them, instead of contending for the office of teaching others, ought to be seriously considering how to correct themselves. Here, again, there is the strangest contradiction between their professions and their practice. Clement of Rome seems to have this passage in his mind when he writes (c. A.D. 97) to the Church of Corinth, "Wherefore are there strifes and wraths, and factions and divisions, and war among you?" (xlvi.).

"Wars" (πόλομοι) and "fightings" (μάχαι) are not to be understood literally. When the text is applied to international warfare between Christian states in modern times, or to any case of civil war, it may be so interpreted without doing violence to its spirit; but that is not the original meaning of the words. There was no civil war among the Jews at this time, still less among the Jewish Christians. St. James is referring to private quarrels and law-suits, social rivalries and factions, and religious controversies. The subject-matter of these disputes and contentions is not indicated, because that is not what is denounced. It is not for having differences about this or that, whether rights of property, or posts of honour, or ecclesiastical questions, that St. James rebukes them, but for the rancorous, greedy, and worldly spirit in which their disputes are conducted. Evidently the lust of possession is among the things which produce the contentions. Jewish appetite for wealth is at work among them.

It was stated in a former chapter that, there are places in this Epistle in which St. James seems to go beyond the precise circle of readers addressed in the opening words, and to glance at the whole Jewish nation, whether outside Palestine or not, and whether Christian or not. These more comprehensive addresses are more frequent in the second half of the Epistle than in the first, and one is inclined to believe that the passage before us is one of them. In that case we may believe that the bitter contentions which divided Pharisees, Sadducees, Herodians, Essenes, Zealots, and Samaritans from one another are included in the wars and fightings, as well as the quarrels which disgraced Christian Jews. In any case we see that the Jews who had entered the Christian Church had brought with them that contentious spirit which was one of their national characteristics. Just as St. Paul has to contend with Greek love of faction in his converts at Corinth, so St. James has to contend with a similar Jewish failing among the converts from Judaism. And it would seem as if he hoped through these converts to reach many of those who were not yet converted. What he wrote to Christian synagogues would possibly be heard of and noted in synagogues which were not Christian. At any rate this Epistle contains ample evidence that the grievous scandals which amaze us in the early history of the Apostolic Churches of Corinth, Galatia, and Ephesus were not peculiar to converts from heathenism: among the Christians of the circumcision, who had had the advantage of life-long knowledge of God and of His law, there were evils as serious, and sometimes very similar in kind. The notion that the Church of the Apostolic age was in a condition of ideal perfection is a beautiful but baseless dream.[74]

"Whence wars, and whence fightings among you? come they not hence, even of your pleasures which war in your members?" By a common transposition, St. James, in answering his own question, puts the pleasures which excite and gratify the lusts instead of the lusts themselves, in much the same way as we use "drink" for intemperance, and "gold" for avarice. These lusts for pleasures have their quarters or camp in the members of the body, *i.e.* in the sensual part of man's nature. But they are there, not to rest, but to make war, to go after, and seize, and take for a prey that which has roused them from their quietude and set them in motion. There the picture, as drawn by St. James, ends. St. Paul carries it a stage farther, and speaks of the "different law in my members, warring *against the law of my mind*" (Rom. vii. 23). St. Peter does the same, when he beseeches his readers, "as sojourners and pilgrims, to abstain from fleshly lusts, which war *against the soul*" (1 Peter ii. 11); and some commentators would supply either "against the mind" or "against the soul" here. But there is no need to supply anything, and if one did supply anything the "wars and sightings *among you*" would rather lead us to understand that the lusts in each one's members make war against everything which interferes with their gratification, and such would be the possessions and desires of other people. This completion of St. James's picture agrees well also with what follows: "Ye lust, and have not: ye kill and covet, and cannot obtain." But it is best to leave the metaphor just where he leaves it, without adding anything. And the fact that he does not add "against the mind" or "against the soul" is some slight indication that he had not seen either the passage in Romans or in the Epistle of St. Peter.

In the *Phædo* of Plato (66, 67) there is a beautiful passage, which presents some striking coincidences with the words of St. James. "Wars, and factions, and sightings have no other source than the body and its lusts. For it is for the getting of wealth that all our wars arise, and we are compelled to get wealth because of our body, to whose service we are slaves; and in consequence we have no leisure for philosophy, because of all these things. And the worst of all is that if we get any leisure from it, and turn to some question, in the midst of our inquiries the body is everywhere coming in, introducing turmoil and confusion, and bewildering us, so that by it we are prevented from seeing the truth. But indeed it has been proved to us that if we are ever to have pure knowledge of anything we must get rid of the body, and with the soul by itself must behold things by themselves. *Then*, it would seem, we shall obtain the wisdom which we desire, and of which we say that we are lovers; when we are dead, as the argument shows, but in this life not. For if it be impossible while we are in the body to have pure knowledge of anything, then of two things one—either knowledge is not to be obtained at all, or after we are dead; for then the soul will be by itself, apart from the body, but before that not. And in this life, it would seem, we shall make the nearest approach to knowledge if we have no communication or fellowship whatever with the body, beyond what necessity compels, and are not filled with its nature, but remain pure from its taint, until God Himself shall set us free. And in this way shall we be pure, being delivered from the foolishness of the body, and shall be with other like souls, and shall know of ourselves all that is clear and cloudless, and that is perhaps all one with the truth."

Plato and St. James are entirely agreed in holding that wars and fightings are caused by the lusts that have their seat in the body, and that this condition of fightings without, and lusts within, is quite incompatible with the possession of heavenly wisdom. But there the agreement between them ceases. The conclusion which Plato arrives at is that the philosopher must, so far as is possible, neglect and excommunicate his body, as an intolerable source of corruption, yearning for the time when death shall set him free from the burden of waiting upon this obstacle between his soul and the truth. Plato has no idea that the body may be sanctified here and glorified hereafter; he regards it simply as a necessary evil, which may be minimized by watchfulness, but which can in no way be turned into a blessing. The blessing will come when the body is annihilated by death. St. James, on the contrary, exhorts us to cut ourselves off, not from the body, but from friendship with the world. If we resist the evil one, who tempts us through our ferocious lusts, he will flee from us. God will give us the grace we need, if we pray for that rather than for pleasures. He will draw nigh to us if we draw nigh to Him; and if we purify our hearts He will make His Spirit to dwell in them. Even in this life the wisdom that is from above is attainable, and where that has found a home factions and fightings cease. When the passions cease to war, those who have hitherto been swayed by their passions will cease to war also. But those whom St. James addresses are as yet very far from this blessed condition.

"Ye lust, and have not: ye kill and covet, and cannot obtain: ye fight and war." In short, sharp, telling sentences he puts forth the items of his indictment; but it is not easy to punctuate them satisfactorily, nor to decide whether "ye kill" is to be understood literally or not. In none of the English versions does the punctuation seem to bring out a logical sequence of clauses. The following arrangement is suggested for consideration: "Ye lust, and have not; ye kill. And ye covet, and cannot obtain; ye fight and war." In this way we obtain two sentences of similar meaning, which exactly balance one another. "Ye lust, and have not," corresponds with, "Ye covet, and cannot obtain," and "ye kill" with "ye fight and war;" and in each sentence the last clause is the consequence of what precedes. "Ye lust, and have not; *therefore* ye kill." "Ye covet, and cannot obtain; *therefore* ye fight and war." This grouping of the clauses yields good sense, and does no violence to the Greek.

"Ye lust, and have not; therefore ye kill." Is "kill" to be understood literally? That murder, prompted by avarice and passion, was common among the Christian Jews of the Dispersion, is quite incredible. That monstrous scandals occurred in the Apostolic age, especially among Gentile converts, who supposed that the freedom of the Gospel meant lax morality, is unquestionable; but that these scandals ever took the form of indifference to human life we have no evidence. And it is specially improbable that murder would be frequent among those who, before they became Christians, had been obedient to the Mosaic Law. St. James may have a single case in his mind, like that of the incestuous marriage at Corinth; but in that case he would probably have expressed himself differently. Or again, as was suggested above, he may in this section be addressing the whole Jewish race, and not merely those who had become converts to Christianity; and in that case he may be referring to the brigandage and assassination which a combination of causes, social, political, and religious, had rendered common among the Jews, especially in Palestine, at this time. Of this evil we have plenty of evidence both in the New Testament and in Josephus. Barabbas and the two robbers who were crucified with Christ are instances in the Gospels. And with them we may put the parable of the man "who fell among robbers," and was left half-dead between Jerusalem and Jericho; for no doubt the parable, like all Christ's parables, is founded on fact, and is no mere imaginary picture. In the Acts we have Theudas with his four hundred followers (B.C. 4), Judas of Galilee (A.D. 6), and the Egyptian with his four thousand "Assassins," or *Sicarii* (A.D. 58); to whom we may add the forty who conspired to assassinate St. Paul (v. 36, 37; xxi. 38; xxiii. 12-21). And Josephus tells us of another Theudas, who was captured and put to death with many of his followers by the Roman Procurator Cuspius Fadus (c. A.D. 45); and he also states that about fifty years earlier, under Varus, there were endless disorders in Judæa, sedition and robbery being almost chronic. The brigands inflicted a certain amount of damage on the Romans, but the murders which they committed were on their fellow-countrymen the Jews (*Ant.* XVII. x. 4, 8; XX. v. i).[75]

In either of these ways, therefore, the literal interpretation of a "kill" makes good sense; and we are not justified in saying, with Calvin, that "kill in no way suits the context." Calvin, with Erasmus, Beza, Hornejus, and others, adopts the violent expedient of correcting the Greek from "kill" (φονεύετε) to "envy" (φθονεῖτε), a reading for which not a single MS., version, or Father can be quoted. It is accepted, however, by Tyndale and Cranmer and in the Genevan Bible, all of which have, "Ye *envy* and have indignation, and cannot obtain." Wiclif and the Rhemish of course hold to the *occiditis* of the Vulgate, the one with "slay," and the other with "kill."

But although the literal interpretation yields good sense, it is perhaps not the best interpretation. It was pointed out above that "ye kill" balances "ye fight and war," and that "wars and fightings" evidently are *not* to be understood literally, as the context shows. If then, "ye fight and war" means "ye quarrel, and dispute, and intrigue, and go to law with one another," ought not "ye kill" to be explained in a similar way? Christ had said, "Ye have heard that it was said by them of old time, Thou shalt not kill; and whosoever shall kill shall be in danger of the judgment: but I say unto you, That every one who is angry with his brother shall be in danger of the judgment" (Matt. v. 21, 22). And St. John tells us that "every one who hateth his brother is a murderer" (1 John iii. 15). "Every one who hateth" (πᾶς ὁ μισῶν) is an uncompromising expression, and it covers all that St. James says here. Just as the cherished lustful thought is adultery in the heart (Matt. v. 28), so cherished hatred is murder in the heart.

But there is an explanation, half literal and half metaphorical, which is well worth considering. It has been pointed out how frequently St. James seems to have portions of the Book of Ecclesiasticus in his mind. We read there that "the bread of the needy is the life of the poor: he that defraudeth him thereof is a man of blood. He that taketh away his neighbour's living slayeth him (φονεύων); and he that defraudeth the labourer of his hire is a blood-shedder" (xxxiv. 21, 22). If St. James was familiar with these words, and still more if he could count on his readers also being familiar with them, might he not mean, "Ye lust, and have not; and then, to gratify your desire, you deprive the poor of his living"? Even Deut. xxiv. 6 might suffice to give rise to such a strong method of expression: "No man shall take the mill or the upper millstone to pledge: for he taketh a man's life to pledge." Throughout this section the language used is strong, as if the writer felt very strongly about the evils which he condemns.

While "ye lust, and have not, and thereupon take a man's livelihood from him," would refer specially to *possessions*, "Ye covet (or envy) and cannot obtain, and thereupon fight and war," might refer specially to *honours, posts,* and *party advantages.* The word rendered "covet" (ζηλοῦτε) is that which describes the thing which love never does: "Love *envieth* not" (1 Cor. xiii. 4). When St. James was speaking of the wisdom from below (iii. 14-16) the kind of quarrels which he had chiefly in view were party controversies, as was natural after treating just before of sins of the tongue. Here the wars and fightings are not so much about matters of controversy as those things which minister to a man's "pleasures," his avarice, his sensuality, and his ambition.

How is it that they have not all that they want? How is that there is any need to despoil others, or to contend fiercely with them for possession? "Ye have not, because ye ask not. Ye ask, and receive not, because ye ask amiss." *That* is the secret of these gnawing wants and lawless cravings. They do not try to supply their needs in a way that would cause loss to no one, viz. by prayer to God; they prefer to employ violence and craft against one another. Or if they do pray for the supply of their earthly needs, they obtain nothing, because they pray with evil intent. To pray without the spirit of prayer is to court failure. That God's will may be done, and His Name glorified, is the proper end of all prayer. To pray simply that our wishes may be satisfied is not a prayer to which fulfilment has been promised; still less can this be the case when our wishes are for the glorification of our lusts. Prayer for advance in holiness we may be sure is in accordance with God's will. About prayer for earthly advantages we cannot be sure; but we may pray for things so far as they are to His glory and for our own spiritual welfare. Prayer for earthly goods, which are to be used as instruments, not of His pleasure, but of ours, we may be sure is not in accordance with His will. To such a prayer we need expect no answer, or an answer which at the same time is a judgment; for the fulfilment of an unrighteous prayer is sometimes its most fitting punishment.

St. James is not blaming his readers for asking God to give them worldly prosperity. About the lawfulness of praying for temporal blessings, whether for ourselves or for others, there is no question. St. John prays that Gaius "in all things may prosper and be in health, even as his soul prospereth" (3 John 2), and St. James plainly implies that when one has temporal needs one *ought* to bring them before God in prayer, only with a right purpose and in a right spirit. In the next chapter he specially recommends prayer for the recovery of the sick. The asking amiss consists not in asking for temporal things, but in seeking them for a wrong purpose, viz. that they may be squandered in a life of self-indulgence. The right purpose is to enable us to serve God better. Temporal necessities are often a hindrance to good service, and then it is right to ask God to relieve them. But in all such things the rule laid down by Christ is the safe one, "Seek ye *first* the kingdom of God, and His righteousness; and all these things shall be added unto you." A life consecrated to the service of God is the best prayer for temporal blessings. Prayer that is offered in a grasping spirit is like that of the bandit for the success of his raids.

[74] See the volume on the *Pastoral Epistles* in this series, pp. 264, 265.

[75] If φονεύετε is taken with what follows, it is best to render φονεύετε καὶ ζηλοῦτε "Ye act as Assassins and Zealots," referring both words to the fanatics who a little later killed James himself, and were the hasteners of the downfall of Jerusalem.

CHAPTER XIX
THE SEDUCTIONS OF THE WORLD, AND
THE JEALOUSY OF THE DIVINE LOVE

"Ye adulteresses, know ye not that the friendship of the world is enmity with God? Whosoever, therefore, would be a friend of the world maketh himself an enemy of God. Or think ye that the Scripture speaketh in vain? Doth the Spirit which He made to dwell in us long unto envying? But he giveth more grace. Wherefore the Scripture saith, God resisteth the proud, but giveth grace to the humble." —St. James iv. 4-6.

THE Revisers are certainly right in rejecting, without even mention in the margin, the reading, "Ye *adulterers and* adulteresses." The difficulty of the revised reading pleads strongly in its favour, and the evidence of MSS. and versions is absolutely decisive. The interpolation of the masculine was doubtless made by those who supposed that the term of reproach was to be understood literally, and who thought it inexplicable that St. James should confine his rebuke to female offenders.

But the context shows that the term is not to be understood literally. It is not a special kind of sensuality, but greed and worldliness generally, that the writer is condemning. It is one of the characteristics of the letter that being addressed to Jewish, and not Gentile converts, and occasionally to Jews whether Christians or not, it says very little about the sins of the flesh; and "adulteresses" here is no exception. The word is used in its common Old Testament sense of spiritual adultery—unfaithfulness to Jehovah regarded as the Husband of His people. "They that are far from Thee shall perish: Thou hast destroyed all them that go a-whoring from Thee" (Ps. lxxiii. 27). "Thus will I make thy lewdness to cease from thee, and thy whoredom brought from the land of Egypt" (Ezek. xxiii. 27). "Plead with your mother, plead; for she is not My wife, neither am I her Husband" (Hos. ii. 2). The fifty-seventh chapter of Isaiah contains a terrible working out of this simile; and indeed the Old Testament is full of it. Our Lord is probably reproducing it when he speaks of the Jews of His own time as an "adulterous and sinful generation" (Matt. xii. 39; xvi. 4; Mark viii. 38). And we find it again in the Apocalypse (ii. 22).

But why does St. James use the feminine? Had he accused his readers of adultery, or called them an adulterous generation, the meaning would have been clear enough. What is the exact meaning of "Ye adulteresses"?

St. James wishes to bring home to those whom he is addressing that not only the Christian Church as a whole, or the chosen people as a whole, is espoused to God, but that each individual soul stands to Him in the relation of a wife to her husband. It is not merely the case that they belong to a generation which in the main has been guilty of unfaithfulness, and that in this guilt they share; but each of them, taken one by one, has in his or her own person committed this sin against the Divine Spouse. The sex of the person does not affect the relationship: any soul that has been wedded to God, and has then transferred its affection and allegiance to other beings, is an unfaithful wife. St. James, with characteristic simplicity, directness, and force, indicates this fact by the stern address, "Ye adulteresses."

"Know ye not that the friendship of the world is enmity with God?" He implies that they might know this, and that they can scarcely help doing so; it is so obvious that to love His opponent is to be unfaithful and hostile to Him. At the beginning of the section St. James had asked whence came the miserable condition in which his readers were found; and he replied that it came from their own desires, which they tried to gratify by intrigue and violence, instead of resorting to prayer; or else from the carnal aims by which they turned their prayers into sin. Here he puts the same fact in a somewhat different way. This vehement pursuit of their own pleasures, in word, and deed, and even in prayer—what is it but a desertion of God for Mammon, a sacrifice of the love of God to the friendship (such as it is) of the world? It is a base yielding to seductions which ought to have no attractiveness, for they involve the unfaithfulness of a wife and the treason of a subject. There can be no true and loyal affection for God while some other than God is loved, and not loved for His sake. If a woman "shall put away her husband, and marry another, she committeth adultery" (Mark xi. 12); and if a soul shall put away its God, and marry another, it committeth adultery. A wife who cultivates friendship with one who is trying to seduce her becomes the enemy of her husband; and every Christian and Jew ought to know "that the friendship of the world is enmity with God."

St. John tells us (and the words are probably not his, but Christ's) that "God loved the world" (John iii. 16). He also charges us *not* to love the world (1 John ii. 15). And here St. James tells us that to be friends with the world is to be the enemy of God. It is obvious that "the world" which God loves is not identical with "the world" which we are told not to love. "World" (κόσμος) is a term which has various meanings in Scripture, and we shall go seriously astray if we do not carefully distinguish them.

Sometimes it means the whole universe in its order and beauty; as when St. Paul says, "For the invisible things of Him since the creation of the world are clearly seen, being perceived through the things that are made" (Rom. i. 20). Sometimes it means this planet, the earth; as when the evil one showed to Jesus "all the kingdoms of the world, and the glory of them" (Matt. iv. 8). Again, it means the inhabitants of the earth; as when Christ is said to "take away the sin of the world" (John i. 2; 1 John iv. 14). Lastly, it means those who are alienated from God—unbelievers, faithless Jews and Christians, and especially the great heathen organization of Rome (John viii. 23; xii. 31). Thus a word which originally signified the natural order and beauty of creation comes to signify the unnatural disorder and hideousness of creatures who have rebelled against their Creator. The world which the Father loves is the whole race of mankind, His creatures and His children. The world which we are not to love is that which prevents us from loving Him in return, His rival and His enemy. It is from this world that the truly religious man keeps himself unspotted (i. 25). Sinful men, with their sinful lusts, keeping up a settled attitude of disloyalty and hostility to God, and handing this on as a living tradition, is what St. Paul, and St. James, and St. John mean by "the world."

This world has the devil for its ruler (John xiv. 30). It lies wholly in the power of the evil one (1 John v. 19). It cannot hate Christ's enemies, for the very reason that it hates Him (John vii. 7). And for the same reason it hates all those whom He has chosen out of its midst (xv. 18, 19). Just as there is a Spirit of God, which leads us into all the truth, so there is a "spirit of the world," which leads to just the opposite (1 Cor. ii. 12). This world, with its lusts, is passing away (1 John ii. 17), and its very sorrow worketh death (2 Cor. vii. 10). "The world is human nature, sacrificing the spiritual to the material, the future to the present, the unseen and the eternal to that which touches the senses and which perishes with time. The world is a mighty flood of thoughts, feelings, principles of action, conventional prejudices, dislikes, attachments, which have been gathering around human life for ages, impregnating it, impelling it, moulding it, degrading it. Of the millions of millions of human beings who have lived, nearly every one probably has contributed something, his own little addition, to the great tradition of materialized life which St. [James] calls the world. Every one, too, must have received something from it. According to his circumstances the same man acts upon the world, or in turn is acted on by it. And the world at different times wears different forms. Sometimes it is a solid compact mass, an organization of pronounced ungodliness. Sometimes it is a subtle, thin, hardly suspected influence, a power altogether airy and impalpable, which yet does most powerfully penetrate, inform, and shape human life."[76]

There is no sin in a passionate love of the ordered beauty and harmony of the universe, as exhibited either in this planet or in the countless bodies which people the immensity of space; no sin in devoting the energies of a lifetime to finding out all that can be known about the laws and conditions of nature in all its complex manifestations. Science is no forbidden ground to God's servants, for all truth is God's truth, and to learn it is a revelation of Himself. If only it be studied as His creature, it may be admired and loved without any disloyalty to Him.

Still less is there any sin in "the enthusiasm of humanity," in a passionate zeal for the amelioration of the whole human race. A consuming love for one's fellow-men is so far from involving enmity to God that it is impossible to have any genuine love of God without it. "He that loveth not his brother whom he hath seen cannot love God whom he hath not seen" (1 John iv. 20). The love of the world which St. James condemns is a passion which more than anything else renders a love of mankind impossible. Its temper is selfishness, and the principle of its action is the conviction that every human being is actuated by purely selfish motives. It has no belief in motives of which it has no experience either in itself or in those among whom it habitually moves. Next to a cultivation of the love of God, a cultivation of the love of man is the best remedy for the deadly paralysis of the heart which is the inevitable consequence of *choosing* to be a friend of the world.

This choice is a very important element in the matter. It is lost in the Authorized Version, but is rightly restored by the Revisers. "Whosoever, therefore, *would be* (βουλληθῇ εἶναι) a friend of the world *maketh himself* (καθίσταται) an enemy of God." It is useless for him to plead that he has no wish to be hostile to God. He has of his own free will adopted a condition of life which of necessity involves hostility to Him. And he has full opportunity of knowing this; for although the world may try to deceive him by confusing the issue, God does not. The world may assure him that there is no need of any choice: he has no need to abandon God; it is quite easy to serve God, and yet remain on excellent terms with the world. But God declares that the choice must be made, and that it is absolute and exclusive. "And now, Israel, what doth the Lord thy God require of thee, but to fear the Lord thy God, to walk in all His ways, and to love Him, and to serve the Lord thy God with *all* thy heart and with *all* thy soul, to keep the commandments of the Lord, and His statutes, which I command thee this day for thy good?" (Deut. x. 12, 13; comp. vi. 5 and xxx. 6).

The next two verses are a passage of known difficulty, the most difficult in this Epistle, and one of the most difficult in the whole of the New Testament. In the intensity of his detestation of the evil against which he is inveighing, St. James has used condensed expressions which can be understood in a variety of ways, and it is scarcely possible to decide which of the three or four possible meanings is the one intended. But the question has been obscured by the suggestion of explanations which are not tenable. The choice lies between those which are given in the margin of the Revised Version and the one before us in the text; for we may safely discard all those which depend upon the reading "*dwelleth* in us" (κατῴκησεν), and we must stand by the reading "*made to dwell* in us" (κατῴκισεν).

The questions which cannot be answered with certainty are these: 1. Are two Scriptures quoted, or only one? and if two are quoted, where is the first of them to be found? 2. Who is it that "longeth" or "lusteth?" is it God, or the Holy Spirit, or our own human spirit? 3. What is it that is longed for by God or the Spirit? Let us take these three questions in order.

1. The words which follow "Think ye that the Scripture speaketh in vain?" do not occur in the Old Testament, although the sense of them may be found piecemeal in a variety of passages. Therefore, either the words are not a quotation at all, or they are from some book no longer extant, or they are a condensation of several utterances in the Old Testament.[77] The first of these suppositions seems to be the best, but neither of the others can be set aside as improbable. We may paraphrase, therefore, the first part of the passage thus:—

"Ye unfaithful spouses of Jehovah! know ye not that to be friendly with the world is to be at enmity with Him? Or do ye think that what the Scripture says about faithlessness to God is idly spoken?" But as regards this first question we must be content to remain in great uncertainty.

2. Who is it that "longeth" or "lusteth" (ἐπιποθεῖ)? To decide whether "longeth" or "lusteth" is the right translation will help us to decide this second point, and it will also help us to decide whether the sentence is interrogative or not. Is this word of desiring used here in the good sense of longing or yearning, or in the bad sense of lusting? The word occurs frequently in the New Testament, and in every one of these passages it is used in a good sense (Rom. i. 11; 2 Cor. v. 2; ix. 14; Phil. i. 8; ii. 26; 1 Thess. iii. 10; 2 Tim. i. 4; 1 Peter ii. 2). Nor is this the whole case. Substantives and adjectives which are closely cognate with it are fairly common, and these are all used in a good sense (Rom. xv. 23; 2 Cor. vii. 7; vii. 11; Phil. iv. 1). We may therefore set aside the interpretations of the sentence which require the rendering "lusteth," whether the statement that man's spirit lusteth enviously, or the question, Doth the Divine Spirit in us lust enviously? The word here expresses the mighty and affectionate longing of the Divine love.

And it is the *Spirit* which God made to dwell in us which longeth over us with a jealous longing. If we make the sentence mean that *God* longeth, then we are compelled to take the Spirit which He made to dwell in us as that for which He longs; God has a jealous longing for His own Spirit implanted in us. But this does not yield very good sense; we decide, therefore, for the rendering, "Even unto jealousy doth the Spirit which He made to dwell in us yearn over us." "Even unto jealousy;" these words stand first, with great emphasis. No friendship with the world or any alien object can be tolerated.

3. The third question has been solved by the answer to the second. That which is yearned for by the Spirit implanted in us is ourselves. The meaning is not that God longs for man's spirit (the human spirit would hardly be spoken of as that which God "made to dwell in us"), or that He longs for the Holy Spirit in us (a meaning which would be very hard to explain), but that His Holy Spirit yearns for us with a jealous yearning. God is a jealous God, and the Divine love is a jealous love; it brooks no rival. And when His Spirit takes up its abode in us it cannot rest until it possesses us wholly, to the exclusion of all alien affections.

At one of the conferences between the Northern and the Southern States of America during the war of 1861-1866 the representatives of the Southern States stated what cession of territory they were prepared to make, provided that the independence of the portion that was not ceded to the Federal Government was secured. More and more attractive offers were made, the portions to be ceded being increased, and those to be retained in a state of independence being proportionately diminished. All the offers were met by a steadfast refusal. At last President Lincoln placed his hand on the map so as to cover all the Southern States, and in these emphatic words delivered his ultimatum: "Gentlemen, this Government *must have the whole.*" The constitution of the United States was at an end if any part, however small, was allowed to become independent of the rest. It was a vital principle, which did not admit of exceptions or degrees. It must be kept in its entirety, or it was not kept at all.

Just such is the claim which God, by the working of His Spirit, makes upon ourselves. He cannot share us with the world, however much we may offer to Him, and however little to His rival. If a rival is admitted at all, our relation to Him is violated and we have become unfaithful. His government *must have the whole.*

Do these terms seem to be harsh? They are not really so, for the more we surrender, the more He bestows. We give up the world, and that appears to us to be a great sacrifice. "But He giveth more grace." Even in this world He gives far more than we give up, and adds a crown of life in the world to come (i. 12). "Verily I say unto you, There is no man that hath left house, or brethren, or sisters, or mother, or father, or children, or lands, for My sake, and for the Gospel's sake, but he shall receive a hundredfold now in this time, houses, and brethren, and sisters, and mothers, and children, and lands, with persecutions; and in the world to come eternal life" (Mark x. 29, 30). "God resisteth the proud, but giveth grace to the humble." Those who persist in making friends with the world, in seeking its advantages, in adopting its standards, in accepting its praise, God resists. By choosing to throw in their lot with His enemy they have made themselves His enemies, and He cannot but withstand them. But to those who humbly submit their wills to His, who give up the world, with its gifts and its promises, and are willing to be despised by it in order to keep themselves unspotted from it, He gives grace—grace to cling closer to Him, in spite of the attractions of the world; a gift which, unlike the gifts of the world, never loses its savour.

Was St. James acquainted with the *Magnificat*? May not he, the Lord's brother, have sometimes heard the Mother of the Lord recite it? The passage before us is almost like an echo of some of its words: "His mercy is unto generations and generations of them that fear Him. He hath showed strength with His arm; He hath scattered the proud in the imagination of their heart. He hath put down princes from their thrones, and hath exalted them of low degree. The hungry He hath filled with good things; and the rich He hath sent empty away." At any rate the *Magnificat* and St. James teach the same lesson as the Book of Proverbs and St. Peter, who, like St. James, quotes it (1 Peter v. 5), that God resists and puts down those who choose to unite themselves with the world in preference to Him, and gives more and more graces and blessings to all who by faith in Him and His Christ have overcome the world. It is only by faith that we *can* overcome. A conviction that the things which are seen are the most important and pressing, if not the only realities, is sure to betray us into a state of captivity in which the power to work for God, and even the desire to serve Him, will become less and less. We have willed to place ourselves under the world's spell, and such influence as we possess tells not for God, but against Him. But a belief that the chief and noblest realities are unseen enables a man to preserve an attitude of independence and indifference towards things which, even if they are substantial advantages, belong to this world only. He knows how insignificant all that this life has to offer is, compared with the immeasurable joys and woes of the life to come, and he cannot be guilty of the folly of sacrificing a certain and eternal future to a brief and uncertain present. The God in whom he believes is far more to him than the world which he sees and feels. "This is the victory which hath overcome the world, even his faith."

[76] Liddon, *Easter Sermons*, vol. ii., pp. 56, 57 (Rivingtons, 1885).

[77] Comp. 1 Cor. ii. 9; ix. 10; Eph. v. 14, in all which places we have quotations the source of which cannot be determined. Similar phenomena are frequent in patristic literature. See A. Resch's *Agrapha; Aussercanonische Evangelienfragmente* in *Texte und Untersuchungen z. Gesch. d. Altchr. Lit.* (Leipzig, 1889), p. 256.

CHAPTER XX
THE POWER OF SATAN AND ITS LIMITS.HUMILITY THE FOUNDATION OF PENITENCE AND OF HOLINESS

"Be subject therefore unto God; but resist the devil, and he will flee from you. Draw nigh to God, and He will draw nigh to you. Cleanse your hands, ye sinners; and purify your hearts, ye double-minded. Be afflicted, and mourn, and weep: let your laughter be turned to mourning, and your joy to heaviness. Humble yourselves in the sight of the Lord, and He shall exalt you." —St. James iv. 7-10.

SUBMISSION to God is the beginning, middle, and end of the prodigal's return from disastrous familiarity with the world to the security of the Father's home. A readiness to submit to whatever He may impose is the first step in the conversion, just as unwillingness to surrender one's own will is the first step towards revolt and desertion. "I am no more worthy to be called Thy son: make me as one of Thy hired servants." As soon as the resolve to make this act of submission is formed, the turning-point between friendship with the world and fidelity to God has been passed. The homeward path is not an easy one, but it is certain, and those who unflinchingly take it are sure of a welcome at the end of it. The prodigal was tenderly received back by his offended father, and these adulterous souls will be admitted to their old privileges again, if they will but return. God has given them no bill of divorcement to put them away for ever (Isa. l. 1). "If a man put away his wife, and she go from him and become another man's, shall he return unto her again? Shall not that land be greatly polluted? But thou hast played the harlot with many lovers; yet return again to Me, saith the Lord" (Jer. iii. 1). An amount of mercy and forgiveness which cannot be shown by an earthly husband to his unfaithful wife is readily promised by God.

But the return must be a complete one. There must be every guarantee that the penitent is in earnest and has utterly broken with the past. And St. James with affectionate sternness points out the necessary steps towards reconciliation. He will not be guilty of the crime of those who "have healed the hurt of the daughter of My people lightly, saying, Peace, peace; when there is no peace" (Jer. viii. 11). The results of intimacy with the world cannot be undone in a day, and there is painful work to be done before the old relationship can be restored between the soul and its God.

Among the most grievous consequences of yielding to the world and its ways are the weakening of the will and the lowering of the moral tone. They come gradually, but surely; and they act and react upon one another. The habitual shirking of the sterner duties of life, and the living in an atmosphere of self-indulgence, enervate the will; and the conscious adoption of a standard of life which is not approved by conscience is in itself a lowering of tone. And this is one of the essential elements of worldliness. The pleas that "I can't help it," and that "everybody does it," are among the most common excuses urged by those whose citizenship is not in heaven (Phil. iii. 20) but in that commonwealth of which Satan is the presiding power. They like to believe that temptations are irresistible, and that there is no obligation to rise above the standard of morality which those about them profess to accept. Such men deliberately surrender to what they know to be evil, and place what they think to be expedient above what they know to be right, forgetting that even the worldlings who set them this low standard, and openly defend it, very often do not really approve it, but despise while they applaud the man that conforms to it.

St. James enters an earnest and simple protest against the weak plea that temptations are irresistible. To maintain *that* is to assert that the evil one has more will and power to destroy mankind than God has to save them. The truth is exactly the other way. God not only allows to Satan no power to coerce a man into sin, but He Himself is ever ready to aid when He is faithfully prayed to do so. Every Christian is endowed with sufficient power to withstand Satan, if only the will to withstand is present, because he has the power to summon God to his assistance. "Resist the devil, and he will flee from you;" that is one side of the blessed truth; and the other is its correlative: "Draw nigh to God, and He will draw nigh to you."

It will be observed that St. James, quite as much as St. Peter, or St. Paul, or St. John, speaks of the chief power of evil as a *person*. The passage is not intelligible on any other interpretation; for there is a manifest and telling antithesis between the devil who yields to opposition, and the God who responds to invitation. It is a contrast between two personal agencies. Whether St. James was aware of the teaching of the Apostles on this point is not of great moment; his own teaching is clear enough. As a Jew he had been brought up in the belief that there are evil spiritual beings of whom Satan is the chief, and since he became a Christian he had never been required to revise this belief. He was probably well aware of the teaching of Jesus Christ as to the real source of temptations. He may have heard Christ's own interpretation of the birds in the parable of the Sower: "And when they have heard, straightway cometh Satan, and taketh away the word which hath been sown in them" (Mark iv. 15). He probably had heard of Christ's declaration to St. Peter, "Simon, Simon, behold, Satan asked to have you, that he might sift you as wheat: but I made supplication for thee, that thy faith fail not" (Luke xxii. 31), where we have a contrast similar to this, an infernal person on one side, and a Divine Person on the other, of the man assailed by temptation. How easy to have interpreted the birds in the parable as the impersonal solicitations of a depraved nature, the hearers' own evil tendencies; and perhaps if we had not possessed Christ's own explanation we should so have explained the birds by the wayside. But Christ seems to have made use of this, the queen of all the parables (Mark iv. 13), in order to teach that a personal enemy there is, who is ever on the watch to deprive us of what will save our souls. And the warning to St. Peter might easily have been given in a form that would not have implied a personal tempter. Nor do these two striking passages stand alone in our Lord's teaching. How unnecessary to speak of the woman who "was bowed together, and could in nowise lift up herself," as one "whom Satan had bound," unless He desired to sanction and enforce this belief (Luke xiv. 11, 16). And why speak of having "beheld Satan fall as lightning from heaven" (Luke x. 18), unless He had this desire? When the Jews said that He cast out devils by the aid of the prince of the devils, it would have been a much more complete contradiction to have replied that no such person existed, than to argue that Satan was not likely to fight against his own interests. If the belief in personal powers of evil is a superstition, Jesus Christ had ample opportunities of correcting it; and He not only steadfastly abstained from doing so, but in very marked ways, both by His acts and by His teaching, He did a great deal to encourage and inculcate the belief. He showed no sympathy with the scepticism of the Sadducees about such things. He argued convincingly against them as regards the doctrine of the resurrection and a future life, and He gave full sanction to the belief in angels and spirits, both good and bad. There is no need to lay much stress upon the disputed meaning of the last petition in the Lord's Prayer; the evidence is quite ample without that. Yet those who are convinced that "Lead us not into temptation, but deliver us from the evil," must mean, "Lead us not into temptation, *but* deliver us from *the tempter*," have a very important piece of evidence to add to all the rest. Is a gross superstition embodied in the very wording of the model prayer?

In the volume in this series which treats of the Pastoral Epistles is a passage on this subject respecting which a very friendly critic has said that he cannot quite see the force of it.[78] As the argument is of value, it may be worth while to state it here more clearly. The statement criticized is the concluding sentence of the following passage: "It has been said that if there were no God we should have to invent one; and with almost equal truth we might say that if there were no devil we should have to invent one. Without a belief in God bad men would have little to induce them to conquer their evil passions; *without a belief in a devil good men would have little hope of ever being able to do so.*"[79] The meaning of the last statement is this, that if good men were compelled to believe that all the devilish suggestions which rise up in their minds come *from themselves alone,* they might well be in despair of ever getting the better of themselves or of curing a nature capable of producing such offspring. But when they know that "a power, *not* themselves, which makes for" wickedness is the source of these diabolical temptations, then they can have confidence that their own nature is not so hopelessly corrupt but that, with the help of "the Power, not themselves, that makes for *righteousness*" they will be able to gain the victory.

The plea that the devil is irresistible, and that therefore to yield to temptation is inevitable, is only another form of the fallacy, against which St. James has already protested, of trying to shift the responsibility of temptation from oneself to God (i. 13-15). It is the old fallacy carried a stage farther. The former plea has reference to the temptation; the present one has reference to the fall. As regards both the facts are conclusive. We often provoke our own temptations; we always can resist them if we in faith draw nigh to God for protection. "To this end the Son of man was manifested, that He might destroy the works of the devil" (1 John iii. 8). And the Son of God preserveth every child of God, "and the evil one toucheth him not" (1 John v. 18). But the man himself must consent and co-operate, for God saves no man against his will. "Return unto Me, and I will return unto you," is the principle of the Old Covenant (Zech. i. 3); and "Draw nigh to God, and He will draw nigh to you," is the principle of the New.

The converse of this is true also, and it is a fact of equal solemnity and of great awfulness. Resist *God,* and He will depart from you. Draw nigh to the *devil,* and he will draw nigh to you. If we persist in withstanding God's grace, He will at last leave us to ourselves. His Spirit will not always strive with us; but at last He Himself hardens the heart which we have closed against him, for He allows things to take their course, and the heart which refuses to be softened by the dew of His grace must become harder and harder. And the more we place ourselves in the devil's way, by exposing ourselves to needless temptations, the more diligently he will seek us and abide with us. Those who voluntarily take up their abode in the tents of ungodliness have surrendered all claim to be kept unspotted from the world. They have lost their right to join in the cry, "Why standest Thou afar off, O Lord? why hidest Thou Thyself in times of trouble?"

But the hands which one raises in prayer to God must be cleansed by withholding them from all evil practices, and from all grasping after the contaminating gifts of the world; and the heart must be purified by the quenching of unholy desires and the cultivation of a godly spirit. In this St. James is but repeating the principles laid down by the Psalmist: "Who shall ascend into the hill of the Lord? and who shall stand in His holy place? He that hath *clean hands* and a *pure heart*" (Ps. xxiv. 3, 4). And in similar language we find Clement of Rome exhorting the Corinthians, "Let us therefore approach Him in *holiness of soul*, lifting up *pure and undefiled hands* unto Him" (xxix.). In all these instances the external instruments of human conduct are mentioned along with the internal source of it.

St. James is not addressing two classes of people when he says, "Cleanse your hands, ye *sinners*; and purify your hearts, ye *double-minded*." Every one whose hands have wrought unrighteousness is a sinner who needs this cleansing; and every one who attempts to draw nigh to God, without at the same time surrendering all unholy desires, is a double-minded man who needs this purification. The "halting between two opinions," between God and Mammon, and between Christ and the world, is fatal to true conversion and efficacious prayer. What is necessary, therefore, for these sinners of double mind, is outward amendment of life and inward purification of the desires. "The sinner that goeth two ways" must with "a single eye" direct his path along the narrow way. "Whoso walketh uprightly shall be delivered; but he that walketh perversely in two ways shall fall at once" (Prov. xxviii. 18). The whole exhortation is in spirit very similar to the second half of the second chapter of Ecclesiasticus. Note especially the concluding verses: "They that fear the Lord will prepare their hearts and humble their souls in His sight, saying, We will fall into the hands of the Lord, and not into the hands of men; for as His majesty is, so is His mercy."

There must be no "light healing," or treatment of the grievous sins of the past as of no moment. There must be genuine sorrow for the unfaithfulness which has separated them so long from their God, and for the pride which has betrayed them into rebellion against Him. "Be afflicted, and mourn, and weep." The first verb refers to the inward feeling of wretchedness, the other two to the outward expression of it. These two are found in combination in several passages, both in the Old Testament and in the New (2 Sam. xix. 2; Neh. viii. 9; Mark xvi. 10; Luke vi. 25; Rev. xviii. 15, 19). The feelings of satisfaction and self-sufficiency in which these friends of the world have hitherto indulged, and the glowing complacency which has been manifest in their demeanour, have been quite out of place, and must be exchanged for feelings and manifestations of grief. Their worldly merriment also must be abandoned; those who have cut themselves off from God have no true spring of joy. "Let your laughter be turned to mourning, and your joy to heaviness." The last word (κατήφεια), which occurs nowhere else in Scripture, refers primarily to the dejected look which accompanies heaviness of heart. The writer of the Book of Wisdom uses the adjective (κατηφής) to express the "*gloomy* phantoms with unsmiling faces" which he supposes to have appeared to the Egyptians during the plague of darkness (xvii. 4). The term admirably expresses the opposite of boisterous lightheartedness.

St. James ends as he began, with submission to the Almighty. He began his exhortation as to the right method of conversion with "Be subject unto God." He ends with "Humble yourselves in the sight of the Lord, and He will exalt you." The root of their worldliness and their grasping at wealth and honour is pride and self-will, and the cure for that is self-abasement and self-surrender. If it is God's will that they should occupy a lowly place in society, let them humbly accept their lot, and not try to change it by violence or fraud. If they will but remember their own transgressions against the Lord, they will admit that the humblest place is not too humble for their merits; and it is the humble whom God delights to honour. Here, again, St. James is reproducing the teaching of his Divine Brother: "Every one that exalteth himself shall be humbled; and he that humbleth himself shall be exalted" (Luke xiv. 11; Matt. xxiii. 12). And the Old Testament teaches the same lesson. "The humble person He shall save," says Eliphaz the Temanite (Job xxii. 29); and the Psalmist gives us both sides of the Divine law of compensation: "Thou wilt save the afflicted people; but the haughty eyes Thou wilt bring down" (xviii. 27).

"Humble *yourselves;*" "He that humbleth *himself.*" Everything depends on that. It must be *self*-abasement. There is nothing meritorious in chancing to be in a humble position, still less in being *forced* to descend to one. It is the voluntary acceptance, or the choice, of a lowly place that is pleasing to God. We must choose it as knowing that we deserve nothing better, and as wishing that others should be promoted rather than ourselves. And this must be done "*in the sight of the Lord;*" not in self-consciousness, to "to be seen of men," which is "the pride that apes humility," but in the consciousness of the ineffable presence of God. That is the source of all true self-abasement and humility. To realize that we are in the presence of the All-holy and All-pure, in whose sight the stars are not clean, and who charges even the angels with folly, is to feel that all differences of merit between man and man have faded away in the immeasurable abyss which separates our own insignificance and pollution from the majesty of His holiness. "Now mine eye seeth Thee. Wherefore I abhor myself, and repent in dust and ashes," is the language of Job (xlii. 5, 6). And it was the same feeling which wrung from St. Peter, as he fell down at Jesus' knees, the agonizing cry, "Depart from me, for I am a sinful man, O Lord" (Luke v. 8). Hence it is that the most saintly persons are always the most humble; for they realize most perfectly the holiness of God and the ceaselessness of His presence, and are therefore best able to appreciate the contrast between their own miserable imperfections and His unapproachable purity. The language which they at times use about themselves is sometimes suspected of unreality and exaggeration, if not of downright hypocrisy; but it is the natural expression of the feelings of one who knows a great deal about the difference between a creature who is habitually falling into sin and One who, in holiness, as in wisdom and power, is absolute and infinite perfection. Humility is thus the beginning and end of all true religion. The sinner who turns to God must be humble; and this is the humility which St. James is urging. And the saint, as he approaches nearer to God, will be humble; for he knows what the approach has cost him, and how very far off he still remains.

"And He will exalt you." This is the result, not the motive. To strive to be humble *in order* to be exalted would be to poison the virtue at its source. Just as the conscious pursuit of happiness is fatal to its attainment, so also the conscious aim at Divine promotion. The way to be happy is not to think about one's own happiness, but to sacrifice it to that of others; and the way to be exalted by God is not to think of one's own advancement, but to devote oneself to the advancement of others. The exaltation is sure to come, if only humility is attained; an exaltation of which there is a foretaste even in this life, but the full fruition of which lies in those unknown glories which await the humble Christian in the world to come.

Note.—It may be that in the phrase "Resist the devil" we have an echo of another unrecorded utterance of Christ, of which we have possible traces also in St. Paul's "Stand against the wiles of the devil" (Eph. vi. 11), and St. Peter's "Whom withstand, steadfast in your faith" (1 Peter v. 9). Comp. Shepherd of Hermas, *Mand.* XII. v. 2; iv. 7; Testament of the Twelve Patriarchs, *Neph.* viii., where James iv. 7 (or its source) would seem to be quoted.

[78] *Sunday School Chronicle,* March 15th, 1889; also the *Durham Chronicle,* Jan. 31st, 1890.

[79] *Expositor's Bible: Pastoral Epistles* (Hodder and Stoughton, 1888), p. 80.

CHAPTER XXI
SELF-ASSURANCE AND INVASION OF DIVINE PREROGATIVES INVOLVED IN THE LOVE OF CENSURING OTHERS

"Speak not one against another, brethren. He that speaketh against a brother, or judgeth his brother, speaketh against the law, and judgeth the law: but if thou judgest the law, thou art not a doer of the law, but a judge. One only is the Lawgiver and Judge, even He who is able to save and to destroy: but who art thou that judgest thy neighbour?"—St. James iv. 11, 12.

FROM sins which are the result of a want of love to God St. James passes on, and abruptly, to some which are the result of a want of love for one's neighbour. But in thus passing on he is really returning to his main subject, for the central portion of the Epistle is chiefly taken up with one's duty towards one's neighbour. And of this duty he again singles out for special notice the necessity for putting a bridle on one's tongue (i. 26; iii. 1-12). Some have supposed that he is addressing a new class of readers; but the much gentler address, "brethren," as compared with "ye adulteresses" (ver. 4), "ye sinners," "ye double-minded" (ver. 8), does not at all compel us to suppose that. After a paragraph of exceptional sternness, he returns to his usual manner of addressing his readers (i. 2, 16, 19; ii. 1, 5, 14; iii. 1, 10, 12; v. 7, 9, 10, 12, 19), and with all the more fitness because the address "brethren" is in itself an indirect reproof for unbrotherly conduct. It implies what Moses expressed when he said, "Sirs, ye are brethren; why do ye wrong one to another?" (Acts vii. 26).

"Speak not against one another, brethren." The context shows what kind of adverse speaking is meant. It is not so much abusive or calumnious language that is condemned, as the *love of finding fault*. The censorious temper is utterly unchristian. It means that we have been paying an amount of attention to the conduct of others which would have been better bestowed upon our own. It means also that we have been paying this attention, not in order to help, but in order to criticize, and criticize unfavourably. It shows, moreover, that we have a very inadequate estimate of our own frailty and shortcomings. If we knew how worthy of blame we ourselves are, we should be much less ready to deal out blame to others. But over and above all this, censoriousness is an invasion of the Divine prerogatives. It is not merely a transgression of the royal law of love, but a setting oneself above the law, as if it were a mistake, or did not apply to oneself. It is a climbing up on to that judgment-seat on which God alone has the right to sit, and a publishing of judgments upon others which He alone has the right to pronounce. This is the aspect of it on which St. James lays most stress.

"He that speaketh against a brother, or judgeth a brother, speaketh against the law and judgeth the law." St. James is probably not referring to Christ's command in the Sermon on the Mount, "Judge not, that ye be not judged. For with what judgment ye judge, ye shall be judged" (Matt. vii. 1, 2). It is a law of far wider scope that is in his mind, the same as that of which he has already spoken, "the perfect law, the law of liberty" (i. 25); "the royal law, according to the Scripture, Thou shalt love thy neighbour as thyself" (ii. 8). No one who knows this law, and has at all grasped its meaning and scope, can suppose that observance of it is compatible with habitual criticism of the conduct of others, and frequent utterance of unfavourable judgments respecting them. No man, however *willing* he may be to have his conduct laid open to criticism, is *fond* of being constantly subjected to it. Still less can any one be fond of being made the object of slighting and condemnatory remarks. Every man's personal experience has taught him that; and if he loves his neighbour as himself, he will take care to inflict on him as little pain of this kind as possible. If, with full knowledge of the royal law of charity, and with full experience of the vexation which adverse criticism causes, he still persists in framing and expressing unfriendly opinions respecting other people, then he is setting himself up as superior, not only to those whom he presumes to judge, but to the law itself. He is, by his conduct, condemning the law of love as a bad law, or at least as so defective that a superior person like himself may without scruple disregard it. In judging and condemning his brother he is judging and condemning the law; and he who condemns a law assumes that he is in possession of some higher principle by which he tests it and finds it wanting. What is the higher principle by which the censorious person justifies his contempt for the law of love? He has nothing to show us but his own arrogance and self-confidence. *He* knows what the duty of other persons is, and how signally they fall short of it. To talk of "hoping all things, and enduring all things," and of "taking not account of evil," may be all very well theoretically of an ideal state of society; but in the very far from ideal world in which we have to live it is necessary to keep one's eye open to the conduct of other people, and to keep them up to the mark by letting them and their acquaintances know what we think of them. It is no use mincing matters or being mealy-mouthed; wherever abuses are found, or even suspected, they must be denounced. And if other persons neglect their duty in this particular, the censorious man is not going to share such responsibility. This is the kind of reasoning by which flagrant violations of the law of love are frequently justified. And such reasoning, as St. James plainly shows, amounts really to this, that those who employ it know better than the Divine Lawgiver the principles by which human society ought to be governed. He has clearly promulgated a law; and they ascend His judgment-seat, and intimate that very serious exceptions and modifications are necessary; indeed, that in some cases the law must be entirely superseded. *They*, at any rate, are not bound by it.

This proneness to judge and condemn others is further proof of that want of humility about which so much was said in the previous section. Pride, the most subtle of sins, has very many forms, and one of them is the love of finding fault; that is, the love of assuming an attitude of superiority, not only towards other persons, but towards the law of charity and Him who is the Author of it. To a truly humble man this is impossible. He is accustomed to contrast the outcome of his own life with the requirements of God's law, and to know how awful is the gulf which separates the one from the other. He knows too much against himself to take delight in censuring the faults of others. Censoriousness is a sure sign that he who is addicted to it is ignorant of the immensity of his own shortcomings. No man who habitually considers his own transgressions will be eager to be severe upon the transgressions of others, or to usurp functions which require full authority and perfect knowledge for their equitable and adequate performance.

Censoriousness brings yet another evil in its train. Indulgence in the habit of prying into the acts and motives of others leaves us little time and less liking for searching carefully into our own acts and motives. The two things act and react upon one another by a natural law. The more seriously and frequently we examine ourselves, the less prone we shall be to criticize others; and the more pertinaciously we busy ourselves about the supposed shortcomings and delinquencies of our neighbours, the less we are likely to investigate and realize our own grievous sins. All the more will this be the case if we are in the habit of *giving utterance* to the uncharitable judgments which we love to frame. He who constantly expresses his detestation of evil by denouncing the evil doings of his brethren is not the man most likely to express his detestation of it by the holiness of his own life; and the man whose whole life is a protest against sin is not the man most given to protesting against sinners. To be constantly speculating, to be frequently deciding, to be ready to make known our decisions, as to whether this man is "awakened" or not, whether he is "converted" or not, whether he is a "Catholic" or not, whether he is a "sound Churchman" or not—what is this but to climb up into the White Throne, and with human ignorance and prejudice anticipate the judgments of Divine Omniscience and Justice, as to who are on the right hand, and who on the left?

"One only is Lawgiver and Judge, even He who is able to save and to destroy." There is one and only one Source of all law and authority, and that Source is God Himself. Jesus Christ affirmed the same doctrine when He consented to plead, as a prisoner charged with many crimes, before the judgment-seat of His own creature, Pontius Pilate. "Thou wouldest have no power against Me, except it were given thee from above" (John xix. 11). It was Christ's last word to the Roman Procurator, a declaration of the supremacy of God in the government of the world, and a protest against the claim insinuated in "I have power to release Thee, and I have power to crucify Thee," to be possessed of an authority that was irresponsible. Jesus declared that Pilate's power over Himself was the result of a Divine commission; for the possession and exercise of all authority is the gift of God, and can have no other origin. And this sole Fount of authority, this one only Lawgiver and Judge, has no need of assessors. While He delegates some portions of His power to human representatives, He requires no man, He allows no man, to share his judgment-seat, or to cancel or modify His laws. It is one of those cases in which the possession of power is proof of the possession of right. "He who is *able* to save and to destroy," who has the power to execute sentences respecting the weal and woe of immortal souls, has the right to pronounce such sentences. Man has no right to frame and utter such judgments, because he has no power to put them into execution; and the practice of uttering them is a perpetual usurpation of Divine prerogatives. It is an approach to that sin which brought about the fall of the angels.

Is not the sin of a censorious temper in a very real sense diabolical? It is Satan's special delight to be "the accuser of the brethren" (Rev. xii. 10). His names, Satan ("adversary") and devil (διάβολος = malicious accuser"), bear witness to this characteristic, which is brought prominently forward in the opening chapters of the Book of Job.[80] It is of the essence of censoriousness that its activity is displayed with a sinister motive. The charges are commonly uttered, not to the person who is blamed, but to others, who will thereby be prejudiced against him; or if they are made to the man's own face, it is with the object of inflicting pain, rather than with the hope of thereby inducing him to amend. It is no "speaking truth in love" (Eph. iv. 15), but reckless or malevolent speaking evil, without much caring whether it be true or false. It is a poisoning of the wells out of which respect and affection for our fellow-men flow. Thus the presumption which grasps at functions that belong to God alone leads to a fall and a course of action which is indeed Satanical.

"One only is the Lawgiver and the Judge, even He who is able to save and to destroy." St. Peter and St. Paul teach the same doctrine in those Epistles which (as has been already pointed out) it is *possible* that the writer of this Epistle may have seen. "Be subject to every ordinance of man for the Lord's sake: whether it be to the king, as supreme (*i.e.* to the Roman Emperor); or unto governors, as sent by him" (1 Peter ii. 13). However much of human origination (κτίσις ἀνθρωπίνη) there may be about civil government, yet its sanctions are Divine. And St. Paul affirms that its real origin is Divine also: "There is no power but of God; and the powers that be are ordained of God" (Rom. xiii. 1). The ultimate sanction of even Pilate's misused jurisdiction was "from above;" and it was to inhabitants of Rome, appalled by the frantic atrocities of Nero, that St. Paul declared that the authority of their Emperor existed by "the ordinance of God." If to resist this delegated authority be a serious matter, how much more to attempt to anticipate or to contradict the judgments of Him from whom it springs!

"But who art thou, that judgest thy neighbour?" St. James concludes this brief section against the sin of censoriousness by a telling *argumentum ad hominem*. Granted that there are grave evils in some of the brethren among whom and with whom you live; granted that it is quite necessary that these evils should be noticed and condemned; are you precisely the persons that are best qualified to do it? Putting aside the question of authority, what are your personal qualifications for the office of a censor and a judge? Is there that blamelessness of life, that gravity of behaviour, that purity of motive, that severe control of tongue, that freedom from contamination from the world, that overflowing charity which marks the man of pure religion? To such a man finding fault with his brethren is real pain; and therefore to be *fond* of finding fault is strong evidence that these necessary qualities are not possessed. Least of all is such a one fond of disclosing to others the sins which he has discovered in an erring brother. Indeed, there is scarcely a better way of detecting our own "secret faults" than that of noticing what blemishes we are most prone to suspect and denounce in the lives of our neighbours. It is often our own personal acquaintance with iniquity that makes us suppose that others must be like ourselves. It is our own meanness, dishonesty, pride, or impurity that we see reflected on what is perhaps only the surface of a life whose secret springs and motives lie in a sphere quite beyond our grovelling comprehension. Here, again, St. James is quite in harmony with St. Paul, who asks the same question: "Who art thou that judgest the servant of another? to his own lord he standeth or falleth.... But thou, why dost thou judge thy brother? or thou again, why dost thou set at nought thy brother? for we shall all stand before the judgment-seat of God?" (Rom. xiv. 4, 10).

But are not St. James and St. Paul requiring of us what is impossible? Is it not beyond our power to avoid forming judgments about our brethren? Certainly this is beyond our power, and we are not required to do anything so unreasonable as to attempt to avoid such inevitable judgments. Whenever the conduct of others comes under our notice we necessarily form some kind of an opinion of it, and it is out of these opinions and judgments, of which we form many in the course of a day, that our own characters are to a large extent slowly built up; for the way in which we regard the conduct of others has a great influence upon our own conduct. But it is not this necessary judging that is condemned. What is condemned is the inquisitorial examination of our neighbours' views and actions, undertaken without authority and without love. Such judging is sinister in its purpose, and is disappointed if it can find nothing to blame. It is eager, rather than unwilling, to think evil, its prejudices being against, rather than in favour of, those whom it criticizes. To discover some grievous form of wrong-doing is not a sorrow, but a delight.

But what both St. James and St. Paul condemn, even more than the habit of forming these unfavourable judgments about our neighbours, is the giving effect to them. "*Speak* not one against another." "Why dost thou *set at nought* thy brother?" This at any rate we all can avoid. However difficult, or impossible, it may be to avoid forming unfavourable opinions of other people, we can at any rate abstain from publishing such opinions to the world. The temper which delights in communicating suspicions and criticisms is even more fatal than the habit of forming and cherishing them; it is the difference between a disease which is infectious, and one which is not. The bitterness and misery which are caused by the love of evil speaking is incalculable. It is one enormous item in that tragic sum of human suffering which is entirely preventable. Much of human suffering is inevitable and incurable; it may be compensated or consoled, but it can be neither escaped nor remedied. There is much, however, that need never be incurred at all, that is utterly wanton and gratuitous. And this pathetic burden of utterly needless misery in great measure consists of that which we heedlessly or maliciously inflict upon one another by making known, with quite inadequate reason, our knowledge or suspicion of the misconduct of other people. Experience seems to do little towards curing us of this fault. Over and over again we have discovered, after having communicated suspicions, that they are baseless. Over and over again we have found out that to disclose what we know to the discredit of a neighbour does more harm than good. And not infrequently we have ourselves had abundant reason to wish that we had never spoken; for curses are not the only kind of evil speaking that is wont to "come home to roost." And yet, each time that the temptation occurs again, we persuade ourselves that it is our duty to speak out, to put others on their guard, to denounce an unquestionable abuse, and so forth. And forthwith we set the whisper in motion, or we write a letter to the papers, and the supposed delinquent is "shown up." An honest answer to the questions, "Should I say this of him if he were present? Why do I not speak to him about it, instead of to others? Am I sorry or glad to make this known?" would at once make us pause, and perhaps abstain. They would lead us to see that we are not undertaking a painful duty, but needlessly indulging an unchristian censoriousness, and thereby inflicting needless pain. It is not given to many of us to do a great deal towards making other persons holier; but it is within the power of all of us to do a very great deal towards making others happier; and one of the simplest methods of diminishing the miseries and increasing the joys of society is to maintain a firm control over our tempers and our tongues, and to observe to the utmost St. James's pregnant rule, "Speak not one against another, brethren."

> [80] Dr. Hatch thinks that in both the Septuagint and the New Testament διάβολος, when used as a proper name, has "the general connotation of enmity, and without implying accusation, whether true or false." As an adjective it has its usual meaning of "slanderous" (1 Tim. iii. 11; 2 Tim. iii. 3; Titus ii. 3) (*Biblical Greek* pp. 46, 47).

CHAPTER XXII
SELF-ASSURANCE AND INVASION OF DIVINE PREROGATIVES INVOLVED IN PRESUMING UPON OUR FUTURE. THE DOCTRINE OF PROBABILISM

"Go to now, ye that say, To-day or to-morrow we will go into this city, and spend a year there, and trade, and get gain: whereas ye know not what shall be on the morrow. What is your life? For ye are a vapour, that appeareth for a little time, and then vanisheth away. For that ye ought to say, If the Lord will, we shall both live, and do this or that. But now ye glory in your vauntings: all such glorying is evil. To him therefore that knoweth to do good, and doeth it not, to him it is sin." —St. James iv. 13-17.

WORLDLINESS and want of humility are the two kindred subjects which form the groundwork of this portion of the Epistle. This fourth chapter falls into three main divisions, of which the third and last is before us; and these two subjects underlie all three. In the first the arrogant grasping after the pleasures, honours, and riches of the world, in preference to the love of God, is condemned. In the second the arrogant judging of others in defiance of the Divine law of charity is forbidden. In the third arrogant trust in the security of human undertakings, without consideration of God's will, is denounced. The transition from the false confidence which leads men to judge others with a light heart, to the false confidence which leads men to account the future as their own, is easily made; and thus once more, while we seem to be abruptly passing to a fresh topic, we are really moving quite naturally from one branch of the main subject to another. The assurance which finds plenty of time for censuring others, but little or none for censuring self, is closely akin to the assurance which counts on having plenty of time for all its schemes, without thought of death or of the Divine decrees. This, then, is the subject before us—presumptuous security as to future undertakings. The future is God's, not ours, just as to judge mankind belongs to Him, and not to us. Therefore to think and speak of the future as if we had the power to control it is as presumptuous as to think and speak of our fellow-men as if we had the power to judge them. In both cases we assume a knowledge and an authority which we do not possess.

"Go to now" (ἄγε νῦω) is a vigorous form of address, which occurs nowhere in the New Testament, excepting here and at the beginning of the next section. Although originally an imperative singular, it has become so completely an adverb that it can be used, as here, when a number of persons are addressed. It serves to attract attention. Those who think that they can acquit themselves of the charge of censoriousness have yet another form of presumptuous confidence to consider. The parable of the Rich Fool, who said to his soul, "Soul, thou hast much good laid up for many years; take thine ease, eat, drink, and be merry" (Luke xii. 19), should be compared with this exhortation. And it is remarkable that it was just after our Lord had refused to be made a judge over two contending brothers that He spoke the parable of the Rich Fool.

There is no special emphasis on "ye that *say*," as if the meaning were, "ye who not only have these presumptuous thoughts, but dare to utter them." In the previous section giving utterance to unfavourable judgments about one's neighbours is evidently worse than merely thinking them, and is a great aggravation of the sin; but here thinking and saying are much the same. The presumptuous people look far ahead, think every step in the plan quite secure, and speak accordingly. To-day and to-morrow are quite safe. The journey to the proposed city is quite safe. That they will spend a year there is regarded as certain, and that they will be able to spend it as they please, viz. in trading. Lastly, they have no doubts as to the success of the whole enterprise; they will "get gain." All this is thought of and spoken of as being entirely within their own control. They have only to decide on doing it, and the whole will be done. That there is a Providence which needs to be considered is entirely left out of sight. That not even their own lives can be counted on for a single day is a fact that is equally ignored.

It was long ago remarked that "All men are mortal" is a proposition which each man believes to be true of every one excepting himself. Not that any one seriously believes that he himself will be exempt from death; but each one of us habitually thinks and acts as if in his case death were such an indefinite distance off that practically there is no need to take account of it—at any rate at present. The young and the strong rarely think of death as a subject that calls for serious attention. Those who are past the prime of life still think that they have many years of life in store. And even those who have received the solemn warning which is involved in reaching man's allotted threescore and ten years remember with satisfaction that many persons have reached fourscore and ten or more, and that therefore there is good reason for believing that they themselves have a considerable portion of life still in front of them. Perhaps the man of ninety finds himself sometimes thinking, if not talking to others, of what he means to do, not only to-morrow, but next year.

Such habits of thought and language are very common, and a man has to be carefully on the watch against himself, in order to avoid them. They are entirely opposed to the spirit of both the Old and the New Testament, and in the most literal sense of the term may be stigmatized as *godless*. The security which ignores the will of God in its calculations, and thinks and acts as an independent power, is godless. Dependence upon God is the centre both of Judaism and of Christianity. A story of the Rabbinists brings this out as clearly on the Jewish side as the parable of the Rich Fool does on the Christian. At his son's circumcision a Jewish father set wine that was seven years old before his guests, with the remark that with this wine he would continue for a long time to celebrate the birth of his son. The same night the Angel of Death meets the Rabbi Simeon, who accosts him and asks him, "Why art thou thus wandering about?" "Because," said the angel, "I slay those who say, We will do this or that, and think not how soon death may come upon them. The man who said that he would continue for a long time to drink that wine shall die in thirty days." It is in this way that "the *careless ease* of fools shall destroy them" (Prov. i. 32). And hence the warning, "Boast not thyself of to-morrow; for thou knowest not what a day may bring forth" (Prov. xxvii. 1). The man who makes plans for the future without taking account of Providence is not far removed from "the fool, who says in his heart, There is no God" (Ps. xiv. 1; liii. 1). "Set not thy heart upon thy goods; and say not, I have enough for my life. Follow not thine own mind and thy strength, to walk in the ways of thy heart; and say not, Who shall control me? for the Lord will surely avenge thy pride" (Ecclus. v. 1-3). "There is that waxeth rich by his wariness and pinching, and this is the portion of his reward. Whereas he saith, I have found rest, and now will eat continually of my good; and yet he knoweth not what time shall come upon him, and that he must leave those things to others, and die" (Ecclus. xi. 18, 19).

The Cyrenaics and their more refined followers the Epicureans started from the same premises, viz. the utter uncertainty of the future, and the inability of man to control it, but drew from them a very different conclusion. Dependence upon God was one of the last doctrines likely to be inculcated by those who contended that there is no such thing as Providence, for the gods do not concern themselves with the affairs of men. True wisdom, they said, will consist in the skilful, calm, and deliberate appropriation of such pleasure as our circumstances afford moment by moment, unruffled by passion, prejudice, or superstition. The present alone is ours, and we must resolutely make the most of it, without remorse for a past which we can never alter, and without disquietude about a future which we cannot determine, and may never possess. This is not very profound as philosophy, for in the wear and tear of life it can neither fortify nor console; and as a substitute for religion it is still less satisfying. The whole difference which separates Paganism from Christianity lies between two such stanzas as these;—

> "Quid sit futurum cras, fuge quærere; et
>
> Quem Fors dierum cunque dabit, lucro
>
> Appone, nec dulces amores
>
> Sperne puer neque tu choreas;"

and—

> "Lead, kindly Light, amid th' encircling gloom,
>
> Lead Thou me on:
>
> The night is dark, and I am far from home;
>
> Lead Thou me on.
>
> Keep Thou my feet; I do not ask to see
>
> The distant scene; one step enough for me."[81]

"We will go into this city, *and* spend a year there, *and* trade, *and* get gain." The frequent conjunctions separate the different items of the plan, which are rehearsed thus one by one with manifest satisfaction. The speakers gloat over the different steps of the programme which they have arranged for themselves. St. James selects trading and getting gain as the end of the supposed scheme, partly in order to show that the aims of these presumptuous schemers are utterly worldly, and partly because a restless activity in commercial enterprise was a common feature among the Jews of the Dispersion. Such pursuits are not condemned; but they are liable to become too absorbing, especially when not pursued in a God-fearing way; and it is this which St. James denounces.

"Whereas ye know not what shall be on the morrow. What is your life? For ye are a vapour, that appeareth for a little time, and then vanisheth away." It is not easy to determine the original Greek text with certainty, but about the general sense there is no doubt. It is possible, however, that we ought to read, "Whereas ye know not as to the morrow of what kind your life will be: for ye are a vapour," etc. In any case "Whereas ye know not" represents words which literally mean, "Since ye are people *of such nature* as not to know" (οἵτινες οὐκ ἐπίστασθε). As human beings, whose life is so full of changes and surprises, it is impossible for them to know what vicissitudes the next day will bring. The real uncertainty of life is in marked contrast to their unreal security.

"What is your life?" Of what kind is it? What is its nature (ποῖα)? Bede remarks that St. James does not ask, "What is *our* life?" He says, "What is *your* life?" It is the value of the life of the godless that is in question, not that of the godly. Those who, by their forgetfulness of the Unseen, their desire for material advantages, and their friendliness with the world, have made themselves enemies of God—what is their life worth? Such persons "are a vapour, that appeareth for a little time, and then vanisheth away." But it may be doubted whether St. James is here speaking of the emptiness of an *ungodly* life. He is addressing godless persons, and in rebuking them reminds them how unstable and fleeting life is, not merely to them, but to all men. It is the same thought as we find in Job's complaint, "As the cloud is consumed and vanisheth away, so he that goeth down to the grave shall come up no more" (vii. 9); and we shall see that in the next two sections (v. 1-6, 7-11) there are coincidences with the Book of Job (see pp. 281, 291). But it is perhaps the Book of Wisdom that is specially in the writer's mind: "Our life shall pass away as the trace of a cloud, and shall be dispersed as a mist, that is driven away with the beams of the sun, and overcome with the heat thereof" (ii. 4). "For the hope of the ungodly is like dust that is blown away with the wind; like a thin froth that is driven away with the storm; like as the smoke which is dispersed here and there with a tempest, and passeth away as the remembrance of a guest that tarrieth but a day" (v. 14). And if these passages *are* the source of St. James's metaphor, Bede's interpretation becomes more probable; for in both of them it is the life of the ungodly that is likened to everything that is unsubstantial and transitory.[82]

"For that ye ought to say, If the Lord will, we shall both live, and do this or that." We must beware of understanding these words in such a way as to lose the spirit of them. It is one of many passages of Scripture which are often taken according to the letter, when the letter is of little or no importance. As in so much of the teaching in the Sermon on the Mount, we have a *principle* given in the form of a *rule*. Rules are given that they may be observed literally. Principles are given that they may be applied intelligently and observed according to their spirit. We do not obey Christ when we allow the thief who has taken our upper garment to have our under one also; nor do we obey St. James when we say, "If the Lord will," or "Please God," of every future event, and make a plentiful use of "D.V." in all our correspondence. Nor is it enough to say that everything depends upon the *spirit* in which the second garment is surrendered, and in which the "Please God" is uttered, or the "D.V." written. It is quite possible to keep Christ's precept without ever surrendering the second garment at all; and indeed we ought not to surrender it. And it is quite possible to keep His brother's precept without ever writing "D.V." or saying "Please God," the habitual use of which would be almost certain to generate formalism and cant in ourselves, and would be quite certain to provoke needless criticism and irreverent ridicule. St. James means that we should habitually feel that moment by moment we are absolutely dependent upon God, not only for the way in which our lives are henceforth to be spent, but for their being prolonged at all. At any instant we may be called upon to surrender, not only all the materials of enjoyment which He has bestowed upon us, but life itself, which is equally His gift; and whenever He does so call upon us we shall have neither the right nor the power to resist. "Shall He not do what He will with His own?" "The Lord gave; and the Lord may take away. Blessed be the name of the Lord."

The man who is thoroughly impressed with the fact of his utter dependence upon God for life and all things is sure to express this in his bearing, his tone, and his manner of speaking about the future, even although such phrases as "Please God" and "If the Lord will" never come from his lips or his pen. Indeed, the more complete his realization of this truth is, the less likely will he be to be constantly expressing it in a formula. It is the habitual setting of his thoughts, and does not need to be stated any more than the conditions of time and space. On rare occasions it may be well to remind others of this truth by giving expression to it in words; but in most cases it will be wisest to retain it as an unforgotten but unexpressed premise in the mind. But it is for each one of us to take care that it is *not* forgotten. Only those who have it constantly in their hearts can safely absolve themselves from the obligation of obeying the words of St. James literally.

"But now ye glory in your vauntings: all such glorying is evil." The carnal self-confidence with which people serenely talk about what they mean to do next year, or many years hence, is only part of a general spirit of arrogance and worldliness which pervades their whole life and conduct; it is one of the results of the thoroughly vitiated moral atmosphere which they have chosen for themselves, and to the noxiousness of which they are constantly contributing. The word here rendered "vaunting," and in 1 John ii. 16 "vainglory," (ἀλαζονεία), indicates insolent and empty assurance; and here the assurance lies in presumptuous trust in the stability of oneself and one's surroundings. Pretentious ostentation is the radical signification of the word, and in Classical Greek it is the pretentiousness which is most prominent, in Hellenistic Greek the ostentation. There is manifest ostentation in speaking confidently about one's future; and seeing how transitory everything human is, the ostentation is empty and pretentious. To be guilty of such vaunting is serious enough; but these fellow-countrymen of St. James, with their minds absorbed in material interests, gloried in their godless view of life. The simple character of his comment makes its severity all the more impressive: "all such glorying is evil." He uses the very word which is commonly used to express "the evil one" (ὁ πονηρός), and thereby indicates the character and source of such glorying.

In concluding this section of his letter, St. James brings the conduct which he has been condemning within the sweep of a very comprehensive principle: "To him, therefore, that knoweth to do good, and doeth it not, to him it is sin." No Jew, whether Christian or not, could plead ignorance as an excuse for his transgressions in this matter. Every human being has experienced the uncertainty of the future and the transitoriness of human life; and every Jew was well instructed in the truth that man and all his surroundings are absolutely dependent upon the Divine will. Moreover, those whom St. James is addressing prided themselves on their spiritual knowledge (i. 19); they were professed hearers of God's Word (i. 22, 23), and were anxious to become teachers of others (iii. 1). Theirs is the case of servants who knew their master's will, and neglected to do it (Luke xii. 47). They themselves declared, "We see;" and the rejoinder is, "Your sin remaineth" (John ix. 41). They knew, long before St. James instructed them on the subject, what was seemly for human beings living as creatures in dependence upon their Creator; and they neglected to do what is seemly. To them this neglect is sin.

The passage is very commonly understood as applying to all sins of omission; and no doubt it is very capable of such application, but it does not follow that St. James was thinking of more than the particular case before him. The words may be interpreted in three different degrees of comprehensiveness, and St. James may have meant one, or two, or all three of them.

1. The relation in which a creature ought to stand to the Creator is one of humility and entire dependence; and he who knows that he is a creature, and adopts an attitude of self-confidence and independence, sins.

2. In all cases of transgression knowledge of what is right aggravates the sin, which is then a sin against light. "If I had not come and spoken unto them, they had not had sin: but now they have no excuse for their sin" (John xv. 22).

3. This applies not only to transgressions, but to omissions. Knowledge of what is evil creates an obligation to avoid it, and knowledge of what is good constitutes an obligation to perform it. The latter truth is not so readily admitted as the former. Everyone recognizes that an opportunity of doing

evil is not a thing about which any choice is allowable. We are not permitted to use the opportunity or not, just as we please; we must on no account make use of it. But not a few persons imagine that an opportunity of doing *good* is a thing about which they have full right of choice; that they may avail themselves of the opportunity or not, just as they please; whereas there is no more freedom in the one case than in the other. We are bound to make use of the opportunity of doing good. "To him that knoweth to do good, and doeth it not, to him it is sin."

Some of those who think that St. James knew the Epistle to the Romans see here an allusion to the principle which St. Paul there lies down: "Whatsoever is not of faith is sin" (xiv. 23). For reasons already stated it must remain doubtful whether St. James had knowledge of that Epistle; and even if he had, we could not by any means be sure that he had it in his mind when he wrote the words before us. But his words and St. Paul's, when combined, give us a complete statement of a great moral principle respecting the possession or non-possession of knowledge as to what is right and wrong in any given case. So long as we have *no* knowledge that a given act is right, *i.e.* so long as we are in doubt as to whether it is allowable or not, it is sin to do it. As soon as we *have* knowledge that a given act is right it is sin to leave it undone.

This principle cuts at the root of that unwholesome growth which in moral theology is known as the doctrine of *Probabilism*, and which has worked untold mischief, especially in the Roman Church, in which its chief supporters are to be found. This doctrine teaches that in all cases in which there is doubt as to whether a given act is allowable or not the less safe course may be followed, even when the balance of probability is against its being allowable, if only there are grounds for believing that it *is* allowable. And some supporters of this doctrine go so far as to maintain that the amount of probability need not be very great. So long as it is not certain that the act in question is forbidden it may be permitted. The object of which teaching is not that which ought to be the object of all moral teaching, viz. to save beings with immortal souls from making serious mistakes of conduct, but to enable beings with strong desires and passions to gratify them without scruple. The moral law is not so much explained as explained away. The very titles of some of the treatises in which the doctrine of Probabilism is advocated indicate their tendency, *e.g.* "The Art of Perpetual Enjoyment."[83] To all such special pleading, and making the Word of God of none effect by human glosses, the simple principles laid down by St. Paul and St. James are the best antidote: "Whatsoever is not of faith is sin;" and "To him that knoweth to do good, and doeth it not, to him it is sin."

[81] Horace, *Odes* I. ix. 13. J. H. Newman, *Verses on Various Occasions*, "The Pillar of the Cloud," June 16th, 1833.

[82] In commenting on Wisdom ii. 4, Farrar quotes Gregory Nazianzen: "We are a flitting dream, a phantom that cannot be grasped, the scud of a passing breeze, a ship that leaves no trace on the sea, dust, vapour, morning dew, a flower that now blossoms, and now is done away" (*Speaker's Commentary, Apocrypha*, I., p. 431).

[83] *Ars Semper Gaudendi*, by Alphonso de Sarasa, a Flemish theologian of Spanish extraction, 1741. For the fullest account of the history of Probabilism see the great work by Döllinger and Reusch, *Geschichte der Moralstreitigkeiten in der Römisch-katholischen Kirche* (Nördlingen, 1889).

CHAPTER XXIII
THE FOLLIES AND INIQUITIES OF THE RICH; THEIR MISERABLE END

"Go to now, ye rich, weep and howl for your miseries that are coming upon you. Your riches are corrupted, and your garments are moth-eaten. Your gold and your silver are rusted; and their rust shall be for a testimony against you, and shall eat your flesh as fire. Ye have laid up your treasure in the last days. Behold, the hire of the labourers who mowed your fields, which is of you kept back by fraud, crieth out: and the cries of them that reaped have entered into the ears of the Lord of Sabaoth. Ye have lived delicately on the earth, and taken your pleasure; ye have nourished your hearts in a day of slaughter. Ye have condemned, ye have killed the righteous one; he doth not resist you."—St. James v. 1-6.

HERE, if anywhere in the Epistle, the writer glances aside from the believing Jews of the Dispersion, to whom the letter as a whole is addressed, and in a burst of righteous indignation which reminds us of passages in the old Hebrew Prophets, denounces members of the twelve tribes who not even in name are Christians. In the preceding section such a transition is in preparation. When he is condemning the godless presumption of those seekers after wealth who dared, without thought of their own frailty and of God's absolute control over their lives and fortunes, to think and speak confidently of their schemes for future gains, he seems to be thinking almost as much of unbelieving Jews as of those who have accepted the Gospel. Here he appears for the moment to have left the latter entirely out of sight, and to be addressing those wealthy Jews who not only continued the policy and shared the guilt of the opponents and murderers of Christ, but by scandalous tyranny and injustice oppressed their poor brethren, many of whom were probably Christians. The severity of the condemnation is not the only or the main reason for thinking that the paragraph is addressed to unconverted Jews. The first ten verses of chapter iv. are very severe; and there also, as here, the affectionate form of address, "brethren," so frequent elsewhere in the Epistle, is wanting; but there is no doubt that those ten verses, like the paragraphs which immediately precede and follow them, are addressed to Christians. What is so exceptional in the passage now under consideration is *the entire absence of any exhortation to repentance*, or of any indication that there is still hope of being reconciled to the offended Jehovah. They are to "weep and howl," not in penitence, but in despair. The end is at hand; the day of reckoning is approaching; and it is a fearful account which awaits them. In this respect there is a very marked difference between this paragraph and the one which follows it. In both the nearness of the Day of Judgment is the motive; but this nearness is to "the rich" a terror, to "the brethren" a comfort. This difference would be very difficult to explain if both paragraphs were addressed to believing Jews.

Throughout the Epistle there are strains which sound like echoes from the Prophets of the Old Testament, with whom St. James has much in common; but the passage before us is specially in their spirit. It would not surprise us to meet with it in Isaiah or Jeremiah. One or two similar passages are worth comparing: "Woe to thee that spoilest, and thou wast not spoiled; and dealest treacherously, and they dealt not treacherously with thee! When thou hast ceased to spoil, thou shalt be spoiled; and when thou hast made an end to deal treacherously, they shall deal treacherously with thee" (Isa. xxxiii. 1). "Woe to him that getteth an evil gain for his house, that he may set his nest on high, that he may be delivered from the hand of evil! Thou hast consulted shame to thy house, by cutting off many peoples, and hast sinned against thy soul. For the stone shall cry out of the wall, and the beam out of the timber shall answer it" (Hab. ii. 9). In the New Testament the passage which most resembles it is our Lord's denunciation of the scribes and Pharisees (Matt. xxiii. 13-36).

"Go to now, ye rich, weep and howl for your miseries that are coming upon you." We have the same combination of words in Isaiah: "In their streets they gird themselves with sackcloth: on their housetops, and in their broad places, every one *howleth, weeping* abundantly" (xv. 3). And in an earlier chapter we have a still closer parallel to the spirit of this verse: "*Howl ye; for the day of the Lord is at hand*" (xiii. 6). The miseries to which St. James alludes are those which shall befall them at "the coming of the Lord" (ver. 8). It is the impending judgment of the tyrannous rich that is primarily in his mind. He may also have foreseen something of the horrors of the Jewish war and the destruction of Jerusalem, and in accordance with Christ's prophecy may have considered these calamities typical of the judgment, or part and parcel of it. In the Jewish war the wealthy classes suffered terribly. Against them, as having been friendly to the Romans, and having employed Roman influence in oppressing their own countrymen, the fury of the fanatical party of the Zealots was specially directed; and although the blow fell first and heaviest upon the Jews in Jerusalem and Judæa, yet it was felt by all Jews throughout the world.

They imagined themselves to be rich; they were really most poor and most miserable. So sure is the doom that is coming upon them, that in prophetical style St. James begins to speak of it as already here; like a seer, he has it all before his eyes. "Your riches are corrupted, and your garments are moth-eaten. Your gold and your silver are rusted." We have here three kinds of possessions indicated. First, stores of various kinds of goods. These are "corrupted;" they have become rotten and worthless. Secondly, rich garments, which in the East are often a very considerable portion of a wealthy man's possessions. They have been stored up so jealously and selfishly that insects have preyed upon them and ruined them. And thirdly, precious metals. These have become tarnished and rusted, through not having been put to any rational use. Everywhere their avarice has been not only sin, but folly. It has failed of its sinful object. The unrighteous hoarding has tended not to wealth, but to ruin. And thus the rust of their treasures becomes "a testimony against them." In the ruin of their property their own ruin is portrayed; and just as corruption, and the moths, and the rust consume their goods, so shall the fire of God's judgment consume the owners and abusers of them. They have reserved all this store for their selfish enjoyment, but God has reserved them for His righteous anger.

"Ye laid up your treasure in the last days." *There* was the monstrous folly of it. The end of all things was close at hand; "the last days" had already begun; and these besotted graspers after wealth were still heaping up treasures which they would never have any opportunity of using. The Authorized Version spoils this by a small, but rather serious, mistranslation. It has, "Ye have heaped up treasure together *for* the last days," instead of "*in* the last days" (ἐν ἐσχάταις ὑμέραις). The case is precisely that which Christ foretold: "As were the days of Noah, so shall be the coming of the Son of man. For as in those days which were before the flood they were eating and drinking, marrying and giving in marriage, until the day that Noah entered into the ark, and they knew not until the flood came, and took them all away; so shall be the coming of the Son of man" (Matt. xxiv. 37-39). "Likewise even as it came to pass in the days of Lot; they ate, they drank, they bought, they sold, they planted, they builded; but in the day that Lot went out from Sodom it rained fire and brimstone from heaven, and destroyed them all: after the same manner shall it be in the day that the Son of man is revealed" (Luke xvii. 28-30).

That the "last days" mean the days immediately preceding the Second Advent can scarcely be doubted. The context renders this very probable, and the exhortation in the next section renders it practically certain. "Be ye also patient; stablish your hearts: for *the coming of the Lord is at hand.* Murmur not, brethren, one against another, that ye be not judged: behold, *the Judge standeth before the doors."* That the first Christians believed that Jesus Christ would return in glory during the lifetime of many who were then living, will hardly be disputed by any one who is acquainted with the literature of the Apostolic age and of the period immediately following. Nor, perhaps, will many at the present time care to dispute that this erroneous opinion was shared, for a time at any rate, even by Apostles. "Ye are guarded through faith unto a salvation ready to be revealed in the last time," says St. Peter (1 Peter i. 5). "We that are alive, that are left unto the coming of the Lord, shall in nowise precede them that are fallen asleep" (1 Thess. iv. 15; *cf.* 1 Cor. xv. 51); and again, writing some years later, "In the last days grievous times shall come," about which Timothy is to be on his guard, says St. Paul (2 Tim. iii. 1). And much nearer to the close of the Apostolic age we have St. John telling his little children that "it is the last hour" (1 John ii. 18). Some twenty or thirty years later St. Ignatius writes to the Ephesians, "These are the last times. Henceforth let us be reverent; let us fear the longsuffering of God, lest it turn into a judgment against us. For either let us fear the wrath which is to come, or let us love the grace which now is" (xi.).

Only very gradually did the Christian Church attain to something like a true perspective as to the duration of Christ's kingdom upon earth. Only very gradually did even the Apostles obtain a clear vision as to the nature of the kingdom which their Lord had founded and left in their charge, for them to occupy until He came. Pentecost did not at once give them perfect insight into the import of their own commission. Much still remained to be learned, slowly, by experience. And if this was the case with Apostles, we need not wonder that it was so with James, the Lord's brother. It is remarkable that Christ's solemn warning against speculating as to the time of His return seems to have made only partial impression upon the disciples. "Of that day or that hour knoweth no one, not even the angels in heaven, neither the Son, but the Father. Take ye heed, watch and pray: for ye know not when the time is" (Mark xiii. 32, 33). But it is our gain that they were allowed for a time to hold a belief that the Lord would return very speedily. The Epistles and Gospels were written by men under the influence of that belief, and such influence is a very considerable guarantee for the honesty of the writers. It was because the rich whom St. James here denounces had no such belief in a speedy judgment, indeed had very little thought of a judgment at all, that they were guilty of such folly and iniquity.

Having indicated their folly in amassing wealth which was no blessing to themselves or others, but simply deteriorated by being hoarded, St. James passes on to point out their iniquity. And first of all he mentions the gross injustice which is frequently inflicted by these wealthy employers of labour upon those who work for them. The payment of the wages which have been earned is either unfairly delayed or not paid at all. "Behold, the hire of the labourers who mowed your fields, which is of you kept back by fraud, crieth out." Several passages in the Old Testament appear to be in the writer's mind. "Thou shalt not oppress an hired servant that is poor and needy, whether he be of thy brethren, or of thy strangers that are in thy land within thy gates: *in his day thou shalt give him his hire,* neither shall the sun go down upon it; for he is poor, and setteth his heart upon it: lest he *cry* against thee unto the Lord, and it be sin unto thee" (Deut. xxiv. 14, 15; cf. 17, and Lev. xix. 13). "And I will come near you to judgment; and I will be a swift witness against ... those that *oppress the hireling in his wages,* the widow and the fatherless, and that turn away the stranger from his right, and fear not Me, saith the Lord" (Mal. iii. 5; *cf.* Jer. xxii. 13). Perhaps also, "Their cry came up unto God by reason of the bondage" (Exod. ii. 23); and "The voice of thy brother's blood crieth unto me from the ground" (Gen. iv. 10). The frequency with which the subject is mentioned[84] seems to show that the evil which St. James here denounces had long been a common sin among the Jews. Tobit, in his charge to his son, says, "What is hateful to thee do not thou to others. Let not the wages of any man, which hath wrought for thee, tarry with thee (abide with thee all night), but give him it out of hand" (Tobit iv. 14). And in Ecclesiasticus, which St. James seems so often to have in his thoughts, we read, "The bread of the needy is the life of the poor: he that defraudeth him thereof (ὁ ἀποστερῶν αὐτήν) is a man of blood. He that taketh away his neighbour's living slayeth him; and he that defraudeth the labourer of his hire (ὁ ἀποστερῶν μισθόν μισθίου)[85] is a blood-shedder" (Ecclus. xxxiv. 21, 22).

But none of these passages determine for us a point of some interest in the construction used by St. James. The words translated "*of you,*" in "of you kept back by fraud," literally mean "*from* you" (ἀφ' ὑμῶν, not ὑφ' ὑμῶν). Two explanations are suggested: 1. The fraudulent action proceeds *from* them, and hence "from" becomes nearly equivalent to "by;" and the use of "from" (ἀπό), rather than "by" (ὑπό), is all the more natural because the word for "kept back by fraud" has the former preposition compounded with it. 2. "From you," being placed between "kept back by fraud" and "crieth out" (ὁ ἀπεστερημένος ἀφ' ὑμῶν κράζει), may go with either, and it will be better to take it with "crieth out:" "The hire kept back by fraud *crieth out from you.*" The wrongfully detained wages are with the rich employers, and therefore it is from the place where they are detained that their cry goes up to heaven. The passage quoted above from Exodus ii. 23 slightly favours this view, for there the Septuagint has, "Their cry came up unto God *from their labours*" (ἀπὸ τῶν ἔργων); but the passages are not really parallel.

The word used for "fields" (χώρας) is worth noting. It implies extensive lands, and therefore adds point to the reproach. The men who own such large properties are not under the temptations to fraud which beset the needy, and it is scandalous that those who can so well afford to pay what is due should refuse. Moreover, the labour of mowing and reaping such fields must be great, and therefore the labourers have well earned their wage. The words "into the ears of the Lord of Sabaoth" probably come from Isaiah (v. 9), and perhaps St. James was led to them by the thought that these extensive fields are the result of fraud or violence; for the verse which precedes the words in Isaiah runs thus: "Woe unto them that join house to house, that lay field to field, till there be no room, and ye be made to dwell alone in the midst of the land!" No other New Testament writer uses the expression "the Lord of Sabaoth," although St. Paul once quotes it from Isaiah (Rom. ix. 29). Bede may be right in thinking that its point here is that the rich fancy that the poor have no protector; whereas the Lord of hosts hears their cry. And there is possibly another point in mowers and reapers being selected as the representatives of all hired labourers. Calvin suggests that it is specially iniquitous that those whose toil supplies us with food should themselves be reduced to starvation; and to this it has been added that the hard-heartedness of the grasping employers is indeed conspicuous when not even the joy of the harvest moves them to pay the poor who work for them their hardly earned wage.

The second feature in the iniquity of the rich is the voluptuous and prodigal life which they lead themselves, at the very time that they inflict such hardships upon the poor. "Ye lived delicately on the earth, and took your pleasure; ye nourished your hearts in a day of slaughter." The aorists should perhaps be translated as aorists throughout these verses: "Ye laid up your treasure, ... ye lived delicately," etc. rather than, "Ye *have* laid up, ye *have* lived," etc. The point of view is that of the Day of Judgment, when these wealthy sinners are confronted by the enormities which they committed during their lives. But it is a case in which it is quite permissible to render the Greek aorist by the English perfect. "On the earth" may either mean "during your lifetime," or may be in contrast to "entered into the ears of the Lord of Sabaoth." All the while that the cry against their iniquity was ascending to *heaven*, as an accumulating charge that would at last overwhelm them, they were living in luxury *on earth*, thinking nothing of the wrath to come. It was the converse of the old Epicurean doctrine, so graphically described by the Laureate in "The Lotus-eaters." There it is the gods who "lie beside their nectar" in ceaseless enjoyment, "careless of mankind," who send up useless lamentations, which provoke no more than a smile among the neglectful deities. Here it is the men who revel in boundless luxury, careless of the righteous God, whose vengeance they provoke by persistent neglect of His commands.

The meaning of "in a day of slaughter" is not easily determined. The "as" — "as in a day of slaughter" — must certainly be omitted. It was inserted to make more evident one of the possible interpretations of "day of slaughter." "Ye fattened your heart with perpetual banqueting, as if life were made up of killing and eating." "And in that day did the Lord, the Lord of hosts, call to weeping and to mourning, and baldness, and to girding with sackcloth: and behold, joy and gladness, slaying oxen and killing sheep, eating flesh and drinking wine: let us eat and drink, for to-morrow we die" (Isaiah xxii. 12, 13). If this be the idea which is expressed by the words in question, then the meaning would be, "Ye fared sumptuously every day." But it is possible that "in a day of slaughter" here balances "in the last days" just above. As the folly of heaping up treasure was augmented by the fact that it was done when the end of all things was at hand, so the iniquity of voluptuous living was augmented by the fact that their own destruction was at hand. In this case the wealthy owners, like stalled oxen, were unconsciously fattening themselves for the slaughter. Instead of sacrificing themselves to God's love and mercy, they had sacrificed and devoured their poor brethren. They had fed themselves, and not the flock; and unwittingly they were preparing themselves as a sacrifice to God's wrath. *For a sacrifice, either willingly or unwillingly, every one must be.*

Did any of those whom St. James here condemns remember his words when, a few years later, thousands of the Jews of the Dispersion were once more gathered together at Jerusalem for the sacrifice of the Passover, and there became unwilling sacrifices to God's slow but sure vengeance? As already pointed out, it was the wealthy among them who specially suffered. Their prosperity and their friendship with the Romans provoked the envy and enmity of the fanatical Zealots, and they perished in a day of slaughter. Josephus tells us that it was all one whether the richer Jews stayed in the city during the siege or tried to escape to the Romans; for they were equally destroyed in either case. Every such person was put to death, on the pretext that he was preparing to desert, but in reality that the plunderers might get his possessions. People who were evidently half-starved were left unmolested, when they declared that they had nothing; but those whose bodies showed no signs of privation were tortured to make them reveal the treasures which they were supposed to have concealed (*Bell. Jud.* V. x. 2).

"Ye condemned, ye killed the righteous one; he doth not resist you." Does this refer to the condemnation and death of Jesus Christ? This interpretation has found advocates in all ages — Cassiodorus, Bede,

Œcumenius, Grotius, Bengel, Lange, and other modern commentators; and it is certainly attractive. St. Peter, addressing the Jews in Solomon's Porch, says, "But ye denied the Holy and *Righteous One*, and asked for a murderer to be granted unto you, and killed the Prince of Life" (Acts iii. 14, 15). St. Stephen, in his speech before the Sanhedrin, asks, "Which of the prophets did not your fathers persecute? and they killed them which showed before of the coming of *the Righteous One*; of whom ye have now become betrayers and murderers" (Acts vii. 52; *cf.* xxii. 14, and 1 Pet. iii. 18). It is certainly no objection to this interpretation that St. James uses the aorist—"ye condemned, ye killed." That tense might fittingly be used either of a course of action in the past, as in the aorists immediately preceding, or of a single action, as of Abraham's offering Isaac (ii. 21). Nor is it any objection that in "He doth not resist you" St. James changes to the present tense. In any case the change from past to present has to be explained, and it is as easy to explain it of the present long-suffering of Christ, or of His abandoning them to their wickedness, as of the habitual meekness of the righteous man. Nor, again, is it any objection that the Jews addressed in this Epistle could not rightly be charged with the condemnation and death of Christ, for twenty or thirty years had elapsed since that event. It is by no means improbable that among the Jews then living there were many who had cried "Crucify Him" on Good Friday; and even if there were not, the words of St. James are quite justifiable. The Crucifixion was in a very real sense the act of the whole nation, far more so than was the murder of Zacharias the son of Jehoiada, and yet Jesus says to the Jews respecting Zacharias, "whom ye slew between the sanctuary and the altar." If at the present day the English might be told that they condemned and killed Charles I., and the French be told that they condemned and killed Louis XVI., much more might the Jews in the middle of the first century be said to have condemned and killed Jesus Christ.

But nevertheless, this attractive and tenable interpretation is probably not the right one; the context is against it. It is the evil that is inherent in class tyrannizing over *class* that is condemned, the rich oppressing the poor, and the godless persecuting the godly. "The righteous one" is here not an individual, but the representative of a class. The iniquitous violence which slew Jesus Christ and His martyrs, James the son of Zebedee and Stephen, *illustrates* what St. James says here, just as his own martyrdom does; but it does not follow from this that he is alluding to any one of these events in particular. The Book of Wisdom seems once more to be in the writer's mind: "Let us oppress the poor righteous man; let us not spare the widow, nor reverence the ancient grey hairs of the aged.... Let us lie in wait for the righteous; because he is not for our turn, and he is clean contrary to our doings: he upbraideth us with our offending the law, and objecteth to our infamy the transgressions of our education.... He is grievous to us even to behold: for his life is not like other men's; his ways are of another fashion.... Let us examine him with despitefulness and torture, that we may know his meekness, and prove his patience. Let us condemn him with a shameful death; for by his own saying he shall be respected" (ii. 10-20).

Julius Cæsar on one occasion stated his financial position by confessing that he needed half a million of money in order to be worth nothing. The spiritual condition of many prosperous men might be expressed in a similar way. Cæsar never allowed lack of funds to stand between him and his political aims; when he had nothing he borrowed at enormous interest. So also with us. In pursuing our worldly aims we sink deeper and deeper in spiritual ruin, and accumulate debts for an eternal bankruptcy. Riches are not a whit less perilous to the soul now than they were in the first century, and yet how few among the wealthy really believe that they are perilous at all. The wisdom of our forefathers has placed in the Litany a petition which every well-to-do person should say with his whole heart: "In all time of our *wealth, Good Lord, deliver us.*"

[84] In addition to the passages quoted in the text see Job vii. 1, 2; ix. 24; xii. 5, 6; xxiv. 1-12; xxxi. 38, 39.

[85] It is uncertain whether the word which St. James uses is ἀπεστερημένος or ἀφυστερημένος.

CHAPTER XXIV
PATIENCE IN WAITING. THE ENDURANCE
OF JOB.THE SIGNIFICANCE OF THE
MENTION OF JOB BY ST. JAMES

"Be patient therefore, brethren, until the coming of the Lord. Behold, the husbandman waiteth for the precious fruit of the earth, being patient over it, until it receive the early and latter rain. Be ye also patient; stablish your hearts: for the coming of the Lord is at hand. Murmur not, brethren, one against another, that ye be not judged; behold, the Judge standeth before the doors. Take, brethren, for an example of suffering and of patience, the prophets who spake in the Name of the Lord. Behold, we call them blessed which endured: ye have heard of the endurance of Job, and have seen the end of the Lord, how that the Lord is full of pity, and merciful." —St. James v. 7-11.

"BE patient, therefore, brethren." The storm of indignation is past, and from this point to the end of the Epistle St. James writes in tones of tenderness and affection. In the paragraph before us he, as it were, rounds off his letter, bringing it back to the point from which he started; so that what follows (vv. 12-20) is of the nature of a postscript or appendix. He began his letter with the exhortation, "Count it all joy, my brethren, when ye fall into manifold trials; knowing that the proof of your faith worketh patience. And let patience have its perfect work, that ye may be perfect and entire, lacking in nothing" (i. 2-4). He draws to a close with the charge, "Be patient therefore, brethren, until the coming of the Lord".

The "therefore" shows that this sympathetic exhortation of the brethren is closely connected with the stern denunciation of the rich in the preceding paragraph. The connexion is obvious. These brethren are in the main identical with the righteous poor who are so cruelly oppressed by the rich; and St. James offers them consolation mainly on two grounds: First, their sufferings will not last for ever; on the contrary, the end of them is near at hand. Secondly, the end of them will bring not only relief, but reward.

As has been already pointed out St. James evidently shared the belief, which prevailed in the Apostolic age, that Jesus Christ would very speedily return in glory to punish the wicked and reward the righteous. This belief, as Neander observes, was very natural: "Christ Himself had not chosen to give any information respecting the time of his coming. Nay, He had expressly said that the Father had reserved the decision to Himself alone (Mark xiii. 32); that even the Son could determine nothing respecting it. But still, the longing desire of the Apostolic Church was directed with eager haste to the appearing of the Lord. The whole Christian period seemed only as the transition-point to the eternal, and thus as something that must soon be passed. As the traveller, beholding from afar the object of all his wanderings, overlooks the windings of the intervening way, and believes himself already near his goal, so it seemed to them, as their eye was fixed on that consummation of the whole course of events on earth."

Thus, by a strange but unperceived incongruity, St. James makes the unconscious impatience of primitive Christianity a basis for his exhortation to conscious patience. Early Christians, in their eagerness for the return of their Lord, impatiently believed that His return was imminent; and St. James uses this belief as an argument for patient waiting and patient endurance. It is only for a short time that they will have to wait and endure, and then the rich reward will be reaped. Ploughing and harrowing are toilsome and painful, but they have to be gone through, and then, after no intolerable waiting, the harvest comes.

Above, when St. James was rebuking his readers for their presumptuous confidence respecting their future plans, he reminded them of the shortness of life. "What is your life? For ye are a vapour, that appeareth for a little time, and then vanisheth away" (iv. 14). Here the shortness of the interval between the present moment and the end of all things is urged as a reason both for circumspection and for patience. In both cases, with his characteristic fondness for illustrations drawn from nature, he employs physical phenomena to enforce his lesson. In the one case life is a vapour, not substantial at any time, and soon dispersed;[86] in the other case life is the work and the waiting which must precede the harvest.

The key-note of the whole passage is *patience*, which in one form or another occurs six times in five verses In the original two different words are used—one (μακροθμεῖν and μακροθμία) four times in the first four verses; and the other (ὑπομένειν and ὑπομενή) twice in the last verse, where we certainly need "the *endurance* of Job" rather than "the *patience* of Job," in order to preserve the transition from the one word to the other. "Take, brethren, for an example of suffering and of *patience* (μακροθυμίας) the prophets who spake in the Name of the Lord. Behold, we call them blessed which *endured* (τοὺς ὑπομείναντας): ye have heard of the *endurance* (ὑπομενήν) of Job." It was perhaps because "the *patience* of Job" has become a proverbial formula that the Revisers banished "endurance" to the margin, instead of placing it in the text.[87] The two words are not infrequently found together (2 Cor. vi. 4-6; Col. i. 11; 2 Tim. iii. 10; Clement of Rome, lviii.; Ignatius, *Ephes.* iii.). The difference between the two is, on the whole, this, that the first is the long-suffering which does not retaliate upon oppressive persons, the second the endurance which does not succumb under oppressive things. The persecuted prophets exhibited the one; the afflicted Job exhibited the other. The oppressed and poor Christians whom St. James addresses are able to practise both these forms of patience, which Chrysostom extols as the "queen of the virtues."

There is a remarkable diversity of readings in the illustration about the husbandman's waiting. Some authorities make him wait for the early and latter *rain*, others for the early and latter *fruit*. The best witnesses leave the substantive to be understood, and this is doubtless the original reading; it accounts for the other two. Some copyists thought that rain was to be understood, and therefore inserted it; while others for a similar reason inserted fruit. No doubt it is rain that is intended, in accordance with several passages in the Old Testament (Deut. xi. 14; Jer. v. 24; Joel ii. 23; Zech. x. 1). The rains of autumn and of spring are meant, not "morning rain and evening rain" as Luther renders it in his version; and no moral or spiritual facts are symbolized by these natural phenomena, such as the penitential tears of youth and of old age, which would not fit the context. The point of the simile lies in the patient waiting, not in that which is waited for.

"Murmur not, brethren, one against another." The literal meaning of the Greek is *"Groan* not;" that is, "Grumble not." Earlier English versions have "Grudge not;" and "grudge" once had the meaning of "murmur," as in "They will run here and there for meat, and *grudge* if they be not satisfied" (Ps. lix. 15). It is altogether a mistake to suppose that "one against another" includes the wealthy oppressors spoken of in the preceding section. It is the common experience of every one that men who are irritated and exasperated by trying persons or circumstances are liable to vent their vexation on those who are in no way responsible for what tries them. St. James is well aware of this danger, and puts his readers on their guard against it. "Be long-suffering," he says, "and do not retaliate on those who maltreat you; and do not let the smart of your troubles betray you into impatience towards one another. He who is to judge your oppressors will judge you also, and He is close at hand." We can hardly doubt that Christ's saying, "Judge not, *that ye be not judged*" (Matt. vii. 1), is in his mind. The way to lighten one's burden is not to groan over it, still less to murmur against those who are in the same case, but to try to console and help them. "Bear ye one another's burdens, and so fulfil the law of Christ." It is a good thing to take as an example of patience the prophets and others among God's suffering saints; but it is a still better thing to give such an example ourselves.

By the prophets St. James no doubt means the prophets of the Old Testament—Elijah, Jeremiah, and others. It is not likely that he includes any of the persecuted disciples of the New Testament, such as James the son of Zebedee, and Stephen. Here again we seem to have an echo of Christ's words: "*Blessed* are ye when men shall reproach you, and persecute you" (comp. "We call them *blessed* which endured"): "for so persecuted they the *prophets* which were before you" (Matt. v. 11, 12). It is the ceaseless reproach against the Jews that they boasted that theirs were the prophets, and yet were the persecutors of the prophets. "The children of Israel ... have slain Thy prophets with the sword," says Elijah (1 Kings xix. 10, 14). "That I may avenge the blood of My servants the prophets," says God to Elisha (2 Kings ix. 7). They "slew Thy prophets which testified against them to turn them again to Thee," says Nehemiah, in his prayer (Neh. ix. 26). "Your own sword hath devoured your prophets, like a destroying lion," is the accusation of Jeremiah (ii. 30). "O Jerusalem, Jerusalem, which killeth the prophets, and stoneth them that are sent unto her!" is the lamentation of Christ (Matt. xxiii. 37). And Stephen, just before he was himself added to the number of the slain, asks, "Which of the prophets did not your fathers persecute? and they killed them which showed before of the coming of the Righteous One" (Acts vii. 52). Certainly those who try to do God's work in the world have no lack of examples of patient suffering for such work. The reasonable question would seem to be, not, "Why should I be made to suffer for endeavouring to do good?" but, "Why should I *not* be made to suffer? Seeing what others have had to endure, why should I be spared?"

"Ye have heard of the endurance of Job." It is possible that this refers specially to the reading of the Book of Job in public service; but there is no need to restrict the hearing to such occasions. We need not doubt that the endurance of Job was a familiar topic among the Jews long before this Epistle was written, and independently of the book being read in the synagogues. Yet, in spite of this familiarity, the passage before us is the only reference in the whole of the New Testament to the story of Job, and there is only one quotation from the Book: "He taketh the wise in their own craftiness" (Job v. 13) is quoted by St. Paul (1 Cor. iii. 19). There are several loose quotations from it in the Epistle of Clement of Rome (xvii., xx., xxvi., xxxix., lvi.); and the remarkable insertion in the Vulgate Version of Tobit ii. 12-15 is worthy of quotation: "This trial the Lord *therefore* permitted to happen to him, that an example might be given to posterity of his patience, as also of holy Job. For whereas he had always feared God from his infancy, and kept His commandments, he repined not against God because the evil of blindness had befallen him, but continued immovable in the fear of God, giving thanks to God all the days of his life. For as the kings[88] insulted over holy Job, so his relations and kinsmen mocked at his life, saying, Where is thy hope, for which thou gavest alms, and buriedest the dead? But Tobias rebuked them, saying, Speak not so; for we are the children of saints, and look for that life which God will give to them that never change their faith from Him."

"Ye have heard of the endurance of Job, and have seen the end of the Lord, how that the Lord is full of pity, and merciful." A well-supported, but, on the whole, less probable reading, gives us the imperative, "*see* the end of the Lord," instead of the indicative, "ye have seen" (ἴδετε, instead of εἴδετε). If it be correct, it may be taken either with what precedes or with what follows: either, "Ye have heard of the endurance of Job: see also the end of the Lord, how that the Lord is full of pity, and merciful;" or, "Ye have heard of the endurance of Job and the end of the Lord: see that the Lord is full of pity, and merciful."

But a more important question than either the reading or the division of the clauses is the meaning of the expression "the end of the Lord." Bede follows Augustine in understanding it of the death of Christ, which no doubt many of the readers of the Epistle had witnessed —"*Exitum quoque Domini in cruce quem longanimiter suscepit, adstantes ipsi vidistis*": and in this interpretation Bede is followed by Wetstein, Lange, and some other modern writers. It cannot be considered as probable. St. James would hardly couple the endurance of Job with the death of Christ in this abrupt way; and the words which follow —"that the Lord is full of pity, and merciful" — do not fit on to this interpretation. "The end of the Lord" much more probably means the end to which the Lord brought the sufferings of Job. It may have special reference to the concluding portion of the Book of Job, in which Jehovah is represented as bringing the argument to a close: "Then the Lord answered Job out of the whirlwind, and said, Who is this that darkeneth counsel by words without knowledge?" etc., etc. (xxxviii.-xlii.). This appearance of Jehovah to end the trials of Job would then be analogous to the appearance of Christ to end the trials of the persecuted Christians; and it is possible that the combination "ye have heard ... and have seen" was suggested by the last words of Job: "*I have heard of* Thee by the hearing of the ear; but now mine eye *seeth* Thee. Wherefore I abhor myself, and repent in dust and ashes" (xlii. 5, 6).

Stier remarks that the mention of Job in Ezekiel (xiv. 14, 16, 20), and here by St. James, shows us "that the man Job actually lived, like Noah, Daniel, and all the prophets; that the narrative of his life is not a didactic poem, but a real history." But is that a necessary conclusion? Let us leave on one side the question whether or no there really was such a person as Job, who experienced what is recorded in the book which bears his name, and let us consider whether the mention of him by Ezekiel and by St. James proves that there was such a person. It proves nothing of the sort. It shows no more than this, that the story of Job was well known, and was employed for moral and spiritual instruction. Let us suppose that the Book of Job is a parable, like that of Dives and Lazarus. Would the fact that its contents are not historical prevent Ezekiel or St. James from speaking of Job as a well-known person of exemplary life? There would be nothing unnatural in coupling together Dives, who is probably an imaginary person, and the rich young man, who is certainly a real person, as examples of men to whom great wealth has proved disastrous, nor, again, in speaking of Lazarus and the penitent thief as instances of souls that had passed from great earthly suffering to the rest of Paradise. Such combinations would not commit the writer or speaker who made use of them to the belief that Dives and Lazarus were historical persons. Why, then, should the fact that an inspired writer couples Job with Noah and Daniel commit *us* to the belief that Job is a real person? He may have been so, just as Lazarus may have been so, but the mention of him by Ezekiel and by St. James does not prove that he was. We know too little about the effects of inspiration to be justified in saying dogmatically that an inspired writer would never speak of an unhistorical person as an example to be imitated. Is the merchant who sold all that he had in order to buy one pearl of great price an historical person? and is he not put before us as an example to be imitated? It is quite possible that the story of Job is in the main a narrative of facts, and not an inspired fiction; but the mention of him by Ezekiel and by St. James is no proof of it. It is neither fair nor prudent to cite either of them as witnesses to the historical character of the Book of Job. It is not fair, because we are ignorant of their opinion on the subject, and are also ignorant as to whether their opinion on the subject would be under the direct inspiration of the Holy Spirit. And it is not prudent, because it may be demonstrated hereafter that the story of Job is not historical; and then we shall have pledged the testimony of inspired persons to the truth of a narrative which is, after all, fictitious. If St. Paul may cite Jannes and Jambres as instances of malignant opposition to the truth, without compelling us to believe that those names are historical,[89] St. James may quote Job as an example of patient endurance, without obliging us to believe that Job is an historical personage. In each case the historical character of the illustrations must be decided on other grounds than the fact that they are employed by writers who were inspired.[90]

Questions of this kind are among the many spheres in which we need that virtue on which St. James here insists with such simple earnestness—patience. When certainty has not been attained, and perhaps is not attainable, let us learn to wait patiently in uncertainty. Was there ever such a person as Job? Who wrote the Book of Job? What is its date? Does inspiration produce infallibility? and if so, what are the limits to such infallibility? There are men to whom uncertainty on such questions as these seems intolerable. They cannot "learn to labour and to wait;" they cannot work patiently, and wait patiently, until a complete solution is found. And hence they hurry to a definite conclusion, support it by evidence that is not relevant, and affirm that it is demonstrated by what is perhaps relevant, but is far short of proof. Intellectual probation is part of our moral probation in this life, and it is a discipline much needed in an age of great mental activity. Impatience of the intellect is a common blemish, and it is disastrous both to him who allows himself to be conquered by it and to the cause of truth. He does good service both to himself and to others, who cultivates a dread of jumping to unproved conclusions, and who in speaking and writing watchfully distinguishes what is certain from what is only probable, and what is probable from what is only not known to be untrue.

The great example of patience is not given by St. James, although we can read it into his words. In a sense not meant by him there is the Husbandman, who waiteth for the precious fruit of the earth, until it receive the early and the latter rain. There is that precious harvest of human souls which must receive and welcome the dew of God's grace before it is ready for His garner. On some it has never yet fallen; on some it has fallen, but as yet in vain; and meanwhile the Husbandman waiteth, "being patient over it," until it receive the one thing needful. Through long, long centuries He has been waiting, and He continues so doing. St. Augustine tells us why. God is "patient, because He is eternal" (*patiens quia æternus*). He who is "from everlasting to everlasting" can afford to wait. He waits patiently for us, generation after generation. Can we not wait for Him one hour? Let us patiently abide until "the end of the Lord" comes, the end which He has prepared for us, and towards which all things under His guiding hand are working. When we have seen it we shall once more see "that the Lord is full of pity, and merciful."[91]

> [86] As already pointed out, this metaphor is perhaps a reminiscence of the Book of Job, to which St. James alludes in the passage before us. He was evidently fond of the sapiential writings, to which Job is akin. "My days are swifter than a weaver's shuttle, and are spent without hope. As the cloud is consumed and vanisheth away, so he that

goeth down to Sheol shall come up no more" (Job vii. 6, 9). See [footnote [84]].

[87] The Rhemish Version distinguishes the words—"be patient" and "patience" for the one, "suffer" and "sufferance" for the other, the Vulgate having *patientia* and *sufferentia*.

[88] *Reges.* "So Job's friends are here called, because they were princes in their respective territories." Note in the Douay Version, from which the translation of the passage is taken.

[89] See *The Pastoral Epistles*, in this series, pp. 379-84 (Hodder and Stoughton, 1888).

[90] That the Book of Job is not pure history is plain from (1) the dialogue between Jehovah and Satan, and the addresses ascribed to the Almighty in the body of the poem; (2) the dramatic character of Job's calamities, man and nature alternately inflicting blows at him, and in each case just one messenger escaping; (3) the dramatic character of his compensation, his goods being exactly doubled, and his family being made exactly what it was before; (4) the elaboration of the dialogue between Job and his friends. On the other hand, it is not likely that it is pure invention. We have no evidence of literary power equal to such invention at the early date to which the Book of Job must be assigned, viz. before the Return from the Captivity; and the writer's object would be better attained if he took an historical person, than if he invented one, as his centre.

[91] The word for "full of pity" (πολύσπλαγχνος) was possibly coined by St. James himself; it occurs nowhere else. It might be rendered "large-hearted." A few inferior MSS. have πολυεύσπλαγχνος, a word which is found in ecclesiastical and Byzantine writers. The simpler εὔσπλαγχνος occurs 1 Pet. iii. 8; Eph. iv. 32; and in the Prayer of Manasses; ὅτι σὺ εἶ κύριοσ ὕψιστος, εὔσπλαγχνος, μακρόθυμος, καὶ πολυέλεος. The unique πολύσπλαγχνος looks like a combination of πολυέλεοσ and εὔσπλαγχνος. Comp. Joel ii. 13; Jonah iv. 2. The word for "merciful" occurs Luke vi. 36 (comp. Col. iii. 12) and frequently in the Septuagint; *e.g.* Ecclus. ii. 11; οἰκτίρμων καὶ ἐλεήμων ὁ κύριος.

CHAPTER XXV
THE PROHIBITION OF SWEARING. THE RELATION OF THE LANGUAGE OF ST. JAMES TO RECORDED SAYINGS OF CHRIST

"But above all things, my brethren, swear not, neither by the heaven, nor by the earth, nor by any other oath: but let your yea be yea, and your nay, nay; that ye fall not under judgment."—St. James v. 12.

THE main portion of the Epistle is already concluded. St. James has worked through his chief topics back to the point from which he started, viz. the blessedness of steadfast and patient endurance of trials and temptations. But one or two other subjects occur to him, and he reopens his letter to add them by way of a farewell word of counsel.

One of the leading thoughts in the letter has been warning against sins of the tongue (i. 19, 26; iii. 1-12; iv. 11, 13; v. 9). He has spoken against talkativeness, unrestrained speaking, love of correcting others, railing, cursing, boasting, murmuring. One grievous form of sinful speech he has not mentioned particularly; and about this he adds a strong word of warning in this postscript to the Epistle: "Above all things, my brethren, swear not."

Two questions are raised by this remarkable prohibition—first, the exact meaning of it, especially whether it forbids swearing for any purpose whatever; and secondly, its relation to the almost identical prohibition uttered by Christ in the Sermon on the Mount (Matt. v. 35, 36). It will be obvious that whatever this relation may be, the meaning of our Lord's injunction determines the meaning of St. James in his injunction. It is hardly worth arguing that he did not mean either more or less than Christ meant.

I. The immediate context of the prohibition is worth noting in each case; it seems to throw light upon the scope of the prohibition. Jesus Christ, after saying "Swear not at all; neither by the heaven, ... nor by the earth.... But let your speech be, Yea, yea; Nay, nay," goes on to forbid retaliation of injuries, and to enjoin love towards enemies. St. James enjoins long-suffering towards enemies, thence goes on to forbid swearing, and then again returns to the subject of how to behave under affliction and ill-treatment: "Is any among you suffering? let him pray." Prayer, not cursing and swearing, is the right method of finding relief. There is, therefore, some reason for thinking that both in the Sermon on the Mount and here the prohibition of swearing has special reference to giving vent to one's feelings in oaths when one is exasperated by injury or adversity. No kind of oath is allowable for any such purpose.

But it is quite clear that this is not the whole meaning of the injunction in either place. "But let your speech be, Yea, yea; Nay, nay;" and, "But let your yea be yea, and your nay, nay," manifestly refers to strengthening affirmations and negations by adding to them the sanction of an oath. There was an old saying, now unhappily quite grotesque in its incongruity with facts, that "an Englishman's word is as good as his bond." What Christ and St. James say is that a Christian's word should be as good as his oath. There ought to be no need of oaths. Anything over and above simple affirming or denying "cometh of the evil one." It is because Satan, the father of lies, has introduced falsehood into the world that oaths have come into use. Among Christians there should be no untruthfulness, and therefore no oaths. The use of oaths is an index of the presence of evil; it is a symptom of the prevalence of falsehood.

But the use of oaths is not only a sign of the existence of mischief, it is also apt to be productive of mischief. It is apt to produce a belief that there are two kinds of truth, one of which it is a serious thing to violate, viz. when you are on your oath; but the other of which it is a harmless, or at least a venial thing to violate, viz. when falsehood is only falsehood, and not perjury. And this, both among Jews and among Christians, produces the further mischievous refinement that some oaths are more binding than others, and that only when the most stringent form of oath is employed is there any real obligation to speak the truth. How disastrous all such distinctions are to the interests of truth, abundant experience has testified: for a common result is this;—that people believe that they are free to lie as much as they please, so long as the lie is not supported by the particular kind of oath which they consider to be binding.

Thus much, then, is evident, that both our Lord and St. James forbid the use of oaths (1) as an expression of feeling, (2) as a confirmation of ordinary statements; for the prohibitions plainly mean as much as this, and we know from other sources that these two abuses were disastrously common among both Jews and Gentiles at that time. That converts to Christianity were exempt from such vices is most improbable; and hence the need that St. James should write as he does on the subject.

But the main question is whether the prohibition is *absolute*; whether our Lord and St. James forbid the use of oaths *for any purpose whatever*;

and it must be admitted that the first impression which we derive from their words is that they do. This view is upheld by not a few Christians as the right interpretation of both passages. Christ says, "Swear not *at all* (μὴ ὀμόσαι ὅλως).... But let your speech be, Yea, yea; Nay, nay." St. James says, "Swear not, neither by the heaven, nor by the earth, *nor by any other oath* (μήτε ἄλλον τινὰ ὅρκον): but let your yea be yea, and your nay, nay." In both cases we have an unqualified prohibition of what is to be avoided, followed by a plain command as to what is to be done.

But further investigation does not confirm the view which is derived from a first impression as to the meaning of the words. Against it we have, first, the fact that the Mosaic Law not only allowed, but enjoined the taking of an oath in certain circumstances; and Christ would hardly have abrogated the law, and St. James would hardly have contradicted it, without giving some explanation of so unusual a course; secondly, the indisputable practice of the early Church, of St. Paul, and of our Lord Himself.

In Deuteronomy we read, "Thou shalt fear the Lord thy God; and Him shalt thou serve, and *shalt swear by His Name*" (vi. 13); and, "to Him shalt thou cleave, and *by His Name shalt thou swear*" (x. 20). The Psalmist says, "The king shall rejoice in God; every one that sweareth by Him shall glory: but the mouth of them that speak lies shall be stopped" (lxiii. 11). Isaiah says, "He that sweareth in the earth shall swear by the God of truth" (lxv. 16); and still more strongly Jeremiah: "Thou shalt swear, As the Lord liveth, in truth, in judgment, and in righteousness" (iv. 2); and, "If they will diligently learn the ways of My people, to swear by My Name, As the Lord liveth; even as they taught My people to swear by Baal; then shall they be built up in the midst of My people" (xii. 16. Comp. xxiii. 7, 8). An absolute prohibition of all swearing would have been so surprisingly at variance with these passages of Scripture that it is difficult to believe that it would have been made without any allusion to them. Even the Essenes, who were very strict about swearing, and considered it to be worse than perjury (for a man is condemned already who cannot be believed except upon his oath), imposed "terrific oaths" (ὅρκους φρικώδεις) upon those who wished to enter their community, before admitting them (Josephus, *Bell. Jud.* II. viii. 6, 7; *Ant.* XV. x. 4); and we can hardly suppose that St. James means to take up a more extreme position than that of the Essenes.

But even if we suppose that he does mean this we have still to explain the *practice* of those who were well aware of Christ's command respecting swearing, and certainly had no intention of deliberately violating it. If the first Christians were willing on certain occasions to take certain oaths, it must have been because they were fully persuaded that Jesus Christ had not forbidden them to do so. When called upon by heathen magistrates to take an oath, the distinction which they drew was not between swearing and not swearing, but between taking oaths that committed them to idolatry and oaths which did nothing of the kind. The latter oaths they were willing to take. Thus Tertullian says that they would not swear by the *genii* of the emperors, because these were supposed to be demons; but by the safety of the emperors they were willing to swear (*Apol.* xxxii.). Origen writes to much the same effect (*Con. Celsum*, viii., lxv.). The oath by the *genius*, or *numen*, or "fortune" (τύχη) of the emperor was recognized as a formula for abjuring Christianity. Thus the proconsul presses Polycarp again and again: "Swear by the genius of Cæsar; swear the oath, and I will release thee" (*Mart. Pol.* ix., x.); and the fear of being betrayed into an act of idolatry was one of the main reasons why the early Christians disliked taking oaths. But there was also the feeling that for Christians oaths ought to be quite unnecessary. Thus Clement of Alexandria says that the true Christian ought to maintain a life calculated to inspire such confidence in those without that an oath would not even be demanded of him. And of course, when he swears, he swears truly; but he is not apt to swear, and rarely has recourse to an oath. And his speaking the truth on oath arises from his harmony with the truth (*Strom.* vii., viii.). Pelagius maintained that all swearing was forbidden; but Augustine contends, on the authority of Scripture, that oaths are not unlawful, although he would have them avoided as much as possible (*Ep.* clvii. Comp. *Epp.* cxxv., cxxvi.).

But there is not only the evidence as to how the primitive Church understood the words of Christ and of St. James; there is also the practice of St. Paul, who frequently calls God to witness that he is speaking the truth (2 Cor. i. 23; xi. 31; xii. 19; Gal. i. 20; Phil. i. 8), or uses other strong asseverations which are certainly more than plain Yea and Nay (Rom. ix. i.; 1 Cor. xv. 31; 2 Cor. i. 18; xi. 10). Augustine quotes St. Paul in defence of swearing, but adds that St. Paul's swearing, when there was weighty reason for it, is no proof that we may swear whenever we think proper to do so. And in the Epistle to the Hebrews the fact that men swear in order to settle disputes is mentioned without any intimation that the practice is utterly wrong. On the contrary, we are told that God has condescended to do the same, in order to give us all the assurance in His power (vi. 16-18).

Lastly, we have the convincing fact that Jesus Christ allowed Himself to be put upon His oath. After having kept silence for a long time, He was *adjured* by the High Priest to answer; and then He answered at once. The full meaning of the High Priest's words are, "I exact an oath of Thee (ἐξορκίζω σε) by the Living God" (Matt. xxvi. 63, 64). Had this been an unlawful thing for the High Priest to do, our Lord would have kept silence all the more, or would have answered under protest.

II. It remains to consider the relation of the prohibition of swearing in this Epistle to the almost identical prohibition in the Sermon on the Mount. Is St. James quoting Christ's words? and if so, whence did he derive his knowledge of them?

No one who compares the two passages will believe that the similarity between them is accidental. Even if such an hypothesis could reasonably be entertained, it would be shattered by the number of other coincidences which exist between passages in this Epistle and the recorded words of Christ. In this instance we have the largest amount of coincidence; and therefore the discussion of this point has been reserved until this passage was reached, although numerous other cases of coincidence have already occurred.

The remark is sometimes made that there are more quotations of Christ's words in the Epistle of St. James than in all the Epistles of St. Paul, or than in all the other books of the New Testament other than the Gospels. It would be better to word the remark somewhat differently, and say that there are more coincidences which cannot be fortuitous between this Epistle and the recorded words of Christ than in all the Epistles of St. Paul; or that there is far more evidence of the influence of Christ's discourses upon the language of St. James than there is of any such influence upon the language of St. Paul. St. Paul tells us much about Christ and His work, but he very rarely reproduces any of His sayings. With St. James it is exactly the opposite; he says very little indeed about Christ, but, without quoting them as such, he frequently reproduces His words. It will be found that the largest number of these coincidences are between St. James and sayings that are recorded by St. Matthew, especially in the Sermon on the Mount. But this does not warrant us in asserting that St. James must have seen St. Matthew's Gospel or any other written Gospels. The coincidences, as will be seen, are not of a character to show this. Moreover, it is extremely doubtful whether any of the Gospels were written so early as A.D. 62, the latest date which can be given to our Epistle; and if any earlier date be assigned to it, the improbability of the writer's having seen a written Gospel becomes all the greater. The resemblances between the words of St. James and the recorded words of Christ are such as would naturally arise if he had himself heard Christ's teaching, and was consciously or unconsciously reproducing what he remembered of it, rather than such as would be found if he had had a written document to quote from. If this be so, we have a strong confirmation of the view adopted at the outset, that this Epistle is the work of the Lord's brother, who had personal experience of Christ's conversation, and was independent of both the oral and the written tradition of His teaching. It will be worth while to tabulate the principal coincidences, so that the reader may be able to judge for himself as to their significance. They suffice to show how full the mind of St. James must have been of the teaching of Jesus Christ, and they lead to the highly probable conjecture that in other parts of the Epistle we have reminiscences of Christ's words of which we have no record in the Gospels.[92] It is not likely that St. James has remembered and reproduced only those sayings of which there is something recorded by the Evangelists.

ST. MATTHEW.	ST. JAMES.
1. Blessed are they that have been persecuted for righteousness' sake: for theirs is the kingdom of heaven. Blessed are ye when men shall reproach you, and persecute you, and say all manner of evil against you falsely, for My sake. Rejoice and be exceeding glad: for great is your reward in heaven: for so persecuted they the prophets which were before you (v. 10-12).	Count it all joy, my brethren, when ye fall into manifold temptations; knowing that the proof of your faith worketh patience (i. 2, 3). Take, brethren, for an example of suffering and of patience, the prophets who spake in the name of the Lord. Behold, we call them blessed which endured (v. 10, 11).
2. Ye therefore shall be perfect, as your heavenly Father is perfect (v. 48).	And let patience have its perfect work, that ye may be perfect and entire, lacking in nothing (i. 4).
3. Ask, and it shall be given you; seek, and ye shall find; knock, and it shall be opened unto you: for every one that asketh receiveth (vii. 7, 8).	But if any of you lacketh wisdom, let him ask of God, who giveth to all liberally and upbraideth not; and it shall be given him (i. 5).
4. Blessed are the poor in spirit: for theirs is the kingdom of heaven (v. 3. Comp. Luke vi. 20).	Let the brother of low degree glory in his high estate (i. 9). Did not God choose them that are poor as to the world to be rich in faith, and heirs of the kingdom? (ii. 5).
5. Not every one that saith unto Me, Lord, Lord, shall enter into the kingdom of heaven; but he that doeth the will of My Father which is in heaven.... And every one that heareth these words of Mine, and doeth them not, shall be likened unto a foolish man, which built his house upon the sand (vii. 21, 26).	Be ye doers of the word, and not hearers only, deluding your own selves. For if any one is a hearer of the word, and not a doer, he is like unto a man beholding his natural face in a mirror (i. 22, 23).

6. Blessed are the merciful: for they shall obtain mercy (v. 7).	So speak ye, and so do, as men that are to be judged by a law of liberty. For judgment is without mercy to him that hath showed no mercy: mercy glorieth against judgment (ii. 12, 13).
If ye forgive not men their trespasses, neither will your Father forgive your trespasses (vi. 15).	
With what judgment ye judge, ye shall be judged (vii. 2).	
7. Do men gather grapes of thorns, or figs of thistles? (vii. 16).	Can a fig-tree, my brethren, yield olives, or a vine figs? (iii. 12).
8. No man can serve two masters: for either he will hate the one, and love the other; or else he will hold to one, and despise the other. Ye cannot serve God and Mammon (vi. 24).	Know ye not that the friendship of the world is enmity with God? Whosoever, therefore would be a friend of the world maketh himself an enemy of God (iv. 4).
9. Whosoever shall humble himself shall be exalted (xxiii. 12).	Humble yourselves in the sight of the Lord, and He shall exalt you (iv. 10).
10. Be not therefore anxious for the morrow (vi. 34).	Whereas ye know not what shall be on the morrow (iv. 14).
11. Lay not up for yourselves treasures upon the earth, where moth and rust doth consume (vi. 19).	Your riches are corrupted, and your garments are moth-eaten. Your gold and your silver are rusted (v. 2, 3).
12. Swear not at all; neither by the heaven, for it is the throne of God; nor by the earth, for it is the footstool of His feet; nor by Jerusalem, for it is the city of the great King. Neither shalt thou swear by thy head, for thou canst not make one hair white or black. But let your speech, be Yea, yea; Nay, nay: and whatsoever is more than these is of the evil one (v. 34-37).	But above all things, my brethren, swear not, neither by the heaven, nor by the earth, nor by any other oath.

But let your yea be yea, and your nay, nay; that ye fall not under judgment (v. 12). |

These twelve parallels are by no means exhaustive, but they are among the most striking. The following are worthy of consideration, although those which have been quoted above are more than sufficient for our purpose:—

St. Matthew	St. James
i. 19	v. 19
i. 20	v. 22
ii. 8	vii. 12
ii. 10, 11	v. 27

Let us now consider some coincidences between the language of St. James and our Lord's words as recorded by the other three Evangelists.

ST. MARK.	ST. JAMES.
13. Whosoever shall say unto this mountain, Be thou taken up and cast into the sea; and shall not doubt (διακριθῇ) in his heart, but shall believe that what he saith cometh to pass; he shall have it (xi. 23).	If any of you lacketh wisdom, let him ask of God, who giveth to all liberally and upbraideth not. But let him ask in faith, nothing doubting (διακρινόμενος): for he that doubteth etc. (i. 5, 6).
14. They shall deliver you up to councils; and in synagogues shall ye be beaten (xiii. 9).	Do not the rich oppress you, and themselves drag you before the judgment-seats? (ii. 6).
15. Know ye that he is nigh, even at the doors (xiii. 29; Matt. xxiv. 33).	Behold, the Judge standeth before the doors (v. 9).

ST. LUKE.	ST. JAMES.
16. Woe unto you, ye that laugh now! for ye shall mourn and weep (vi. 25).	Let your laughter be turned to mourning, and your joy to heaviness (iv. 9).
17. Woe unto you that are rich for ye have received your consolation (vi. 24).	Go to now, ye rich, weep and howl for your miseries that are coming upon you (v. 1).

ST. JOHN.	ST. JAMES.
18. If ye know these things, blessed are ye if ye do them (xiii. 17).	Being not a hearer that forgetteth, but a doer that worketh, this man shall be blessed in his doing (i. 25).
19. If ye were of the world, the world would love its own: but because ye are not of the world, ... therefore the world hateth you (xv. 19. Comp. xvii. 14).	Know ye not that the friendship of the world is enmity with God? Whosoever therefore would be a friend of the world maketh himself an enemy of God (iv. 4).

It will be observed that these reminiscences of the teaching of Christ are all of one kind. They are all of them concerned with the morality of the Gospel, with Christian conduct and Christian life. Not one of them is doctrinal, or gives instruction as to the Christian creed. This, again, is what we might expect if the brother of the Lord is the writer of the Epistle. At the time when he listened to his Divine Brother's teaching he did not believe on Him. The doctrinal part of His discourses was precisely that part which did not impress him; it seemed to him as the wild fancies of an enthusiast (Mark iii. 21). But the moral teaching of Jesus impressed many of those who rejected His claims to be the Messiah, and it is this element which St. James remembers.

Before concluding, let us return to the moral precept contained in the verse which we have been considering: "Above all things, my brethren, swear not." The prohibition has not ceased to be necessary, as our daily experience proves. The vice of profane swearing (and all swearing about ordinary matters is profane) is a strange one. Where is the pleasure of it? Where, before it becomes a fashion or a habit, is the temptation to it? Where, in any case, is the sense of it? There is pleasure in gluttony, in drunkenness, in lust, in pride, in avarice, in revenge. But where is the pleasure in an oath? The sensualist, the hypocrite, the miser, and the murderer can at least plead strong temptation, can at least urge that they get something, however pitiful, in exchange for eternal loss. But what can the blasphemer plead? what does he get in exchange for his soul? In times of strong excitement it is no doubt a relief to the feelings to use strong language; but what is gained by making the strong language trebly culpable by adding blasphemy to it? Besides which, there is the sadly common case of those who use blasphemous words when there is no temptation to give vent to strong feeling in strong language, who habitually swear in cold blood. Let no one deceive himself with the paltry excuse that he cannot help it, or that there is no harm in it. A resolution to do something disagreeable every time an oath escaped one's lips would soon bring about a cure. And let those who profess to think that there is no harm in idle swearing ask themselves whether they expect to repeat that plea when they give an account for every idle word at the day of judgment (Matt. xii. 36).

[92] See Salmon's *Introduction to the N.T.*, pp. 221, 500, 4th ed., 1889.

CHAPTER XXVI
WORSHIP THE BEST OUTLET AND REMEDY FOR EXCITEMENT.THE CONNEXION BETWEEN WORSHIP AND CONDUCT

"Is any among you suffering? let him pray. Is any cheerful? let him sing praise." —St. James v. 13.

THE subject of this verse was probably suggested by that of the preceding one. Oaths are not a right way of expressing one's feelings, however strong they may be, and of whatever kind they may be. There is, however, no need to stifle such feelings, or to pretend to the world that we have no emotions. In this respect, as in many others, Christianity has no sympathy with the precepts of Stoicism or Cynicism. It is not only innocent, but prudent, to seek an outlet for excited feelings; the right and wrong of the matter lie in the *kind* of outlet which we allow ourselves. Language of some kind, and in most cases articulate language, is the natural instrument for expressing and giving vent to our feelings. But we need some strong safeguard, or the consequences of freely giving expression to our emotions in speech will be calamitous. This safeguard is clearly indicated by the rules here laid down by St. James. Let the expression of strongly excited feelings be an act of *worship*; then we shall have an outlet for them which is not likely to involve us in harmful results. By the very act in which we exhibit our emotions we protect ourselves from the evil which they might produce. The very mode of expressing them moderates them, and serves as an antidote to their capacity for evil. Prayer and praise, or (in one word) worship, according to St. James, is the Christian remedy for "allaying or carrying off the fever of the mind." In all cases in which the mind is greatly agitated, whether painfully or pleasantly, whether by sorrow, anger, regret, or by joy, pleasure, hope, —the wise thing to do is to take refuge in an act of worship.

Mental excitement is neither right nor wrong, any more than physical hunger or thirst. Everything depends on the method of expressing the one or gratifying the other. It will be easy in both cases to indulge a legitimate craving in such a way as to turn a natural and healthy symptom into a disease. Neither a heated mind nor a heated body can without danger be kept heated, or treated as if they were at their normal temperature. The advice of St. James is that in all cases in which our minds are agitated by strong emotion we should turn to Him who gave us minds capable of feeling such emotion; we should cease to make ourselves our own centre, and turn our thoughts from the causes of our excitement to Him who is the unmoved Cause of all movement and rest.

We need not tie ourselves to the distribution of prayer and praise expressed in the text. It is the most natural and most generally useful distribution; but it is not the only one, and perhaps it is not the highest. The precept will hold good with equal truth if we transpose the two conclusions: "Is any among you suffering? let him sing praise. Is any cheerful? let him pray." "In *everything* give thanks," says St. Paul; which involves our frequently giving thanks in suffering. This was what Job, to whom St. James has just directed his readers, did in his trouble. He "fell upon the ground and worshipped: and he said, Naked came I out of my mother's womb, and naked shall I return thither: the Lord gave, and the Lord hath taken away; blessed be the name of the Lord" (i. 20, 21). And the Psalmist teaches much the same lesson as St. Paul: "I will bless the Lord *at all times*; His praise shall continually be in my mouth" (xxxiv. 1). But if praise is as suitable as prayer for suffering, prayer is as suitable as praise for cheerfulness. He who is cheerful has indeed great reason to bless and praise God. He has a priceless gift, which is a blessing to himself and to all around him, a gift which makes life brighter to the whole circle in which he moves. We most of us take far too little pains to cultivate it, to retain it when it has been granted to us, to regain it when we have lost it or thrown it away. Yet cheerfulness has its dangers. The light-hearted are apt to be light-headed, and to be free from care leads to being free from carefulness. The cheerful may easily lose sobriety, and be found off their guard. The remedy is prayer. Prayer steadies without dimming the bright flame of cheerfulness; and just as thanksgiving sweetens sorrow, so supplication sanctifies joy. "Is any suffering? let him sing praise. Is any cheerful? let him pray."

But there is another advantage in making religious worship, whether public or private, the outlet for our emotions. It secures a real connexion between worship and life. Missionaries tell us that this is a frequent difficulty in their work. It is a hard enough thing to win converts from heathenism; but it is perhaps still harder to teach the newly converted that the worship of God has any bearing whatever upon their conduct. This idea is quite strange to them, and utterly alien to their whole mode of thought. They have never been taught anything of the kind before. They have been accustomed to regard the worship of the gods as a series of acts which must be religiously performed in order to win the favour of the deities, or at least to avert their wrath. But it has never occurred to them, nor have their priests impressed upon them, that their lives must be in accordance with their worship, or that the one has any connexion with the other, any more than the colour of their clothes with the amount that they eat and drink. From this it follows that when the idolater has been induced to substitute the worship of God for the worship of idols, there still remains an immense amount to be done. The convert has still to be taught that there can no longer be this divorce of religion from conduct, but that prayer and praise must go hand in hand with work and life.

Converts from heathenism are by no means the only persons who are in need of this lesson. We all of us require to be reminded of it. All of us are apt to draw far too strong a line of distinction between Church and home, between Sunday and week-day, between the time that we spend on our knees and that which we spend in work and recreation. Not, alas! that we are too scrupulous about allowing worldly thoughts to invade sacred times and places, but that we are very jealous about allowing thoughts of God and of His service to mingle with our business and our pleasures, or at least take no pains to bring about and keep up any such mingling. Our worship is often profaned by being shared with the world; our work is rarely consecrated by being shared with God.

What St. James recommends here is a remedy for this. There can be no wall of partition between conduct and religion if our feelings of joy and sorrow, of elation and despondency, of hope and fear, of love and dislike, are daily and hourly finding expression in praise and prayer. Our emotions will thus become instruments for moving us towards God. So much of life is filled with either vexation or pleasure, that one who has learned to carry out the directions here given of turning suffering into prayer, and cheerfulness into praise, will have gone a long way towards realizing the Apostolic command, "Pray without ceasing." As Calvin well observes, St. James "means that there is no time in which God does not invite us to Himself. For afflictions ought to stimulate us to pray; prosperity supplies us with an occasion to praise God. But such is the perverseness of men, that they cannot rejoice without forgetting God, and when afflicted they are disheartened and driven to despair. We ought, then, to keep within due bounds, so that the joy which usually makes us forget God may induce us to set forth the goodness of God, and that our sorrow may teach us to pray."

The word used by St. James for "to sing praise" (ψάλλειν) is worthy of notice. It is the source of the word "psalm." Originally it meant simply to *touch*, especially to *make to vibrate* by touching; whence it came to be used of playing on stringed instruments. Next it came to mean to *sing to the harp*; and finally to sing, whether with or without a stringed accompaniment. This is its signification in the New Testament (Rom. xv. 9; 1 Cor. xiv. 15;

Eph. v. 19);—to sing praise to God. St. James, therefore, regards music as a natural and reasonable mode of expressing joyous feelings; and few will care to dispute that it is so; and it is evident that he is thinking chiefly, if not exclusively, of the joyous Christian singing by himself, rather than of his joining in psalms and hymns in the public worship of the congregation. A portion of Hooker's noble vindication of music as a part of religious worship may here with advantage be quoted.

"Touching musical harmony, whether by instrument or by voice, it being but of high and low in sounds a due proportionable disposition, such, notwithstanding, is the force thereof, and so pleasing effects it hath in that very part of man which is most divine, that some have been thereby induced to think that the soul itself, by nature, is or hath in it harmony. A thing which delighteth all ages and beseemeth all states; a thing as seasonable in grief as in joy; as decent being added unto actions of greatest weight and solemnity, as being used when men most sequester themselves from action. The reason hereof is an admirable facility which music hath to express and represent to the mind, more inwardly than any other sensible mean, the very standing, rising, and falling, the very steps and inflexions every way, the turns and varieties of all passions whereunto the mind is subject; yea, so to imitate them that whether it resemble unto us the same state wherein our minds already are, or a clean contrary, we are not more contentedly by the one confirmed, than changed and led away by the other.... So that although we lay altogether aside the consideration of ditty or matter, the very harmony of sounds being framed in due sort, and carried from the ear to the spiritual faculties of our souls, is by a native puissance and efficacy greatly available to bring to a perfect temper whatsoever is there troubled, apt as well to quicken the spirits as to allay that which is too eager, sovereign against melancholy and despair, forcible to draw forth tears of devotion if the mind be such as can yield them, able both to move and to moderate all affections.

"The Prophet David having therefore singular knowledge, not in poetry alone, but in music also, judged them both to be things most necessary for the house of God, left behind him to that purpose a number of Divinely indited poems, and was farther the author of adding unto poetry melody both vocal and instrumental, for the raising up of men's hearts, and the sweetening of their affections towards God. In which considerations the Church of Christ doth likewise at this present day retain it as an ornament to God's service, and an help to our own devotion. They which, under pretence of the Law ceremonial abrogated, require the abrogation of instrumental music, approving nevertheless the use of vocal melody to remain, must show some reason wherefore the one should be thought a legal ceremony, and not the other" (*Eccles. Pol.*, V. xxxviii. 1, 2).

It hardly needs to be stated that it is not necessary to be able to sing in order to observe this precept of St. James. The "singing and making melody with our hearts to the Lord" of which St. Paul writes to the Ephesians (v. 19) is all that is necessary; "giving thanks always for all things in the name of our Lord Jesus Christ to God, even the Father." The lifting up of the heart is enough, without the lifting up of the voice; and if the voice be lifted up also, it is of little account, either to the soul or to God, whether its tones be musical, always provided that he who thus offers praise is alone, and not in the congregation. Those who have no music in their voices, and yet persist in joining aloud in the singing of public service, are wanting in charity. In order to gratify themselves, they disturb the devotions of others. And that principle applies to many other things in public worship, especially to details of ritual other than those which are generally observed. There would be much less difficulty about such things if each member of the congregation were to ask, "By doing this, or by refusing to do it, am I likely to distract my neighbours in their worship?" Ought not the answer to that question to be conclusive as regards turning or not turning to the East at the creed, bowing or not bowing the head at the *Gloria Patri*, and the like? We come to church to be calmed, sobered, soothed, not to be fretted and vexed. Let us take care that our own behaviour is such as not to irritate others. By our self-will we may be creating or augmenting mental excitement, which, as St. James tells us, worship, whether public or private, ought to cure.

CHAPTER XXVII
THE ELDERS OF THE CHURCH. THE ANOINTING OF THE SICK AND EXTREME UNCTION

"Is any among you sick? let him call for the elders of the Church; and let them pray over him, anointing him with oil in the name of the Lord: and the prayer of faith shall save him that is sick, and the Lord shall raise him up; and if he have committed sins, it shall be forgiven him." —St. James v. 14-15.

TWO subjects stand out prominently in this interesting passage— the elders of the Church, and the anointing of the sick. The connexion of the passage with what immediately precedes is close and obvious. After charging his readers in general terms to resort to prayer when they are in trouble, St. James takes a particular and very common instance of trouble, viz. bodily sickness, and gives more detailed directions as to the way in which the man in trouble is to make use of the relief and remedy of prayer. He is not to be content with giving expression to his need in private prayer to God; he is to "call for *the elders of the Church.*"

I. The first thing to be noted in connexion with this sending for the elders of the congregation by the sick man is, that in this Epistle, which is one of the very earliest among the Christian writings which have come down to us, we already find a *distinction made between clergy and laity*. This distinction runs through the whole of the New Testament. We find it in the earliest writing of all, the First Epistle to the Thessalonians, in which the Christians of Thessalonica are exhorted "to know them that labour among you, and are over you in the Lord, and admonish you; and to esteem them exceeding highly in love for their work's sake" (v. 12, 13). And here St. James assumes as a matter of course, that every congregation has elders, that is a constituted ecclesiastical government. Compare with these the precept in the Epistle to the Hebrews, "Obey them that have the rule over you, and submit to them: for they watch in behalf of your souls, as they that shall give account" (xiii. 17); and the frequent directions in the Pastoral Epistles (1 Tim. iii. 1-13; iv. 6, 13, 14; v. 17, 19, 22; Tit. i. 5-9; ii. 15; 2 Tim. i. 6, 14; ii. 2; iv. 5). What the precise functions of the clergy were is not told us with much detail or precision; but it is quite clear, from the passage before us, and those which have been quoted above, that whatever the functions were, they were spiritual rather than secular, and were duties which a select minority had to exercise in reference to the rest; they were not such as any one might exercise towards any one. In the present case the sick person is not to send for any members of the congregation, but for certain who hold a definite, and apparently an official position. If *any* Christians could discharge the function in question, St. James would not have given the sick person the trouble of summoning the elders rather than those people who chanced to be near at hand. And it is quite clear that not all Christians are over all other Christians in the Lord; that not all are to rule, and all to obey and submit; therefore not all have the same authority to "admonish" others, or to "watch in behalf of their souls, as they that shall give account."[93]

The reason why the elders are to be summoned is stated in different ways by different writers, but with a large amount of substantial agreement. "As being those in whom the power and grace of the Holy Spirit more particularly appeared," says Calvin. "Because when they pray it is not much less than if the whole Church prayed," says Bengel. St. James, says Neander, "regards the presbyters in the light of organs of the Church, acting in its name;" and, "As the presbyters acted in the name of the whole Church, and each one as a member of the body felt that he needed its sympathy and intercession, and might count upon it; individuals should therefore, in cases of sickness, send for the presbyters of the Church. These were to offer prayer on their behalf." The intercession which St. James recommends, says Stier, is "intercession for the sick on the part of the representatives of the Church, ... not merely the intercession of friends or brethren as such, but in the name of the whole community, one of whose members is suffering." It is altogether beside the mark to suggest that the elders were summoned as people of the greatest experience, who perhaps also were specially *skilled in medicine*. Of that there is not only no hint, but the context excludes the idea. If that were in the writer's mind, why does he not say at once, "Let him call for the physicians"? If the healing art is to be thought of at all in connexion with the passage, the case is one in which medicine has already done all that it can, or in which it can do nothing at all. St. James would doubtless approve the advice given by the son of Sirach: "My son, in thy sickness be not negligent; but pray unto the Lord, and He will make thee whole" (Ecclus. xxxviii. 9). This exactly agrees with the precept, "Is any among you suffering? let him pray." "Then give place to the physician, for the Lord hath created him: let him not go from thee, for thou hast need of him. There is a time when in their hands there is good success" (12, 13). To this there is no equivalent in St. James; but he says nothing that is inconsistent with it. Then, after the physician has done his part, and perhaps in vain, would come the summoning of the elders to offer prayer. But it is simpler to suppose that the physician's part is left out of the account altogether.

II. The second point of interest is the anointing of the sick person by the elders. That what is said here affords no Scriptural authority for the Roman rite of Extreme Unction, is one of the commonplaces of criticism. One single fact is quite conclusive. The object of the unction prescribed by St. James is the recovery of the sick person; whereas Extreme Unction, as its name implies, is never administered until the sick person's recovery is considered to be almost or quite hopeless, and death imminent; the possibility of bodily healing is not entirely excluded, but it is not the main purpose of the rite. The only other passage in the New Testament in which the unction of the sick is mentioned is equally at variance with the Roman rite. We are told by St. Mark that the Twelve, when sent out by Christ two and two, "anointed with oil many that were sick, and healed them" (vi. 13). Here also recovery, and not preparation for death, was the purpose of the anointing, which the Apostles seem to have practised on their own responsibility, for it is not mentioned in the charge which Christ gave them when He sent them out (7-11).

But there is this amount of connexion between these two passages of Scripture and the Roman sacrament of Extreme Unction, viz. that the latter *grew out of ecclesiastical practices which were based upon these passages.* As in not a few other instances, development has brought about a state of things which is inconsistent with the original starting-point. But in order to understand the development we must understand the starting-point, and that requires us to find an answer to the question, What purpose was the oil intended to serve? Was it purely symbolical? and if so, of what? Was it merely for the refreshment of the sick person, giving relief to parched skin and stiffened limbs? Was it medicinal, with a view to a permanent cure by natural means? Was it the channel or instrument of a supernatural cure? Was it an aid to the sick person's faith? One or both of the last two suggestions may be accepted as the most probable solution. And the reason why oil was selected as a channel of Divine power and an aid to faith was, that it was believed to have healing properties. It is easier to believe when visible means are used than when nothing is visible, and it is still easier to believe when the visible means appear to be likely to contribute to the desired effect. Christ twice used spittle in curing blindness, probably because spittle was believed to be beneficial to the eyesight. And that oil was supposed to be efficacious as medicine is plain from numerous passages both in and outside of Holy Scripture. "From the sole of the foot even unto the head there is no soundness in it; but wounds, and bruises, and festering sores: they have not been closed, nor bound up, neither mollified with oil" (Isa.

i. 6). The Good Samaritan poured wine and oil into the wounds of the man who fell among robbers (Luke x. 34). A mixture of oil and wine was used for the malady which attacked the army of Ælius Gallus, and was applied both externally and internally (Dion Cass. LIII. 29; Strabo XVI., p. 780). His physicians caused Herod the Great to be bathed in a vessel full of oil when he was supposed to be at death's door (Josephus, *Ant.* XVII. vi. 5). Celsus recommends rubbing with oil in the case of fevers and some other ailments (*De Med.* II. 14, 17; III. 6, 9, 19, 22; IV. 2).[94] But it is obvious that St. James does not recommend the oil merely as medicine, for he does not say that the oil shall cure the sick person, nor yet that the oil with prayer shall do so; but that "the prayer of faith shall save him that is sick," without mentioning the oil at all. On the other hand, he says that the anointing is to be done by the elders "in the name of the Lord." If the anointing were merely medicinal, it might have been performed by any one, without waiting for the elders. And it can hardly be supposed that oil was believed to be a remedy for all diseases.

On the other hand, it seems to be too much to say that the anointing had nothing to do with bodily healing at all, and was simply a means of grace for the sick. Thus Döllinger says, "This is no gift of healing, for that was not confined to the presbyters; and for that Christ prescribed not unction, but laying on of hands. Had he meant that, St. James would have bidden or advised the sick to send for one who possessed this gift, whether presbyter or layman.... What was to be conveyed by this medium was, therefore, only sometimes recovery or relief, always consolation, revival of confidence and forgiveness of sins, on condition, of course, of faith and repentance" (*First Age of the Church*, p. 235, Oxenham's translation, 2nd ed.: Allen, 1867). But although the gift of healing was not confined to the elders, yet in certain cases they may have exercised it; and although Christ prescribed the laying on of hands (Mark xvi. 18), yet the Apostles sometimes healed by anointing with oil (Mark vi. 13). And that "shall *save* him that is sick" (σώσει τὸν κάμνοντα) means "shall *cure* him," is clear both from the context, and also from the use of the same word elsewhere. "Daughter, be of good cheer; thy faith hath *saved* thee," to the woman with the issue of blood (Matt. ix. 22). Jairus prays, "Come and lay Thy hands on her, that she may be *saved*" (Mark v. 23). The disciples say of Lazarus, "Lord, if he is fallen asleep, he will be *saved*" (John xi. 12). And "the Lord shall raise him up" makes this interpretation still more certain. The same expression is used of Simon's wife's mother (Mark i. 31). "The Lord" is Christ, not the Father, both here and "in the Name of *the Lord*." Thus St. Peter says to Æneas, "*Jesus Christ* healeth thee" (Acts ix. 34. Comp. iii. 6, 16; v. 10).

That St. James makes the promise of recovery without any restriction may at first sight appear to be surprising; but in this he is only following the example of our Lord, who makes similar promises, and leaves it to the thought and experience of Christians to find out the limitations to them. St. James is only applying to a particular case what Christ promised in general terms. "All things, whatsoever ye pray and ask for, believe that ye have received them, and ye shall have them" (Mark xi. 24. Comp. Matt. xvii. 20). "If ye shall ask [Me] anything in My Name, I will do it" (John xiv. 14). "If ye shall ask anything of the Father, He will give it you in My Name" (John xvi. 23). The words "in My Name" point to the limitation; they do not, of course, refer to the use of the formula "through Jesus Christ our Lord," but to the exercise of the spirit of Christ: "Not My will, but Thine be done." The union of our will with the will of God is the very first condition of successful prayer. The Apostles themselves had no indiscriminate power of healing. St. Paul did not heal Epaphroditus, much as he yearned for his recovery (Phil. ii. 27). He left Trophimus at Miletus sick (2 Tim. iv. 20). He did not cure his own thorn in the flesh (2 Cor. xii. 7-9). How, then, can we suppose that St. James credited the elders of every congregation with an unrestricted power of healing? He leaves it to the common sense and Christian submission of his readers to understand that the elders have no power to cancel the sentence of death pronounced on the whole human race. To pray that any one should be exempt from this sentence would be not faith, but presumption.

Of the employment of the rite here prescribed by St. James we have very little evidence in the early ages of the Church. Tertullian mentions a cure by anointing, but it is not quite a case in point. The Emperor Septimius Severus believed that he had been cured from an illness through oil administered by a Christian named Proculus Torpacion, steward of Evodias, and in gratitude for it he maintained him in the palace for the rest of his life (*Ad. Scap.* iv.). Origen, in the second Homily on Leviticus (iv.), quotes the passage from St. James, and seems to understand the sickness to be that of sin. He interpolates thus: "Let him call for the elders of the Church, and *let them lay their hands on him*, anointing him with oil," etc. This perhaps tells us how the rite was administered in Alexandria in his time; or it may mean that Origen understood the "pray *over* him" (ἐπ' αὐτόν) of St. James to signify imposition of hands. With him, then, the forgiveness of sins is the healing. A century and a half later Chrysostom takes a further step, and employs the passage to show that priests have the power of absolution. "For not only at the time when they regenerate us, but afterwards also, they have authority to forgive sins." And then he quotes James v. 14, 15 (*De Sacerd.* III. 6). It is evident that this is quite alien to the passage. The sickness and the sins are plainly distinguished by St. James, and nothing is said about absolution by the elders, who pray for his recovery, and (no doubt) for his forgiveness.

When we reach the sixth century the evidence for the custom of anointing the sick with holy oil becomes abundant. At first any one with a reputation for sanctity might bless the oil—not only laymen, but women. But in the West the rule gradually spread from Rome that the sacred oil for the sick must be "made" by the bishop. In the East this has never been observed. Theodore of Tarsus, Archbishop of Canterbury, says that according to the Greeks it is lawful for presbyters to make the chrism for the sick. And this rule continues to this day. One priest suffices; but it is desirable to get seven, if possible.

But the chief step in the development is taken when not only the blessing of the oil, but the administering of it to the sick, is reserved to the clergy. In Bede's time this restriction was not yet made, as is clear from his comments on the passage, although even then it was customary for priests to administer the unction. But by the tenth century this restriction had probably become general. It became connected with the communion of the sick, which of course required a priest, and then with the *Viaticum*, or communion of the dying; but even then the unction seems to have preceded the last communion. The name "Extreme Unction" (*unctio extrema*), as a technical ecclesiastical term, is not older than the twelfth century. Other terms are "Last Oil" (*ultimum oleum*) and "Sacrament of the Departing" (*sacramentum exeuntium*). But when we have reached these phrases we are very far indeed from the ordinance prescribed by St. James, and from that which was practised by the Apostles. Jeremy Taylor, in the dedication of the *Holy Dying*, says fairly enough, "The fathers of the Council of Trent first disputed, and after their manner at last agreed, that Extreme Unction was instituted by Christ; but afterwards being admonished by one of their theologues that the Apostles ministered unction to infirm people before they were priests, for fear that it should be thought that this unction might be administered by him that was no priest, they blotted out the word 'instituted,' and put in its stead 'insinuated' this sacrament, and that it was published by St. James. So it is in their doctrine; and yet in their anathematisms they curse all them that shall deny it to have been instituted by Christ. I shall lay no prejudice against it, but add this only, that there being but two places of Scripture pretended for this ceremony, some chief men of their own side have proclaimed these two invalid as to the institution of it;" and he mentions in particular Suarez and Cajetan. But he states more than he can know when he declares of Extreme Unction that "since it is used when the man is above half dead, when he can exercise no act of understanding, it must needs be nothing." Those who receive the rite are not always unconscious; and is it certain that an unconscious person "can exercise no act of the understanding," or that prayer for one who can exercise no act of the understanding "must needs be nothing"? With similar want of caution Stier speaks of "the *superstition* which sends for the minister to 'pray over the sick,' when these have scarce any consciousness left." Whether or no Extreme Unction is an edifying ceremony is a question worthy of argument, and nothing is here urged on either side; but we are going beyond our knowledge if we assert that it *can* have no effect on the dying man; and we are unduly limiting the power of prayer if we affirm that to pray for one who has lost consciousness is a useless superstition. All that is contended for here is, that the Roman rite is something very different from that which is ordered by St. James.[95]

"And if he have committed sins, it shall be forgiven him." We ought perhaps rather to translate, "Even if he have committed sins, it shall be forgiven him." (The Greek is not καὶ ἐάν or ἐὰν δέ, but κἄν, for which comp. John viii. 14; x. 38; xi. 25). The meaning would seem to be, "even if his sickness has been produced by his sins, his sin shall be forgiven, and his sickness cured." It is possible, but unnatural, to join the first clause of this sentence with the preceding one: "the Lord shall raise him up, even if he have committed sins." In that case "It shall be forgiven him" forms a very awkward independent sentence, without conjunction. The ordinary arrangement of the clauses is much better: even if the malady is the effect of the man's own wrong-doing, the prayer offered by faith—his faith, and that of the elders—shall still prevail. St. Paul tells the Corinthians that their misconduct respecting the Lord's Supper had caused much sickness among them, and not a few deaths (1 Cor. xi. 30); and such direct punishments of sin were not confined to the Corinthian Church nor to the Apostolic age. They still occur in abundance, and those who experience them have the assurance of Scripture that if they repent and pray in faith their sins will certainly be forgiven, and their punishment possibly removed.

[93] The question of the Origin of the Christian Ministry has been discussed in another volume of this series. See the *Pastoral Epistles*, pp. 104-117 (Hodder and Stoughton, 1888).

[94] For additional evidence see J. C. Wolf, *Curæ Philol. et Crit.* V., pp. 79-81; Lightfoot, *Horæ Hebr.* II., pp. 304, 444, on Matt. vi. 17 and Mark vi. 13; Launoi, *De Sacramento Unctionis Infirmorum*, I., p. 444.

[95] See letters in the *Guardian* of Mar. 12, 19, Apr. 9, 16, 23, May 7, 1890; pp. 447, 481, 594, 633, 682, 763.

In the Visitation of the Sick in the First Prayer Book of Edward VI. there is provision for the older rite: "If the sicke person desyre to be annoynted, then shall the priest annoynte him upon the forehead or breast only, making the signe of the crosse, saying thus, As with this visible oyle thy body outwardly is annoynted: so our heavenly father almyghtye God graunt of his infinite goodnesse, that thy soule inwardly may be annoynted with the holy gost, who is the spirite of al strength, comforte, reliefe, and gladnesse. And vouchsafe for his great mercy (yf it be his blessed will) to restore unto thee thy bodely helth and strength, to serve him," etc.

Readers of the *Confessions* will remember how St. Augustine on one occasion asked his friends to pray that he might be freed from great pain, and forthwith found relief. "I have neither forgotten nor will be silent about the severity of Thy scourge, and the marvellous speed of Thy mercy. Thou didst then torture me with toothache (he says elsewhere that this was so grievous that he could learn nothing fresh, but could only think of what he already knew), and when the pain became so severe that I was unable to speak the thought rose in my heart to urge all my friends who were present to pray for me to Thee, the God of all health. And I wrote this on a waxen tablet, and gave it to them to read. Presently, as with suppliant desire we bowed our knees, that great pain fled away. But what pain? and how did it flee? I confess, my Lord and my God, that it frightened me; for from my earliest days I had experienced nothing like it" (IX. iv. 12).

CHAPTER XXVIII
THE PUBLIC AND PRIVATE CONFESSION OF SINS.THE LAWFULNESS OF PRAYERS FOR RAIN

"Confess therefore your sins one to another, and pray one for another, that ye may be healed. The supplication of a righteous man availeth much in its working. Elijah was a man of like passions with us, and he prayed fervently that it might not rain; and it rained not on the earth for three years and six months. And he prayed again; and the heaven gave rain, and the earth brought forth her fruit." —St. James v. 16-18.

THE connexion of this passage with the preceding one is very close. This is evident even in the Authorized Version; but it is made still more manifest by the Revisers, who have restored the connecting "therefore" to the text upon overwhelming authority. St. James is passing from the particular case of the sick person to something more general, viz. mutual confession of sins. If we draw out his thought in full, it will be something of this kind: "Even if the sick person be suffering the consequences of his sins, nevertheless the faith and prayers of the elders, combined with his own, shall prevail for his forgiveness and healing. Of course he must confess and bewail his sins: if he does not admit them and repent of them, he can hope for nothing. *Therefore* you ought all of you habitually to confess your sins to one another, and to intercede for one another, in order that when sickness comes upon you, you may the more readily be healed." It is not quite certain that the word rendered "ye may be healed" (ἰαθῆτε) ought to be limited to bodily healing; but the context seems to imply that the cure of bodily disorders is still in the mind of St. James. If, however, with various commentators, we take it to mean "that your *souls* may be healed," then there is no need to supply any such thought as "when sickness comes upon you."

It might surprise us to find that the practice of auricular confession to a priest is deduced from the precept, "Confess your sins one to another," if we had not the previous experience of finding the rite of Extreme Unction deduced from the precept respecting the anointing of the sick. But here also Cajetan has the credit of admitting that no Scriptural authority for the Roman practice can be found in the words of St. James. The all-important "to one another" (ἀλλήλοις) is quite fatal to the interpretation of confession to a priest. If the confession of a layman to a priest is meant, then the confession of a priest to a layman is *equally meant*: the words, whether in the Greek or in the English, cannot be otherwise understood. But the injunction is evidently quite general, and the distinction between clergy and laity does not enter into it at all: each Christian, whether elder or layman, is to confess to other Christians, whether elders or laymen, either to one or to many, as the case may be. When the sick person just spoken of confessed his sins, he confessed them to the elders of the Church, because they were present; they did not come to receive his confession, but to pray for him and to anoint him. He sent for them, not because he wished to confess to them, but because he was sick. Even if he had had nothing to confess to them—a case evidently contemplated by St. James as not only possible, but common—he would still have sent for them. So far from its being among their functions as elders to hear the sick man's confession, St. James seems rather to imply that he ought to have made it previously to others. If Christians habitually confess their sins to one another, there will be no special confession required when any of them falls ill. But granting that this interpretation of his brief directions is not quite certain, it is quite certain that what he commends is the confession of any Christian to any Christian, and not the confession of laity to presbyters. About that he says nothing, either one way or the other, for it is not in his mind. He neither sanctions nor forbids it, but he gives a direction which shows that as regards the duty of confession to man, the normal condition of things is for any Christian to confess to any Christian. The important point is that the sinner should not keep his guilty secret locked up in his own bosom; to whom he should tell it is left to his own discretion. As Tertullian says, in his treatise *On Penance*, "Confession of sins lightens as much as concealment (*dissimulatio*) aggravates them. For confession is prompted by the desire to make amends; concealment is prompted by contumacy" (viii.). Similarly Origen, on Psalm xxxvii.: "See, therefore, what the Divine Scripture teaches us, that we must not conceal sin within us. For just as, it may be, people who have undigested food detained inside them, or are otherwise grievously oppressed internally, if they vomit, obtain relief, so they also who have sinned, if they conceal and retain the sin, are oppressed inwardly. But if the sinner becomes his own accuser, accuses himself and confesses, he at the same time vomits out both the sin and the whole cause of his malady" (*Homil.* II. 6). In much the same strain Chrysostom writes, "Sin, if it is confessed, becomes less; but if it is not confessed, worse; for if the sinner adds shamelessness and obstinacy to his sin, he will never stop. How, indeed, will such a one be at all able to guard himself from falling again into the same sins, if in the earlier case he was not conscious that he sinned.... Let us not merely call ourselves sinners, but let us make a reckoning of our sins, counting them according to their kind, one by one.... If thou art of the persuasion that thou art a sinner, this is not able so much to humble thy soul as the very catalogue of thy sins examined into according to their kind" (*Homil. xxx. in Ep. ad Hebr.*)

All these writers have this main point in common, that a sinner who does not confess what he has done amiss is likely to become careless and hardened. And the principle is at least as old as the Book of Proverbs: "He that covereth his transgressions shall not prosper: but whoso confesseth and forsaketh them shall obtain mercy" (xxviii. 13). But, as the context clearly shows in each case, they are each of them writing of a different kind of confession. The confession (*exomologesis*) which Tertullian so urgently recommends is public confession before the congregation; that which Origen advises is private confession to an individual, particularly with a view to deciding whether public confession is expedient. What Chrysostom prefers, both here and elsewhere in his writings, is secret confession to God: "I say not to thee, Make a parade of thyself; nor yet, Accuse thyself in the presence of the others.... Before God confess these things; before the Judge ever confess thy sins, praying, if not with the tongue, at any rate with the heart, and in this way ask for mercy." All which is in accordance with the principle laid down by St. John, "If we confess our sins" —our sins in detail, not the mere fact that we have sinned—"He is faithful and righteous to forgive us our sins, and to cleanse us from all unrighteousness" (1 John i. 9). Bellarmine has the courage to claim not only St. James, but St. John, as teaching confession to a priest (*De Pænit.* III. iv.); but it is manifest that St. John is speaking of confession to God, without either approving or condemning confession to man, and that St. James is speaking of the latter, without saying anything about the former. But just as St. James leaves to the penitent's discretion the question to whom he shall confess, whether to clergy or laity, so also he leaves it to his discretion whether he shall confess to one or to many, and whether in private or in public.[96] In the second, third, and fourth centuries public confession was commonly part of public penance. And the object of it is well stated by Hooker: "Offenders in secret" were "persuaded that if the Church did direct them in the offices of their penitency, and assist them with public prayer, they should more easily obtain that they sought than by trusting wholly to their own endeavours." The primitive view, he holds, was this: "Public confession they thought necessary by way of *discipline*, not private confession as in the nature of a *sacrament*" (*Eccl. Pol.*, VI. iv. 2, 6). But experience soon showed that indiscriminate public confession of grievous sins was very mischievous. Therefore in the East, and (if Sozomen is correct) at Rome also, penitentiary presbyters were appointed to decide for penitents whether their sins must be confessed to the congregation or not. Thus, what Origen advises each penitent to do for himself, viz. seek a wise adviser respecting the expediency of public confession and penance, was formally done for every one. But in A.D. 391, Nectarius, the predecessor of Chrysostom in the see of Constantinople, was persuaded to abolish the office, *apparently* because a penitentiary presbyter had sanctioned public confession in a case which caused great scandal; but neither Socrates (V. xix.) nor Sozomen (VII. xvi.) makes this point very clear. The consequence of the abolition was that each person was left to his own discretion, and public penance fell into disuse.

But public confession had other disadvantages. Private enmity made use of these confessions to annoy, and even to prosecute the penitent. Moreover, the clergy sometimes proclaimed to the congregation what had been told them in confidence; that is, they made public confession on behalf of the sinner without his consent. Whereupon Leo the Great, in a letter to the Bishops of Apulia and Campania, March 6th, A.D. 459, sanctioned the practice of private confession (*Ep.* clxviii. [cxxxvi.]). Thus, in the West, as previously in the East, a severe blow was given to the practice of public confession and penance.

But it is probable that the origin, or at least the chief encouragement, of the practice of auricular confession is rather to be looked for in *monasticism*. Offences against the rule of the Order had to be confessed before the whole community; and it was assumed that the only other grave offences likely to happen in the monastic life would be those of thought. These had to be confessed in private to the abbat. The influences of monasticism were by no means bounded by the monastery walls; and it is probable that the rule of private confession by the brethren to the abbat had much to do with the custom of private confession by the laity to the priest. But it is carefully to be noted that for a considerable period the chief considerations are the penitent's admission of his sins and the fixing of the penance. Only gradually does the further idea of the absolution of the penitent by the body or the individual that hears the confession come in; and at last it becomes the main idea. Confession once a year to a priest was made compulsory by the Lateran Council in 1215; but various local synods had made similar regulations at earlier periods; *e.g.* the Council of Toulouse in 1129, and of Liège in 710.[97] But when we have reached these regulations we have once more advanced very far indeed beyond what is prescribed by St. James in this Epistle.

There cannot be much doubt what is the main idea with St. James: "Confess therefore your sins one to another, and *pray* one for another, that ye may be healed. The *supplication* of a righteous man availeth much in its working. Elijah ... *prayed fervently*.... And he *prayed again*," etc. It is in order that we may *induce others to pray for us* that we are to confess our sins to them; and this is the great motive which underlies the public confession of the primitive Church. As Hooker well expresses it, "The greatest thing which made men forward and willing upon their knees to confess whatever they had committed against God ... was their fervent desire to be helped and assisted with the prayers of God's saints." And the meaning of these prayers is strikingly expressed by Tertullian, who thus addresses the penitent in need of such intercession: "Where one and two meet, there is a Church; and a Church is Christ. Therefore, when thou dost stretch forth thy hands to the knees of thy brethren, it is Christ that thou touchest, Christ on whom thou prevailest. Just so, when *they* shed tears over *thee*, it is Christ who feels compassion, Christ who is entreating the Father. Readily doth He ever grant that which the Son requests" (*De Pœnit.* x.). To unburden his own heart was one benefit of the penitent's confession; to obtain the intercession of others for his forgiveness and recovery was another; and the latter was the chief reason for confessing to man; confession to God might effect the other. The primitive forms of absolution, when confession was made to a priest, were precatory rather than declaratory. "May the Lord absolve thee" (*Dominus absolvat*) was changed in the West to "I absolve thee," in the twelfth century. From the Sarum Office the latter formula passed into the First Prayer Book of Edward VI., in the Visitation of the Sick, and has remained there unchanged; but in 1552 the concluding words of the preceding rubric, "and the same forme of absolucion shalbe used in all pryvate confessions," were omitted.[98] In the Greek Church the form of absolution after private confession is precatory:—

"O my spiritual child, who dost confess to my humility, *I, a humble sinner, have no power on earth to remit sins. This God alone can do.* Yet by reason of that Divine charge which was committed to the Apostles after the resurrection of our Lord Jesus Christ, in the words, Whose soever sins ye forgive, etc., and by that encouraged, *we* say, Whatsoever thou hast confessed to my most lowly humility, and whatsoever thou hast omitted to confess, either through ignorance or any forgetfulness, *may God forgive thee*, both in this world and in that which is to come." And this is followed by a prayer very similar to the absolution: "God ... forgive thee, by the ministry of me a sinner, all thy sins, both in this world and in that which is to come, and present thee blameless at His dread tribunal. Go in peace, and think no more of the faults which thou hast confessed." The "*we* say" holds fast to the doctrine that it is to the Church as a whole, and not to Peter or any individual minister, that the words, "Whose soever sins ye forgive, they are forgiven unto them" (John xx. 23), were spoken.

"The supplication of a righteous man availeth much in its working." "The effectual earnest prayer" of the Authorized Version cannot be justified: either "effectual" or "earnest" must be struck out, as there is only one word (ἐνεργουμένη) in the original; moreover, the word for "prayer" is not the same as before (δέησις, not εὐχή). But it may be doubted whether "earnest" is not better than "in its working." Perhaps "in its earnestness" would be better than either: "Great is the strength of a righteous man's supplication, in its earnestness."

The example by which St. James proves the efficacy of a righteous man's prayer is interesting and important in two respects:—

1. It is the only evidence that we have that the great drought in the time of Ahab was prayed for by Elijah, and it is the only direct evidence that he prayed for the rain which put an end to it. We are told that Elijah *prophesied* the drought (1 Kings xvii. 1) and the rain (1 Kings xviii. 41); and that before the rain he put himself in an attitude of prayer, with his face between his knees (ver. 42); but that he prayed, and for the rain which he had foretold, is not stated. Whether the statement made by St. James is an inference from these statements, or based on independent tradition, must remain uncertain. We read in Ecclesiasticus of Elijah that by "the word of the Lord he shut up (held back) the heaven" (xlviii. 3); but that seems to refer to prophecy rather than to prayer. The difference, if there be any, between the duration of the drought as stated here and by St. Luke (iv. 25), and as stated in the Book of the Kings, will not be a stumbling-block to any who recognize that inspiration does not necessarily make a man infallible in chronology. Three and a half years (= 42 months = 1,260 days) was the traditional duration of times of great calamity (Dan. vii. 25; xii. 7; Rev. xi. 2, 3; xii. 6, 14; xiii. 5).

2. This passage supplies us with *Biblical authority for prayers for changes of weather*, and the like; for the conduct of Elijah is evidently put before us for our imitation. St. James carefully guards against the objection that Elijah was a man gifted with miraculous powers, and therefore no guide for ordinary people, by asserting that he was a man of like nature (ὁμοιοπαθής) with ourselves. And let us concede, for the sake of argument, that St. James may have been mistaken in believing that Elijah prayed for the drought and for the rain; yet still the fact remains that an inspired New Testament writer puts before us, for our encouragement in prayer, a case in which prayers for changes of weather were made and answered. And he certainly exhorts us to pray for the recovery of the sick, which is an analogous case. This kind of prayer seems to require special consideration.

"Is it, then, according to the Divine will that when we are individually suffering from the regularity of the course of nature—suffering, for instance, from the want of rain, or the superabundance of it—we should ask God to interfere with that regularity? That in such circumstances we should pray for submission to the Divine will, and for such wisdom as shall lead to compliance with it in the future, is a matter of course, and results inevitably from the relation between the spiritual Father and the spiritual child. But ought we to go farther than this? Ought we to pray, expecting that our prayer will be effectual, that God may interfere with the fixed sequences of nature? Let us try to realize what would follow if we offered such prayer and prevailed. In a world-wide Church each believer would constitute himself a judge of what was best for himself and his neighbour, and thus the order of the world would be at the mercy everywhere of individual caprice and ignorance. Irregularity would accordingly take the place of invariableness. No man could possibly foretell what would be on the morrow. The scientist would find all his researches for rule and law baffled; the agriculturist would find all his calculations upset; nature, again, as in the days of ignorance, would become the master of man; like an eagle transfixed by an arrow winged by one of its own feathers, man would have shackled himself with the chains of his ancient servitude by the licentious employment of his own freedom, and would have reduced the cosmos of which God made him the master to a chaos which overwhelmed him by its unexpected blows" (the Bishop of Manchester, September 4th, 1887, in Manchester Cathedral, during a meeting of the British Association).

The picture which is here drawn sketches for us the consequences of allowing each individual to have control over the forces of nature. It is incredible that God could be induced to allow such control to individuals; but does it follow from this that He never listens to prayers respecting *His* direction of the forces of nature, and that consequently all such prayers are presumptuous? The conclusion does not seem to follow from the premises. The valid conclusion would rather be this: No one ought to pray to God to give him absolute control of the forces of nature. The prayer, "Lord, in *Thy* control of the forces of nature have mercy upon me and my fellow men," is a prayer of a very different character.

The objection to prayers for rain, or for the cessation of rain, and the like, is based on the supposition that we thereby "ask God to interfere with the regularity of the course of nature." Yet it is admitted that to "pray for submission to the Divine will, and for such wisdom as shall lead to compliance with it in the future, is a matter of *course*, and results *inevitably* from the relation between the spiritual Father and the spiritual child." But is there no regularity about the things thus admitted to be fit objects of prayer? Are human character and human intellect not subject to law? When we pray for a submissive spirit and for wisdom, are we not asking God to "interfere with that regularity" which governs the development of character and of intelligence? Either the prayer is to obtain more submission and more wisdom than we should otherwise get, or it is not. If it is to obtain it, then the regularity which would otherwise have prevailed is interrupted. If our prayer is not to obtain for us more submission and more wisdom than we should have obtained if we had not prayed, then the prayer is futile.

It will perhaps be urged that the two cases are not strictly parallel. They are not; but for the purposes of this argument they are sufficiently parallel. It is maintained that we have no right to pray for rain, because we thereby propose to interfere with the regularity of natural processes; yet it is allowed that we may pray for wisdom. To get wisdom by prayer is quite as much an interference with the regularity of natural processes as to get rain by prayer. Therefore, either we ought to pray for neither, or we have the right to pray for both. And so far as the two cases are not parallel, it seems to be more reasonable to pray for rain than to pray for submissiveness and wisdom. God has given our wills the awful power of being able to resist His will. Are we to suppose that He exercises less control over matter, which cannot resist Him, than over human wills, which He allows to do so; or that He will help us or not help us to become better and wiser, according as we ask Him or do not ask Him for such help, and yet will never make any change as to giving or withholding material blessings, however much, or however little, we may ask Him to do this?

The objection is sometimes stated in a slightly different form. God has arranged the material universe according to His infinite wisdom; it is presumptuous to pray that He will make any change in it. The answer to which is, that if that argument is valid against praying for rain, it is valid against all prayer whatever. If I impugn infinite wisdom when I pray for a change in the weather, do I not equally impugn it, when I pray for a change in the life or character of myself or of my friends? God knows without our asking what weather is best for us; and He knows equally without our asking what spiritual graces are best for us.

Does not the parallel difficulty point to a parallel solution? What right have we to assume that in either case effectual prayer interferes with the regularity which seems to characterize Divine action? May it not be God's will that the prayer of faith should be a force that can influence other forces, whether material or spiritual, and that its influence should be according to *law* (whether natural or supernatural) quite as much as the influence of other forces? A man who puts up a lightning-conductor brings down the electric current when it might otherwise have remained above, and brings it down in one place rather than another; yet no one would say that he interferes with the regularity of the course of nature. Is there anything in religion or science to forbid us from thinking of prayer as working in an analogous manner—according to a law too subtle for us to comprehend and analyse, but according to a law none the less? In the vast network of forces in which an all-wise God has constructed the universe a Christian will believe that one force which "availeth much," both in the material and in the spiritual world, is the earnest prayer of the righteous. It is better for us that we should be able to influence by our prayers God's direction of events than that we should be unable to do so; therefore a merciful Father has placed this power within our reach.[99]

[96] In the *Dict. of Chr. Biogr.*, I., p. 615, Tertullian's account of public confession is given at some length, and then the question is asked, "Is not this, clearly, the *exomologesis* which St. James enjoins?" To this one replies that St. James enjoins confession, but says nothing about publicity.

[97] The Council of Trent anathematizes any one "who denies that sacramental confession was instituted of Divine right, or that it is necessary to salvation, or who says that the manner of confessing secretly to a priest alone, *which the Church has ever observed from the beginning*, and doth observe, is alien from the institution and command of Christ, and is a human invention" (Canon VI. ii. 165).

[98] Moreover, "shall absolve hym after this *forme*" was changed to "shall absolve hym after thys *sorte*," as if allowing another form in the Visitation of the Sick.

[99] Dean Plumptre has pointed out an "interesting coincidence" between this mention of Elijah and the account given by Josephus of Caligula's mad attempt to set up his statue in the Temple. P. Petronius Turpilianus had been appointed Governor of Syria in the room of Vitellius, and was commissioned to erect the statue; but he was much impressed by the earnestness of the Jews in opposing the proposed outrage, and promised large multitudes of them at Tiberias that he would do all in his power to induce Caligula to desist. It was a year of great drought, no rain falling even when the sky was overcast; but on this day, although there had been no previous signs of it, abundance of rain fell directly Petronius had finished his speech to the Jews. Josephus speaks of this as God showing His presence (παρουσία) to Petronius, and says that Petronius recognized it as a Divine manifestation (ἐπιφάνεια) of God's care of the

Jews. Dr. Plumptre says that the people—"Christians, we may believe, as well as Jews"—had been praying for rain, and that Petronius regarded the rain "partly as an answer to the prayers of the people;" which may have been so, but *it is not so stated by Josephus*. "According to the date which, on independent grounds, has here been assigned to St. James's Epistle, the event referred to must have happened but a *few months* before, or but a *few months* after it. If before, he may well have had it in his thoughts; if after, it may well have been in part the effect of his teaching." Dr. Plumptre thinks that the Epistle was written between A.D. 44 and 51. The events recorded by Josephus took place A.D. 39. Caligula was assassinated January 24th, A.D. 41. The coincidence, therefore, breaks down upon examination. (1) The unexpected rain is represented, not as an answer to prayer, but as a sign of God's approval of the decision of Petronius. (2) Even if we place the Epistle as early as A.D. 45, it was written *six years* after the sudden rain at Tiberias; and St. James did not need that occurrence (of which he had possibly never heard) in order to be reminded of the drought and the rain prophesied by Elijah.

CHAPTER XXIX
THE WORK OF CONVERTING SINNERS;
ITS CONDITIONS AND REWARDS

"My brethren, if any among you do err from the truth, and one convert him, let him know, that he which converteth a sinner from the error of his way shall save a soul from death, and shall cover a multitude of sins." —St. James v. 19, 20.

ST. JAMES has just been speaking of the case of a man who is sick, and needs the prayers of others for his healing, both in body and soul; for it may be that the sick man has sins to be repented of as well as ailments to be cured. This leads naturally enough to the common case of those who, whether sick in body or not, feel their consciences burdened by sin. They are to make known their trouble to one or more of the brethren, in order that efficacious prayers may be offered to God on their behalf. But these cases do not by any means cover the whole ground. Besides those who feel and make known their bodily sickness, and those who feel and make known their spiritual sickness, in order that their fellow Christians may pray to God for their healing, there is the common case of those who either do not feel, or if they feel do not confess, that their souls are sick unto death. There are many who have left the path of life, and are going steadily, and perhaps rapidly, to destruction, who are ignorant of their piteous condition; and there are others who are aware of their peril, but are either too hardened to desire any serious change, or too proud to own their condition to others and ask their help towards recovery. Are such unhappy persons to be left to themselves, and allowed to go on their way to perdition, for want of the aid which they are too insensate or to haughty to ask?

Certainly not, says the writer of this Epistle. The reclaiming of such sinners is one of the noblest tasks which a Christian can undertake; and the successful accomplishment of it is fraught with incalculable blessings, the thought of which ought to move us to undertake such work. To save one immortal soul from eternal death is worth the labour of a lifetime. If to lead one soul astray is to share the devil's work and incur guilt to which a violent death would be preferable (Matt. xviii. 6; Mark ix. 42; Luke xvii. 2), to lead one soul back from death is to share Christ's work (2 Cor. vi. 1) by blotting out from God's sight the sins which cry for punishment.

We shall obtain a clearer view of the meaning of St. James in these concluding verses of his Epistle if we begin with the last words of the passage, and from them work back to what precedes.

"Shall cover a multitude of sins." Whose sins? Not the sins of him who converts the erring brother. This view, which is perhaps the one which most readily occurs to those who merely listen to the passage as it is read in church, but have never studied it, may safely be rejected, although it has the sanction of Erasmus and to some extent also of the Venerable Bede. There are two reasons, each of which would suffice to condemn this explanation, and which taken together are almost unanswerable. (1) Nowhere else in Scripture do we find any such doctrine, that a man may cover his own sins by inducing another sinner to repent. On the contrary, it is one of the terrible possibilities which attend the work of the ministry that a man may preach successfully to others, and yet himself be a castaway (1 Cor. ix. 27), and may move many hearts, while his own remains as hard as the nether millstone. It is altogether misleading to quote Matt. vi. 14 in connexion with this passage. There Christ says, "If ye forgive men their trespasses, your heavenly Father will also forgive you." What has that to do with converting sinners from their sins? Is "Forgive, that ye may be forgiven," even parallel to "*Convert*, that ye may be forgiven"? It is very far indeed from being equivalent to it. The exact parallel would be, "Convert, that ye may be converted;" and where in either the Old or the New Testament do we find any such teaching as that? What we *do* find is the converse of it: "Be converted, that ye may convert. Cast out first the beam out of thine own eye; and then shalt thou see clearly to cast out the mote out of thy brother's eye" (Matt. vii. 5). And this brings us to the other reason why this interpretation ought to be set aside. (2) We cannot suppose that St. James would contemplate, not merely as a possible case, but as the normal condition of things, that a Christian would undertake the task of converting others while his own conscience was burdened with a multitude of sins. He no doubt assumed, and meant his readers to assume, that before taking this very glorious, but also very difficult work upon themselves, Christians would at least have repented of their own sins, and thus have won the assurance that they were covered and forgiven. As we have seen, St. James shows an intimate personal knowledge of the teaching of Christ, and especially of that portion of it which is contained in the Sermon on the Mount. It is difficult to believe that any one who was acquainted with the fundamental principle involved in the saying just quoted, about the mote and the beam, would end his exhortations to the Church with a declaration which, according to the view of Erasmus and others, would mean that it is precisely those who have a beam in their own eye who should endeavour to convert sinners from the error of their ways, for in this way they may get the beam removed, or at least overlooked.

It is the sins of the converted sinner that are covered when a brother has had the happiness of converting him. The saying "cover sins" is a proverbial one, and seems to have been common among the Jews. St. Peter also makes use of it (1 Peter iv. 8); and this is one of the points which make some persons think that the writer of this Epistle had seen that of St. Peter, and others that St. Peter had seen this one. The source of the saying appears to be Prov. x. 12, "Hatred stirreth up strifes: but *love covereth all transgressions.*" It is, however, by no means certain that St. James is consciously quoting this saying, although his evident fondness for the sapiential books of Scripture would incline us to think that he is doing so. But the Septuagint of the passage in Proverbs has a different reading: "Friendship shall cover those who love not strife." A similar expression to the one before us occurs twice in the Psalms: "Thou hast forgiven the iniquity of Thy people; Thou hast covered all their sin" (lxxxv. 2): "Blessed is he whose transgression is forgiven, whose sin is covered" (xxxii. 1). The fact that the phrase occurs so frequently renders it impossible for us to determine the precise passage which suggested the use of the words in this place. (See note at the end of this chapter.)

The statement that the converted sinner had "a multitude of sins" which are covered by his returning from "the error of his way" shows us plainly what is meant by "the error of his way" and by his "erring" or "being led astray[100] from the truth." St. James is evidently not thinking of purely dogmatic error, about which his Epistle is almost, if not entirely, silent. It is conviction as expressed in *conduct* with which he deals throughout. As we have seen again and again, the evils which he denounces are those of a sinful life: with the evils of erratic speculation he does not deal at all. Quite in harmony, therefore, with the practical character of the Epistle, we find that with him to "err from the truth" means the apostasy that is involved in a life of sin. "Of His own will God brought us forth by *the word of truth,* that we should be a kind of firstfruits of His creatures" (i. 18); and those who allow themselves to be seduced into sinful courses dishonour their Divine parentage and desert their Father's home. To recover such from the path of destruction is the blessed work to which St. James wishes to incite and encourage his readers.

It is important to recognize the fact that it is the *lives* of notorious *sinners*, and not the *views* of those who *differ from us*, that we are urged to correct. The latter interpretation is not an uncommon one. The expression "err from the truth" seems at first sight to countenance it; and to many of us the work of winning over others to accept our religious opinions is much more congenial employment than that of endeavouring to reclaim the profligate. But the duty to which St. James here exhorts us is one of universal obligation. It is one which every Christian must recognize, and according to his opportunities perform; and it is one which every one, however ignorant, simple, and insignificant he may be, is able in some measure to fulfil. But comparatively few of us are qualified to deal with the erroneous opinions of others. Not infrequently those which we think to be erroneous are nearer the truth than those which we hold ourselves. Even where this is not the case, the errors may be much less hurtful than we suppose, because, with happy inconsistency, men allow the goodness of their hearts to direct their conduct, rather than the erratic convictions of their heads. And again, our efforts to change the erroneous opinions of others may do more harm than good, for it is much more easy to unsettle than to establish. We may take away a plank, without being able to supply an ark; and an inadequate or even faulty principle is better than no principle at all. The man who endeavours to act up to erroneous convictions is in a much healthier state than the man who has lost all convictions whatever. And this is the danger which always lies before us when we attempt to win others over from sincere and steadfast beliefs which seem to us to be untrue. We may succeed in shaking these beliefs; but it by no means follows that we shall be equally successful in giving them better beliefs in exchange for them. We may accomplish no more than the miserable result of having convinced them that in religion everything is uncertain.

Of course there are times when it is our duty to do what we can to bring others over to opinions which we are persuaded are much sounder and safer than those which they at present hold; but such times are very much less frequent than many of us are inclined to believe. It is obviously our duty to undertake this difficult task when other people consult us as to their religious convictions; but the mere fact that we know what their convictions are, and that we hold them to be perilously unsound, does not establish a right on our part to attempt to change them. And as regards the passage before us, it is quite clear, both from the context and from the tenour of the whole Epistle, that the rare occasions on which we are under the obligation of endeavouring to convert others to our own ways of thinking are not the occasions to which St. James refers in these concluding sentences of his letter.

The duty of reclaiming the lost grows out of the condition of brotherhood which is assumed all through the Epistle as being the relation which exists between those who are addressed. This is manifestly the case here. "My *brethren*, if any among *you* do err from the truth." If it be right to clothe and feed the naked and hungry brother, to pray for the sick brother, and for those who confess their faults to us, much more must it be right to do all that is possible to bring back from the way of death those who are walking in it, to convert them, turn them right round, and induce them to go in the opposite direction. To believe in God, to believe that we are His children, and yet to act as if the bodies and souls of others, who are equally His children, are in no degree in our keeping, and that their condition is no concern of ours—this is indeed to have that faith which, being apart from works, is dead.

How is the conversion of the erring brother to be effected? St. James gives no explicit directions, but leaves all matters of detail to the discretion of the worker. Yet he does not leave us altogether without guidance as to what are the best methods. One of these is intimated by what immediately precedes, and the other by the general import of the letter. These two efficacious means for the conversion of sinners are, not rebuke or remonstrance, not exhortation or advice, not anger or contempt, but—*prayer* and *good example*. It is by prayer that the sick may be restored to health; it is by prayer that sinners who confess their sins may be healed; and it is by prayer that sinners, who as yet will not confess and repent, may be won over to do so. And here the appropriateness of the example of Elijah becomes evident. Elijah was a prophet, and he knew that when he prayed for drought and for rain he was praying for what was in accordance with the will of God; and it is such prayers that are sure of fulfilment. We are not prophets, and when we pray for changes of weather we cannot be sure that what we ask is in accordance with God's will. All that we can do is to submit humbly to His will, and to beg that, so far as they are in harmony with it, our desires may be granted. But when we pray for the conversion of sinners we are in the same position as Elijah. We know from the outset that we are praying for something which it is His will to grant, if only the rebellious wills of impenitent sinners do not prove insuperable: for He forces no one to be converted; He will have voluntary service, or none at all. When, therefore, we ask Him for the assistance of His Holy Spirit in bringing back sinners from the error of their ways, we may have the greatest confidence that we are desiring that which He would have us desire, and are uniting our wills to His. This, then, is one great instrument for the conversion of our erring brethren—the *prayer of faith*, which can remove mountains of sin out of God's sight, by bringing the sinner, who has piled them up during years of sinning, to confess, and repent, and be forgiven.

The case of St. Monica, praying for the conversion of her sinful and heretical son Augustine, will occur to many as a beautiful illustration of the principle here indicated. He himself tells us of it in his immortal *Confessions*

(III. xi., xii. 20, 21); how that for years, especially from his nineteenth to his twenty-eighth year, he went on seduced and seducing, deceived and deceiving, in various lusts; and how his mother continued to pray for him. "And her prayers entered into Thy presence; and yet Thou didst leave me to wallow deeper and deeper in that darkness." Then she went to a certain bishop, and entreated him to reason with her son; but he declined, saying that the time for that had not yet come. "Leave him alone for a time; only pray to God for him." But she was not satisfied, and continued to implore him with tears that he would go and see Augustine, and try to move him. At which he somewhat lost patience, and sent her away, saying, "Go, leave me, and a blessing go with thee: it is impossible that the son of such tears should perish." Which answer, as she often told her son afterwards, she accepted as if it were a voice from heaven; and all Christendom knows how her prayer was heard. He himself attributed all that was good in him to his mother's tears and prayers.

The other great instrument in accomplishing this blessed work is a *good example*. A holy life is the best sermon, the most effectual remonstrance, the strongest incentive, the most powerful plea. Without it words are of little avail; with it words are scarcely necessary. This is the instrument which St. James throughout this Epistle commends. Not words, but works; not professions, but deeds; not fair speeches, but kind acts (i. 19, 22, 27; ii. 1, 15, 16, 26; iii. 13; iv. 17). Nothing that we can say will ever make such impression upon others as what we *do* and what we *are*. Eloquence, reasoning, incisiveness, pathos, persuasiveness, all have their uses, and may be of real service in the work of winning back sinners from the error of their ways, but they are as nothing compared with holiness. It is when deep calls to deep, when life calls to life, when the life of manifest devotion at once shames and attracts the life of flagrant sin, that spirits are moved, that the loathing for vice and the longing for virtue are excited. The man whose own habitual conduct most often makes other men ashamed of themselves is the man who not only has the best of all qualifications for winning souls to God, but is actually accomplishing this work, even when he is not consciously attempting it. And such a one, when he does attempt it, will have a large measure of the requisite wisdom. The earnestness of his own life will have given him a knowledge of his own heart, and that is the best of all keys to a knowledge of the hearts of others.

There is something fatally wrong about us if we have no strong desire to bring back sinners to God. We cannot be Christ's disciples without having it. The man who would go to heaven *alone* is already off the road thither. The man whose one consuming thought is to save his *own* soul has not yet found out the best means of saving it. The surest road to personal happiness is to devote oneself to promoting the happiness of others, and the best way to secure one's own salvation is to devote oneself to the Divine work of helping forward the salvation of others. Let the fear of giving scandal to others keep us from sin; let the hope of being a help to others encourage us in well-doing; and let our prayers be more for others than for ourselves. As Calvin says, on this passage, "We must take heed lest souls perish through our sloth whose salvation God puts in a manner in our hands. Not that we can bestow salvation on them, but that God by our ministry delivers and saves those who seem otherwise to be nigh destruction."

What is the reward which St. James holds out to us to induce us to undertake the work of converting a sinner? He offers nothing; he promises nothing. The work itself is its own reward. To win back an erring brother is a thing so blessed, so glorious, so rich in incalculable results, that to have been enabled to accomplish it is reward enough—is a prize sufficient to induce any true hearted Christian to work for it. It is no less than the "saving of a soul from death;" and who can estimate what that means? It is the "covering of a multitude of sins."

There is no need to make this last phrase include the sins which the man would otherwise have committed had he not been converted. Sins not committed cannot be covered. It is quite true that by conversion a man is saved from sins into which he would certainly have fallen; and this is a very happy result, but it is not the result pointed out by St. James. The sins which have been committed during the daily walk towards destruction are what he has in his mind; and they are not one or two here and there, but a *multitude*. To aid a brother to get rid of these by confession and repentance is an end that amply repays all the trouble that we can take in attaining to it.

"But the number of renegades is so enormous; the multitude of impenitent sinners is so overwhelming: how is it possible to convert them?" St. James says nothing about converting multitudes; he speaks only of converting *one*. "If any (ἐάν τις) among you do err from the truth, and one convert *him*." To bring over *one* soul from eternal death to eternal life may be within the power of any one earnest Christian. Is each one of us making the attempt? Are we making our lives as beneficent, as sympathetic, as unselfish as our opportunities admit of? Do we give a generous, or even a moderate share of encouragement to the numerous agencies which are at work to lessen the temptations and increase the means of grace for those who are living in sin, and to help and encourage those who, in however feeble a way, are making a fight against it?

"Know ye,[101] that he which converteth a sinner from the error of his way shall save a soul from death, and shall cover a multitude of sins." With these words St. James abruptly takes leave of those whom he addresses. The letter has no formal conclusion; not because it is unfinished, or because the conclusion has been lost, but because St. James wishes by means of a sudden close to leave his last words ringing in the hearts of his readers. In this respect the Epistle reminds us of the First Epistle of St. John. "Guard yourselves from the idols" is the only farewell which the last of the Apostles has for his "little children;" and a very summary statement of what the conversion of one sinner means is the farewell of St. James to his "brethren." In both cases it is the abruptness of emphasis, as if the writer said, "If all else that I have written be forgotten, at least remember this."

How beautiful to find one noble soul, and enter into frequent communion with it! how happy to be the means of preserving it from defilement! but most blessed of all to be instrumental in rescuing it from degradation and destruction! "I say unto you, That there shall be joy in heaven over one sinner that repenteth, more than over ninety and nine righteous persons, which need no repentance."

Note.—It is by no means impossible that in the phrase "cover a multitude of sins" neither St. James is quoting St. Peter, nor St. Peter St. James, nor either of them quoting Psalms or Proverbs, but that each of them is reproducing a saying of Christ's which is not recorded in the Gospels. The phrase occurs in both Clement of Rome (XLV.) and Clement of Alexandria (*Strom.* I. xxvii.; II. xv.; IV. xviii.; *Quis Div. Salv.* xxxviii.), in all which places it may be a quotation from 1 Peter iv. 8. But in one place (*Pædag.* III. xii.) he seems to give it as a saying of our Lord's, for he couples it with a saying which is certainly His (Luke xx. 25). Clement's wording is as follows: "Love, He saith, covereth a multitude of sins; and respecting citizenship, Render to Cæsar the things that are Cæsar's, and to God the things that are God's;" where one and the same "He saith" (φησί) covers both sayings. In the *Didascalia* (II. iii.) the saying is explicitly attributed to Christ: "Because the Lord saith, Love covereth a multitude of sins." See Resch, *Agrapha; Aussercanonische Evangelienfragmente* (Leipzig, 1889), pp. 248, 249.

> [100] πλανηθῇ. This aorist passive *may* have a middle signification, but it is simpler to allow it to be passive: the man has been led astray by evil influences, and he is led back by good influences. It matters not whether we regard him as led astray by sin (Bengel), or Satan, or wicked companions.
>
> [101] This is probably the true reading.

THE GENERAL EPISTLE OF ST. JUDE

CHAPTER XXX
THE AUTHENTICITY OF THE
EPISTLE OF ST. JUDE

"Judas, a servant of Jesus Christ, and brother of James, to them that are called, beloved in God the Father, and kept for Jesus Christ: mercy unto you and peace and love be multiplied."—St. Jude 1, 2.

Precisely as in the case of the Epistle of St. James, the question as to the authenticity of this letter resolves itself into two parts: Is the Epistle the veritable product of a writer of the Apostolic age? If it is, which of the persons of that age who bore the name of Judas is the author of it? Both of these questions can be answered with a very considerable amount of certainty.

Let us remember the right way of putting the first of these two questions. Not, Why should we believe that this Epistle was written by an Apostle or a contemporary of the Apostles? but, Why should we refuse to believe this? What reason have we for rejecting the verdict of ecclesiastics and theologians of the fourth and fifth centuries, who were well aware of the doubts which had been raised respecting the authority of the Epistle, and after full and prolonged consideration decided that it possessed full canonical authority. Not only were they in possession of evidence which is no longer available, and which rendered it probable that their decision would be correct; but the universal acceptance of their decision in all the Churches proves that their decision was admitted to be correct by those who had ample means of testing its soundness.

The Epistle of St. Jude, like that of St. James, is reckoned by Eusebius as one of the six or seven "disputed" (ἀντιλεγόμενα) books of the New Testament, which fact, while it proves that misgivings had existed in some quarters respecting the authority of the letter, at the same time proves that it was not admitted into the canon by an oversight. The difficulties respecting it were well known, and were considered to be by no means fatal to its otherwise strong claim to be accepted And the difficulties respecting the two Epistles were similar in kind. 1. Many Churches remained for a considerable time without any knowledge of one or other of the two Epistles; but whereas it was in the West that the Epistle of St. James was least known, it was Eastern Churches that remained longest without knowledge of that of St. Jude. 2. Even when the Epistle did become known it remained doubtful whether the writer was a person of authority. He was possibly not an Apostle, and if he was not such, what were his claims to be heard? 3. To these two difficulties, which were common to both Epistles, must be added another which was peculiar to that of St. Jude. It may be stated in Jerome's words. "Because in it Jude derives a testimony from the Book of Enoch, which is apocryphal, it is rejected by some"[102] (*Catal. Scr. Eccl.* iv.). As we shall see hereafter, it probably makes use of yet another apocryphal book; and it was not unreasonably doubted whether an Apostolic writer would compromise himself by the use of such literature. If he were inspired, he would know it to be apocryphal, and would abstain from quoting it; and if he did not know its apocryphal character, how could he be inspired, or his words be of any authority?

That so brief a letter should remain for a considerable time quite unknown to some Churches, is not at all surprising. Its evident Jewish tone would render it less attractive to Gentile Christians. Its making no claim to Apostolic authority raised a doubt whether it had any authority whatever, and this doubt was increased by the fact that it quotes apocryphal writings. Consequently those Christians who knew the Epistle would not always be ready to promote its circulation. Even if we were compelled to infer that silence respecting it implies ignorance of its existence, such ignorance would in most cases be very intelligible: but this perilous inference from silence in some cases can be shown to be incorrect. Hippolytus may *possibly* have remained ignorant of it; but if, as Bishop Lightfoot suggests,[103] he is the author of the supposed Greek original of the Muratorian Canon, he testifies strongly (note the *sane*) to the general reception of the Epistle. This holds good, however we may deal with the ambiguous *in catholica*, which may possibly mean "in the Catholic Church," or be a mistake for *in catholicis*, "among the Catholic Epistles." Cyprian, who never quotes the Epistle of St. Jude, must have known of it from the celebrated passage in "the master" Tertullian, whose works he was always reading. And it is quite incredible that Chrysostom, who in all his voluminous writings does not chance to quote it even once, was not familiar with its contents. The brevity of the Epistle is sufficient to explain a great deal of the silence respecting it.

The most serious item in the external evidence against the Epistle is its absence from the Peshitto, or ancient Syriac Version. The considerations already mentioned go a long way towards explaining this absence, and it is a great deal more than counterbalanced by the strong external evidence in its favour. This is surprisingly strong, especially when compared with that in favour of the Epistle of St. James. In both cases the troubles which overwhelmed the Church of Jerusalem and Jewish Christianity in the reign of Hadrian interfered with the circulation of the letters; but it is the shorter letter and the letter of the less-known writer which (so far as extant testimony goes) seems in the first instance to have obtained the wider circulation and recognition. The Muratorian Canon, as we have seen, contains it; so also does the old Latin Version. Tertullian (*De Cult. Fem.* I. iii.) vehemently contends that the Book of Enoch ought to be accepted as canonical, and he clenches his argument with the fact that it is quoted by "the Apostle Jude." This appeal would have seemed dangerous rather than conclusive, if in North Africa there had been any serious misgivings about the authority of Jude's Epistle. Tertullian evidently entertained nothing of the kind. In a similar spirit Augustine asks, "What of Enoch, the seventh from Adam? Does not the canonical Epistle of the Apostle Jude declare that he prophesied?" (*De Civ. Dei*, xviii. 38). Clement of Alexandria quotes it as Scripture (*Pæd.* III. viii., and *Strom.* III. ii.), and commented upon it in his *Hypotyposeis* (Eus. H. E. VI. xiv. 1), of which we probably still possess some translations into Latin made under the direction of Cassiodorus. Origen, although he was aware that it was not universally received, for in one place he uses the cautious expression, "If any receive the Epistle of Jude," yet accepted it thoroughly himself, as the frequent citations of it in his works show. In one passage he speaks of it as "an Epistle of but few lines, yet full of the strong words of heavenly grace" (*Comm.* on Matt. xiii. 55). Athanasius places it in his list of the canonical Scriptures without any mark of doubt. And Didymus, head of the Catechetical School at Alexandria, and instructor of Jerome and Rufinus, condemns the opposition which some offered to the Epistle on account of the statement respecting the body of Moses (ver. 9), just as Jerome virtually condemns those who opposed it because of the quotation from the Book of Enoch.

This evidence, it will be observed, is mostly Western. The blank as regards the East is to some extent filled by the letter of the Synod at Antioch against Paul of Samasota, A.D. 269. Portions of this letter have been preserved by Eusebius, and Malchion, the presbyter who chiefly composed it, seems to have had the Epistle of Jude in his mind when he wrote. This is chiefly evident in the tone of the letter; but here and there the wording approaches that of St. Jude; *e.g.* "denying his God [and Lord]" reminds us of "denying our only Master and Lord" (Jude 4); and "not guarding the faith which he once held" may be suggested by "contend earnestly for the faith which was once for all delivered unto the saints" (Jude 3). The quotations from Jude in Ephrem Syrus (c. A.D. 308-73) are somewhat discredited, for they occur only in the Greek translations of his works, some of which, however, were made in his lifetime; but the quotations may be insertions made by translators.

That so short a letter should have so much testimony in its favour is remarkable; and although it may be a slight exaggeration to say, with Zahn, that about A.D. 200 it was accepted "in the Church of all lands round the Mediterranean Sea" (*Gesch. d. Neutest. Kanons*, I., p. 321), yet even Harnack admits that this is not much in excess of the truth. The only abatement which he suggests is that the misgivings to which Origen on one single occasion bears witness, show that the Epistle was not *everywhere* in the East part of the New Testament Scriptures (*Das N.T. um d. Jahr 200*, p. 79). We may take it, therefore, as sufficiently proved that this letter was written by one who belonged to the Apostolic age. Had it been a forgery of the second century, it would not have found this general acceptance. Moreover, a forger would have chosen some person of greater fame and greater authority as the supposed writer of the Epistle, or would at least have made Jude an Apostle; and above all, he would have betrayed some *motive* for the forgery. There is nothing in the letter to indicate any such motive. Renan accepts the Epistle as a genuine relic of the Apostolic age, and indeed places it as early as A.D. 54; yet his view of it would lead other people to regard it as a forgery, for it supplies a strong motive. Renan considers it to be an attack on St. Paul. The Clementine literature shows us how a heretic of the second century can make a covert attack on the Apostle of the Gentiles; and if we could believe that the writer of this Epistle had St. Paul in his mind when he denounced those who "in their dreamings defile the flesh, and set at nought dominion, and rail at dignities," we should be ready enough to believe that he was not really "Judas, brother of James," but one who did not dare to say openly in the Church the accusations which he tried to insinuate. But no critic has accepted this strange theory of Renan's, and it is hardly worth while asking, Why was not St. Peter or St. John taken as the authority wherewith to counteract the influence of St. Paul? Of what weight would the words of the unknown Jude be in comparison with his? Renan's literary acuteness recognizes in this Epistle a veritable product of the first century: his prejudices respecting anti-Pauline tendencies among the Apostolic writers lead him amazingly astray as to the meaning of its contents.

It remains to consider the second part of the question respecting the authenticity of this Epistle. We are justified in believing that it is a writing of the Apostolic age, by a person bearing the name of Judas or Jude. But to which of the persons who bore that name in the first age of the Church is the letter to be assigned? Only two persons have to be considered—(1) "Judas not Iscariot," who seems also to have been called Lebbæus or Thaddæus, for in the lists of the Apostles Thaddæus or Lebbæus (the readings are confused) stands in Matthew x. and Mark iii. as the equivalent of "Judas [the son] of James" in Luke vi. and Acts i.; and (2) Judas one of the four brethren of the Lord; the names of the other three being James, Joseph or Joses, and Simon (Matt. xiii. 55; Mark vi. 3). These two are sometimes identified, but the identification is highly questionable, although the Authorized Version encourages us to make it by giving to "Judas of James" the improbable meaning, "Judas the *brother* of James," instead of the usual meaning, "Judas the *son* of James."[104] In other words, the Authorized Version assumes that the writer of this Epistle is the Apostle "Judas not Iscariot;" the writer calls himself "brother of James," and the Authorized Version makes this Apostle to be "the brother of James."

We have seen already that both Tertullian and Augustine speak of the writer of this Epistle as an Apostle. So also does Origen, but only in two passages, of which the Greek original is wanting (*De Principiis*, III. ii. 1; *Comm. on Romans* v. 13, vol. iv., 549). In no passage of the Greek works, and in no other passage of the Latin translations, does he call Jude an Apostle; so that the addition of Apostle in these two places may be an insertion of his not very accurate translator Rufinus. But even if the authority of Origen is to be added to that of Tertullian and Augustine, the opinion that the author of this letter was an Apostle is not probable. Had he been such, it would have been natural to mention the fact as a claim on the attention of his readers, instead of merely contenting himself with naming his relationship to his much more distinguished brother James. It is not to the point to urge that St. Paul does not always call himself an Apostle in his Epistles. He was a well-known person, especially after his four great Epistles had been published, in all of which he styles himself an Apostle. In the two to the Thessalonians he does not, probably because he there associates Silvanus and Timothy with himself (but see 1 Thess. ii. 6). St. Jude was comparatively unknown, having written nothing else, and having probably travelled little. The charge, "Remember ye the words which have been spoken before by the Apostles of our Lord Jesus Christ" (ver. 17), although it does not necessarily imply that the writer himself is not one of these Apostles, yet would be more suitable to one who did not possess Apostolic rank. And when we ask what *James* is meant, when he styles himself "brother of James," the answer cannot be doubtful; it is James the brother of the Lord, one of the three "Pillars" of the Jewish Christian Church, first overseer of the Church of Jerusalem, and author of the Epistle which bears his name. The Epistle of Jude is evidently by a Jewish Christian, who, while writing to all that have been called to the faith, evidently has Jewish Christians chiefly in his mind. To such a writer it was well worth while to mention that he was brother of that James who was so revered by all his fellow countrymen. Reasons have been given already for believing that this James was not an Apostle, and these will confirm us in the opinion that his brother Jude was not such. The question of their relationship to Jesus Christ has also been discussed, and need not be reopened here. If it be argued that, had St. Jude been the brother of the Lord, he would have mentioned the fact, we may securely answer that he would not have done so. "As the author of the *Adumbrationes* centuries ago remarked, religious feeling would deter him, as it did his brother James, in his Epistle, from mentioning this. The Ascension had altered all Christ's human relationships, and His brethren would shrink from claiming kinship after the flesh with His glorified body. This conjecture is supported by facts. Nowhere in primitive Christian literature is any authority claimed on the basis of nearness of kin to the Redeemer. He Himself had taught Christians that the lowliest among them might rise above the closest of such earthly ties (Luke xi. 27, 28); to be spiritually the "servant of Jesus Christ" was much more than being His actual brother."[105]

We may suppose that Jude, like the rest of his brethren (John vii. 5), did not at first believe in the Messiahship of Jesus, but was converted by the convincing event of the Resurrection (Acts i. 14). We know that he was married, not merely from the general statement made by St. Paul respecting the brethren of the Lord (1 Cor. ix. 5), but from the interesting story told by Hegesippus, and preserved by Eusebius (*H. E.* III. xx. 1-8), that two grandsons of Jude were taken before Domitian as being of the royal family of David, and therefore dangerous to his rule. "For," says Hegesippus, "he was afraid of the appearance of the Christ, as Herod was." In answer to his questions, they stated that they were indeed of the family of David, but were poor and humble persons, who supported themselves by their own labour; in proof of which they showed their horny hands. When further questioned respecting the Christ and His kingdom, they said that it was not earthly, but heavenly, and would arise at the end of the world, when He came to judge the living and the dead. Whereupon Domitian contemptuously dismissed them as too simple to be dangerous, and ordered that the persecution of the descendants of David should cease. These two men were afterwards honoured in the Churches, both as confessors and as being near of kin to the Lord. A fragment of Philip of Side (*c.* A.D. 425) lately discovered says that Hegesippus gave the names of these two men as Zocer and James (*Texte und Untersuchungen*, V. 2, p. 169).

This narrative implies that both St. Jude and the father of these grandsons were already dead, and this gives us a terminus respecting the date of the Epistle. St. Jude was almost certainly dead when Domitian came to the throne, in A.D. 81, and therefore this letter was written before that date. Whether, as Hilgenfeld and others would have us believe, the Epistle is aimed at Gnostic errors which did not arise until the second century, will be considered hereafter, when the nature of the evils denounced by St. Jude is discussed; but the evidence which has been examined thus far entirely agrees with the supposition that the letter was written during the Apostolic age.

It is not impossible that in calling himself "brother of James" St. Jude is thinking of his brother's *Epistle*, and wishes his readers to consider that the present letter is to be taken in conjunction with that of St. James. Both letters are Palestinian in origin and Jewish in tone; and they are almost entirely practical in their aim, dealing with grave errors in conduct. Those which are denounced by St. Jude are of a grosser kind than those denounced by St. James, but they resemble the latter in being errors of behaviour rather than of creed. They are to a large extent the *outcome* of pernicious principles; but it is the vicious lives of these "ungodly men" that are condemned more than their erroneous beliefs. St. Jude, therefore, may be appealing not only to his brother's position and authority as a recommendation for himself, but also to his brother's Epistle, which many of his readers would know and respect.

The attempts which have been made to find a locality for St. Jude's readers altogether fail. Palestine, Asia Minor, Alexandria have all been suggested; but the letter does not offer sufficient material for the formation of a reasonable opinion. "To them that are called, beloved in God the Father, and kept for Jesus Christ," is a formula which embraces *all* Christians, whether Jews or Gentiles, and whether inside or outside Palestine. The topics introduced are such as would chiefly interest Jewish Christians, and it is probable that the writer has the Jewish Christians of Palestine and the adjoining countries chiefly in his mind; but we have no right to limit the natural meaning of the formal address which he himself has adopted. All Christians, without limitation, are the objects of St. Jude's solicitude.

[102] *A plerisque rejicitur.* Possibly this means "is rejected by *very many*;" it certainly ought not to be rendered "is rejected by *most*." "Most" is the classical meaning of *plerique*; but in Tacitus it means no more than "very many" (*Hist.* iv. 84, etc.), and in Jerome and his contemporaries it need mean no more than "some." Thus in Jerome's letter to Dardamus (*Ep.* cxxix.) we have *licet plerique eam vel Barnabæ vel Clementis arbitrentur* (of the Epistle to the Hebrews), where *plerique* = the τινές of Eusebius and Origen (*H. E.* VI. xx. 3; xxv. 14).

[103] See the *Academy* of September 21st, 1889, where he shows how much of the Fragment can be turned quite literally into Greek verse, and suggests that the εἰς πάσας τὰς γράφας, "Odes referring to all the Scriptures," mentioned among the works of Hippolytus whose titles are inscribed on his chair (see Kraus, *Real. Encykl. der Chris. Alterthümer*, I., pp. 661-64), refers to metrical compositions on the contents of the Old and New Testaments. The Fragment says respecting this Epistle, "Epistola sane Iude et superscrictio (*sic*) Iohannis duas in catholica habentur", where *superscrictio* is a clerical error for *superscripti*, "the John mentioned above."

[104] The Genevan Version introduced this rendering. Previous versions either leave the meaning doubtful, "Judas of James," as Wiclif, or translate "James' *sonne*," as Tyndale and Cranmer. Luther also is for "son."

[105] These words are quoted from a commentary which the writer of this volume wrote in 1879 for Messrs. Cassell, in the *New Testament Commentary for English Readers*, edited by Bishop Ellicott (p. 505), of which, through the courtesy of the publishers, he is allowed to make use for the present work.

CHAPTER XXXI
THE PURPOSE OF THE EPISTLE.—THE FAITH ONCE FOR ALL DELIVERED AND THE DEVELOPMENT OF CHRISTIAN DOCTRINE

"Beloved, while I was giving all diligence to write unto you of our common salvation, I was constrained to write unto you exhorting you to contend earnestly for the faith which was once for all delivered unto the saints."—St. Jude 3.

THE Greek of the opening sentence of this passage, in which St. Jude explains his reason for writing this Epistle, is ambiguous. The words "of our common salvation" (περὶ τῆς κοινῆς ἡμῶν σωτηρίας) may go either with what precedes or with what follows. But there is little doubt that both the Authorized and the Revised Versions are right in taking them with what precedes. The true connexion is, not, "While I was giving all diligence to write unto you, I was constrained to write unto you of our common salvation," but, "While I was giving all diligence to write unto you of our common salvation, I was constrained to write unto you exhorting you to contend earnestly for the faith." This Epistle can scarcely be called a letter "about our common salvation." The meaning is that St. Jude had intended to write such a letter, but the crisis created by the entrance of these ungodly men into the Church constrained him to write a letter of a different kind, viz. the one which lies before us. That he had already *begun* to write a letter "respecting our common salvation," and that we have here to lament the loss of another Epistle besides the lost Epistles of St. Paul and St. John (1 Cor. v. 9; 3 John 9), is neither stated nor implied.[106] St. Jude had been thinking very earnestly about writing a more general and comprehensive Epistle, when he realized that the presence of a very serious evil required immediate action, and accordingly he writes at once to point out the existing peril, and to denounce those who are the authors of it. It is the duty of all Christians to be on their guard, and to be unflinching in their defence of the truth which has been committed to them to preserve and cherish.

"The faith which was once for all delivered unto the saints." This does not mean, which was delivered by God to the Apostles, but which was delivered by the Apostles to the Church. "The saints" here, as so often in the New Testament (Acts ix. 13, 32, 41; xxvi. 10; Rom. viii. 27; xiii. 13; xv. 25, 26, 31; etc., etc.), means *all* Christians. If the whole nation of the Jews was a "holy people" (λαὸς ἅγιος), "a peculiar treasure unto Jehovah from among all peoples" (Exod. xix. 5), by reason of their special election by Him (Deut. vii. 6; xiv. 2, 21); if they were "saints of the Most High" (Dan. vii. 18, 22, 25), much more might this be said of Christians, who had inherited all the spiritual privileges of the Jews, and had received others in abundance, far exceeding any that the Jews had ever possessed. Christians also, in a still higher sense, were "an elect race, a royal priesthood, a holy nation, a people for God's own possession" (1 Peter ii. 9). The Christians of Corinth, Ephesus, and Colossæ, in spite of the enormous evils which they practised or sanctioned, or at least tolerated, are still called "saints." They are holy, not as being persons of holy life, but as being devoted to God. Of course such persons *ought* to be holy in conduct, but to call them "saints" does not assert that they are so. The name asserts the fact of being set apart by God for Himself, and implies what ought to be the result of such separation. "Thus the main idea of the term is *consecration.* But though it does not assert moral qualifications as a fact in the persons so designated, it implies them as a duty."[107] To each individual Christian, therefore, the name is at once an honour, an exhortation, and a reproach. It tells of his high calling, it exhorts him to live up to it, and it reminds him of his grievous shortcomings.

"The faith *once for all delivered* unto the saints" (τῇ ἅπαξ παραδοθείσῃ τοῖς ἁγίοις πίστει): both the adverb, "once for all," and the aorist participle, "delivered," are worthy of special notice. "The faith" does not mean any set formula of articles of belief, nor the internal reception of Christian doctrine, but the *substance* of it; it is equivalent to what St. Paul and the Evangelists call "the Gospel," viz. that body of truth which brings salvation to the soul that receives it. This Faith, or this Gospel, has been once for all delivered to Christians. No other will be given, for there is no other. Whatever may be delivered by any one in future cannot be a gospel at all. The one true Gospel is complete and final, and admits of no successors and no supplements (Gal. i. 6-9).

"The faith which was once for all delivered unto the saints." Does this exclude all possibility of a "development of Christian doctrine"? That depends upon what one means by "development." The expression has been interpreted to mean "that the increase and expansion of the Christian creed and ritual, and the variations which have attended the process in the case of individual writers and Churches, are the necessary attendants on any philosophy or polity which takes possession of the intellect and heart, and has had any wide or extended dominion; that from the nature of the human mind, time is necessary for the full comprehension *and perfection* of great ideas; and that the highest and most wonderful truths, though communicated to the world once for all by inspired teachers, could not be comprehended all at once by the recipients, but, as received and transmitted by minds not inspired and through media which were human, have required only the longer time and deeper thought for their full elucidation."[108] If the ambiguous expression "and perfection" be omitted, one may readily allow that development of Christian doctrine in this sense has taken place. To say that time is needed for the *full comprehension* of the great truths which were communicated to the Church once for all by the Apostles is one thing; to say that time is needed for the *perfection* of those truths may or may not be quite another. And the manner in which the subject is treated in the famous Essay from which the passage just quoted is taken shows that what is meant by the "perfecting" of the truths is a very different thing from the full comprehension of their original contents; it means making additions to the original contents in order to remedy supposed deficiencies. In this sense it may be confidently asserted, and as loyal Christians we are bound to assert, that there is no such thing as development of Christian doctrine. If there be such a thing, then we cannot stop short with those developments which can in some measure be called Christian. The author himself reminds us that "no one has power over the issues of his principles; we cannot manage our argument, and have as much of it as we please, and no more". If the faith once for all delivered to the saints was defective, and needed to be supplemented by subsequent additions, why may not Christianity itself be, as some have maintained, only a phase in the development of religion, which in process of time is to be superseded by something wholly unchristian? The transition is easily made from the position of the *Essay on the Development of Christian Doctrine* to that of Channing, that "it makes me smile to hear immortality claimed for Catholicism or Protestantism, or for any past interpretations of Christianity: as if the human soul had exhausted itself in its infant efforts; as if the men of one or a few generations could bind the energy of human thought and affection for ever;"[109] and thence to the position of Strauss, who, in his latest and most dreary work, on *The Old and the New Faith*, asks the question, "Are we still Christians?" and answers it emphatically in the negative. The chief doctrines of Christianity are to him childish or repulsive beliefs, which thoughtful men have long since left behind. We may still in some sense be religious; but Christianity has done its work, and is rightly being dismissed from the stage.[110] This is the advanced thinking of which St. John writes in his Second Epistle: "Everyone that *goeth onward* (πᾶς ὁ προάγων), and *abideth not in the doctrine of Christ*, hath not God" (ver. 9). There is an advance which involves desertion of first principles; and such an advance is not progress, but apostasy.

But *does* the development of doctrine, in the sense contended for by the author of the celebrated Essay, mean making actual additions to the faith once for all delivered, as distinct from arriving at a better comprehension of the contents and logical consequences of the original deposit? This question must be answered in the affirmative, for various reasons. The whole purpose of the Essay, and the actual expressions used in it, require this meaning; and that this is the obvious meaning has been assumed by Roman Catholic as well as Protestant critics, and (so far as the present writer is aware) this interpretation has never been resented as illegitimate by the author. The whole argument is admittedly "an hypothesis to account for a difficulty," "an expedient to enable us to solve what has now become a necessary and an anxious problem", viz. the enormous difference between the sum total of Roman Catholic doctrines and those which can be found in the Christian documents of the first two or three centuries. The Essay is believed by its author to furnish "a solution of such a number of the reputed corruptions of Rome as might form a fair ground for trusting her where the investigation had not been pursued". And that the faith once for all delivered is regarded as in need of supplements and additions seems to be implied in such language as the following: "In whatever sense the need and its supply are a proof of design in the visible creation, in the same do *the gaps*, if the word may be used, *which occur in the structure of the original creed of the Church,* make it probable that those developments, which grow out of the truths which lie around them, were intended to complete it". It is the business of succeeding ages of the Church to "keep what was exact, and *supply what was deficient*".

The author of the *Essay on the Development of Christian Doctrine* states in another of his works that when he was admitted to the Church of Rome he embraced volumes containing the writings of the Christian Fathers, crying out that now they were really his own. The action and exclamation were thoroughly inconsistent with the position maintained throughout the Essay, and since then adopted by numbers of Roman controversialists. He ought rather to have cleared his shelves of the works of the Fathers, and to have consigned them to the lumber-room, with the remark, "Now I need never look at you any more." As Bishop Cornelius Mussus (Musso) said long ago, "For my part, to speak quite frankly, I would give more credence to a single Pope than to a thousand Augustines, Jeromes, and Gregorys" (*In Epist. ad Rom.* xiv., p. 606, Venet., 1588, quoted in Hardwick's edition of Archer Butler's *Letters on Romanism*, p. 394). It is the latest and most modern works on Roman theology, especially those which expound the utterances of the most recent Popes, that deserve to be studied, if the theory of the development be correct. According to that theory, the teaching of the primitive Church was certainly immature and defective, and possibly even erroneous. In order to find out what primitive writers meant, or *ought to have meant*, we must look to the latest developments. *They* are the criteria by which to test the teaching of the early Church; it is beginning at the wrong end to test the developments by Christian antiquity. In former times Romanists were at great pains to show that traces of their peculiar tenets could be found in the writers of the first few centuries; and in not a few cases the works of these primitive writers were interpolated, in order to make out a fair case. Criticism has exposed these forgeries, and it has been demonstrated that the early Christian teachers were ignorant of whole tracts of Roman doctrine and practice. Roman controversy has therefore entirely shifted its ground. It now freely admits that these things were unknown to Irenæus, Cyprian, Chrysostom, Athanasius, and Augustine; but for the simple reason that, when they wrote, these things had not yet been revealed. The Church was still ignorant that the Blessed Virgin was conceived without sin, was taken bodily to heaven after her death, and ought to be invoked in prayer; it was still ignorant of the doctrine of purgatory, of indulgences, and of the necessity of being in communion with the Church of Rome. It will not do to say that Christ and His Apostles planted the *germs* of these things, and that for centuries the germs did not expand and fructify, and therefore remained unnoticed. For, first, how can there be *a germ of an historical fact,* such as the supposed removal of the Virgin's body to heaven, which is most happily named an "assumption"? Secondly, now that the fruit *has* appeared, we ought to be able to trace it back to the germ which for so long was ignored. And thirdly, if the germs were really deposited by Christ and His Apostles, they would have developed in a *somewhat* similar manner in all parts of Christendom. Different surroundings will account for some variety of development, but not for absolute difference in kind. The germ respecting communion with the Church of Rome, if there was one, developed in the East, where all germs were in the first instance planted, into the doctrine that no such communion was necessary.[111] Therefore, from the Roman point of view, it is necessary to maintain that the development of Christian doctrine involves, not merely the better comprehension of the contents of doctrines, and the expansion of seeds and germs of truth, but the admission of actual supplements and additions, derived from new revelations of fresh items of truth. As the Jesuit Father Harper said, in his reply to Dr. Pusey's *Eirenicon,* "Christ grew in wisdom daily. So does the Church, not in mere appearance, but of truth. Her creed, therefore, can never shrink back to the dimensions of the past, but must ever enlarge with the onward future."

Hence the necessity for the doctrine of Infallibility. For Roman developments are not the only ones. The Eastern Churches have theirs;

Protestant Churches have theirs; and outside these there are other developments, both non-Christian and anti-Christian. Unless there is some authority which can say, "Our developments are Divinely inspired and necessary, while all others are superfluous or wrong," the doctrine of Development may be used with as much force against Rome as for her. Consequently, we find the author of the Essay using the theory of Development as an argument for that of the Infallibility. "If the Christian doctrine, as originally taught, admits of true and important developments, ... this is a strong antecedent argument in favour of a provision in the Dispensation for putting a seal of authority upon those developments.... If certain large developments of it are true, they must surely be accredited as true".

This is further proof that what is contemplated in this theory is not mere logical deductions from revealed truth; for logical deductions vindicate themselves by an appeal to the reason, and need no sanction from an infallible authority. Developments are indeed said to follow by way of "logical sequence," but this term is made to receive an enlarged meaning. "It will include any progress of the mind from one judgment to another, as, for instance, *by way of moral fitness*, which may not admit of analysis into premiss and conclusion" . Thus the "deification of St. Mary" is a "logical sequence" of our Lord's Divinity. "The votaries of Mary do not exceed the true faith, unless the blasphemers of her Son came up to it. The Church of Rome is not idolatrous, unless Arianism is orthodoxy". The following criticism, therefore, does not seem to be unjust: "However the theory may be modified by the subsequent additional supposition of infallible guidance, it is quite evident that, considered in itself, its internal spirit and scope (especially as illustrated by its alleged Roman instances) are nothing short of this, that *everything* which *certain* good men in the Church, or men assumed to be such, can by reasoning *or feeling* collect from a revealed truth is, by the mere fact of its recognition [*i.e.* by the supposed infallible guide], admissible and authoritative."[112] This is indeed a wide door to open for the reception of additions to the faith!

That St. Jude lays much stress on the fact that the sum total of the Gospel, and not merely the elementary portions of it, have been once for all committed to the Church, is shown, not only by the prominence which he gives to the thought here, but by his repetition of it a few lines later, when he begins the main portion of his Epistle: "I desire to put you in remembrance, though ye know *all things once for all*" (ver. 5). Any teaching of new doctrines is not only unnecessary, it is also utterly inadmissible. And every Christian has his responsibilities in this matter. He is to "contend earnestly" (ἐπαγωνίζεσθαι), with all the energy and watchfulness of an athlete in the arena, for the preservation of this sacred deposit, lest it be lost or corrupted. And the manner in which this earnest contest is to be maintained is not left doubtful; not with the sword, as Beza rightly remarks, nor with intemperate denunciation or indiscriminate severity, but with the mighty influence of a holy life, built upon the foundation of our "most holy faith" (vv. 20-23). It is in this way that lawful development of Christian doctrine is secured; not by additions to what was once for all delivered, but by a deeper and wider comprehension of its inexhaustible contents. "If any man willeth to do His will, he shall know of the doctrine."

Note.—In connexion with the subject treated above, chapter ix. of R. H. Hutton's sketch of *Cardinal Newman* (Methuen & Co., 1891) may be profitably read.

[106] This is an assumption of De Wette, who in this followed Sherlock, and was followed by Brückner. It is worth noting that the Vulgate here is as ambiguous as the original Greek: "*Omnem solicitudinem faciens scribendi vobis de communi vestra salute necesse habui scribere vobis,*" etc.

[107] Lightfoot, *Philippians*, note on i. 1.

[108] J. H. Newman, *An Essay on the Development of Christian Doctrine* (London, Toovey, 1845), p. 27.

[109] *Letter on Catholicism: Complete Works* (Routledge, 1884), p. 346.

[110] *Der alte und der neue Glaube* (Leipzig, 1872), pp. 13-91: see especially pp. 90, 91.

[111] See Dr. Salmon's admirable work on *The Infallibility of the Church* (Murray, 1888), pp. 33-41.

[112] Archer Butler's *Letters on Romanism*, Revised by Rev. Charles Hardwick (Macmillan, 1858), p. 91.

CHAPTER XXXII
THE PERSONS DENOUNCED IN THE
EPISTLE. ITS RELATION TO 2 PETER

"For there are certain men crept in privily, even they who were of old set forth unto this condemnation, ungodly men, turning the grace of our God into lasciviousness, and denying our only Master and Lord, Jesus Christ." —St. Jude 4.

WE have here the *occasion* of the letter stated very plainly. St. Jude was meditating a letter on a more general subject, when the grave peril created by the anti-Christian behaviour of the persons condemned in the text constrained him to write at once on this more urgent topic. An insidious invasion of the Christian Church has taken place by those who have no right to a place within it, and who endanger its peace and purity; and he dare not keep silence. The strong must be exhorted to withstand the evil; the weak must be rescued from it.

These invaders are in one respect like those who are condemned in the Epistle to the Galatians, in another respect are very unlike them. They are "false brethren privily brought in, who came in privily" (ii. 4); but they have come in, not "to spy out our liberty which we have in Christ Jesus, that they might bring us into bondage," but to "turn the grace of our God into lasciviousness." The troublers of the Galatian Church were endeavouring to *contract* Christian liberty, whereas these ungodly men were *straining* it to the uttermost. Both ended in destroying it. The one turned the "freedom with which Christ set us free" into an intolerable yoke of Jewish bondage; the other turned it into the polluting anarchy of heathen, or worse than heathen, licence. How utterly alien these latter are from Christianity, or even from Judaism, is indicated by St. Jude's pointed introduction of the pronoun "our" in two clauses in this verse: "turning the grace of *our* God into lasciviousness, and denying *our* only Master and Lord, Jesus Christ." Jehovah is "*our* God," not theirs; they are "without God in the world." And Christ is "*our* only Master and Lord," but not theirs; they have denied and rejected Him, choosing to "walk after their own lusts" (ver. 16), rather than to "walk even as He walked" (1 John ii. 6). They have repudiated His easy yoke, that they may follow their own bestial desires.

Who are these "ungodly men"? Clement of Alexandria (*Strom.* III. ii. *sub fin.*) thinks that St. Jude is speaking prophetically of the abominable doctrines of the Gnostic teacher Carpocrates. Some modern writers adopt this view, with the omission of the word "prophetically," and thus obtain an argument against the genuineness of the Epistle. If the writer knew the teaching of Carpocrates, he cannot have been Jude the brother of James and the brother of the Lord. The date of Carpocrates is too uncertain to make this a perfectly conclusive argument, even if we admit the assumption that the writer of this Epistle *is* alluding to his teaching; for he is sometimes placed before Cerinthus, who was contemporary with St. John. But it may be allowed as probably correct that St. Jude was dead before Carpocrates was known as a teacher of Antinomian Gnosticism. There is, however, nothing whatever to show that it is to his teaching that St. Jude is alluding. He says nothing whatever about the *teaching* of these "ungodly men," who perhaps were not teachers at all; still less does he indicate that they belonged to those Gnostics who, from the Oriental doctrine of the absolutely evil character of matter and everything material, drew the practical conclusion that man's material body may be made to undergo every kind of experience, no matter how shameless, in order that the soul may gain knowledge; that the soul is by enlightenment too pure, and the body by nature too impure, to be capable of pollution; that filth cannot be defiled; and that pure gold remains pure, however often it may be plunged in filthiness. No such doctrine is hinted at by St. Jude. Dorner, therefore, goes beyond what is written when he says that "the persons whom Jude opposes are not merely such as have practically swerved from the right way; they are also teachers of error" (*Doctrine of the Person of Christ*, Intr., p. 72, Eng. Tr.: T. and T. Clark, 1861). It is more reasonable, with De Wette, Brückner, Meyer, Kühl, Reuss, Farrar, Salmon, and others to regard these "ungodly men" as just what St. Jude describes them, and no more; libertines, who ought never to have been admitted into the Church at all; who maintained that Christians were free to live lives of gross sensuality; and who, when rebuked by the elders or other officers of the Church for their misconduct, not only refused to submit, but reviled those who were set over them. They were "teachers of error," but by their bad example, not by systematic preaching. They "screened their immoral conduct by blasphemous assumptions," because they assumed that "having been called for freedom," they might "use their freedom for an occasion to the flesh" (Gal. v. 13), not because they assumed that they ought to disobey the commandments of the Creator of the material universe. And for the same reason they may be called "libertines" on principle. When St. Jude says that they "denied our only Master[113] and Lord, Jesus Christ," he means that they denied Him by their lives. It is altogether unreasonable to read into this simple phrase, which is sufficiently explained by the context, a dogmatic denial of the Incarnation. That the germs of Antinomian Gnosticism are here indicated may be true enough; but they have not yet developed into a body of doctrine. Still less have those who are tainted by these germs developed into an heretical sect.[114]

It is with the verse before us that the marked resemblance between the Epistle of St. Jude and the central portion of the Second Epistle of St. Peter begins; and it continues down to ver. 18. In this short letter of twenty-five verses, only the first three and last seven verses, *i.e.* about a third of the whole, have no intimate relations with 2 Peter. The last word has not yet been spoken upon this perplexing subject. The present writer confesses that he remains still uncertain as to the true relation between the two, and that he has inclined sometimes to the one, and sometimes to the other of the two rival hypotheses. Thus much of what he wrote on the subject more than ten years ago may be repeated now:—

"The similarity, both in substance and wording, is so great that only two alternatives are possible—either one has borrowed from the other, or both have borrowed from a common source. The second alternative is rarely, if ever, advocated; it does not explain the facts very satisfactorily, and critics are agreed in rejecting it. But here agreement ends. On the further question, as to which writer is prior, there is very great diversity of opinion. One thing, therefore, is certain, that whichever writer has borrowed, he is no ordinary borrower. He knows how to assimilate foreign material so as to make it thoroughly his own. He remains original, even while he appropriates the words and thoughts of another. He controls them, not they him. Were this not so, there would be little doubt about the matter. In any ordinary case of appropriation, if both the original and copy are forthcoming, critics do not doubt long as to which is the original. It is when the copy itself is a masterpiece, as in the case of Holbein's Madonna, that criticism is baffled. Such would seem to be the case here; and the present writer is free to confess his own uncertainty."[115]

Other persons are able to write with much more confidence. Dean Mansel says, "Some eminent modern critics have attempted, on the very precarious evidence of style, to assign the priority in time of writing to St. Jude; but there are two circumstances which appear to me to prove most conclusively that St. Jude's Epistle was written after that of St. Peter, and with express reference to it. The first is, that the evils which St. Peter speaks of as partly future St. Jude describes as now present. The one says, 'There *shall* be false teachers among you' (2 Peter ii. 1; the future tense being continued through the two following verses); the other says, 'There *are* certain men crept in unawares.' The other circumstance is still more to the point. St. Peter, in his Second Epistle, has the remarkable words, 'Knowing this first, that in the last days mockers (ἐμπαῖκται) shall come with mockery, walking after their own lusts' (iii. 3). St. Jude has the same passage, repeated almost word for word, but expressly introduced as a citation of Apostolic language: 'But ye, beloved, remember ye the words which have been spoken before by the Apostles of our Lord Jesus Christ; how that they said to you, In the last time there shall be mockers (ἐμπαῖκται), walking after their own ungodly lusts' (vv. 17, 18). The use of the plural number (τῶν ἀποστόλων) may be explained by supposing that the writer may also have intended to allude to passages similar in import, though differently expressed, in the writings of St. Paul (such as 1 Tim. iv. 1, 2; 2 Tim. iii. 1), but the verbal coincidence can hardly be satisfactorily explained, unless we suppose that St. Jude had principally in his thoughts, and was actually citing the language of St. Peter" (*The Gnostic Heresies of the First and Second Centuries*, Murray, 1875, pp. 69, 70). Hengstenberg puts forward the same arguments, and considers the second to be decisive as to the priority of 2 Peter.

Not less confident is Archdeacon Farrar that exactly the opposite hypothesis is the right one. "After careful consideration and comparison of the two documents it seems to my own mind *impossible to doubt* [the italics are Dr. Farrar's] that Jude was the earlier of the two writers.... I must confess my inability to see how any one who approaches the inquiry with no ready-made theories can fail to come to the conclusion that the priority in this instance belongs to St. Jude. It would have been impossible for such a burning and withering blast of defiance and invective as his brief letter to have been composed on principles of modification and addition. All the marks which indicate the reflective treatment of an existing document are to be seen in the Second Epistle of St. Peter. In every instance of variation we see the reasons which influenced the later writer.... The notion that St. Jude endeavoured to 'improve upon' St. Peter is, I say, a literary impossibility; and if in some instances the phrases of St. Jude seem more antithetical and striking, and his description clearer, I have sufficiently accounted for the inferiority—if it be inferiority—of St. Peter by the supposition that he was a man of more restrained temperament; that he wrote under the influence of reminiscences and impressions; and that he was warning against forms of evil with which he had not come into so personal a contact" (*The Early Days of Christianity*, Cassell and Co., 1882, i., pp. 196-203).

The main arguments in favour of the view that the Second Epistle of St. Peter was used by St. Jude, besides those stated by Dean Mansel, are the following:—

(1) If 2 Peter is genuine, it is more probable that St. Jude should borrow from St. Peter than that the chief of the Apostles should borrow from one who was not an Apostle at all.

If 2 Peter is not genuine, it is improbable that the forger would borrow from a writing which from the first was regarded with suspicion, because it quoted apocryphal literature.

(2) St. Jude tells us (ver. 3) that he wrote under pressure to meet a grave emergency, and therefore he would be more likely to make large use of suitable material ready to his hand, than one who was under no such necessity.

The main arguments on the other side are these:—

(1) It is more probable that the chief portion of a short letter should be used again with a great deal of additional matter, than that one section only of a much longer letter should be used again with very little additional matter.

(2) It is more probable that the writer of 2 Peter should omit what seemed to be difficult or likely to give offence, than that St. Jude should insert such things; *e.g.* "*clouds* without water" (Jude 12) is a contradiction in terms, and therefore is naturally corrected to "*wells* without water" (2 Pet. ii. 17); the particular way in which the angels fell (Jude 6), the allusion to certain Levitical pollutions (ver. 23), and the citations from apocryphal books (vv. 9, 14, 15) are either entirely omitted by the writer of 2 Peter, or put in a way much less likely to seem offensive (ii. 4, 11). And Jude 9 has been so toned down by the writer of 2 Peter that without St. Jude's statement respecting Michael and the devil we should scarcely understand 2 Peter ii. 11.

Besides these points, there are two arguments which are used on *both* sides of the question:—

(i) There are certain elements in St. Jude's Epistle of which the writer of 2 Peter would probably have made use, had he seen them; *e.g.* the ironical play upon the word "kept" in "the angels which *kept* not (μὴ τηρήσαντας) their own principality.... He hath *kept* (τετήρηκεν) in everlasting bonds;" the telling antithesis in ver. 10, that what these sinners do not know, and cannot know, they abuse by gross irreverence; and what they know, and cannot help knowing, they abuse by gross licentiousness; and the metaphor of "wandering stars" (ver. 13), which would fit the false teachers, who lead others astray, in 2 Peter, much better than the ungodly men, who are not leaders at all, in Jude. As the writer of 2 Peter makes no use of these points, the inference is that he had never seen them.

But, on the other hand, there are certain elements in 2 Peter of which St. Jude would probably have made use, had he seen them; *e.g.* the destruction of "the world of the ungodly" by the Flood; the "eyes full of an adulteress;" and the explanation of the "great swelling words" as "promising them liberty," which would exactly have suited St. Jude's purpose in condemning those who turned liberty into license. As St. Jude makes no use of these points, the inference is that he had not seen them.

(ii) St. Jude, as will be shown presently, groups nearly everything in threes. It is scarcely an exaggeration to say that wherever he can make a threefold arrangement he does so. Is this artificial grouping a mark of originality or not? Some would urge that it is the writer who is using up another's material who would be likely to add this fanciful arrangement, and that, therefore, St. Jude is the borrower. Others would urge that such triplets would be just the things to be overlooked or disregarded by the borrower, and that, therefore, St. Jude is the original.

About the existence of the triplets in Jude, and their absence in 2 Peter, there can be no question, whatever view we may hold as to their significance. They begin in the very first verse of our Epistle, and continue to the last verse, although those at the close of the letter are lost in the Authorized Version, owing to the fact that the translators used a faulty Greek text. It will be worth while to run through them. (1) Judas, a servant ... and brother. (2) To them that are called, beloved, ... and kept. (3) Mercy unto you and peace and love. (4) Ungodly men, turning, ... and denying. (5) Israelites, angels, cities of the plain. (6) Defile, ... set at nought, ... and rail. (7) Cain, Balaam, Korah. (8) These are.... These are.... These are.... (9) They who make separations, sensual, having not the Spirit. (10) Building up yourselves, ... praying, ... looking for the mercy, (11) On some have mercy; ... and some save; ... and on some have mercy with fear. (12) Before all time, and now, and for evermore.

Before parting with this verse it will be well to put readers on their guard against a misinterpretation of the phrase, "They who were of old set forth unto this condemnation;" a misinterpretation all the more likely to be made by those who use the Authorized Version, which has, "Who were before of old *ordained* to this condemnation." The text is a favourite one with Calvinists; but when rightly translated and understood, it gives no support to extreme predestinarian theories. When literally rendered it runs, "Who have been of old *written down beforehand* for this *sentence;*" or possibly, "Who have been written *up* beforehand;" for the metaphor may be borrowed from the custom of posting up the names of those who had to appear before the court for trial. Be this as it may, "of old" (πάλαι) cannot refer to the eternal counsel and decree of Almighty God, but to something in human history, something remote from St. Jude's own day, but in time, and not in eternity. Perhaps some of the warnings and denunciations in the prophets of the Old Testament or in the *Book of Enoch* are in his mind. "Condemnation" is a justifiable rendering of the Greek word (κρίμα), because it is manifest from the context that the sentence or judgment intended is one of condemnation, and not of acquittal; but this word when coupled with "ordained" is likely to be grievously misunderstood. "Ordained to condemnation" suggests with fatal facility "predestined to damnation"—a doctrine which has perhaps been a more fruitful cause of the rejection of Christianity than all the doctrines included in the creeds.

Probably in all ages of the Church there have been men such as St. Jude here describes—nominal members of the Church who are nothing but a scandal to it, and professing Christians whose whole life is one flagrant denial of Christ. Such persons certainly trouble Christendom now. By their luxury and licentiousness they set an evil example and create a pestilential moral atmosphere. They practise no self-control, and sneer at self-denial in others. They reject all Christian discipline, and mock at those who endeavour to maintain it. And sometimes they are not at once recognized in their true character. They are plausible and amusing, obviously not strict, but not obviously scandalous in their manner of life. It is then that such men become specially dangerous. Such may have been the case in the Churches which St. Jude has in mind. Therefore he strips off all this specious disguise, and describes these profligate scoffers according to their true characters. Moreover, we must remember that there were some, and perhaps many, who, like Simon Magus (Acts viii. 13), accepted baptism without any real appreciation of the meaning of Christianity, and who remained either Jews or heathen at heart, long after they had enrolled themselves as Christians. Where dangerous material of this kind abounded, it was necessary to put the faithful on their guard about the danger; and hence the strength and vehemence of St. Jude's language. A sharp, clear statement of the evil was necessary to put the weak and the unwary on their guard against a peril to which they might easily succumb, before they were fully aware of its existence. We all of us need such warnings still, not merely to form a truer estimate of the nature and tendency of certain forms of evil, and thus keep on our guard against courting needless temptation, but also to preserve us from becoming in our own persons, through manifest self-indulgence and carelessness of life, a snare and a stumbling-block to our brethren.

Note.—On the question as to which of the two Epistles is prior, the opinion of scholars has been greatly divided; but a comparison of the following lists will show that among more recent critics the decision is commonly in favour of the priority of our Epistle:—

For the priority of 2 Peter: Bauer, Beausobre, Benson, Bloomfield, Dahl, Dietlein, Dodwell, Estius, Fronmüller, Hänlein, Hengstenberg, Heydenreich, Hofmann, Lange, Lenfant, Lumby, Luthart, Luther, Mansel, Michaelis, Mill, Œcumenius, Pott, Schaff, Schmid, Schoff, Schulze, Semler, Steinfass, Stier, Stolz, Storr, Thiersch, Wetstein, Wolf, Wordsworth, Zachariæ, and others.

For the priority of St. Jude: Alford, Angus, Arnaud, Bleek, Brückner, Caffin, Credner, Davidson, De Wette, Eichhorn, Ewald, F. W. Farrar, Guerike, Hatch, Herder, Hilgenfeld, Hug, Huther, Kühl, Kurz, Mayerhoff, Neander, Plumptre, Reuss, Salmon, Schenkel, Sieffert, Thorold, Weiss, Wiesinger, and others. Plumptre makes the remarkable suggestion that St. Jude may have written *both* letters. He first wrote his own Epistle, then was sent with it to St. Peter by St. James, and finally acted as St. Peter's amanuensis in writing 2 Peter (*Cambridge Bible for Schools, Epistle of St. Peter and St. Jude*, 1879, pp. 79, 80, 88, 89).

On this point also Dr. Döllinger changed his mind (see p. 31). In *The First Age of the Church* (pp. 93, 108, Eng. Tr., 2nd ed.) he maintained the priority of 2 Peter. June 22nd, 1879, he wrote to me, "Its priority to the Epistle of Jude I *cannot* believe" (*kann ich gar nicht glauben*).

> [113] The insertion of the word "God" into the authorities followed in the Authorized Version is one of the few instances in which it is possible that the Greek text of the N.T. has been corrupted in the interests of orthodoxy.
>
> [114] See the author's *Epistles of St. John* in the *Cambridge Greek Testament*, pp. xx-xxix and 160-162.
>
> [115] *N.T. Commentary for English Readers*, edited by Bishop Ellicott (Cassell and Co. 1879), iii., p. 506.

CHAPTER XXXIII
DOUBTFUL READINGS AND THE THEORY OF VERBAL INSPIRATION. THREE PALMARY INSTANCES OF DIVINE VENGEANCE UPON GRIEVOUS SIN

"Now I desire to put you in remembrance, though ye know all things once for all, how that the Lord, having saved a people out of the land of Egypt, afterwards destroyed them that believed not. And angels which kept not their own principality, but left their proper habitation, He hath kept in everlasting bonds under darkness unto the judgment of the great day. Even as Sodom and Gomorrah, and the cities about them, having in like manner with these given themselves over to fornication, and gone after strange flesh, are set forth as an example, suffering the punishment of eternal fire." —St. Jude 5-7.

WITH these three verses the main portion of the Epistle begins, the first three verses being introductory. These put before us three instances of Divine vengeance upon those who were guilty of grievous sin—the unbelieving Israelites in the wilderness, the impure angels, and the inhabitants of the cities of the plain; and in the three verses which follow (8-10) St. Jude points out the similarity between the offences of these wicked persons and the offences of the libertines who are provoking God to execute similar vengeance upon them. It is quite possible that we have here the explanation of the words, "Who were of old set forth unto this condemnation" (ver. 4). The doom of these impious profligates has long since been written in the doom of those who sinned in a similar manner.

The Greek text of the opening verse exhibits a great variety of readings, and one may suspect with Westcott and Hort that there has been some primitive error, and that none of the existing readings are correct. Of the points in which they differ from one another three require notice:—

(1) In the words, "The Lord, having saved a people out of the land of Egypt," the authorities vary between "the Lord" (with or without the article), "God," and "Jesus." This last is far the best attested (AB, the best cursives, the Vulgate, both Egyptian Versions, both Ethiopic, the margin

of the Armenian, and several Fathers); but the internal evidence against it is immense. Nowhere else in Scripture is Jesus said to be the Author of anything which took place before the Incarnation. Had St. Jude written "Christ," we might have compared "the rock was Christ" (1 Cor. x. 4). But the general adoption of the reading "Jesus" shows how completely in Christian thought and language the Man Jesus had become identified with the Eternal Son. If "Lord" be correct (κύριος, without the article), it should be understood as meaning Jehovah; and therefore "God," though not likely to be right as the reading, is right as an interpretation. In the Latin translation of the *Hypotyposeis* of Clement of Alexandria we have these two readings combined, *Dominus Deus*, and the Greek of Didymus has "Lord Jesus" combined. Possibly all three readings are insertions, and should be omitted, the true text being simply, "He who saved a people out of the land of Egypt" (ὁ λαὸν ἐκ γῆς Αἰγύπτου σώσας).[116]

(2) In the words, "Though ye know all things once for all," some authorities, which were followed by the translators of 1611, have "this" for "all things," while one authority makes "all" to be masculine instead of neuter (πάντας for πάντα). This last *may* be correct, for the final letter of the masculine might easily be lost (especially in front of ὅτι); and in that case the meaning would be, "though ye all know it," *i.e.*, "know what I am going to point out." There is a similar confusion of reading in 1 John ii. 20, where for "Ye know all things" (οἴδατε πάντα) we should perhaps read, "Ye all know" (οἴδατε πάντες). But here the masculine has too little support to be adopted.

(3) The Sinaitic MS. transposes the "once" or "once for all" (ἅπαξ) from "know" to "saved," and makes it answer to the "afterwards," or "the second time" (τὸ δεύτερον) which follows. In this it is supported by the Armenian Version and a single cursive of the fourteenth century.[117] If it were adopted, the sentence would run thus: "Now I desire to put you in remembrance, though ye know all things, how that the Lord, having *once* saved a people out of the land of Egypt, *afterwards* destroyed them that believed not." The correspondence between "once" and "afterwards" — "having *a single time* saved, ... *the second time* He destroyed" — is at first sight attractive; but it is precisely this superficial attractiveness which has caused the corruption of the text. A recent writer pleads for its adoption, but his reasons are not convincing.[118] The external evidence against the proposed transposition is enormous; and there is no strong internal evidence against the best-attested text (as there is against the reading "Jesus") to turn the scale. "Though ye know all this *once for all*" makes excellent sense; and so also does "He who saved a people out of Egypt, *the second time* (viz. in the wilderness) destroyed them that believed not."

This collection of various readings, out of which it is impossible to select the true text with anything like certainty, is worth remembering in considering the theory of *verbal* inspiration. If every word that St. Jude wrote was supernaturally dictated, why has not every word been supernaturally preserved? It is manifest that God has not, either miraculously or in any other way, secured that the exact words written by St. Jude should come down to us without alteration. The alterations are so ancient, so widely diffused, and so numerous, that we are unable to decide what St. Jude's exact words were. We are not even certain that among the numerous variations we have got his exact words. This is not a common case. The usual problem, when various readings occur, is to select the right reading out of several that have been handed down to us, there being no reason to doubt that one of them is the original reading of the autograph. But there are a few passages, and this is one of them, where one may reasonably doubt whether the original reading has not been altogether lost (Acts vii. 46; xiii. 32 [comp. Heb. xi. 4]; xix. 40; xxvi. 28; Rom. xv. 32; 1 Cor. xii. 2; Col. ii. 18, 23; Heb. iv. 2; x. 1; 1 Tim. vi. 7; 2 Tim. i. 13; 2 Peter iii. 10, 12; Jude 22, 23). This result might easily be produced through an error in the earliest copies made from the original document, or through a slip made by the amanuensis who wrote the original document. There are minds to which this supposition is very repugnant; and there are writers who assure us that in Biblical criticism "*conjectural emendation* must never be resorted to, even in passages of acknowledged difficulty," or that "conjectural criticism is entirely banished from the field." But if the whole of an Apostolic Epistle may have been lost (1 Cor. v. 9; 3 John 9), why may not a word or two of an extant Epistle have been lost? And is it quite natural that there should sometimes be a doubt as to *which* of several existing readings is the original, and yet quite inconceivable that there should ever be a doubt as to whether *any* of them is original? In either case we are left in uncertainty as to the precise words which are inspired; and we are thus confronted with the perplexing result that the Almighty has specially guided a writer to use certain words and phrases, to the exclusion of all others, and yet from very early times has, in not a few cases, allowed Christians to be in doubt as to what these exact words and phrases are. Have we any right to assume that there was this special Divine care to produce a particular wording, when it is quite manifest that there has not been special Divine care to preserve a particular wording?

The theory of verbal inspiration imports unnecessary and insuperable difficulties into the already sufficiently difficult problem as to the properties of inspired writings. It maintains that "the line can never rationally be drawn between the thoughts and words of Scripture;" which means that the only inspired Word of God is the original Hebrew and Greek wording which was used by the authors of the different books in the Bible. Consequently all who cannot read these are cut off from the inspired Word; for the inspired thoughts are, according to this theory, inseparably bound up with the original form of words. But if it is the thought, and not the wording, that is inspired, then the inspired thought may be as adequately expressed in English or German as in Hebrew or Greek. It is the inspired thought, no matter in what language expressed, which comes home to the hearts and consciences of men, and convinces them that what is thus brought to them by a human instrument is indeed in its origin and in its power Divine. "Never *man* thus spake" was said, not of the choice language that was used, but of the meaning which the language conveyed.

In the passage before us there are several points which call for attention, most of which are independent of the differences of reading.

It may be doubted whether the participle (εἰδότας) is rightly rendered "*though* ye know all things once for all." It makes good, and perhaps better sense to understand it in the equally possible signification of "*because* ye know all things once for all." Their being already in full possession of a knowledge of Old Testament history is the reason why St. Jude need do no more than remind them of one or two particulars which throw a terrible light upon the position of those whose conduct is being discussed. That "once" here does not mean "formerly," as the Authorized Version takes it, "though ye *once knew* this," is manifest to every one who knows the meaning of the participle and adverb here used (εἰδότας ἅπαξ). Nor is there much doubt that both here and in ver. 3 it does mean "once for all." This Greek adverb, like its Latin equivalent *semel*, is sometimes "used of what is so done as to be of perpetual validity and never need repetition." It is twice so used in the Epistle to the Hebrews: "For as touching those who were *once* enlightened and tasted of the heavenly gift" (vi. 4); *i.e.* once for all enlightened, so that no second enlightenment is possible. And again, "Because the worshippers, having been *once* cleansed, would have had no more conscience of sins" (x. 2). So also in 1 Peter: "Because Christ also died for sins *once*" (iii. 18). The meaning is similar in both the passages here (vv. 3 and 5). The Gospel was once for all delivered by the Apostles to the Church; for there can be no second Gospel. And this Gospel Christians receive and know once for all.

Doubt has been raised as to the event or events to which St. Jude refers in the words "afterward destroyed them that believed not." Hofmann, Schott, and others, adopting the best-attested reading, "*Jesus*, having saved a people out of the land of Egypt, afterward destroyed them that believed not," interpret the latter clause of the destruction of Jerusalem or of the overthrow of the Jewish nation. It is felt that this makes a very unnatural contrast with the deliverance of Israel from Pharaoh by the hand of Moses, and therefore "saved a people out of the land of Egypt" has to be interpreted to mean "the redemption from the bondage-house of the Law and of sin wrought in Israel and for Israel by Christ's act of salvation" (Schott, Erlangen, 1863, p. 225). This is very forced and improbable. Let us hold by Hooker's "most infallible rule in expositions of sacred Scripture, that where a literal construction will stand, the farthest from the letter is commonly the worst"(*Eccl. Pol.* V. lix. 2). The literal construction of "saved a people out of the land of Egypt" will certainly stand here, and the words must be understood of the passage of the Red Sea and all that accompanied that event. This is the clause of which the meaning is plain, and it must be the interpreter of the clause of which the meaning is less plain: to work backwards from the latter is singularly unreasonable. The "saving" being understood of the deliverance of the Israelites from the tyranny of Pharaoh, the "destroying" is most naturally understood of the overthrow of these same Israelites in the wilderness; not of any one catastrophe, such as followed the matter of Korah (Num. xvi. 49) or of Baal-peor (xxv.), but of the gradual destruction, during the forty years of wandering, of the rebellious and unbelieving, "whose carcases fell in the wilderness. And to whom sware He that they should not enter into His rest, but to them that were disobedient? And we see that they were not able to enter in *because of unbelief*" (Heb. iii. 17-19). It is quite unnecessary to add to this, with Fronmüller, the Babylonish captivity, as if "afterward" or "the second time" (τὸ δεύτερον) referred to *two destructions*. It refers to two Divine acts—one of mercy, and a second of judgment.

"And angels which kept not their own principality, but left their proper habitation, He hath kept in everlasting bonds." This is St. Jude's second instance of God's vengeance upon gross sin, and this and the next are common to both Epistles. For the destruction of the unbelieving Israelites 2 Peter has the Deluge. The Revised Version has several improvements here. It substitutes "principality" for "first estate," in harmony with other passages, where the same word occurs (Rom. viii. 38; Eph. iii. 10; vi. 12; Col. i. 16; ii. 10, 15), and inserts "own"—"their *own* principality" (τὴν ἑαυτῶν ἀρχήν); thereby marking the difference between "own" and "proper"—"their *proper* habitation" (τὸ ἴδιον οἰκητήριον). Above all, it preserves St. Jude's irony in the double use of the word "kept" (τηρεῖν): "angels which *kept* not their own principality.... He hath *kept* in everlasting bonds;" which is destroyed in the Authorized Version by the substitution of "reserved" for the second "kept." The alteration of "chains" into "bonds" is of less moment; but it is worth while marking the difference between two Greek words (ἅλυσις and δεσμός), both of which are frequent in the New Testament, and of which the former is always used in a literal sense (Mark v. 3, 4; Luke viii. 29; Acts xii.

6, 7; etc.), and the other sometimes literally (Luke viii. 29; Acts xvi. 26; xxiii. 29; etc.), and sometimes metaphorically (Mark vii. 35; Luke xiii. 16; Philem. 13). It is the latter which is used here.

It may be regarded as certain that this passage does not refer to the original rebellion of the angels, and their fall from being heavenly powers to being spirits of evil and of darkness. Nor is it a *direct* reference to the Rabbinic interpretation of "the sons of God saw the daughters of men that they were fair; and they took them wives of all that they chose" (Gen. vi. 2, where the best texts of the Septuagint have "angels of God" for "sons of God"). Much more probably it is a reference to a topic which is very prominent in the *Book of Enoch*, which, however, in this particular is based upon the common interpretation of the passage in Genesis. A discussion of this most interesting and perplexing writing is reserved for a later chapter. At present it suffices to say that the work is a composite one, written at different times and by different authors, and that the allusions to it here, and the quotation from it in vv. 14 and 15, are from the first portion of the *Book of Enoch* (chapters i.-xxxvi.), which, together with the last portion (chapters lxxii.-cv.), may safely be considered as the original writing, and undoubtedly pre-Christian. Whether any of the book was composed in the Christian era is doubtful, and that any of it was written by a Christian is very doubtful indeed. Hofmann, Philippi, and Weisse have not succeeded in persuading many people that the whole work is of Christian origin. The portion of which St. Jude makes use may, with a good deal of probability, be assigned to the latter part of the second century before Christ. A sketch of the section respecting the sin of the angels will throw much light on the passage before us. A portion of it had long been known through two considerable extracts, which the Byzantine writer Georgius Syncellus (*c.* A.D. 800) makes from it in his *Chronographia* (pp. 20-23 and 40-42, Dindorf's ed., Bonn, 1829). The quotation in our Epistle and those made by Syncellus constituted all that was known of the *Book of Enoch* in Europe until 1773, when the English traveller Bruce brought home three MSS. of an Ethiopic version of the whole which was still extant in the Abyssinian Church.

The section about the sin of the angels and their punishment (vii.-xxxvi.) begins very abruptly after a short introduction (i.-vi.), in which Enoch blesses the righteous, and states that he received a revelation from the angels in heaven. "And it came to pass, when the sons of men had multiplied, that daughters were born to them, very beautiful. And the angels, the sons of heaven, desired them, and were led astray after them, and said to one another, Let us choose for ourselves wives of the daughters of the men of the earth." Two hundred of them then made a conspiracy, and went down to the earth, and begat an offspring of giants. They imparted a knowledge of sorcery and many baneful arts; and the corruption thus diffused, and the voracity and violence of their offspring, produced the evils which preceded the Deluge. Then the sinful angels are sentenced by the Almighty, and Enoch is commissioned to make the sentence known to them. "Then the Lord said to me, Enoch, scribe of righteousness, go tell the watchers of heaven, *who have deserted the lofty sky, and their holy everlasting station*, who have been polluted with women, ... that on earth they shall never obtain peace and remission of sin." The fallen angels persuade Enoch to intercede for them; but his intercession is not heard, and he is told to repeat the sentence which has been pronounced upon them. The following particulars of their punishment are of interest. Azâzêl (comp. Lev. xvi. 26, R.V.), one of the ringleaders, is to be *bound hand and foot*, thrown into a pit in the wilderness, and *covered with darkness*; there he is to remain, with his face covered, *till the great day of judgment*, when he is to be cast into the fire. The others, after they have seen their offspring kill one another in mutual slaughter, are to be *bound for seventy generations underneath the earth, till the day of their judgment*, when they shall be thrown into the lowest depths of the fire, and be *shut up for ever* (x. 6-9, 15, 16). "Judgment has been passed upon you: your prayer shall not be granted you. From henceforth never shall you ascend to heaven. He hath said that on the earth *He will bind you, as long as the world endures*" (xiv. 2). And Enoch is afterwards shown their punishment in a vision. "These are those of the stars which have transgressed the commandment of the most high God, and *are here bound, until the infinite number of the days of their crimes be completed....* Why art thou alarmed and amazed at this terrific place, at the sight of this place of suffering? This is *the prison of the angels; and here are they kept for ever*" (xxi. 3, 6).

It is specially worthy of remark that it is in these older portions of the *Book of Enoch* that we meet for the first time in Jewish literature with the distinct conception of a general judgment. The idea is very frequent, and is expressed in a great variety of ways. Thus, what St. Jude calls "the Judgment of the Great Day" (κρίσιν μεγάλης ἡμέρας), a phrase which occurs nowhere else in the New Testament, is called in the *Book of Enoch* "the Great Day of Judgment" (x. 9), "the Day of the Great Judgment" (xciii. 8; xcvii. 15; civ. 3), "the Day of the Great Trouble" (xcix. 5), "the Great Day" (xvi. 2); "the Great Judgment" (xxii. 5), "the General Judgment" (xxii. 9).[119] St. Jude of course need not have derived this idea from the *Book of Enoch*; but the fact that it is so very frequent there, especially in connexion with the sin of the impure angels, may have influenced him in writing the passage before us. At any rate all these numerous details will not leave us in much doubt as to the origin of St. Jude's statement, "angels which kept not their own principality, but left their proper habitation, he hath kept in everlasting bonds under darkness unto the judgment of the great day." It comes either directly from the *Book of Enoch*, or from a source of which both the writer of the book and St. Jude make use.

It was "in like manner with these" angels that the inhabitants of Sodom and Gomorrah sinned, going astray after unlawful and unnatural indulgences; and "in like manner with these" angels, they also "are set forth as an example, suffering the punishment of eternal fire." The meaning is not quite clear, but apparently it is this, that the sinful angels are in prison awaiting the day of judgment, when they will be cast into the lake of fire; and that the destruction of the cities of the plain by fire, and their perpetual submersion, are an example of the eternal fire in which the angels will be submerged. Perhaps there is also the idea that under the Dead Sea volcanic fires are burning. It is quite possible to take "of eternal fire" after "example" instead of after "punishment;" and this rendering makes the statement more in accordance with the actual facts: "are set forth as an example of eternal fire, suffering punishment." But the two last words come in rather awkwardly at the end of the sentence, and most commentators decide against this construction (comp. 3 Macc. ii. 5).

The three cases exhibit, not a climax, but great diversity, as regards persons, sin, and punishment. We have both Jews and Gentiles, and between them beings superior to both. The Israelites by unbelief rejected their promised home, and perished slowly in the wilderness. The angels left their proper home, sinned grossly, and are in banishment and in prison, awaiting still worse punishment. The men of Sodom and Gomorrah sinned grossly in their home, and both they and it were suddenly, horribly, and irrevocably destroyed. This great diversity gives point to the moral. No matter who may be the sinners, or what the circumstances of the sin, outrageous offences, such as impurity and rebellion, are certain of Divine chastisement.

If fallen angels are evil spirits actively compassing the ruin of souls, how can fallen angels be "kept in everlasting bonds unto the judgment of the great day"? More than one answer might be given to this question, but the reserve of Scripture on the subject seems to warn us from unprofitable speculation. Even without Scripture the reality of spiritual powers of evil may be inferred from their effects. Scripture seems to tell us that some of these powers are personal, and some not, that some are more free than others, and that all shall be defeated at last. That is enough for our comfort, warning, and assurance. It consoles us to know that much of the evil within us is no part of ourselves, but comes from without. It makes us wary to know that such powers are contending against us. It gives us confidence to know that even Satan and his hosts can be overcome by those who resist steadfast in the faith.[120]

[116] W. & H. point out

that OTI<u>O</u>	=	ὅτι ὁ might easily be corrupted
into OTI<u>IC</u>	=	ὅτι ἰησοῦς,
or into OTIKC	=	ὅτι κύριος.

(vol. ii., p. 106. See also Scrivener, 3rd ed., p. 656).

[117] The Latin translation of Clement of Alexandria has the same reading: "*Quoniam Dominus Deus semel populum de terra Ægypti liberans deinceps eos, qui non crediderunt, perdidit.*"

[118] W. S. Wood, *Problems in the N.T.* (Rivingtons, 1890), pp. 161-164.

[119] Stanton, *The Jewish and the Christian Messiah* (T. and T. Clark, 1886), pp. 139, 140. He seems, however, to be mistaken in saying that "the Judge is not the Messiah," but Jehovah. As in Scripture, *both* are represented as judging. "Then the Lord of the spirits made to sit upon the throne of His glory the Elect One, who shall judge all the works of the holy.... And when He shall lift up His countenance to judge their secret way in the word of the Name of the Lord of spirits," etc. (lx. 10-11. Comp. John v. 22).

[120] On the fall of the angels see Hooker, *Eccl. Pol.* I. iv. 3, and V. Appendix i. 28. For a modern and poetical rendering of what is stated in Gen. vi. 1, 2, see Byron, *Heaven and Earth: a Mystery.*

CHAPTER XXXIV
RAILING AT DIGNITIES. "THE ASSUMPTION OF MOSES." ST. JUDE'S USE OF APOCRYPHAL LITERATURE

"Yet in like manner these also in their dreamings defile the flesh, and set at nought dominion, and rail at dignities. But Michael the archangel, when contending with the devil he disputed about the body of Moses, durst not bring against him a railing judgment,[121] but said, The Lord rebuke thee. But these rail at whatsoever things they know not: and what they understand naturally, like the creatures without reason, in these things are they destroyed. Woe unto them! for they went in the way of Cain, and ran riotously in the error of Balaam for hire, and perished in the gainsaying of Korah." — St. Jude 8-12.

ST. JUDE having given three terrible examples of the punishment of gross sin in Jews, Gentiles, and angels, proceeds to apply these instances to the libertines who in his own day, by their scandalous conduct as Christians, were provoking God to punish them in like manner; and the threefold description of their conduct here given seems to refer to the three instances just given, which are now taken in reverse order. Like the people of Sodom and Gomorrah, these ungodly libertines "defile the flesh;" like the "angels which kept not their own principality," they "set at nought dominion;" and like the unbelieving and rebellious Israelites in the wilderness, they "rail at dignities." In all three particulars they show themselves as "dreamers" (ἐνυπνιαζόμενοι). They are like men who say and do monstrous things in their sleep. They are deadened to all sense of decency and duty, "dreaming, lying down, loving to slumber" (Isa. lvi. 10, where the same word that we have here is used in the LXX.). They are sunk in the torpor of sin (Rom. xiii. 11). The Revisers have done rightly in omitting the epithet "filthy," in adding the word "also," and in substituting "in their dreamings" for "dreamers." The participle represented by "in their dreamings" does not belong to "defile the flesh" exclusively, but to the other two clauses as well; so that "filthy" is not even correct as an interpretation: it is quite unjustifiable as a rendering. There is no reason for suspecting that certain Levitical pollutions are indicated. Seeing that "in their dreamings" they "set at nought dominion, and rail at dignities," dreaming must not be understood of actual sleep. Moreover, St. Jude does not say "defile *their* flesh," but "defile the flesh" (σάρκα μιαίνουσι), which includes more than their own bodies. He perhaps means that they pollute human nature, or even the whole animal world.

Like the men of Sodom, these profligates "defile the flesh." Like the angels who sold their birthright for base indulgences, they "set at nought dominion." But it is by no means easy to determine what this "dominion" or "lordship" (κυριότητα) signifies. Calvin and others interpret this and "dignities" or "glories" (δόξας) of the civil power: "There is a contrast to be noticed, when he says that they defiled or polluted the flesh, that is, that they degraded what was less excellent, and that yet they despised as disgraceful what is deemed especially excellent among mankind. It appears from the second clause that they were seditious men, who sought anarchy, that, being loosed from the fear of the laws, they might sin more freely. But these two things are nearly always connected, that they who abandon themselves to iniquity do also wish to abolish all order. Though, indeed, their chief object is to be free from every yoke, it yet appears from the words of Jude that they were wont to speak insolently and reproachfully of magistrates, like the fanatics of the present day, who not only grumble because they are restrained by the authority of magistrates, but furiously declaim against all government, and say that the power of the sword is profane and opposed to godliness; in short, they superciliously reject from the Church of God all kings and all magistrates. 'Dignities,' or 'glories,' are orders or ranks eminent in power or honour" (Calvin's *Commentaries on the Catholic Epistles*, Eng. Tr., Edinburgh, 1855, p. 438). But if earthly rulers of any kind are meant by "dominion" and "dignities," it is more probable that St. Jude is thinking of ecclesiastical officers; in which case the meaning would be that these libertines set Church discipline at defiance, and reviled the presbyters or bishops who rebuked them for their evil conduct.

It is, however, more probable that at least "dominion," if not "dignities," refers to unseen and supernatural powers. We must look backwards to ver. 4, and forwards to ver. 10, for a key to the interpretation. These profligates "turn the grace of God into lasciviousness," and thus "defile the flesh;" and they "deny our only Master and Lord, Jesus Christ," and thus "set at nought lordship." Again, "what they understand naturally, like the creatures without reason, in these things are they destroyed," *i.e.* they ruin themselves, body and soul, by their carnal indulgences; while "they rail at whatsoever things they know not," *i.e.* they speak with flippant irreverence respecting the invisible world, reviling angels, and perhaps mocking at Satan. We may, therefore, with some hesitation, but with a fair amount of reason, interpret "dominion," or "lordship," of Christ or of God, and "dignities," or "glories," of angels, remembering that either or both of these may include Christ's ministers and messengers on earth. One of the ways in which these ungodly men denied Christ in their lives was by their contemptuous disregard of the teaching of His Apostles.[122]

It is quite possible that in this particular also St. Jude is under the influence of the *Book of Enoch*. In it we read, "Ye fulfil not the commandments of the Lord; but ye transgress and *calumniate greatness*" (vi. 4); and again, "All who *utter with their mouths unbecoming language against God*, and *speak harsh things of His glory*, here they shall be collected" (xxvi. 2); and again, "My eyes beheld all the sinners, who *denied the Lord of glory*" (xli. 1). And with this last expression should be compared, "*The splendour of the Godhead* shall illuminate them" (i. 8). But of course it does not follow that because St. Jude partly reproduces the language of this writer, therefore he uses it with precisely the same meaning.

"But Michael the archangel, when contending with the devil he disputed about the body of Moses, durst not bring against him a railing judgment, but said, The Lord rebuke thee." The meaning of this illustration is obvious. The profane libertines allow themselves to speak of "dignities" in a way which even an archangel did not venture to adopt in rebuking Satan. It is a very strong argument *à fortiori*. Consequently, the fact that it was an evil angel against whom Michael did not dare to rail by no means proves that it was evil angels against which the libertines did dare to rail. Rather the contrary may be inferred. They use language of good angels which Michael would not use of a bad one. That "dignities," or "glories," may include the fallen angels or evil spirits is perhaps possible; that it refers to them exclusively is very improbable. The word itself is against this; for "glories" is certainly a strange name to give to devils.

But a more interesting question lies before us as to the source from which St. Jude derived the story about Michael the archangel contending with the devil about the body of Moses. It is as unreasonable to suppose that he received a special revelation on the subject as to suppose that St. Paul received a special revelation respecting the names of the Egyptian magicians (see on 2 Tim. iii. 8 in this series, *Pastoral Epistles*, pp. 379-83). St. Jude refers to the incident as something quite familiar to his readers; and this could hardly have been the case if it had been specially revealed to himself. Lardner supposes that the reference is to Zech. ii. 1, 2. But, excepting that the words, "The Lord rebuke thee, O Satan," occur there, the difference between the two incidents is immense. Neither Michael nor the body of Moses is mentioned in Zechariah. The cause of Satan's hostility is the consecration of Joshua the high priest. And it is the Lord, and not the angel, who rebukes the evil one. These differences are conclusive; they leave just the features which need explanation still unexplained. We may safely decide that St. Jude is not alluding to anything contained in the Bible. More probably he is referring to some well-known Jewish story respecting the death and burial of Moses—in other words, to apocryphal literature.

"So Moses the servant of the Lord died there in the land of Moab, according to the word of the Lord. And He buried him in the valley in the land of Moab over against Beth-peor: but no man knoweth of his sepulchre unto this day" (Deut. xxxiv. 5, 6). These words excited the curiosity of the Jews; and as history told them nothing beyond the statement in Deuteronomy, they fell back upon imagination as a substitute, and the mysterious words of Scripture became a centre round which a series of legends in process of time clustered. The *Targum of Jonathan* on the passage says that the grave of Moses was entrusted to the care of Michael the archangel. The *Midrash* on the same states that Sammael, chief of the evil spirits, was impatient for the death of Moses. "And he said, When will the longed-for moment come when Michael shall weep and I shall laugh? And at last the time came when Michael came to Sammael and said: Ah! cursed one! shall I weep while thou laughest? and he made answer in the words of Micah (vii. 8), Rejoice not against me, O mine enemy: when I fall, I shall arise; when I sit in darkness, the Lord shall be a light unto me." The *Midrash* also contains another legend, in which the sin of the impure angels is mentioned in connexion with the death of Moses. The soul of Moses prays that it may not be taken from the body: "Lord of the world, the angels Asa and Asael lusted after daughters of men; but Moses, from the day that Thou appearedst unto him in the bush, led a life of perpetual continence;" the plea being that from so pure a body the soul need not depart. Both Gabriel and Michael shrink from bringing the soul, and Sammael failed to obtain it. "And Moses prayed, Lord of the world, give not my soul over to the angel of death. And there came a voice from heaven, Fear not, Moses; I will provide for thy burial. And Moses stood up and sanctified himself as do the Seraphim, and the Most High came down from heaven, and the three chief angels with Him. Michael prepared the bier, and Gabriel spread out the winding-sheet.... And the Most High kissed him, and through that kiss took his soul to Himself" (Plumptre *in loco*).

These legends bring us a little nearer to the illustration used by St. Jude, for they bring Michael and the evil spirit into connexion with what is related respecting the death and burial of Moses. But the contest between Michael and Satan respecting the body is not there. Origen tells us that this comes from an apocryphal book called *The Assumption* or *The Ascension* (ἀνάληψις or ἀνάβασις) *of Moses*: "In Genesis the serpent is described as having seduced Eve, regarding whom, in *The Assumption of Moses* (a little treatise of which the Apostle Jude makes mention in his Epistle), the archangel Michael, when disputing with the devil regarding the body of Moses, says that the serpent, being inspired by the devil, was the cause of the transgression of Adam and Eve" (*De Princip.* III. ii. *sub init.*). The book was fairly well known in the early Church. Clement of Alexandria quotes it (*Strom.* VI. xv. *sub fin.*); and in the Latin translation of the *Hypotyposeis* his note on Jude 9 is "*Hic confirmat Assumptionem Moysis.*" Didymus of Alexandria says the same as Origen about St. Jude's use of it, and censures those who made this an objection to the Epistle of Jude (*In Epist. Judæ enarratio in Gallandi Biblioth. Patr.* VI. 307). Evodius, Bishop of Uzala, one of Augustine's early friends (*Confess.* IX. viii. 17; xii. 31), in writing to him, speaks of it as the *Mysteries (Secreta) of Moses*, and calls it a writing devoid of authority (Aug. *Ep.* clviii. 6). It was known in the second half of the fifth century to Gelasius of Cyzicus, and in the second half of the eighth to Nicephorus of Constantinople, who, in his *Stichometria Sacrorum Librorum*, tells us that it was about as long as the Apocalypse of St. John. But from that time we hear no more of it until 1861, when Ceriani published about a third of it from a palimpsest in the Ambrosian Library at Milan (*Monumenta Sacra et Prof.* I. i., p. 55). This fragment contains the passage quoted by Gelasius, but most tantalizingly comes to an end before the death of Moses, so that we are still without the passage about the contest between Michael and the devil respecting his body. Nevertheless, we have no reason for doubting the statements of Origen and of Didymus that the book contained this incident, and that this is the source of the illustration used by St. Jude. Such evidence as we have confirms the statements, and there is no evidence on the other side. We know that there were legends connecting Michael and the evil one with the death of Moses. We know that *The Assumption of Moses* contained similar material. Above all, we know that the incident mentioned by St. Jude is not in the canonical Scriptures, and therefore must have come from some apocryphal source, and that elsewhere in his Epistle St. Jude makes use of apocryphal literature. We are not, therefore, creating a difficulty by adopting the all but certain conclusion that this apocryphal work is the source from which St. Jude draws. Even if we reject this highly probable conclusion, the difficulty, such as it is, will still remain.

That *The Assumption of Moses* was written before our Epistle is almost universally admitted. Philippi is almost alone in thinking that its author was a Christian, and that he borrowed from St. Jude. Ewald, Dillmann, Drummond, Schürer, and Wiesler place it between B.C. 4 (the year of the war of Quintilius Varus, to which it almost certainly refers) and A.D. 6. Hilgenfeld, Merx, Fritzsche, and Lucius place it at different points between

A.D. 44 and 70. But the earlier date is the more probable. The large fragment in Latin which we now possess was evidently made from a Greek document, and Hilgenfeld has attempted to restore the Greek from the Latin. But this Greek document may itself have been a translation from the Aramaic. In either case St. Jude would be able to read it.[123]

That any true tradition on the subject should have been handed down orally through fifteen centuries, *"without leaving the slightest trace in a single passage in the Old Testament,"* is utterly improbable. This hypothesis, and the still more violent supposition of a special revelation made to St. Jude, are devices prompted by a reverent spirit, but thoroughly uncritical and untenable, to avoid the unwelcome conclusion that an inspired writer has quoted legendary material. Have we any right to assume that inspiration raises a writer to the intellectual position of a critical historian, with power to discriminate between legend and fact? St. Jude probably believed the story about the dispute between Michael and Satan to be true; but even if he knew it to be a myth, he might nevertheless readily use it as an illustrative argument, seeing that it was so familiar to his readers. If an inspired writer were living now, would it be quite incredible that he should make use of Dante's *Purgatory*, or Shakespeare's *King Lear*? Inspiration certainly does not preserve those who possess it from imperfect grammar, and we cannot be certain that it preserves them from other imperfections which have nothing to do with the truth that saves souls. Besides which, it may be merely our prejudices which lead us to regard the use of legendary material as an imperfection. Let us reverently examine the features which inspired writings actually present to us, not hastily determine beforehand what properties they *ought* to possess. We not unnaturally fancy that when the Holy Spirit inspires a person to write for the spiritual instruction of men throughout all ages, He also preserves him from making mistakes as to the authenticity of writings of which he makes use, or at least would preserve him from misleading others on such points; but it does not follow that this natural expectation of ours corresponds with the actual manner of the Spirit's working. "We follow a very unsafe method if we begin by deciding in what way it seems to us most fitting that God should guide His Church, and then try to wrest facts into conformity with our preconceptions."[124]

[121] Dr. Field, in his most valuable *Otium Novicense* (iii., pp. 154, 155), argues strongly in favour of translating κρίσιν ἐπενεγκεῖν βλασφημίας, "bring against him an accusation of blasphemy;" and he quotes various passages to show that κρίσιν ἐπιφέρειν may mean "to bring an accusation against." But none of them have a genitive after the κρίσιν, and the question still remains whether the genitive is descriptive

and may be treated as an adjective, or expresses the subject-matter of the κρίσις. That the former is right seems to be shown by the context (βλασφημῦσιν in vv. 8 and 10); the libertines do to higher beings what an archangel did not dare to do to Satan; and also by the parallel in 2 Peter ii. 11 (βλασφημον κρίσιν). And on what grounds would Michael not dare to charge Satan with blasphemy? That he did not dare to rail at him is intelligible.

[122] The variety of interpretation as regards these two expressions is remarkable. Some, as Beza, Calvin, Erasmus, and Grotius, interpret both "dominion" and "dignities" of civil magistrates; others, as Hammond, include ecclesiastical rulers; others, as Lumby, interpret both of Apostles and elders, and through them Christ; others, as Ritsch, apply "dominion" to God or Christ, and "dignities" to good angels. Wiesinger and Huther apply "dominion" to God or Christ, and "dignities" to bad angels. Alford, Bengel, Brückner, and De Wette explain both of good angels; while Schott apparently explains both of bad angels. Œcumenius is not quite alone in suggesting that "dignities" may mean the Old and New Testament; Plumptre would make the word include both good and bad angels.

[123] The Latin fragment has been several times published since Ceriani made it known in 1861; by Hilgenfeld in 1866 and 1876; by Volkmar in 1867; Schmidt and Merx in 1868; and by Fritzsche in 1871. A very full summary of literature on the subject is given in Schürer, *The Jewish People in the Time of Jesus Christ* (T. and T. Clark, 1886), Div. II., vol. iii., pp. 80-83. See also Herzog, Plitt, and Hauck (*Real-Encykl.*, vol. xii. pp. 352, 353).

[124] Salmon, *Introduction to the N.T.*, 4th ed., Murray (1889), p. 528.

CHAPTER XXXV
THE DESCRIPTION CORRESPONDING TO CAIN:THE LIBERTINES AT THE LOVE-FEASTS. THE BOOK OF ENOCH

"These are they who are [hidden] rocks in your Love-feasts when they feast with you, [shepherds] that without fear feed themselves, clouds without water, carried along by winds; autumn trees without fruit, twice dead, plucked up by the roots; wild waves of the sea, foaming out their own shame; wandering stars, for whom the blackness of darkness hath been reserved for ever.

"*But* to these also Enoch, the seventh from Adam, prophesied, saying, Behold, the Lord came with ten thousands of His holy ones, to execute judgment upon all, and to convict all the ungodly of all their works of ungodliness which they have ungodly wrought, and of all the hard things which ungodly sinners have spoken against Him." —St. Jude 12-15.

ST. JUDE leaves off comparing the libertines with other sinners— Cain and the Sodomites, Balaam and the impure angels, Korah and the unbelieving Israelites—and begins an independent description of them. Nevertheless, there is reason for believing that he has Cain, Balaam, and Korah in his mind in framing this new account of them. The description falls into three parts, of which this is the first. Each of the three parts begins in the same way: "These are" (οὗτοί εἰσιν). And each is balanced by something said on the other side, which is introduced with a "But" (δέ). In the case before us the "But" introduces a warning given prophetically to these libertines by Enoch (vv. 14, 15). In the second case St. Jude quotes a warning given prophetically to his readers by the Apostles (vv. 17, 18). In the third he exhorts his readers himself (vv. 20-23). This threefold division has been rather generally ignored. It is quite obliterated in the Revised Version by the division of the paragraphs, and also by the substitution of an "And" for the first "But:" "*And* to these also Enoch prophesied." The Vulgate is right with *autem* in all three places, followed by Wiclif with "Forsothe" in all three places. Luther is not only right in his rendering of the conjunction with *aber* in all three places, but also in his division of the paragraphs. But since Wiclif all English versions have obscured this threefold description of the ungodly with the three corresponding warnings or exhortations.[125]

"These are they who are hidden rocks in your love-feasts when they feast with you." The difference between this and the parallel passage in 2 Peter is of special interest here; for it looks as if whichever writer used the work of the other remembered the sound rather than the sense. We have here ἐν ταῖς ἀγάπαις ... σπιλάδες; but in 2 Peter ii. 13 σπίλοι ... ἐν ταῖς ἀπάταις (with ἀγάπαις as a various reading, probably taken from this passage). It is possible that there may be no difference of meaning between σπιλάδες and σπίλοι. The former, which is St. Jude's word, almost invariably means "rocks," but in an Orphic poem of the fourth century means "spots." The latter, which is used in 2 Peter ii. 13 and Eph. v. 27, generally means "spots," but sometimes means "rocks." So that "spots" may be the right rendering in both Epistles, and "rocks" may be right in both. More probably, however, we should understand "spots" in 2 Peter, and "rocks" here. The Revised Version inserts "hidden" as an epithet—"*hidden* rocks in your love-feasts"—which is hardly justifiable, because the word seems to mean reefs over which the sea dashes, as distinct from rocks which are wholly covered (so in the *Anthologia Palatina*, ii. 390; and in a fragment of Sophocles the word has the epithet "lofty," ἐφ' ὑψηλαῖς σπιλάδεσσι, and "lofty hidden rocks" would be almost a contradiction in terms). Moreover, "hidden" does not seem to be right even as an interpretation; for these profligates were not at all hidden; they were utterly notorious and scandalous. They made no secret of their misconduct, but gloried in it and defended it. Yet this fact does not make the name "rocks," or "reefs," inappropriate. A reef may be a very dangerous thing, although it is always visible. It may be impossible to avoid going near it; and proximity to such things is always perilous. So also with these ungodly men: St. Jude's readers could not wholly avoid them, either in society or in the public services of the Church, but their presence disturbed and polluted both. The whole purpose of the love-feasts was wrecked by these men. Like Cain, they turned the ordinances of religion into selfishness and sin.

We cannot doubt that when St. Jude wrote the eucharist was still part of the agape or love-feast, as when St. Paul wrote to the Corinthians (A.D. 57, 58). It was still "the Lord's *Supper*" not merely in name, but in fact (1 Cor. xi. 17-34; Acts xx. 7-11). It is almost certain that when Ignatius wrote his Epistles (*c.* A.D. 112) the eucharist was still united with the love-feast. He writes to the Church of Smyrna, "It is not lawful without the bishop either to baptize or to hold a love-feast" (viii.). This must refer to the two sacraments, the administration of which are the chief functions of the priestly office. Ignatius cannot have meant that a love-feast apart from the eucharist might not be held without the bishop. When Justin Martyr wrote his First Apology (c. A.D. 140) it is evident that the two had been separated; his description of the eucharist (lxv.-lxvii.) implies that no love-feast accompanied it (see Lightfoot, *St. Ignatius and St. Polycarp*, I., pp. 52, 387; II., p. 312: Macmillan, 1885). We may regard it, therefore, as certain that even if this Epistle be placed late in the first century, St. Jude is here referring to a state of things very similar to that which St. Paul rebukes in the Church of Corinth; the love-feast accompanied by the eucharist was profaned by the shameless indulgence of these libertines.

The love-feast symbolized the brotherhood of Christians. It was a simple meal, in which all met as equals, and the rich supplied the necessities of the poor. Anything like excess was peculiarly out of place, and it was the duty of the rich to see that the poorer members of the congregation were satisfied. But it would seem as if these profligates (1) brought with them luxurious food, thus destroying the Christian simplicity of the meal; and (2) brought this, not for the benefit of all, but for their own private enjoyment, thus destroying the idea of Christian brotherhood and equality. There is nothing in the word used for "feasting with you" (συνευωχούμενοι) which necessarily implies revelry or excess, but in this connexion it implies censure. To turn the love-feast into a banquet was wrong, however innocent a banquet might be in itself. We might translate the word "when they feast *together*," instead of "when they feast *with you*;" and this would imply that at the love-feast they kept to themselves, and did not mix with their poorer brethren. This makes good sense; but if this translation is adopted, we must beware of interpreting it to mean that these libertines had become schismatics, and had set up a love-feast of their own. They could not be "rocks in your love-feasts" if they did not attend the love-feasts.

There are two other uncertainties in these opening clauses—one of construction, and one of translation. (1) Ought we to take "without fear" with what precedes, or with what follows—"when they feast with you without fear," or "that feed themselves without fear"? As in ver. 7, with regard to "of eternal fire," we are unable to decide with certainty. Both constructions make excellent sense, and nothing can be urged as being strongly in favour of either. English versions are divided. The Rhemish has "feasting together without fear." Purvey, the Authorized, and the Revised take "without fear" with "feeding themselves." Tyndale, Cranmer, and the Genevan aim at being as ambiguous as the Greek; they place "with out feare" between the two clauses with a comma on each side of it. (2) Does "feeding themselves" mean that they fed themselves *instead of feeding the flock*? (Ezek. xxxiv. 2, 8; Isa. lvi. 11). If so, the Revisers give the right interpretation with "shepherds that without fear feed themselves;" but this is interpretation rather than translation. Or does it mean that they fed themselves, *instead of waiting to be fed by the shepherds*? If so, it is quite misleading to call them shepherds. As we have seen already there is no reason for thinking that these profligates set up as teachers or pastors. We shall be safer if we render the Greek participle (ἑαυτοὺς ποιμαίνοντες) by a participle: "pasturing themselves," or "shepherding themselves." Lucifer, as Dr. Salmon points out, renders it *semetipsos regentes*, which shows that he understood it in the latter sense. Yet this second view does not imply anything schismatical in their conduct, but merely that they were selfish and disorderly. They kept their own good food, and consumed it among themselves at the love-feast, instead of throwing it into the common store, and allowing it to be distributed to all by the elders. With full recognition of the fact that there is much to be said for other views, the following rendering may be accepted as on the whole preferable: "These are they who are rocks in your love-feasts, feasting together without fear, pasturing their own selves."

In what follows St. Jude piles metaphor on metaphor and epithet on epithet, in the effort to express his indignation and abhorrence. But we cannot say that "no doubt also in the comparisons which he employs he has an eye to the original intention of the love-feast." It is somewhat forced to say that the love-feast "was to have the blessing of the rain from heaven; it was meant to be a cause of much fruit in the whole Christian community." But assuming that "waterless clouds" and "fruitless trees" may be made to refer to the love-feasts, what are we to make of "wild waves" and "wandering stars" in that connexion? It is better to regard the subject of the love-feasts as ended, and to take the similes which follow as quite independent. These men are ostentatious, but they do no good. It was perhaps expected that their admission to the Church would be a great gain to Christendom; but they are as disappointing as clouds that are carried *past* (παραφερόμεναι) by winds without giving any rain; and in the East that is one of the most grievous among common disappointments.

How the framers of the Authorized Version came to perpetrate such a contradiction in terms as "trees whose fruit withereth, without fruit," it is not easy to see. No earlier English version is guilty of it; nor the Vulgate (*arbores autumnales, infructuosæ*); nor Beza, with whom Calvin agrees (*arbores emarcidæ, infrugiferæ*); nor Luther (*kahle unfruchtbare Bäume*). The Greek (δένδρα φθινοπωρινά) means literally "autumn-withering trees;" *i.e.* just at the time when fruit is expected they wither and are without fruit. The parable of the barren fig-tree (Luke xiii. 6-9) is perhaps in St. Jude's mind. The epithets form a natural climax—withering in autumn, fruitless, twice dead, rooted up. These profligates were twice dead, because they had returned after baptism to the death of sin: the end of such men is that they shall be rooted out at the last (Ps. xxx. 28; lii. 5; Prov. ii. 22). When he calls them "wild waves of the sea, foaming out their own shames," St. Jude is perhaps thinking of the words of Isaiah: "The wicked are like the troubled sea; for it cannot rest, and its waters cast up mire and dirt" (lvii. 20). But the wording of the Septuagint is utterly different from that which we have here; it is the thought that is similar.

What are we to understand by "wandering stars"? Not planets, nor comets, neither of which either *seem* to wander while one looks at them, or *do* wander, in St. Jude's sense, as a matter of fact. Both have their orbits, to which they keep with such regularity that their movements can be accurately predicted; so that they are symbols rather of Christian lives than of the course of the ungodly. Much more probably St. Jude means "falling stars," or "shooting stars," which seem to leave their place in the heavens, where they are beautiful and useful, and to wander away into the darkness, to the confusion and dismay of those who observe them. Thus understood, the simile forms a natural transition to the prophecy of Enoch which follows. St. Jude's thoughts have once more gone back to the fallen angels in the *Book of Enoch*. Angels, like stars, have a path to keep, and those who keep it not are punished. "I saw the winds which cause the orb of the sun and of all the stars to set.... I saw the path of the angels.... I perceived a place which had neither the firmament of heaven above it, nor the solid ground underneath it; neither was there water above it, nor anything on wing; but the spot was desolate. And there I saw seven stars, like great blazing mountains, and like spirits entreating me. Then the angel [Enoch's guide] said, This place, until the consummation of heaven and earth, will be the prison of the stars and the host of heaven. The stars which roll over fire are those which transgressed the commandment of God" (xviii. 6, 7, 13-16). In another terrible place he sees stars bound together, and is told that these are "the stars which have transgressed," and that "this is the prison of the angels," in which "they are kept for ever" (xxi. 2, 3, 5, 6). These extracts make it highly probable that when St. Jude compares the ungodly to "wandering stars, for whom the blackness of darkness hath been reserved for ever," he is thinking once more of the "angels which left their proper habitation," who are "kept in everlasting bonds under darkness unto the judgment of the great day" (ver. 6). After this return to the ideas contained in the *Book of Enoch*, the quotation of the prophecy comes quite naturally; and all the more so because, as Irenæus indicates, Enoch forms a splendid contrast to the fallen angels: they lost their heavenly habitation by displeasing God, whereas he was taken up to heaven for pleasing Him. His words show that he was acquainted with the *Book of Enoch*, and accepted it as trustworthy: "But Enoch also without circumcision, by pleasing God, although he was a man, discharged the office of ambassador to angels, and was translated, and is preserved even until now as a witness of the just judgment of God: while angels by transgression fell to earth for judgment; but a man by pleasing Him was translated for salvation" (*Hær.* IV. xvi. 2). Having compared the profligates to the stars, or angels, who fell from heaven to earth, St. Jude passes on readily to quote the warning of one who was taken up from earth to heaven.

And the way in which the prophecy is introduced makes us still more clear as to the source from which St. Jude derived it: "Enoch, *the seventh* from Adam, prophesied." Nowhere in the Old Testament, and nowhere else in the New, is Enoch said to be "the seventh from Adam." But he is called "the seventh" in the *Book of Enoch*, where he is made to say, "I have been born the seventh in the first week" (xcii. 4), although in order to make seven both Adam and Enoch have to be counted (xxxvii. 1). The number seven is possibly symbolical, indicating perfection. Thus Dr. Westcott takes Enoch to be "a type of perfected humanity" (*Dict. of the Bible*). Yet it is also possible that he is called "the seventh" in the *Book of Enoch*, and consequently by St. Jude, in order to mark the extreme antiquity of the prophecy, or to distinguish him from other persons of the same name (Gen. xxv. 4; xlvi. 9).

But a careful comparison of the passage in question, as quoted by St. Jude, and as it stands in the translation of the *Book of Enoch*, is the chief means of determining the source of the quotation. This, however, cannot be made satisfactorily until we can place the Greek, of which the Ethiopic version of the *Book of Enoch* is a translation, side by side with St. Jude's Greek.

ENOCH.	ST. JUDE.
Behold, He cometh with ten thousands of His holy ones, to execute judgment upon them, and to destroy the ungodly and reprove all the carnal [or, and will destroy and convict the ungodly with all flesh], for everything which the sinners and the ungodly have done and committed against Him (chap. ii.).	Behold, the Lord came with ten thousands of his holy ones to execute judgment upon all, and to convict all the ungodly of their works of ungodliness which they have ungodly wrought, and of all the hard things which ungodly sinners have spoken against Him (vv. 14, 15).

It will be observed that there is nothing in the *Book of Enoch* to correspond with the saying about "the hard things which sinners have spoken against God." This in itself is almost conclusive against the hypothesis, which on other grounds is not very probable, that some later writer copied the prophecy as given by St. Jude, and inserted it into the *Book of Enoch*. If so, why did he not copy it exactly? Why did he not only slightly vary the wording, but omit a rather important clause? The passage is very short, and a writer who was anxious to make St. Jude agree with the reputed prophecy would be likely to make the agreement exact. On the other hand, if St. Jude is quoting loosely from memory, or from a Greek or Aramaic original, of which the text varied somewhat from the Ethiopic translation which has come down to us, everything is explained. He would be tenacious of the clause about "hard things spoken against God," as a warning to those who "set at nought dominion and rail at dignities." It is of course possible that both the author of this book and St. Jude independently make use of a traditional saying attributed to Enoch. But seeing that the work was in existence when St. Jude wrote, was probably well known to his readers, and contains most of the passage which he quotes; and seeing that elsewhere in his Epistle he seems to refer to other parts of the book, far the more reasonable view is that he quotes directly from it. The case therefore is parallel to that of the reference to *The Assumption of Moses* in ver. 9. St. Jude probably believed the prophecy to be a genuine prophecy of Enoch, and the writing in which it occurs to be a genuine revelation respecting the visible and invisible world; but even if he knew its apocryphal character, its appositeness to the subject of which he is so full might easily lead him to quote it to persons who would be familiar with it. We have no right to prejudge the question of fitness, and say that inspiration would certainly preserve its instruments from wittingly or unwittingly making use of a fictitious apocalypse. Our business, as reverent and therefore honest students, is to ascertain whether this writer does derive some of his material from the document which, after the lapse of so many centuries, was given back to us about a hundred and twenty years ago. If on critical grounds we find ourselves compelled to believe that this document is the source from which St. Jude draws, then let us beware of setting our own preconceptions above the wisdom of God, who in this case, as in many more, has been pleased to employ an unexpected instrument, and has made a human fiction the means of proclaiming a Divine truth.

It remains to give some further account of the intensely interesting writing which St. Jude appears to have used. The Books of Daniel, Ezekiel, and Zechariah gave to the Jews a love of visions, revelations, and prophecies which at times was almost insatiable; and, when the gift of prophecy came to an end, the three centuries between Malachi and the Baptist, during which it seemed as if Jehovah had departed from His people, and "answered no more, neither by dreams nor by prophets," appeared dreary and intolerable. What had been written by Moses and the Prophets did not satisfy. Fresh revelations were desired; and the reality being absent, fiction attempted to stop the gap. Such writings as the *Book of Enoch, Assumption of Moses*,

Testament of Moses, Eldad and Modad, Apocalypse of Elijah, etc., etc., were the result. This desire for prophecies and revelations passed over from Judaism into the Christian Church, and was quickened rather than satisfied by the Revelation of St. John. During the first two centuries of the Christian era such literature continued to be produced by Jews and Christians alike; and specimens of it still survive in the *Apocalypse of Baruch* and the *Fourth Book of Ezra* on the Jewish side, and the *Shepherd of Hermas* on the Christian; the *Testaments of the Twelve Patriarchs* being apparently a Jewish original with Christian interpolations. But in most cases only the titles survive, and where the revelation or prophecy is attributed to an Old Testament character we are unable to decide whether the fiction was of Jewish or of Christian origin.

It is strange that such a writing as the *Book of Enoch* should have been allowed to disappear entirely from the West after the fourth century, and from the East after the eighth. The quotations in the *Chronographia* of Georgius Syncellus, some portions of which are not found in the recovered Ethiopic Version, are the last traces that we have of it until early in the seventeenth century, when it was rumoured that it was extant in Abyssinia, and late in the eighteenth, when it was found there. The revelations which it professes to make respecting judgment, heaven, and hell might have been expected to make it a special favourite with Christians from the fourth to the tenth century, during which period one of the commonest topics of speculation was the end of the world. Moreover, there was the passage in Jude, with the notices in Barnabas, Irenæus, Tertullian, Clement of Alexandria, Origen, Jerome, and others, to keep the book from being forgotten. But it was generally believed that the end of the world would be heralded by two great signs—the downfall of Rome, and the coming of Antichrist. About these the *Book of Enoch* contains no hint, and the absence of such material may have caused it to pass out of knowledge. Englishmen have the honour of giving it back to Europe. James Bruce brought the Ethiopic translation from Abyssinia in 1773, and Archbishop Laurence published an English translation of it in 1821, and an Ethiopic text in 1838. Since then the scholars who have edited it or commented on it have been almost exclusively Germans.[126]

It is generally acknowledged that the book is a composite one. Probably the original writer incorporated older materials, and his work has probably been interpolated by later hands. Whether any of these supposed interpolations are Christian is still debated; and the question scarcely admits of a decided answer. On the one hand, there are expressions which would come much more naturally from a Christian than from a Jew; on the other, it is difficult to see why a Christian should insert anything at all, if he did not insert what might teach others Christian truth. Messianic passages abound; and in them the Messiah is called, again and again, "the Son of man" and "the Elect One;" twice He is called "the Anointed" (xlvii. 11; li. 4), twice "the Righteous One" (xxxviii. 2; lii. 6; where Laurence translates otherwise); once He is "the Son of the offspring of the mother of the living," *i.e.* Son of the son of Eve (lxi. 10); and once the Lord speaks of Him as "My Son" (civ. 2). This Messiah is the Judge of men and angels, by the appointment of Jehovah. "In those days will the earth give back that which has been entrusted to it, and Sheol will give back that which has been entrusted to it, which it has received, and destruction (Abaddon) will give back what it owes.... And in those days will the Elect One sit upon His throne, and all secrets of wisdom will come forth from the thoughts of His mouth; for the Lord of spirits hath given it to Him, and hath glorified Him" (l. 1, 3). "Then the Lord of spirits made to sit upon the throne of His glory the Elect One, who will judge all the works of the holy" (lx. 10, 11; lxviii. 39). But this Messiah is not much more than a highly exalted angel. He is not the Word; he is not God. That this Son of man has already lived upon the earth is not indicated. Of the name Jesus, the Crucifixion, the Resurrection, or the Ascension, there is not a trace. There is no hint of baptism, or of the eucharist, or of the doctrine of the Trinity. In a word, everything distinctly Christian is absent, even from that section (xxxvii.-lxxi.) which makes the nearest approaches to Christian language, and which is probably a later insertion. It is difficult to see what object a Christian could have in writing just this and no more. The fact that so many of the angels have Hebrew names favours the view that the original was in Hebrew or Aramaic, of which the Greek, from which the Ethiopic version is taken, was only a translation. If so, this also is in favour of Jewish, rather than of Christian origin.

Those who can should read the whole book in Laurence's translation, or still better in Dillmann's. But the more accurately translated portions given in Westcott and in Stanton will give some idea of the whole. The latter have been used in this chapter. The book is manifestly the work of a man of the most earnest convictions, one who believes in God, and fears Him, and is appalled at the practical infidelity and utter godlessness which he finds around him. On two things he is ever insisting: (1) that God's rule extends everywhere, over angels and men, no less than over winds and stars; (2) that this rule is a moral one, for He abundantly rewards righteousness, and fearfully punishes sin. Nothing, therefore, could well be more in harmony with the spirit and purpose of St. Jude, and it ought not to perplex us that he makes use of such a book.

But in any case it may reassure us to remember that, in spite of its being quoted *in* Scripture, the Church has never been allowed to admit it *as* Scripture. The mind of Christendom has never wavered as to the real character of the *Book of Enoch*. It is one of the many eccentricities of Tertullian that he upholds its authority; but his special pleading has misled no one else (*De Cultu Fem.* I. iii.). Justin Martyr apparently knew it (*Apol.* II. v.), but there is nothing to show that he accepted it as a genuine revelation. Origen (*Contra Cels.* V. liv.: comp. *In Numer. Homil.* xxviii. 2; *In Joannem*, tom. vi., cap. xxv.: De la Rue, ii. 384; iv. 142) distinctly marks it as uncanonical and of doubtful value; Augustine (*De Civ. Dei*, XV. xxiii. 4) and Jerome (*De Vir. Illustr.* iv.) reject it as apocryphal; and soon after their time it seems to have disappeared from Western Christendom. As already stated, it is uncertain whether St. Jude was mistaken as to the true nature of the book: it is quite certain that the Church has been preserved from being so.

Note.—For a collection of parallels between the *Book of Enoch* and 2 Peter and Jude see the *New Testament Commentary for English Readers*, edited by Bishop Ellicott, vol. iii., pp. 518, 519 (Cassells, 1879).

[125] Purvey has "But.... And.... But...." Tyndale, Coverdale, Crammer, and the Genevan Version (following the reading of A) omit the conjunction altogether in the first place. It is the Rhemish Version which first introduces "And" into the first place; yet one might have expected that it, being made direct from the Vulgate, would have been correct in this particular.

[126] Hofmann, Gfrörer, Lützelberger, Lücke, Ewald, Köstlin, Hilgenfeld, Weisse, Volkmar, Geiger, Langen, Sieffert, Philippi, Gebhardt, Wieseler, and others, especially Hoffmann and Dillmann, who have published complete translations with notes and explanations. Dillmann's work (Leipzig, 1853) is still the standard work on the subject, but is out of print. Schodde published an English translation with notes at Andover, 1882; and the English reader will find much information in the articles by Westcott in the *Dict. of the Bible* and by Lipsius in the *Dict. of Chr. Biography*; also in Westcott's *Introduction to the Gospels*, pp. 73, 99-109, 7th ed.; in Schürer's *The Jewish People in the Time of Jesus Christ*, Div. II., vol. iii., pp. 54-73; in Stanton's *The Jewish and the Christian Messiah* (T. and T. Clark, 1886), pp. 44-64, 88-95, 139, 140, 170-75, 311-15, 332-35, 347; and in Drummond's *The Jewish Messiah*, 1877, pp. 17-73. Murray's *Enoch Restitutus* (Rivington, 1836) does not seem to be of much value.

CHAPTER XXXVI
THE DESCRIPTION CORRESPONDING TO BALAAM:IMPIOUS DISCONTENT AND GREED OF THE LIBERTINES.THE APOSTOLIC WARNING RESPECTING THEM

"These are murmurers, complainers, walking after their lusts (and their mouth speaketh great swelling words), showing respect of persons for the sake of advantage.

"But ye, beloved, remember ye the words which have been spoken before by the Apostles of our Lord Jesus Christ; how that they said to you, In the last time there shall be mockers, walking after their own ungodly lusts."—St. Jude 16-18.

THESE words form the second part of the threefold description of the libertines; and just as the first part was balanced by a prophetic warning quoted from the *Book of Enoch,* so this part is balanced by a quotation of the prophetic warning given by the Apostles, to the effect that persons like these ungodly men would certainly arise. This second division more clearly corresponds to the case of Balaam mentioned in ver. 11 than the first division of the description corresponds to the case of Cain. This will appear when we come to examine the details.

"These are murmurers." For the second time St. Jude points to the intruders who are disturbing the Church, and shows his readers another group of characteristics by which these dangerous persons, who disgrace the name of Christian, may be known. This second group hangs on closely to what immediately precedes. It seems to have been suggested by the last words of the prophecy quoted from Enoch, "the hard things which ungodly sinners have spoken against Him." The way in which the libertines spoke hard things against God was by murmuring against His decrees and complaining of the dispensations of His Providence. This is the exact meaning of the word which is rendered "complainers" (μεμψίμοιροι), and which occurs nowhere else in the New Testament; "finding fault with their lot," *i.e.* discontented with the condition of life which God had assigned to them, and not only blaming Him for this, but for the moral restrictions which He had imposed upon them and upon all mankind. Men who "walk after their lusts," and shape their course in accordance with these (κατὰ τὰς ἐπιθυμίας αὐτῶν πορευόμενοι), cannot be contented, for the means of gratifying the lusts are not always present, and the lusts themselves are insatiable: even when gratification is possible, it is only temporary; the unruly desires are certain to revive and clamour once more for satisfaction. This was notably the case with Balaam, whose grasping cupidity chafed against the restraints which prevented it from being gratified. As Bishop Butler says of him, "He wanted to do what he knew to be very wicked, and contrary to the express command of God; he had inward checks and restraints, which he could not entirely get over; he therefore casts about for ways to reconcile this wickedness with his duty," (*Sermon* vii.). From a somewhat different point of view J. H. Newman says much the same thing of him: Balaam "would have given the world to have got rid of his duties; and the question was, how to do so without violence" (*Plain Sermons*, Rivingtons, 1868, vol. iv., p. 28). Isaac Williams, who has a sermon on the same subject, puts the matter in yet another way. Balaam "knew what was holy and good, and it may be that he loved it also, but he loved riches more: his knowledge was with God; his will was with Satan.... He wished to proceed together with God and Mammon—God on his lips, and Mammon in his heart" (*The Characters of the Old Testament*, Rivingtons, 1869, pp. 128, 130). The way in which the libertines seem to have set about the impossible task of getting rid of their duties and reconciling the service of God with the service of Satan appears to have been that of roundly declaring that Christian liberty included freedom to gratify one's desires: if it did not do so, it was an empty delusion. In this way they "turned the grace of God into lasciviousness" (ver. 4), and "their mouth spoke great swelling words." In the parallel passage in 2 Peter an explanation of this kind is given of the "great swelling words." By means of them these evil men "enticed others in the lusts of the flesh by lasciviousness, ... *promising them liberty*" (2 Peter ii. 18, 19). According to them, it was the magnificent privilege of Christians to be freed from righteousness and become the slaves of sin. Irenæus attributes doctrine of this kind to Simon Magus and his followers, who, "as being free, live as they please; for men are saved through His grace, and not through their own righteous acts. For righteous actions are not such in the nature of things, but accidentally" (*Hær.* I. xxiii. 3).

"Showing respect of persons for the sake of advantage." This, again, is exactly what Balaam did. He had regard to Balak and the princes whom he sent as ambassadors; and he did this because he hoped to gain the large reward which they were told to promise him if he would but exercise his prophetic power in solemnly cursing Israel. In like manner these blatant profligates, who were loud in their complaints against the treatment which they received from Providence, and equally loud in protesting that the Gospel allowed them and others the licence which they desired, nevertheless became mean flatterers and parasites when there was any chance of getting anything from persons of wealth and distinction. This apparently incongruous combination of arrogant self-assertion with grovelling sycophancy is common enough in men without principle, as Calvin remarks. "When there is no one to check their insolence, or when there is nothing which stands in their way, their pride is intolerable, so that they imperiously arrogate everything to themselves; but they meanly flatter those whom they fear, and from whom they expect some advantage." While they refuse submission where it is due, they give it where it is not due. They rebelliously reject the plain commands of God, and yet servilely cringe to the humours and caprices of their fellow-men.

"But ye, beloved, remember ye the words which have been spoken before by the Apostles of our Lord Jesus Christ." The Revisers have done well to restore the "ye"—"But *ye*, beloved"—which was in all English versions previous to that of 1611, just as in ver. 20. In both cases the pronoun is emphatic, and places the persons addressed in marked contrast to the ungodly men against whom they are being warned. "Whatever they may do, do not you be deceived by their arrogant language and time-serving conduct, for these are the scoffing sensualists against whom you have already been warned beforehand by the Apostles. Their behaviour is amazing, but it ought not to take you by surprise." St. Jude evidently takes for granted that the Apostolic warning which he quotes is well known to his readers. Such an appeal to the authority of the Apostles would certainly be more natural in one who was himself not an Apostle, but it must not be regarded as quite decisive, as if St. Jude had written "how that they said to *us*." Other reasons, however, support the impression which this passage conveys, that the writer is not an Apostle. On the other hand, there is nothing in these words to warrant the conclusion that the writer regards the Apostles as persons who lived long ago, or who gave this warning long ago. All that is implied is that before these ungodly men "crept in privily" into the Church, Apostles had foretold that such persons would arise. "In the last time" is not St. Jude's expression, but theirs; and by it the Apostles certainly did not mean an age remote from their own: the "last time" had already begun when they wrote (see on 2 Tim. iii. 1, 2, in *The Pastoral Epistles*, in this series, pp. 377, 378; and comp. 1 John ii. 18; Heb. i. 2; 1 Peter i. 20).

"How that they said to you" may mean "how that they *used* to say to you" (ἔλεγον ὑμῖν), and may refer to oral teaching; but we cannot be at all certain of this. Still less can we be certain that, if written warnings are included or specially meant, the reference is to 2 Peter iii. 3: "knowing this first, that in the last days mockers shall come with mockery, walking after their own lusts." Both passages may have a common source, or that in 2 Peter may be modelled upon this one. The word for "mockers" is the same in both (ἐμπαῖκται), and it is a very unusual word, not used by profane writers, nor anywhere else in the New Testament; in the Septuagint it occurs only once (Isa. iii. 4), and there apparently in the sense of "childish persons." The Authorized Version unfortunately obscures this close connexion between the wording of 2 Peter iii. 3, and that of this passage, by having "scoffers" in the one, and "mockers" in the other. The particular in which the two passages really differ must not pass without notice. St. Jude writes, "walking after their own *ungodly* lusts," or, more literally, "their own lusts *of ungodlinesses*" (τῶν ἀσεβειῶν). Most probably the genitive here is descriptive, as in James i. 24 and ii. 4; and therefore the substitution of the adjective "ungodly" for it in the English versions is justifiable. But it is possible that "lusts of ungodlinesses" means that they lusted after impieties, and therefore the rendering given in the margin of the Revised Version should not be left unheeded. Wiclif, Purvey, and the Rhemish here differ from other English versions, being made from later texts of the Vulgate, which read, "*secundum desideria sua ambulantes in impietatibus* or *in impietate*," whereas the better text has *impietatum*. However we translate the genitive case, we may regard the word as an echo of the prophecy quoted from the *Book of Enoch*, in which "ungodly" or "ungodliness" occurs with persistent iteration (ver. 15).

The fact that this expression (τῶν ἀσεβειῶν) occurs here, but not in the parallel verse in 2 Peter, is an indication of a much more important difference between the two passages. In spite of the great similarity of wording, the meaning is very different. The mockers in each case mock at totally different things. In 2 Peter we are expressly told that they scoffed at the belief that Christ was coming to judge the world. "What has become of the promise of His coming? Everything goes on just as it has done for generations." There is not a hint of any such notion here; on the contrary, it is implied that these libertines mocked at God's dealings with themselves, and at the belief that the Gospel did not give them full liberty to gratify their sensual desires. They were among those of whom it is written that "fools make a mock at sin" (Prov. xiv. 9). By scoffing at things sacred, and ridiculing the notion that there is any harm in licentiousness, or anything estimable in holiness, they created a moral atmosphere in which men sinned with a light heart, because sin was made to look as if it were a matter of no moment, a thing to be indulged in without anxiety or remorse. It would be more reasonable and less reprehensible to make a mock at carnage or pestilence, and teach men to go with a light heart into a desolating war or plague-stricken neighbourhood. In such cases experience of the manifest horrors would soon cure the light-heartedness. But the horrible nature of sin is not so manifest, and with regard to *that* experience teaches its lesson more slowly. It is like a poisoning of the blood rather than a wound in the flesh, and may have done incalculable mischief before any serious pain is felt, or any grave alarm excited. Hence it is quite easy for many to "walk after their own ungodly lusts," and at the same time "mock at sin" and its consequences. And then the converse of the proverb becomes true, and "sin mocks at the fools" that mocked at it—a meaning which the Hebrew may very well have. In the margin of the Revised Version we read, "Guilt mocketh at the foolish." As Delilah mocked at Samson, so does sin mock at those who have been taken captive by it. There is no folly equal to the foolhardiness of those who make light, either to themselves or to others, of the deadly character of any form of sin. They thereby save the tempter all trouble, and do his work themselves. "His own iniquities shall take the wicked, and he shall be holden with the cords of his sin. He shall die for lack of instruction; and in the greatness of his folly he shall go astray" (Prov. v. 22, 23).

CHAPTER XXXVII
THE DESCRIPTION CORRESPONDING TO KORAH:MAKING SEPARATIONS. EXHORTATION TO THE FAITHFUL TO BUILD UP THEMSELVES, AND THEN RESCUE OTHERS

"These are they who make separations sensual, having not the Spirit.

"But ye, beloved, building up yourselves on your most holy faith, praying in the Holy Spirit, keep yourselves in the love of God, looking for the mercy of our Lord Jesus Christ unto eternal life. And on some have mercy, who are in doubt; and some save, snatching them out of the fire; and on some have mercy with fear; hating even the garment spotted by the flesh." —St. Jude 19-23.

FOR the third and last time St. Jude points his finger at the ungodly intruders who are working such mischief in the Church, and gives another triplet of characteristics by which they may be recognized.

"These are they who make separations." This is the first point; like Korah and his company, these men are separatists (οἱ ἀποδιορίζοντες). They do not actually make a schism *from* the Church, for they frequent the love-feasts and profess membership; but they create a faction *within* it. Even in the public services of the Church they keep aloof from the poorer members of the congregation. At the love-feasts they feed themselves on the good things which they bring with them, instead of handing them over to the ministers to be distributed among all. And in society they care only for persons of rank and wealth, out of whom they hope to gain something. Worst of all, they claim to be specially enlightened members of the Church, having a more comprehensive knowledge of the nature of Christian liberty, while they are turning the fundamental principles of Christian life upside down. Hence, although they are not actual schismatics, who have gone out of the Church and set up a communion of their own, their tendencies are in that direction. They are, in short, much the same kind of people as those against whom St. Paul warns his readers in the Epistle to the Romans: "Now I beseech you, brethren, mark them *which are causing the divisions* and occasions of stumbling, contrary to the doctrine which ye learned: and turn away from them. For they that are such serve not our Lord Christ, but *their own belly*; and by their smooth and fair speech they beguile the hearts of the innocent" (xvi. 17, 18). And again in the Epistle to the Philippians: "For many walk of whom I told you often, and now tell you even weeping, that they are the enemies of the cross of Christ: whose end is perdition, *whose god is the belly*, and whose glory is in their shame, who mind earthly things" (iii. 18, 19). A parallel to nearly every clause in these two descriptions might be found in the account of the libertines given by St. Jude. Indeed, the words in which Bishop Lightfoot sums up St. Paul's description might be adopted verbatim as a summary of the description in our Epistle: "They are described as creating divisions and offences, as holding plausible language, as professing to be wise beyond others, and yet not innocent in their wisdom." They are "Antinomians, who refuse to conform to the Cross, and live a life of self-indulgence." "The unfettered liberty of which they boast, thus perverted, becomes their deepest degradation" (*Philippians*, Notes on iii. 18, 19).

Hooker, in his sermons on this passage, although he adopts the translation of Tyndale, continued by Cranmer and the Genevan Version, "These are makers of sects," yet in his exposition follows the corrupt reading which misled the translators of 1611, "These be they who separate *themselves*" (οἱ ἀποδιορίζοντες ἑαυτούς), "themselves" being absent from almost all the ancient MSS. and versions. He says, "St. Jude, to express the manner of their departure which by apostasy fell away from the faith of Christ, saith, 'They separated themselves;' noting thereby that it was not constraint of others which forced them to depart; it was not infirmity and weakness in themselves, it was not fear of persecution to come upon them, whereat their hearts did fail; it was not grief of torments, whereof they had tasted, and were not able any longer to endure them. No, they voluntarily did separate themselves, with a fully settled and altogether determined purpose never to name the Lord Jesus any more, nor to have any fellowship with His saints, but to bend all their counsel and all their strength to raze out their memorial from amongst them" (*Serm.* v. 11). Here there is a double error in the quotation from St. Jude, and therefore considerable error in the exposition of his meaning. St. Jude does not say that these libertines "separat*ed*," but that they are "those who *are* separat*ing*," *i.e.* are habitually making separations or differences. He uses the present participle, not the aorist or perfect. And, as already noticed, he says nothing about separating *themselves*. So far from implying that they had "a settled and determined purpose never to name the Lord Jesus any more, nor to have any fellowship with His saints," He shows that these men had crept into the Church, and evidently intended to remain there, attending the love-feasts and polluting them, while they put forward the "freedom wherewith Christ had made them free" as a plea for their own licentiousness; thus "turning the grace of God into lasciviousness," and by their conduct denying the Christ in whom they professed to believe. Thus, though they did not formally leave the Church as heretics, schismatics, or apostates, yet they had the heretical and schismatical temper, and were apostates in their manner of life. As Hooker says elsewhere, "Many things exclude from the kingdom of God, although from the Church they separate not" (*Eccl. Pol.* V. lxviii. 6). These men had left the way of salvation to "walk after their own lusts," but they had not separated from the Church, into which they had surreptitiously obtained admission.

"Sensual" (ψυχικοί). This word has been already discussed in a previous chapter, in the exposition of the passage where it occurs in the Epistle of St. James (iii. 15: see pp. 200, 201). "Sensual" persons are those who live in the world of sense, and are ruled by human feeling and human reason. They stand not very much above the carnal, and with them are opposed to the spiritual. In the triplet, *carnalis, animalis, spiritalis*, the second term is far more closely allied with the first than with the third. It is possible that the libertines, in their travesty of the freedom conferred by the Gospel, made a special claim to be "spiritual" persons, who were above the restraints of the moral law. They may have held that to their exalted natures the things of sense were morally indifferent, and might be indulged in without fear of loss or contamination; while they scoffed at those Christians who were on their guard against such things, and called such Christians *psychical* or sensuous, because they were careful about the things of sense. St. Jude tells them that it is they who are sensuous, and not spiritual at all.

"Not having the Spirit." The Revisers maintain this rendering, which does not appear in English versions until the influence of Beza and the Genevan Version made itself felt. Calvin seems to adopt it; but Luther certainly does not ("*die da keinen Geist haben*"). It must be supposed that the arguments in favour of it are very strong, seeing that the alternative translation is not allowed a place in the margin of either Authorized or Revised Version, nor is recommended by the American Committee. Nevertheless, the points in its favour are well worth considering. This alternative translation is, "Having no spirit" (Tyndale, Cranmer), *i.e.* no spiritual nature. "Not having spirit" is Wiclif's rendering. This agrees very well with the context. St. Jude has just stigmatized the libertines as "sensuous," or "psychical." Of the three elements in man's nature, body, soul, and spirit, they are ruled by the two lower, while the third, which ought to be supreme, is persistently ignored. They had allowed the spiritual part of their being to become so bemired with self-indulgence and self-sufficiency, to be so much under the dominion of human emotion and reason, that it was utterly inoperative and practically non-existent. Their power of spiritual insight into things heavenly, of laying hold of the invisible world, and of entering into communion with God, was gone. The Holy Spirit was not only absent, but His seat was overturned and destroyed. The facts that "spirit" has neither article nor epithet in the Greek, and that the negative is subjective, and not objective (πνεῦμα μὴ ἔχοντες), are in favour of man's spirit being meant, and of this clause being an explanation of what precedes. These men are sensuous *because* they have lost all spiritual power. It must not, however, be understood that the absence of article and epithet is any barrier to the rendering, "Having not the Spirit." Phil. ii. 1 is proof of that (comp. Eph. ii. 22; vi. 18; Col. i. 8). Nevertheless, such cases are comparatively rare. The usual expression for the Third Person of the Holy Trinity is either "the Spirit," or "Holy Spirit," or "the Holy Spirit," or "the Spirit of God," or "of the Lord," or "of Jesus Christ," or "of truth," or "of life," etc. Therefore, when we find "spirit" without either article, epithet, or distinguishing genitive, the probabilities are that the spirit of man, and not the Spirit of God, is intended.

It will be observed that the three independent descriptions of the libertines, beginning with the words, "These are," become shorter as they go on. The first is two long verses (12, 13); the second is one long verse (16); the third is one very short verse. It is as if the writer were disgusted with the unpalatable subject which necessity had compelled him to take in hand (ver. 3), and were hurrying through it to the more pleasing duty of exhorting those faithful Christians for whose sake he has undertaken this painful task.

"But ye, beloved, building up yourselves on your most holy faith, praying in the Holy Spirit, keep yourselves in the love of God, looking for the mercy of our Lord Jesus Christ unto eternal life." As in ver. 17, the "But *ye*, beloved" (ὑμεῖς δέ, ἀγαπητοί) makes an emphatic contrast between those whom St. Jude addresses and the sensuous and unspiritual men of whom he has been speaking. He exhorts his readers to endeavour to keep themselves in favour with God by cultivating faith, prayer, and hope; and in this exhortation the main purpose of the letter, as set forth in ver. 3, is fulfilled. The triplet of participles (ἐποικοδομοῦντες—προσευχόμενοι—προσδεχόμενοι) must not be lost sight of, although the fact that the main verb (τηρήσατε) comes in the middle of them, instead of at the end, somewhat obscures the triple construction.

The expression "building up" (ἐποικοδομεῖν) is in the New Testament never used of actual building, but always in the metaphorical sense of believers being united together so as to form a temple. In this temple Christ is sometimes regarded as the foundation (1 Cor. iii. 11), sometimes as that which binds the structure together (Eph. ii. 20; Col. ii. 7). The notion of building up comes from the preposition (ἐπί), one stone being placed upon another, so that upward progress is made. "The faith" here is probably the foundation on which the structure is to rest; but it would be possible to translate "*with* your most holy faith," instead of "*on* your most holy faith;" and in that case the dative would, as in Col. ii. 7, express the cement rather than the foundation. In any case "the faith" is not the internal grace or virtue of faith, but, as both the participle and the adjective show, "the faith which was once for all delivered unto the saints" (ver. 3). It is "*your* faith," because it has been thus delivered to you; and it is "most holy," in marked contrast to the vile and shifty doctrines which the libertines profess and uphold.

"Praying in the Holy Ghost." This is the best arrangement of the words, although the Greek allows us to take "in the Holy Ghost" with the previous clause, a rather clumsy division of the words, which is sanctioned by Luther, Beza, and the Rhemish Version: "building yourselves upon our (*sic*) most holy faith, in the Holy Ghost, praying." The expression "praying in the Holy Ghost" occurs nowhere else; but that is no reason why St. Jude should not have used it here. It means that we are to pray in the power and wisdom of the Spirit. In order that we may pray, and pray aright, He must move our hearts and direct our petitions.

"Keep yourselves in the love of God." Not our love of God is meant, but His love of us. This is rendered probable both by what immediately follows—for "the love of God" should have a meaning similar to that of "the mercy of Jesus Christ"—and also by the opening address, "beloved in God" (ver. 1), which St. Jude perhaps has in his mind; for the whole of the verse before us is closely connected with the first verse of the Epistle. God's love is the region in which all Christians should strive to abide, and it is by faith and prayer that this abode is secured. To be conscious of being beloved by God is one of the greatest protections that the believer can possess.

"Looking for the mercy of our Lord Jesus Christ unto eternal life." That mercy which He will show to all faithful Christians when He returns as Judge at the last day. We may compare "looking for and earnestly desiring the coming of the day of God" (2 Peter iii. 12). Both in this life and in eternity it is mercy that we need and crave. The Psalms are full of this thought, as a reference to the numerous passages in which the word mercy occurs will reveal: see especially Ps. cxxx. And in connexion with this the concise statement respecting the relations of the Persons of the Blessed Trinity to believers must not be overlooked. By prayer in the power of the Holy Spirit we are kept in the love of the Father through the mercy of the Son. "Unto eternal life." It is not a matter of much moment whether we take these words with "keep yourselves," or with "looking," or with "mercy." The first seems to be the best arrangement, "keep yourselves ... unto eternal life;" but in any case the eternal life is reached through the mercy of the Lord Jesus Christ. With a similar thought the author of the Epistle to the Hebrews (ix. 28) writes of Christ's Second Advent as an advent "unto salvation" (εἰς σωτηρίαν). The Divine purpose of both Advents is mercy, and not judgment; but seeing that both Advents are met by some who refuse to believe and repent, judgment is inevitable.

"And on some have mercy, who are in doubt; and some save, snatching out of the fire; and on some have mercy with fear." In hardly any other passage, perhaps, does the Revised Version differ in so many particulars from the Authorized. The main changes are the result of changes in the Greek text, which here is in so corrupt a state that the original cannot be restored with certainty. The readings adopted by the Revisers have the advantage of giving us another triple division, which St. Jude is very likely to have made. This triple division is preserved in the Vulgate, and therefore in Wiclif and the Rhemish Version. Our other translators, with Luther and Beza, not finding it in the inferior Greek MSS. which they used, of course do not give it.[127] With one possible exception, the text adopted by the Revisers seems to be the best that can be framed with our present evidence. It is doubtful whether we ought not to substitute "convict" (ἐλέγχετε) for the first "have mercy" (ἐλεᾶτε). This reading has very powerful support (AC, the best cursives, Vulgate, Memphitic, Armenian, and Ethiopic), and is adopted by many critics. But it may possibly be an early correction of a still earlier corruption, and not a restoration of the original reading. This is one of those passages about which we must be content to remain in doubt as to what the author actually wrote (see above on ver. 5, p. 404).

In any case the writer is giving directions as to how to deal with two or three different classes of persons, who are in danger of being seduced by the libertines; and possibly the libertines themselves are included. We will assume that three classes are named. In the first we are confronted with an uncertainty of translation. The participle rendered "who are in doubt" (διακρινομένους) may also mean "while they contend" with you. Which meaning we prefer will depend partly upon the reading which we adopt for the imperative which governs the accusative. "On some *have mercy*, when they are in *doubt*," makes very harmonious sense; for earnest doubters, who are unable to make up their minds for or against the truth, are to be treated with great tenderness. Again, "And some *convict*, when they *contend* with you," makes very harmonious sense; for it is those who are disposed to be contentious that need to be refuted and convinced of their error. It is in favour of the latter version of the command that the verbs rendered "convict" and "contend" occur, *and in the same sense*, in the earlier part of the Epistle (vv. 9, 15). In either case that which is doubted or contended about is "the faith once for all delivered unto the saints," on which believers are to "build themselves up."

The second class are such as can still be rescued, but by strong measures. No hint, however, is given as to their characteristics; we are merely told that there are some who require to be taken with decision, and perhaps even with violence, out of their perilous surroundings, in order that they may be saved from destruction. We may perhaps think of those who, without being in doubt or inclined to dispute about the faith, are being carried away into licentiousness by intercourse with the libertines. The fire out of which they are to be snatched is not the penal fire of the judgment to come, but the state of perdition in which they are now living. We seem to have here, as in ver. 9, a reminiscence of Zechariah iii. 1, where we read, "Is not this a brand plucked out of the fire?" In Amos iv. 11 we have the same figure, and the context there agrees with the suggestion just made as to the kind of person indicated by St. Jude: "I have overthrown some among you, as when God overthrew Sodom and Gomorrah, and ye were as a brand plucked out of the burning." There are some who need to be rescued in the way that the angels rescued Lot, with urgency and constraint (Gen. xix. 16, 17); and it is specially in reference to temptations such as Lot had gone into that such urgency is needed.

The third class is one which must be treated with great circumspection: "and on some have mercy *with fear*; hating even the garment spotted by the flesh." This does not mean, as Luther supposes, that we must "let them severely alone, and have nothing to do with them," but that in dealing with evil so insidious and so infectious, we must take care that we are not contaminated ourselves. It is quite possible to approach evil with good intentions, and then, through want of proper humility and caution, end in finding it fatally attractive. We must carefully preserve abhorrence for all that is associated with pollution. In the *defiled* garment (comp. James iii. 6, where the same word is used) St. Jude appears once more to have Zechariah iii. 1-3 in his mind; but the Greek of the LXX. is there quite different (ἱμάτια ῥυπαρά, instead of ἐσπιλωμένον χιτῶνα). The garment here mentioned is the *chiton*, or shirt, which came in contact with the body, and would itself be rendered unclean if the body were unclean. It therefore serves well as a symbol for that which has become perilous through being closely connected with evil. But while the evil and that which has been contaminated by it are to be hated, compassion is to be shown to those who have fallen victims to it. To be *shown*, not merely *felt*, as is manifest from the word which St. Jude uses (ἐλεᾶν, not οἰκτείρειν). The passages in which this verb (or its more common form ἐλεεῖν) elsewhere occurs in the New Testament prove that it means "to *have* mercy on, to succour and bring help to," and not merely "to *feel* pity for" without doing anything to relieve the person pitied (Matt. ix. 27; xv. 22; xvii. 15; xviii. 33; xx. 30; Mark x. 47; Luke xvi. 24; xvii. 13; xviii. 38; Phil. ii. 27). It is specially used of God's showing mercy to those who do not deserve it (Rom. ix. 15, 16, 18; xi. 32; 1 Cor. vii. 25; 2 Cor. iv. 1; 1 Tim. i. 13, 16; 1 Peter ii. 10), and therefore fitly expresses the sympathy which ought to be manifested by the faithful towards the fallen. But in some cases this sympathy must be manifested *in fear*. It is by acting in the spirit of godly fear that love of the sinner can be combined with hatred of the sin. Without it sympathy with the sinner is too likely to turn into sympathy with the sin. To put it otherwise: All our efforts for the reformation of others must be begun and continued with self-reformation; and therefore St. Jude insists on the necessity for spiritual progress and prayer, before advising as to the treatment of the fallen. It is while we are earnestly detesting and contending against a particular sin in ourselves that we can most safely and effectually deal with that sin in others.

Finally, it must be noted as specially remarkable that St. Jude, after all the strong language which he has used in describing the wickedness of those who are corrupting the Christian community, does *not*, in this advice as to the different methods which are to be used in dealing with those who are going or have gone astray, recommend denunciation. Not that denunciation is always wrong; in some cases it may be necessary. But denunciation by itself commonly does more harm than good; while other methods, which must be added in order to make denunciation effectual, are often quite as efficacious when no denunciation has been employed. It is quite possible to manifest one's abhorrence of "the garment spotted with the flesh," without public or private abuse of those who are the authors of the defilement.

> [127] Nevertheless, Westcott and Hort reject the triple division, and adopt the text of B, "which involves the incongruity that the first οὕς must be taken as a relative, and the first ἐλεᾶτε as indicative. Some primitive error evidently affects the passage" (ii., p. 107). It is difficult to believe that their text is right.

CHAPTER XXXVIII
THE FINAL DOXOLOGY: PRAISE TO GOD, THE PROTECTOR OF HIS SERVANTS

"Now unto Him that is able to guard you from stumbling, and to set you before the presence of His glory without blemish in exceeding joy, to the only God our Saviour, through Jesus Christ our Lord, be glory, majesty, dominion and power, before all time, and now, and for evermore." Amen.— St. Jude 24, 25.

FROM his severe and sombre warnings and exhortations St. Jude turns in joyous and exulting confidence to Him who alone can make them effectual. He has spoken with sternness and horror of great wickedness which has been manifested both in the past and in the present, and of God's terrible judgments upon it. He has exhorted his readers to beware of it, and not to let their abhorrence of it grow less when they are engaged in the merciful work of rescuing others from it. Now, in conclusion, he offers a fervent tribute of praise to Him who is a God of love as well as of justice, and who is as able and ready to protect those who cling to Him and serve Him as to punish those who murmur and rebel against Him.

The doxologies at the end of the Epistle to the Romans and at the beginning of the First Epistle to Timothy should be compared with this one. The former is nearest to it in form; and it is from the doxology in Romans that the epithet "wise," which the Authorized Version wrongly inserts both here and in 1 Tim. i. 17, probably comes. Doxologies, modelled on those in the New Testament, became elastic in some respects, and stereotyped in others. The formula "to the only wise God" was a common one, and hence scribes inserted the epithet, perhaps almost mechanically, in places where it was not found in the original. It is quite possible that St. Jude knew the Epistle to the Romans, and his doxology, especially in its opening words, may be a conscious or unconscious imitation of it; for the Epistle to the Romans was written some years before the earliest date that can with any probability be assigned to this Epistle.

"To guard you from stumbling;" which in two respects is more than "to keep you from falling." Firstly, "guard" preserves the idea of *protection* against perils, both manifest and secret, more decidedly than "keep;" and secondly, one may have many stumbles without any falls, and therefore to be preserved from even stumbling implies a larger measure of care on the part of the protector. But even "to guard you from stumbling" does not quite do justice to the Greek (φυλάξαι ὑμᾶς ἀπταίστους), nor is it easy to do so. "Guard you so that you are exempt from stumbling and never trip or make a false step" is the full meaning of the expression. The verb which is here negatived is used by St. James (ii. 10): "Whosoever shall keep the whole law, and yet stumble (πταίσῃ) in one point, he is become guilty of all." The Vulgate lets go the metaphor of stumbling, and translates simply "to preserve you without sin" (*conservare sine peccato*). That which is impossible with men is possible with God, and the Divine grace can protect Christians against their own frailty. Christ says of His sheep that they shall assuredly never perish, and that no one, whether powers of evil or human seducers, can snatch them out of His hand (John x. 28). Their wills are free, and they may will to leave Him; but if they determine to abide with Him they will be safe.

"And to set you before the presence of His glory without blemish." This is the blessed result of His protecting them from stumbling. The revised translation, "without blemish" (ἀμώμους), at first sight looks like a needless and vexatious change from the "faultless" of the Authorized Version, and a clumsy one, because it gives two English words for one Greek word. But the change is a real improvement, for the Greek word is a *sacrificial* term, which "faultless" is not. It is frequently used of victims, which must be "without blemish," in order to be suitable for offerings. It is not common in classical Greek, but frequent in the LXX. (Exod. xxix. 1; Lev. i. 3, 10; xxii. 21-24; Num. vi. 14; xix. 2). In 1 Macc. iv. 42 it is used of the priests, and so also in Philo (*De Merc. Mer.* i.; *De Agric.* xxix.: see Lightfoot on μωμοσκοπθέν: Clem. Rom. xli.). In the New Testament it is used sometimes of the sinlessness of Christ (Heb. ix. 14; 1 Peter i. 19), sometimes of the ideal perfection of Christians (Eph. i. 4; v. 27; Phil. ii. 15). In the Epistle to the Colossians St. Paul has almost the same idea as St. Jude—"to *present* you holy and *without blemish* and unreprovable *before Him*" (i. 22); and again in the First Epistle to the Thessalonians—"to the end He may stablish your hearts unblameable in holiness before our God and Father, at the coming of our Lord Jesus with all His saints" (iii. 13). "Before the presence of His glory" refers to the glory of God which shall be revealed at the last day.

"In exceeding joy" is a further consequence from the second point, as the second from the first. To be protected against stumbling leads to being presented without blemish before the judgment-seat, and this is an occasion of intense delight. As St. Peter puts it, "Inasmuch as ye are partakers of

Christ's sufferings, rejoice; that at the revelation of His glory also ye may rejoice with exceeding joy" (1 Peter iv. 13).

"To the only God our Saviour." St. Paul, like St. Jude, speaks of God the Father as our Saviour. He is "an Apostle of Christ Jesus according to the commandment of God our Saviour" (1 Tim. i. 1), and he says that intercession and thanksgiving for others "is good and acceptable in the sight of God our Saviour" (ii. 3). Still more fully he says that "God our Saviour ... saved us ... through Jesus Christ our Saviour (Titus iii. 4-6: comp. i. 3; ii. 10). The work of the Son is the work of the Father; and so in the Old Testament we have Jehovah spoken of as the Saviour and Redeemer of His people (Ps. cvi. 21; Isa. xli. 15, 21; xlix. 26; lx. 16). And this is the meaning of the clause which textual criticism has restored to us in this passage. God is our Saviour *"through Jesus Christ our Lord."* Some take these words with what follows. "To the only God be glory, majesty, dominion and power, through Jesus Christ our Lord;" which makes excellent sense, and is in harmony with the doxology in 1 Peter iv. 11, "that in all things God may be glorified through Jesus Christ." It is no strong objection to this to urge that in that case St. Jude would have reversed the order of the clauses (δόξα μεγαλωσύνη κράτος καὶ ἐξουσία διὰ Ἰησοῦ Χριστοῦ τοῦ κυρίου ἡμῶν). In the doxology at the end of the Epistle to the Romans (which St. Jude *may* have in his mind) "through Jesus Christ" precedes "be the glory," and yet cannot easily be taken with anything else (omitting ᾧ as a probable corruption). The combination "glory and dominion" occurs in other doxologies (1 Peter iv. 11; Rev. i. 6; v. 13); "majesty" and "power" do not occur in any. "Majesty" in the New Testament is found in Hebrews i. 3 and viii. 1 only; but it occurs in the LXX. and in Clement of Rome (xvi. 1). The doxology in 1 Chron. xxix. 11 is specially worthy of notice. The word seems to have been used almost exclusively of the majesty of God, and the four words together sum up the Divine glory and omnipotence. It is a little remarkable that in this case St. Jude abandons his favourite triplets, and gives four attributes rather than three. But he returns in a still more remarkable way to his favourite arrangement in the concluding words.

"Before all time, and now, and for evermore." Thus, in a very comprehensive phrase, eternity is described. Throughout all time, and throughout the ages which precede and follow it, these attributes belong to God. Evil men in their dreamings may "set at nought dominion and rail at glories," and their mouth may "speak great swelling words" about their own superior knowledge and greater liberty, and may mock and scoff at those who will not follow them in "walking after their own ungodly lusts." Nevertheless, ages before they were born, and ages after they shall have vanished from the world which they are troubling by their presence, glory, majesty, dominion, and power belong to Him who saves us, and would save even them, through Jesus Christ our Lord.

They *belong* to Him. This seems to be the meaning rather than that they are *ascribed* to Him. No verb is given in the Greek; neither "is," as in 1 Peter iv. 11 (ᾧ ἐστὶν ἡ δόξα καὶ τὸ κράτος), nor "be" (ἔστω), which in most doxologies may be understood. "To Him be glory *before all time*" is scarcely sense, for our wishes cannot influence the past. "To Him belongs glory before all time" is the statement of a simple fact.

It is those who know their own frailty and liability to sin; who know the manifold temptations which surround them, and the terrible attractiveness which many of them can present; who know from past experience what frequent and grievous falls are possible; that can best understand the statement of fact which this doxology contains, and the significance of it. He who can guard such creatures as we are from stumbling, in such a world as this, must be the only God; must be He who was, and is, and is to come; must possess throughout all time and all eternity the highest powers and glories which the heart of man can conceive. The wonders of the material universe impress us in our more solemn moments with feelings of awe, and reverence, and love for Him who is the Author of them all. How much more should the wonders of the kingdom of heaven do so! Out of sinful man to make a saint is more than to make a world out of nothing; and to keep sinful men from stumbling is more than to keep the stars in their courses. There is a free and rebellious will to be won and retained in the one case, whereas there is nothing but absolute and unresisting obedience in the other. The difference is that which is so beautifully expressed in the 103rd and 104th Psalms. In the latter of these two exquisite songs of praise and thanksgiving Jehovah is praised as the Creator and Regulator of the world, in the former as the Pardoner and Preserver of His servants. In the one case blessing and praise is offered to the Lord—

"Who laid the foundations of the earth,

That it should not be moved for ever.

Thou coveredst it with the deep as with a vesture;

The waters stood above the mountains.

They went up by the mountains,

They went down by the valleys,

Unto the place which Thou hadst founded for them.

Thou hast set a bound that they may not pass over;

That they turn not again to cover the earth.

O Lord, how manifold are Thy works!

In wisdom hast Thou made them all:

The earth is full of Thy riches.

Let the glory of the Lord endure for ever;

Let the Lord rejoice in His works:

Who looketh on the earth, and it trembleth;

He toucheth the mountains, and they smoke."

Ps. civ. 5, 6, 8, 9, 24, 31, 32.

But in the other song the Lord is praised, not so much in relation to the glorious universe which He creates and controls, but in relation to the spirits of men, whom He restores, and of angels, whom He retains, to willing obedience and service.

"Bless the Lord, O my soul,

And forget not all His benefits:

Who forgiveth all thine iniquities;

Who healeth all thy diseases;

Who redeemeth thy life from destruction;

Who crowneth thee with lovingkindness and tender mercies.

He hath not dealt with us after our sins,

Nor rewarded us after our iniquities.

For as the heaven is high above the earth,

So great is His mercy toward them that fear Him.

As far as the east is from the west,

So far hath He removed our transgressions from us.

Bless the Lord, ye angels of His;

Ye mighty in strength, that fulfil His word,

Hearkening unto the voice of His word,

Bless the Lord, all ye His hosts;

Ye ministers of His, that do His pleasure."

Ps. ciii. 2, 3, 4, 10, 11, 12, 20, 21.

It is quite in harmony with such a strain as this that the joyous doxology with which St. Jude's stern letter suddenly ends is written. Its clauses lend themselves to that parallelism which distinguishes Hebrew poetry, and they have not only the spirit, but the form, of a concluding strophe of praise.

"Now unto Him that is able to guard you from stumbling,

And to set you before the presence of His glory without blemish in exceeding joy,

To the only God our Saviour,

Through Jesus Christ our Lord,

Glory, majesty, dominion and power,

Before all time, and now, and for evermore. Amen."

Note.—The "Amen" at the end of this Epistle, as at the end of Romans and 2 Peter, which like this close with a doxology, seems to be genuine (comp. 1 Peter iv. II; v. II); but that at the end of 2 Peter is somewhat doubtful. In all other books of the New Testament, excepting Galatians, the final "Amen" is probably spurious.

INDEX

Auricular confession

Authenticity of the Epistle of St. James, of St. Jude

Azazel

Barnabas, Epistle of

Baur, F. C.

Bede

Bellarmine

Bengel

Beyschlag

Beza

Bias the sage

Bodenstein

British Association

Brother of the Lord

Bruce

Brückner

Building up

Butler, Archer

Butler, Bishop

Cæsar, Julius

Cajetan

Calendars

Caligula

Calvin

Canonical

Canonical Books

Canonical Epistles

Carlyle

Carpocrates

Cassian

Cassiodorus

Catholic

Catholic Epistles

Cave

Hippolytus

Hoffmann

Hofmann

Holzmann

Hooker

Hornejus

Hutton

Ignatius

Inspiration

Intercession

Irenæus

James, The name

James of Alphæus

James the Just

Jealousy

Jealousy, Divine

Jellett

Jeremy Taylor

Jerome

Jerusalem, Destruction of

Job, Character of the Book of

—— Coincidences with the Book of

John, Coincidences with the Gospel of

Josephus

Joy in temptation

Judas not Iscariot

—— of James

Judgment, Day of

Julius Cæsar

Justin Martyr

Keble

Lange

Laodicea, Council of

Lardner